THE HIDDEN PLACES OF THE
PEAK DISTRICT
AND DERBYSHIRE

By Jim Gracie

© Travel Publishing Ltd.

Regional Hidden Places

Cornwall
Devon
Dorset, Hants & Isle of Wight
East Anglia
Lake District & Cumbria
Northumberland & Durham
Peak District and Derbyshire
Yorkshire

National Hidden Places

England
Ireland
Scotland
Wales

Hidden Inns

East Anglia
Heart of England
South
South East
West Country

Country Pubs and Inns

Cornwall
Devon
Sussex
Wales
Yorkshire

Country Living Rural Guides

East Anglia
Heart of England
Ireland
North East of England
North West of England
Scotland
South
South East
Wales
West Country

Other Guides

Off the Motorway

Published by: Travel Publishing Ltd, 7a Apollo House,
Calleva Park, Aldermaston, Berks, RG7 8TN

ISBN 1-904-434-55-X

© Travel Publishing Ltd

First published 1991, second edition 1994,
third edition 1997, fourth edition 1999,
fifth edition 2002, sixth edition 2005,
seventh edition 2007

Printing by: Scotprint, Haddington

Maps by: © Maps in Minutes ™ (2006)
© Crown Copyright, Ordnance Survey 2006

Editor: Jim Gracie

Cover Design: Lines and Words, Aldermaston

Cover Photograph: Winnats Pass, Castleton
© www.picturesofbritain.co.uk

Text Photographs: © www.picturesofbritain.co.uk
and © Bob Brooks, Weston-super-Mare

Foreword

This is the 7th edition of the *Hidden Places of The Peak District and Derbyshire* which has been fully updated. In this respect we would like to thank the many Tourist Information Centres in Derbyshire, Staffordshire and Cheshire for helping us update the editorial content. Regular readers will note that the pages of the guide have been extensively redesigned to allow more information to be presented on the many places to visit in The Peak District and Derbyshire. In addition, although you will still find details of places of interest and advertisers of places to stay, eat and drink included under each village, town or city, these are now cross referenced to more detailed information contained in a separate, easy-to-use section of the book. This section is also available as a free supplement from the local Tourist Information Offices.

The *Peak District National Park* was the very first of Britain's National Parks covering an area of 540 square miles. The *Dark Peak* covering north Derbyshire and small parts of Cheshire and South Yorkshire is an area of windswept moorland, steep river valleys and impressive crags. Futher south is the *White Peak* a limestone-based undulating green landscape criss-crossed by miles of dry stone walls and gently flowing rivers whilst to the west can be found the beautiful valleys and rivers of the *Dales* as well as the *Staffordshire Moorlands*. In contrast the rest of Derbyshire offers the visitor an intriguing mix of villages and towns packed with cultural and industrial heritage and should certainly not be missed.

The **Hidden Places** series is a collection of easy to use local and national travel guides taking you on a relaxed but informative tour of Britain and Ireland. Our books contain a wealth of interesting information on the history, the countryside, the towns and villages and the more established places of interest. But they also promote the more secluded and little known visitor attractions and advertise places to stay, eat and drink many of which are easy to miss unless you know exactly where you are going.

We include hotels, inns, restaurants, public houses, teashops, various types of accommodation, historic houses, museums, gardens, and many other attractions all of which are comprehensively indexed. Most places are accompanied by an attractive photograph and are easily located by using the map at the beginning of each chapter. We do not award merit marks or rankings but concentrate on describing the more interesting, unusual or unique features of each place with the aim of making the reader's stay in the local area an enjoyable and stimulating experience.

Whether you are visiting The Peak District and Derbyshire for business or pleasure or are a local inhabitant, we do hope that you enjoy reading and using this book. We are always interested in what readers think of places covered (or not covered) in our guides so please do not hesitate to use the reader reaction forms provided to give us your considered comments. We also welcome any general comments which will help us improve the guides themselves. Finally if you are planning to visit any other corner of the British Isles we would like to refer you to the order form for other **Hidden Places** titles to be found at the rear of the book and to the Travel Publishing website at www.travelpublishing.co.uk.

Travel Publishing

Contents

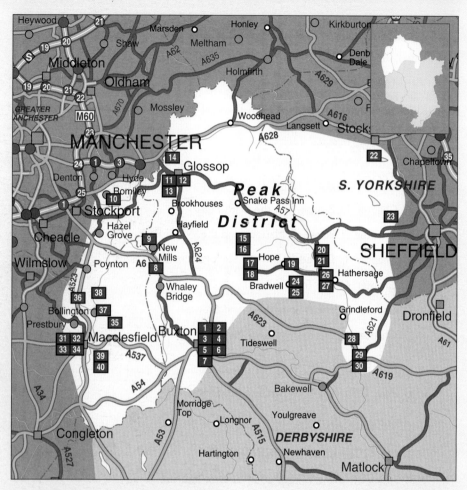

Buxton and the Dark Peak

Situated right at the centre of England, the Peak District and surrounding area is truly a microcosm of the country. It divides the rugged north from the softer pastoral countryside of the south. There are spectacular rock formations, windswept moorland, undulating pastures, country lanes, picturesque villages and historic churches and castles. The Romans left their roads and the remains of their forts and baths, there are Saxon and Norman churches, and the Civil War raged through the area leaving a trail of destruction. Mainly agricultural for hundreds of years, with some coal mining and ironworks, the industrial revolution transformed the place as mills, mines and works sprang up everywhere. As the population of the towns grew, the factory and mine owners built houses for the workforce, churches and grand civic buildings, and left a rich legacy of Victorian architecture.

Kinder Scout

The first of Britain's National Parks, The Peak District itself covers an area of 540 square miles close to the large industrial conurbations of middle England such as Manchester, Stoke-on-Trent and Sheffield. The National Park is scattered with the remains of ancient settlements. The northern area of the Peak District National Park, known as the Dark Peak

---

3

or High Peak, is a landscape of moorland and deep valleys edged with escarpments of dark sandstone and shale. The rugged millstone grit moorland and crags enclose the softer limestone plateau of the White Peak like a horseshoe. The southern section of the Peak District is the beautiful Dovedale. The River Dove is a famous fishing river, first mentioned in Izaak Walton's *The Compleat Angler,* published in 1653. The River Manifold, too, has wonderful scenery including the beautifully preserved estate village of Ilam. The ancient custom of well-dressing is found mainly in these limestone areas of Derbyshire, where the streams frequently disappear through the porous rock.

The Amber Valley, the Erewash and the Trent Valley, to the east and south of Derbyshire, although not part of the National Park, have many pleasant walks and magnificent stately homes for visitors to enjoy. Derbyshire was at the forefront of the Industrial Revolution, and its history is recorded in the Industrial Museum at Derby. It is reflected, too, in many of the villages with their rows of 18th and 19th century workers' cottages. To the northeast of Derbyshire is the heart of the coal-mining area, which prospered during the 19th and early 20th centuries. Sometimes overlooked, this part of Derbyshire is well worth exploring for its industrial architecture alone.

On the southern edge of the Peak District, the undulating pastures and crags of the Staffordshire Moorland are ideal places to walk, cycle or trek. It is a mixture of charming villages, historic market towns, ancient farms and relics of the Industrial Revolution, including the reservoirs of Rudyard and Tittesworth. They were originally the water supply for the Midlands, but are now peaceful havens for wildlife and leisure.

The Dark Peak, or High Peak, is not as forbidding as its name might suggest. These high moors are ripe for exploring on foot, and a walk

from the Kinder Reservoir will lead to the western edge of Kinder Scout. This whole area is really a series of plateaux, rather than mountains and valleys, with the highest point on Kinder Scout being some 2,088 feet above sea level. In this remote and wild area the walker can feel a real sense of freedom - however, it is worth remembering that the moors, with their treacherous peat bogs and unpredictable mists, which can rise quickly even in summer, should not be dismissed as places for a casual ramble.

It was at Kinder Scout, in April 1932, that the single most important action in securing access rights for ordinary people to the English countryside took place. Over 400 walkers took part in what became known as the "Mass Trespass", by walking over what was then private land. They were confronted by gamekeepers on the way, who were easily swept aside. Four of the leaders were later imprisoned, though the action led to legislation which opened up England's countryside to walkers. The Peak District National Park was also formed as a direct result of the trespass, and nowadays the Pennine Way passes directly over Kinder Scout.

To the eastern side of this region are the three reservoirs created by flooding of the upper valley of the River Derwent. Howden, Derwent and Ladybower provide water for the East Midlands but their remote location, along with the many recreational activities found there, make them popular places to visit. The Derwent dam is particularly famous as the site of practice exercises for the Dambusters of the Second World War. Even those who have not visited the area before will be familiar with some of the place names, as they feature heavily in winter weather reports. Snake Pass (the A57), one of the few roads that runs through this northern section of the National Park, is often closed during the winter; even in spring, conditions can deteriorate quickly to make driving hazardous.

BUXTON

With a population of barely 20,000, the elegant Georgian town of Buxton is nonetheless the largest settlement within the boundaries of the Peak District National Park. (The second largest town, Bakewell, has fewer than 5,000 inhabitants.) Referred to as the heart of the Peak District, Buxton, like Bakewell, is right on the divide between the Dark Peak and White Peak areas of the National Park. A large part of the White Peak lies between the two towns. At 1,000 feet above sea level, Buxton is also England's second-highest market town (only Alston in Cumbria is higher), and provides a wealth of things to do.

Buxton's gracious architecture can be attributed mainly to the 5th Duke of Devonshire, who hoped to establish a northern spa town that would rival, and possibly surpass, the attractions of Bath. In both locations it was the Romans who first exploited the healing waters of apparently inexhaustible hot springs as a commercial enterprise. They arrived in AD70, and called the place *Aquae Arnemetiae* - The Spa of the Goddess of the Grove. It is one of only two places in Britain which had the Roman prefix aquae (meaning "waters") - the other being *Aquae Sulis*, or Bath. The waters still bubble up at Buxton, always maintaining a constant temperature of 82 degrees F (28 degrees C). Buxton water is reputed to be particularly pure and especially effective at mitigating the symptoms of rheumatism. Countless rheumatism sufferers are on record attesting that Buxton water has helped to soothe their symptoms – Mary, Queen of Scots, a political prisoner detained at nearby Chatsworth but allowed out on day-release to Buxton, was among them. The people of Buxton also say that it makes the best cup of tea possible, and collect bottles of it to take home. Experts have calculated that the water that bubbles up nowadays fell as rainfall over 5,000 years ago.

In the 18th century, the 5th Duke of Devonshire commissioned the building of **The Crescent** to ensure that visitors would flock here. Designed by John Carr of York, the building is similar to the architecture found in Bath and, after suffering from neglect, underwent a huge restoration programme. It is 240 feet in length and has the coat-of-arms of the Dukes of Devonshire at its centre. Next to The Crescent, the Thermal Baths are now the Cavendish Shopping Centre, and the former town house of Bess of Hardwick and her husband the Earl of Shrewsbury, where Mary Queen of Scots stayed when she visited Buxton, is now the Old Hall Hotel. **Turner's Memorial** stands opposite, and commemorates Samuel Turner, treasurer to the Devonshire Hospital. It was designed by Robert Rippon Duke. In 1959 it was demolished when a motor car crashed into it. When the

1 WHITE LION

Buxton

An old coaching inn that has bags of character, and which is handy for a quiet drink if you're sightseeing, shopping or heading for a show.

❚❙ see page 161

2 CAFÉ NATS AND THE GEORGE

Buxton

Two establishments - a café and a pub - that have married tradition with modern standards of service and value for money.

❚❙ see page 160

3 THE KINGS HEAD

Buxton

A pub that was once a parsonage. Great food all day and an excellent selection of real ales - that's The King's Head!

❚❙ see page 161

5

4 THE OLD SUN INN

Buxton

A 400-year old coaching inn that offers six kinds of real ale and marvellous food, all at reasonable prices.

see page 162

area was pedestrianised some years later however, it was repaired and reinstated.

As with many places, the coming of the railway to Buxton in 1863 marked the height of popularity of the town. Nothing, however, could be done to alter the harsh climate, and the incessant rainfall meant that the Duke's dream of making Buxton the 'Bath of the North', was never truly realised.

Among the other notable architectural features of the town are **The Colonnade** and the

Devonshire Royal Hospital. They were originally built as stables for hotel patrons of The Crescent and, after their conversion by the 6th Duke in 1858, the largest unsupported dome in the world was built to enclose the courtyard in 1880.

The attractive **Buxton Opera House** was designed and built in 1903 by the renowned theatre architect, Frank Matcham. Gertrude Lawrence, Gracie Fields and Hermione Gingold all played here and on one memorable occasion, the famous Hollywood screen stars Douglas Fairbanks and Mary Pickford were in the audience to watch the Russian ballerina, Anna Pavlova. However, in 1932 it became a cinema and, apart from an annual pantomime and a handful of amateur performances, showed films only. In the late 1970s it was restored to its former Edwardian grandeur and was officially opened by Princess Alice in 1979. The Buxton Opera Festival was inaugurated in the same year and is now one of Britain's best-known and largest opera-based festivals. Since 1994, the International Gilbert & Sullivan Festival has been held here in August. Throughout the rest of the year its comprehensive and popular programme has won it a well-deserved reputation nationally and internationally.

The Opera House stands in 23 acres of ornamental gardens in the heart of Buxton. The attractive **Buxton Pavilion Gardens** have a

Pavilion Gardens, Buxton

conservatory (built in 1871) and octagon within the grounds. Antique markets, brass band concerts and arts shows are often held here, and it is a very pleasant place to walk at any time of year. Laid out in 1871 by Edward Milner, with money donated by the Dukes of Devonshire, it includes formal gardens, serpentine walks and decorative iron bridges across the River Wye. The conservatory was reopened in 1982 following extensive renovation; there is also a swimming pool filled with warm spa water.

St John the Baptist Church was built in Greek style, with pediment, in 1811 by Sir Jeffrey Wyatville. That same year Wyatville laid out The Slopes, the area below the Market Place in Upper Buxton. The grand Town Hall was built between 1887 and 1889 and dominates the Market Place. Further down Terrace Road is the **Buxton Museum**, which reveals the long and varied history of the town and its surrounding area. As well as housing an important local archaeology collection, the museum also has a fine collection of Ashford Marble, Blue John ornaments, paintings, prints, pottery and glassware.

It is not known for certain whether well-dressing took place in Buxton before 1840. There are stories that Henry VIII put a stop to the practice, but it has certainly been a part of Buxton's cultural calendar since the Duke of Devonshire provided the townsfolk

with their first public water supply at **Market Place Fountain**. From then on, High Buxton Well (as the fountain came to be called) and St Anne's Well were decorated sporadically. In 1923 the Town Council set about organising a well-dressing festival and carnival that continues to this day. Every year on the second Wednesday in July, this delightful tradition is enacted.

St Anne's Church, built in 1625, reflects the building work here before Buxton's 18th century heyday when limestone was the most common construction material, rather than the mellow sandstone that dominates today.

Buxton is surrounded by some of the most glorious of the Peak District countryside. These moorlands also provide one of the town's specialities - heather honey. Several varieties of heather grow on the moors: there is ling, or common heather which turns the land purple in late summer; there is bell-heather which grows on dry rocky slopes; and there is cross-leaved heather which can be found on wet, boggy ground.

The town is also the starting point for both the Brindley Trail and the Monsal Trail. Covering some 61 miles, the Brindley Trail, which takes its name from the famous canal engineer, leads southwest to Stoke-on-Trent, while the Monsal Trail, beginning just outside Buxton at Blackwell Mill Junction, finishes at Coombs Viaduct near Bakewell, some 8 miles away.

5 THE CAFÉ @ THE GREEN PAVILION

Buxton

The perfect place in Buxton for morning tea or coffee, light snacks and superbly cooked lunches. The prices are right, and the service is friendly and efficient.

see page 162

6 THE HYDRO CAFÉ TEA ROOMS

Buxton

The perfect place in the heart of Buxton for a light lunch, a cream tea or a refreshing cup of coffee, all at affordable prices.

see page 162

7 BUXTON MUSEUM AND ART GALLERY

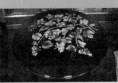

Buxton

Explore the history of the area from pre-history to the Victorian era and enjoy displays of art works.

see page 164

7

AROUND BUXTON

Those who venture to Errwood Reservoir will be surprised to see rhododendrons growing near the banks of a man-made lake. They once stood in the grounds of Errwood Hall, which was built in the 1830s for the Grimshawe family. The house was demolished before the reservoir was flooded, but the gardens were left to grow wild. Not far away can be seen the strange-looking Spanish Shrine. Built by the Grimshawes in memory of their Spanish governess, it is a small stone building with an unusual beehive roof.

To the west of Buxton lies **Axe Edge**, the highest point of which rises to 1,807 feet above sea level. From this spot on a clear day (and the weather here is notoriously changeable) the panoramic views of Derbyshire are overwhelming. Just beyond, at 1,690 feet above sea level, the **Cat and Fiddle Inn** is the second highest pub in England. Axe Edge Moor, which receives an average annual rainfall of over four feet, is strictly for hardened walkers. It should come as no surprise that this moor is the source of several rivers which play important roles in the life of the Peak District. The River Dove and the River Manifold, which join at Ilam, rise not far from one another; the River Wye rises above Buxton to join the Derwent further south; the River Goyt, a major source of the Mersey, rises to the west of Axe Edge. The moor actually spreads over three counties, and at Three Shire's Head, to the south east, the counties of Derbyshire, Staffordshire and Cheshire meet.

The entire length of the River Goyt can be walked, from its source to its confluence with the River Etherow to the north and just outside the boundaries of the National Park. Once marking the boundary between Derbyshire and Cheshire (which now lies just to the west), a walk along the Goyt takes in sections of the riverbank as well as the Errwood and Fernilee reservoirs before leaving Derbyshire just north of New

Mills. Although the two reservoirs look well established and very much part of the landscape, they are relatively recent additions: the Fernilee was opened in 1938 while the Errwood was flooded in 1967.

The highest point in this area is **Shining Tor**, overlooking Errwood Reservoir and standing some 1,834 feet above sea level. To the north is **Pym Chair**, the point at which an old packhorse road running east to west crosses this gritstone ridge. An old salters' route, it was used for transporting salt from the Cheshire plains across the Peak District moorlands to the industrial and well-populated areas of south and west Yorkshire. Pym's chair is said to be named after a highwayman called Pym, who used to sit here awaiting travellers whom he could rob. During the 19th century, the Goyt valley with its natural resources of both coal and water, developed rapidly into one of the nation's major textile production centres. In order to service this growth, the valley also developed an intense system of transport, including canals and railways. The rugged terrain that had to be negotiated has made for some spectacular solutions to major engineering difficulties.

Also to the west of town, on Green Lane, is **Poole's Cavern,** so called for 'The robber Poole', who supposedly lived in the cave in the 15th century. It is a natural limestone cave, said to be over 2 million years old, which was used by tribes from the Neolithic period onwards. Archaeological digs have discovered Stone Age, Bronze Age and Roman artefacts near the cave entrance. Mary, Queen of Scots visited and the 'chair' she used is still in evidence, and pointed out during the regular tours of the cave on offer. The spectacular natural formations in the cavern include a large stalactite called the 'Flitch of Bacon' and the 'Poached Egg Chamber', with blue grey and orange formations, coloured by manganese and iron soaking down from the lime-tips above. Since the 16th century, the cavern has been known as "the first wonder of the Peak".

NORTH OF BUXTON

TAXAL

5 miles NW of Buxton off the A5004

Overlooking the Goyt Valley, Taxal is home to the church of **St James**, the tower of which dates from the 12th century. Inside are a series of fascinating memorials - the earliest to William Jaudrell, who died in 1375, and Roger Jaudrell, a soldier killed at Agincourt in 1415. This is the same family that gave its name to Joddrell Bank, where the radio telescope can be found. An unusual memorial is one dated 1768 to the "Yeoman of the King's Mouth" or "food taster" to George II.

West of Taxal are **Windgather Rocks**, a gritstone outcrop popular with trainee rock-climbers. East of the village is the elegant and gracious **Shallcross Hall**, dating back to the 18th century and at one time home of the Shawcross family.

COMBS

3 miles N of Buxton off the A6

Combs Reservoir southwest of Chapel-en-le-Frith is crossed at one end by Dickie's Bridge. 'Dickie' is said to have resided at a farm in Tunstead where he was known as Ned Dixon. Apparently murdered by his cousin, he nevertheless continued his 'working life' as a sort of guard-skull, alerting the household whenever strangers drew near. Various strange occurrences are said to have ensued when attempts were made to move the skull.

CHAPEL-EN-LE-FRITH

4 miles N of Buxton off the A6

This charming town is often overlooked by travellers on the bypass between Buxton and Stockport, but it repays a closer look.

In 1225 the guardians of the High Peak's Royal Forest purchased land from the Crown and built a chapel here, dedicating it to St Thomas à Becket of Canterbury. A century later the chapel was replaced with a more substantial building; further modernisation took place in the early 1700s. The building of the original chapel led to the foundation of the town and also its name, which is Norman French for 'chapel in the forest'. Although the term 'forest' suggests a wooded area, the frith or forest never really existed, but referred to the Royal Forest of the Peak, hunting grounds which extended over much of north Derbyshire

•

Above Poole's Cavern and about 20 minutes' walk away is Grin Low Country Park and, at the summit of Grin Hill, the prominent folly and scenic viewpoint known as Solomon's Temple. It was built in 1896 by Solomon Mycock as a true folly, having no purpose whatsoever. When the foundations were being dug, it was discovered it was being built on top of a prehistoric burial cairn, as human bones were uncovered.

•

during the Middle Ages.

A curious legacy has been passed down allowing owners of freehold land in the district the right to choose their vicar. The interior of the church boasts 19th century box pews and a monument to 'the Apostle of the Peak', William Bagshawe of nearby Ford Hall, a Nonconformist minister of the late 17th century, who was forced to resign his ministry for refusing to accept the Book of Common Prayer (see also Litton).

In 1648 the church was used as a gaol for 1,500 Scottish prisoners and the dreadful conditions arising from such close confinement caused unimaginable suffering. Their ordeal lasted for 16 days and a total of 44 men died.

Chapel Brow is a steep and cobbled street lined with pictuesque little cottages leading down from the church to Market Street. An ancient market town, the cross still stands in Market Square, as do the town's stocks. This is the true centre of Chapel, surrounded by a variety of old inns and buildings.

South west of the town is the 1,250 feet high **Eccles Pike** (NT), which, every year in August, is the site of the Eccles Pike Fell Race, one of the oldest in the country. From the top, and from Castle Naze, there are magnificent views, even as far as Manchester 20 miles to the north west.

Just a few miles northeast of the town is the **Chestnut Centre**, a fascinating wildlife conservation centre, popular with children and adults alike. It is famed for its otters, with award-winning otter and owl enclosures, set along an extensive circular nature trail, which meanders through some historic wooded parkland.

The Chestnut Centre, Chapel-en-le-Frith

CHINLEY

6 miles N of Buxton off the B6062

This small north Derbyshire village lays claim to the superb **Chinley Viaducts**, a masterpiece of Victorian engineering. Chinley Station was once an important railway junction, as the railway lines from Derby to Manchester and Sheffield linked up here. **Chinley Chapel**, a simple Georgian building, looks deceptively like an ordinary house from the outside.

Nearby Ford Hall was the home of the Revd William Bagshawe, the vicar at Glossop (known as the "Apostle of the Peak"), who was ejected from the church because of the Act of Uniformity in 1662. The Act required that all clergymen in the Church of England should accept all the rites and religious ceremonies in the Book of Common Prayer. Over 2,000 clergymen refused to do so, and were forced to resign. Bagshawe's successor as Nonconformist minister at Chinley, Dr James Clegg, built Chinley Chapel in 1711.

BUXWORTH

6½ miles N of Buxton off the B6062

Once known as Bugsworth, the villagers got tired of the jokes and changed the village's name in 1929. However, in 1999, an attempt was made to restore the old name to commemorate the Millennium, but villagers voted the idea down. Buxworth is the site of the terminal basin for the Peak Forest Canal (see Whaley Bridge), finished in 1800. Buxworth used to have several public houses. Nowadays there is one inn, the Navigation, and a war memorial club known as 'Buggy Club', where sixteen year old members are allowed with parental permission to buy alcohol at the bar.

WHALEY BRIDGE

6 miles N of Buxton off the A5004

This small industrial town, at the gateway to the **Goyt Valley,** grew up around the coal-mining and textile industries. Both have now gone, but the **Peak Forest Canal,** flowing through the town, remains very much the centre of activity. Every year, usually in June, the **Whaley Water Weekend** takes place in and around the canal. A week later the **Rose Queen Carnival** takes place. The 'bridge' of the village's name crosses the River Goyt, on the site of what may once have been a Roman crossing. A map detailing many of the walks in and around Whaley Bridge is available from many outlets in the town.

Many of the old warehouses in Whaley Bridge have been restored and converted to meet modern needs and, where once narrow boats transported goods and raw materials to and from the town, boats can be hired to those who want to explore the delights of the waterways in the area. The **Toddbrook Reservoir** was built in 1831 to be a feeder for the Peak Forest Canal, and is situated to the west of the town. The wharf here is dotted with picturesque narrowboats.

•

The village of Buxworth is popular with visitors attracted by the historic Bugsworth Basin (the original name of the village having been retained) where limestone and lime were brought down from the works up at Dove Holes, to be transported by canal barge. The limestone was carried in small horse-drawn wagons on the Peak Forest Tramway, which was operated in part by the force of gravity. The wagons were rolled down the track to the Basin full and then pulled back up empty by horses. The basin was not used after 1926 but reopened in 1999 thanks to the efforts of the Inland Waterways Preservation Society.

•

8 THE NEW SOLDIER DICK

Furness Vale

A friendly pub that is renowned for its excellent cuisine, its atmosphere and its value for money.

see page 163

Peak Forest Canal, Whaley Bridge

Just outside Whaley Bridge is the curiously named **Roosdyche**, a flat-bottomed valley that seems to have been scooped from the countryside and which runs up towards Eccles Pike. The great scoop taken out of the hillside was the result of glacier erosion, though its distinctive shape gave rise to the theory that it was once a racecourse for Roman chariots.

Above Roosdyche is **Bing Wood**, a charming name until the true meaning of "bing" is revealed - it means 'slag heap' - a name that harkens back to the prominence of the coal industry during the 19th century .

LYME PARK

8 miles NW of Buxton off the A6

Lyme Park is an ancient estate, and though it is in the Peak District, is actually within the county of Cheshire. It is now in the hands of the National Trust, and was given to Sir Thomas Danyers in 1346 by a grateful King Edward III after a battle at Caen. Danyers then passed the estate to his son-in-law, Sir Piers Legh, in 1388. It remained in the family until 1946, when it was given to the Trust. Not much remains of the original Elizabethan manor house; today's visitors are instead treated to the sight of a fantastic Palladian mansion, the work of Venetian architect Giacomo Leoni. Not daunted by the bleak landscape and climate of the surrounding Peak District, Leoni built a corner of Italy here in this much harsher countryside. Inside the mansion there is a mixture of styles: the elegant Leoni-designed rooms with rich rococo ceilings, the panelled Tudor drawing room, and two surviving Elizabethan rooms. Much of the three-dimensional internal carving is attributed to Grinling Gibbons, though a lot of the work was also undertaken by local craftsmen. Another glory of the house is the collection of early 17th century Mortlake tapestries, produced in what was then the village of Mortlake outside London.

As well as the fantastic splendour of the mansion, the estate includes a late 19th century formal garden. The 17-acre Victorian garden is laid out with impressive bedding schemes, a sunken parterre, an Edwardian rose garden, Jekyll-style herbaceous borders, a reflection lake, a ravine garden and Wyatt conservatory. The garden is surrounded by 1,400 acres of medieval deer park of moorland, woodland and parkland, including an early 18th century hunting tower, **Lyme Cage**. It was called this because at one time it was used to lock up poachers. Lyme featured as 'Pemberley' in the 1995 BBC film of Jane Austen's novel, *Pride and Prejudice*. A leaflet has been produced to help you get the best out of the grounds and gardens.

The grounds now form a country park owned and managed by the National Trust and supported by Stockport Metropolitan Borough Council. Though close to the Manchester suburb of Stockport, the estate lies wholly within the Peak District National Park.

NEW MILLS

9 miles N of Buxton off the A6015

Situated by the River Sett, New Mills takes its name from Tudor corn mills that once stood on the riverbanks, though an earlier mill, known as the "Berde Mill", built in 1391, gave it the name New Mill before that. Later, in the 18th and 19th centuries, water power was used to drive several cotton-spinning mills in the town and, as New Mills grew, the textile industry was joined by engineering industries and the confectionery trade. There is still a rich legacy of this industrial heritage to be found in the town. The Torr Mill is featured on the millennium series of postage stamps issued by the

Post Office. The elevated **New Mills Millennium Walkway**, built on stilts rising from the River Goyt, sits directly opposite the Torrs Mill. The walkway answered public demand for a route through the impassable gritstone **Torrs Gorge**, reached by the **Torrs Riverside Park**. The gorge is an area of exceptional natural beauty and unique industrial archaeological heritage. The 175-yard-long steel walkway is fixed to the rock face and adjoining railway retaining wall at a height of about 20 feet from the base of the 100-foot deep gorge. The **New Mills Heritage Centre**, near the walkway, contains a fine model of how the town looked in the 1840s.

The **Little Mill** at Rowarth still retains a working water wheel, although the mill building is now a well-known public house. Opposite the library is the Police Station, where the ringleaders of the 'Kinder Trespassers' were kept in the cells, following their arrest in 1932, after the mass public trespass on Kinder Scout. Although it is now a private house, the site is identified by a plaque on the wall. The trespass was a significant factor in the creation of National Parks, to allow public access to the countryside (see also the introduction to this book).

The serious walker or stroller can use New Mills as a starting point for various way-marked walks. **The Goyt Valley Way** leads south to Buxton via Whaley Bridge and the Goyt Valley north to Marple. There are local signposted

9   THE MASONS ARMS

New Mills

A traditional , no nonsense pub that continues the fine old English traditions of a warm welcome and well kept ales.

see page 164

Kinder Scout

•

Kinder Scout is a high gritstone plateau, rising steeply from the surrounding ground to a height of around 600 metres. The edges are studded with rocky outcrops and crags and the highest point at 631 metres, is Crowden Head. This is also the highest point in the Peak District.

•

walks below the Heritage Centre and the **Sett Valley Trail** follows the line of the old branch railway to Hayfield and then on to Kinder Scout. Opened in 1868, the single track line carried passengers and freight for over 100 years. However, by the late 1960s much of the trade had ceased and the line closed soon afterwards. In 1973, the line was reopened as a trail and is still used by walkers, cyclists and horse riders and it takes in the remains of buildings that were once part of the prosperous textile industry.

HAYFIELD

9 miles N of Buxton off the A624

This small town lies below the exposed moorland of **Kinder Scout**, where the Pennine chain of hills, the "backbone of England", is said to begin. It was once a staging post on the pack-horse route across the Pennines. The old pack-horse route went up the Sett valley and by Edale Cross, where the remains of an old cross can still be seen, down

to Edale by Jacob's Ladder. Some ancient cottages still survive around the centre of the old village, and some local farmhouses date from the 17th century.

Hayfield is a popular centre for exploring the area and offers many amenities for hillwalkers. Like its neighbour New Mills, Hayfield grew up around the textile industry, in this case wool weaving and calico printing. Many of the houses were originally weavers' cottages. A curious building can be found in Market Street, on the left of a small square known as **Dungeon Brow**. Built in 1799 this was the town's lock-up and was referred to as the new prison. However, the stocks in front of the building appear to be somewhat newer than the prison itself.

At the other end of the Sett Valley Trail, the old station site has been turned into a picnic area and information centre. The elegant parish **Church of St Matthew** was completed in 1818, and is a reminder of this Pennine town's former prosperity. It stands on the site of a medieval church built in 1386 at the command of Richard ll. The freemen of the parish had the right to appoint their own vicar, recommending him to the local bishop. This right was given to the freeholders by Richard ll when the church was built. **Bowden Bridge Quarry** was the starting point for the famous 'Mass Trespass' on Kinder Scout and is now a car park with public toilets and a Peak Park camp site opposite.

Three miles northeast of the town is **Kinder Downfall**, at over 90 feet the highest waterfall in the county, where the River Kinder flows off the edge of Kinder Scout. In low temperatures the fall freezes solid - a sight to be seen. In such conditions, climbers use it for ice-climbing training. It is also renowned for its blow-back effect: when the wind blows, the fall's water is forced back against the rock and the water appears to run uphill! Not far from the bottom of the fall is a small lake known as **Mermaid's Pool**. Legend has it that those who go to the pool at midnight on the night before Easter Sunday will see a mermaid, or water sprite, swimming in the dark waters. The legend is said to date back to the times when pools and lakes were places of worship.

CHARLESWORTH

12 miles N of Buxton on the A626

On the western edge of the Pennines and close to the Cheshire border, Charlesworth has many old and typically Pennine cottages. Three storeys tall, they were built as weavers' cottages. Apart from the neat mock-Gothic **St John the Baptist Parish Church** of 1849, there is also a Catholic church, built primarily for the Irish immigrants working in the nearby mills, which stands at the edge of the village in a lovely position near the banks of the River Etherow.

GLOSSOP

13 miles N of Buxton off the A624

Suituated only 14 miles from the centre of Manchester and 24 miles from Sheffield, Glossop stands at the foot of the Snake Pass and is an interesting mix of styles: the industrial town of the 19th century with its towering Victorian mills and the 17th century village with its charming old cottages and cobble streets. Its name is first mentioned as "Glotts Hop" in about AD650. Further back in time, the Romans came here and established a fort, now known as **Melandra Castle**, but probably then called Ardotalia. Built to guard the entrance to Longdendale, little survives today but the stone foundations. The settlement developed further as part of the monastic estates of Basingwerk Abbey in north Wales and the village received its market charter in 1290. Subsequently there was a decline in its importance, and little now remains of Old Glossop except the medieval parish **Church of All Saints**.

Planned as a new town in the 19th century by the Duke of Norfolk, the original village stood on the banks of the Glossop Brook at the crossing point of three turnpike roads. The brook had already been

10 THE DUKE OF YORK

Stockport

A former coaching inn on the banks of the Peak Forest canal that serves real ale and traditional English cuisine.

see page 164

11 ROYAL OAK INN

Glossop

A fine old early 19th century coaching inn that upholds the tradition of great hospitality, good food and good drink

see page 165

Melandra Castle Roman Fort, Glossop

15

12 THE RAINBOW BISTRO

Glossop

An intimate, welcoming establishment close to Glossop town centre that has a great reputation for its tea and coffee, lunches and dinners.

🍴 see page 166

13 THE OLD GLOVE WORKS

Glossop

A real gem of a pub that has a great programme of entertainment as well as good food and drink.

🍴 see page 167

14 THE CHIEFTAIN

Hadfield

A friendly, modern pub that welcomes all visitors, and sells great food and well-kept ales.

🍴 see page 168

harnessed to provide power for the cotton mills, as this was one of the most easterly towns of the booming Lancashire cotton industry. Many still refer to the older Glossop as Old Glossop and the Victorian settlement as Howard Town, named after the Duke, Bernard Edward Howard.

The **Glossop Heritage Centre** in Henry Street highlights the way the town has developed over the years, and has an art gallery and café. There are also resources for family history research.

DINTING

13 miles N of Buxton off the A624

The impressive **Dinting Arches**, a viaduct built to carry the main Sheffield to Manchester railway line, stands 120 feet high. The village church of the Holy Trinity was built in 1875 in Victorian gothic style and has a tall and elegant spire.

HADFIELD

14 miles N of Buxton off the A624

The small village of Hadfield is the terminus of the **Longdendale Trail**, which follows the line of the former Manchester to Sheffield railway line and is part of the Trans-Pennine Trail. It is now a safe, traffic-free trail for biking and walking. Its level sandy surface makes it suitable for wheelchair users and less agile people, as well as for families with small children and pushchairs. **Old Hall,** in The Square, is the oldest building in the village, built in 1646. The Roman Catholic Church of St Charles was built in 1868 by Baron Howard of Glossop; members of the Howard family are buried here.

The Longdendale Trail continues eastward from here. Longdendale itself is the valley of the River Etherow, and is a favourite place for day-trippers. Along the footpath through this wild and desolate valley there are many reminders of the past, including **Woodhead Chapel**, the graveyard of which has numerous memorials to the navvies, and their families, who died in an outbreak of cholera in 1849 while working on the two tunnels on the Sheffield to Manchester railway line. The chapel was originally built in 1487, though it has been rebuilt several times since.

Hadfield is where the TV comedy *The League of Gentlemen* was filmed.. In the series, the town was known as Royston Vasey , and some of the local shops have maps showing the locations of many of the scenes, as well as souvenirs of the programme.

NORTH EAST OF BUXTON

From Glossop, the A57 east is known as Snake Pass, and is an exhilarating stretch of road, with hair-pin bends. The road is frequently made impassable by landslides, heavy mist and massive snowfalls in winter but, weather permitting, it is an experience not to be missed. For much of the length of the turnpike road that Thomas Telford built across Snake

Pass in 1821, the route follows the line of an ancient Roman road, known as Doctor's Gate, which ran between Glossop and a fort at Brough. The route was so named after it was rediscovered, in the 16th century, by Dr Talbot, a vicar from Glossop. The illegitimate son of the Earl of Shrewsbury, Talbot used the road with great frequency as he travelled from Glossop to his father's castle at Sheffield.

Grindsbrook Booth Packhorse Bridge, Edale

EDALE

8 miles NE of Buxton off the A625

In the valley of the River Noe, Edale marks the start of the **Pennine Way**. Opened in 1965, this long-distance footpath follows the line of the backbone of Britain for some 270 miles from here to Kirk Yetholm, just over the Scottish border. Though the footpath begins in the lush meadows of this secluded valley, it is not long before walkers find themselves crossing the wild and bleak moorland of featherbed Moss before heading further north to Bleaklow. At Fieldhead is the Peak District National Park's information centre and campsite.

Many travellers have spoken of Derbyshire as a county of contrasts, and nowhere is this more apparent than at Edale. Not only does the landscape change dramatically within a short distance from the heart of the village, but the weather - as all serious walkers will know - can alter from brilliant sunshine to snowstorms in the space of a couple of hours.

The village, nestling at the foot

of Kinder Scout, is in the heart of dairy-farming and stock-rearing country, began as a series of scattered settlements that had grown around the shepherds' shelters or bothies. The true name of the village is actually Grindsbrook Booth, but it is commonly known by the name of the valley. Tourism first came to Edale with the completion of the Manchester to Sheffield railway in 1894, though at that time there was little in the way of facilities for visitors. Today there are several hotels, camping sites, a large youth hostel and adventure and walking centres.

Not far from the village is the famous **Jacob's Ladder**, overlooking the River Noe. Nearby is the tumbledown remains of a hill farmer's cottage; this was the home of Jacob Marshall, who some 200 years ago cut the steps into the hillside leading up to **Edale Cross**, an ancient boundary marker erected by the monks of Holywell abbey, Flintshire, who owned lands here in medieval times.

15 THE OLD NAG'S HEAD

Edale

One of the "100 great pubs of England" and a place where you are sure of good, honest food, self catering accommodation and drinks at affordable prices.

🍴 🛏 *see page 169*

16 THE RAMBLER COUNTRY HOUSE HOTEL

Edale

A hotel that marries comfort, great service and a warm welcome with outstanding value for money.

🛏 🍴 *see page 170*

17

17 CAUSEWAY HOUSE

Castleton

A superb B&B establishment within Castleton that offers value-for-money accommodation as well as a warm and friendly welcome.

see page 171

CASTLETON

8 miles NE of Buxton off the A625

Situated at the head of the Hope Valley, Castleton is sheltered by the Norman ruin of **Peveril Castle** (English Heritage). It was originally built in 1080 by William Peveril, king's bailiff for the Royal Manor of the Peak and thought to be the illegitimate son of William the Conquerer. In 1155 Henry ll, thinking that the Peverils had become too powerful, seized the castle and its lands, and it has formed part of the estate of the Duchy of Lancaster ever since. In 1157 King Malcolm of Scotland met Henry at Peveril Castle, and paid homage to him. In 1832 Sir Walter Scott published *Peveril of the Peak*, set in and around the castle.

The village is overlooked by Mam Tor, from which there are tremendous views. Known as the "shivering mountain", it rises to a height of 1,691 feet, and has the remains of an Iron Age fort at the top. Approaching Castleton from

the west along the A625, the road runs through the **Winnats Pass**, a narrow limestone gorge hemmed in on both sides by steep limestone hills. It is thought to have been created when huge caverns, carved out by swift flowing underground rivers, collapsed. The gorge, over a mile in length, has been used as a road for centuries and is still the only direct route to the village from the west.

Originally laid out as a planned town below its castle, the shape of the village has changed little over the years and it has become a popular tourist centre. **St Edmund Parish Church** was heavily restored in 1837, but retains its box pews and a fine Norman arch, as well as a Breeches Bible.

Two and a half miles west of the village at Rushup Edge, is **Lord's Seat,** a Bronze age burial mound.

On Oak Apple Day, 29th May, the ancient ceremony of garlanding takes place in the village, and after the three feet high Garland has been paraded though the streets, it is hoisted to the top of Saint Edmund's Church tower. The ceremony celebrates the ending of winter, and the restoration of Charles II to the throne in 1660 after the rule by the parliamentarians.

The Garland is a wooden frame, with bunches of wild flowers attached and a small wreath of garden flowers on top called the "Queen". The 'King', dressed in Stuart costume, with the garland on his shoulders, tours the village on

Castleton

horseback followed by a procession and a band. At the end of the ceremony the garland is left on the top of the tower of St Edmunds Church to wither and the Queen's wreath is placed on the war memorial. **Castleton Village Museum** in the Methodist Church School Room has a collection of garland memorabilia, including a king's costume worn 200 years ago.

The hills to the west of Castleton are famous for their caves, which have been in the hands of the Ollerenshaw family for many years, and are probably one of Derbyshire's most popular attractions. Amazing trips down into the caves themselves can be made. During these trips, as well as seeing the incredible natural beauty of the caverns and the unique rock formations, there are collections of original 19th century mining tools. Above ground, in the gift shops, various items can be bought made with the distinctive "Blue John" fluorspar with its attractive purplish veining, which is only found in the Castleton area.

The **Blue John Mine** is a natural cavern system with some old workings. The name "blue John" was given to the fluorspar in the 18th century by two miners, John Kirk and Joseph Hall. The best caverns within the system are the Crystallised Cavern and the Variegated Cavern. The **Ollerenshaw Collection** is a collection of huge vases and urns made with the same unique stone. Once prized by the Romans, it is said that Petronius paid the

equivalent of around £40,000 for a wonderfully ornate vase carved from the stone. It is said that in a fit of petty-mindedness, he preferred to smash the vase rather than relinquish it to the Emperor Nero.

At the bottom of Winnats Pass, only 1,000 metres (0.6 miles) from the centre of the village, lies **Speedwell Cavern.** It is a very gentle walk along the road to this former lead mine, which used boats on an underground canal to ferry the miners and lead ore to and from the rock face. Half way along is a small chamber known as Halfway House, which allows boats to pass as they go in and out. The mine had a short life: it started up in 1771 and, following an investment of £14,000, closed in 1790 after only £3,000 worth of iron ore had been extracted. This underground canal is about 800 metres long, finally reaching a glorious cavern with a huge subterranean lake known as the Bottomless Pit.

Treak Cliff Cavern is on the Mam Tor Road, and contains superb stalagmites and stalactites. The cavern is not a natural formation, as it was dug by miners for the Blue John fluorspar. However, while digging in 1926, the miners broke through into some natural caverns, which have some features now known as the Frozen Waterfall and Alladin's Cave.

Peak Cavern, (now again known as The Devil's Arse) is reached by a delightful riverside

18 TREAK CLIFF CAVERN

Castleton

This spectacular underground cavern contains a wealth of rock formations, minerals and fossils. A fascinating day out for all the family.

🏛 see page 171

•

No description of Castleton would be complete without a mention of Mam Tor. The name means 'Mother Hill', and locally the Tor is referred to as "Shivering Mountain", because the immense cliff face near the summit is constantly on the move owing to water seepage. A climb to the top of the ridge shows what a splendid vantage point it provides over the surrounding landscape; in particular of the two diverse rock formations, which differentiate the White (limestone) Peak from the northern Dark (gritstone) Peak.

•

Peveril Castle

walk, and has the widest opening of any cave in Europe. It is the only purely natural cavern in the system, with no mine workings whatsoever, and goes deep into the crag on which Peveril Castle stands. Up until the 17th century, little cottages used to stand within the entrance. The ropemakers who lived in these tiny dwellings used the cave entrance for making rope, the damp atmosphere being a favourable environment for rope making. Bert Marrison, the last rope maker in Castleton, worked here and his ashes, along with some of his tools, are buried here. The ropewalk, which dates back some 400 years, can still be seen and guides re-enact the process of making rope. One ropemaker's cottage still exists. Recently the cave was used by the BBC, who filmed an episode of *The Chronicles of Narnia* series here. Over the years successive kings and queens would entertain deep within the belly of the cave, which would be festooned with candles and other open flames - visitors can see the ledge on which the Royal musicians would

perch. Peak Cavern was originally known as The Devil's Arse, though the Victorians - ever fastidious - felt this was 'inappropriate' and changed it to the name it carries today.

Above Peak Cavern is **Peveril Castle** with its spectacular views over Castleton and the surrounding countryside. The castle, originally called Castle of the Peak, was built as a wooden stockade in 1080 by William Peveril, illegitimate son of William the Conqueror. Later rebuilt in stone, the keep was added by Henry II in 1176. It was originally about 60 feet high and faced with gritstone blocks, which still remain on the east and south sides and still dominates the view across Castleton. In Tudor times the building fell into disrepair, and the keep was used as a courthouse. Soon after, the castle was abandoned completely, with the stone being used for building cottages and dykes. The foundations of the Great Hall and kitchens can be seen inside the courtyard. It remains the only surviving example of a Norman castle in Derbyshire, and is among the best preserved and most complete ruins in Britain.

HOPE

9 miles NE of Buxton off the A625

Tradition says that a great battle took place here in the 7th century between the troops of Mercia, under King Penda, and Northumbrian troops under King Edwin. The tradition further states that two hills to the north of the village, **Win Hill** and **Lose Hill,** were so named because of the battle. However, the village gets its first recorded mention in a charter dated AD 926, where it mentions a great battle won by King Athelstan. By the time of the Domesday survey of 1086, the parish of Hope had extended to embrace much of the High Peak area and included places such as Buxton, Chapel-en-le-Frith and Tideswell, and was one of the largest parishes in England. It remained so until the 19th century, though a market charter was not granted it until 1715. Hope lies at the point where the River Noe meets Peakshole Water, which takes its name from its source in **Peak's Hole,** better known as Peak Cavern.

The parish **Church of St Peter** was built at the beginning of the 13th century. The only part remaining from that original church is the Norman font. Its tower is 14th century with a squat spire on top and, though the chancel was rebuilt in 1881, 14th century piscina and sedilia are incorporated into the walls. The Latin inscription on a chair in the north aisle reads (in translation), 'You cannot make a scholar out of a block of wood', and is said to have been carved for Thomas Bocking, the vicar and schoolmaster here during the 17th century. His name also appears on the fine pulpit, and his Breeches Bible is displayed nearby. From the outside, the squat 14th century

spire gives the church a rather curious shape. In the churchyard can be found the shaft of a Saxon cross.

The **Hope Agricultural Show** is held every year on August Bank Holiday Monday.

BROUGH

9 miles NE of Buxton off the A6187

At the village of Brough can be seen remains of the earthworks of the two-and-a-half acre fort of Navio ("The Place on the River"). At the confluence of the River Noe and Bradwell Brook, this rectangular fort was built in AD 158 to control the Romans' lead mining interests in the area. The site was excavated in the early 20th century.

BAMFORD

11 miles NE of Buxton off the A6187

This charming village situated between the Hope Valley and Ladybower Reservoir, stands at the heart of the Dark Peak below Bamford Edge and close to the Upper Derwent Valley dams. When

Saxon Cross, St Peter's Church, Hope

19 WOODROFFE ARMS

Hope
A delightful inn with comfortable accommodation, good food and a wide selection of drinks.

see page 172

21

20 YE DERWENT HOTEL

Bamford

A friendly, comfortable hotel with comfortable accommodation as well as good food and drink.

 see page 172

21 LADYBOWER INN

Bamford

A superb country inn amidst some lovely scenery that offers guest accommodation, home-ccoked food and real ales.

 see page 173

22 THE CASTLE INN

Bolsterstone

A delightful inn with a warm friendly feel to it that places great emphasis on food, drink and a warm welcome.

 see page 173

the Derwent and Howden dams were built in the early years of the 20th century, the valley of the Upper Derwent was flooded, submerging many farms under the rising waters. The 1,000 or so navvies and their families were housed at Birchinlee, a temporary village which came to be known locally as 'Tin Town', for its plethora of corrugated iron shacks. During the Second World War the third and largest reservoir, the **Ladybower**, was built. This involved the inundating of two villages — Derwent and Ashopton. Many buildings were lost including ancient farms and Derwent Hall, dating from 1672 and made into a youth hostel in 1931. The spire of the parish church was visible at first, but was demolished in 1947.

St John the Baptist Parish Church in Bamford was built between 1856 and 1860, and is unlike any other in Derbyshire. It was designed by the famous church architect William Butterfield, with a slender tower and an extra-sharp spire. It was here, within the churchyard, that the dead from Derwent's church were re-interred. The living were re-housed in Yorkshire Bridge, a purpose-built hamlet located below the embankment of the Ladybower Dam. A viaduct was built to carry the Snake Road over the reservoir at Ashopton and another for the road to Yorkshire Bridge. The packhorse bridge at Derwent, which had a preservation order on it, was moved stone by stone and rebuilt at Slippery Stones at the head of the Howden Reservoir. There is a Visitor Centre at **Fairholmes** (in the Upper Derwent Valley), which tells the story of these 'drowned villages'. The **Derwent Dam**, built in 1935, was the practice site for the Dambusters, who tested their bouncing bombs here.

Also worthy of note, particularly to lovers of industrial architecture, is **Bamford Mill**, just across the road by the river. This cotton mill, built in 1780 and rebuilt in 1971-1792 after a fire, retains its huge waterwheel and also has a 1907 tandem-compound steam engine. It ceased to operate as a cotton mill in 1965 and was used by an electric furnace manufacturer until a few years ago. It has now been converted into flats. The village lies in the heart of hill-farming country, and each Spring Bank Holiday Bamford plays host to one of the most famous of the Peak District sheepdog trials, which draws competition from all over the country. Well dressing takes place every July.

Along the A57 towards Sheffield, the road dips and crosses the gory-sounding **Cutthroat Bridge**. The present bridge dates back to 1830, but its name comes from the late 16th century, when the body of a man with his throat cut was discovered under the then bridge.

BRADWELL

9 miles NE of Buxton off the B6049

Usually abbreviated in the unique Peak District way to 'Bradder' -

Bradwell is a charming little limestone village sheltered by **Bradwell Edge**, from which there are good views. At one time this former lead mining community was famous as the place where miners' hardhats - hard, black, brimmed hats in which candles were stuck to light the way underground - were made; thus these hardhats came to be known as Bradder Beavers. It owes its fortune to the lead mining industry of the 18th and 19th centuries, though other items manufactured in Bradwell include coarse cotton goods, telescopes and opera glasses. It was also the birthplace of Samuel Fox, the 19th century inventor of the folding-frame umbrella. His house is marked with a plaque and lies just off the main street.

The centre of the village, which lies above the stream south of the main road, is a maze of narrow lanes with tiny cottages. Though most of the village dates from the lead mining era, Bradwell had been occupied in Roman times. A narrow street called Smalldale follows the line of the Roman road between Brough and Buxton. Near the New Bath Hotel, where there is a thermal spring, the remains of a Roman Bath were found. Legend has it that Bradwell was also once a Roman slave camp, with the slaves working in the lead mines.

During the period of struggle that followed the Romans' departure, the mysterious fortification to the north of the village, known as **Grey Ditch**, was built. Stretching from Mam Tor to Shatton Edge, it probably marked the boundary between the Anglo-Saxon kingdoms of Northumbria and Mercia. At Eden Tree ("Edwin's Tree") the Northumbrian King Edwin was supposed to have been hanged after a defeat in battle. Though a stronghold of nonconformism, Bradwell became an Anglican parish in 1868, the year **St Barnabas Parish Church** was built.

A key attraction here is the massive **Bagshawe Cavern**, a cave reached by descending a flight of 98 steps through an old lead mine. It was named after Sir William Bagshawe, who owned the land when it was discovered in 1806 by lead miners. For the more adventurous, caving trips are available.

A mile south of the village is the mid-16th century **Hazlebadge Hall**. One of several manors of the Vernon family, whose main seat was at Haddon Hall, their coat of arms can be seen above the upper mullioned windows. The house dates from 1549 and was part of Dorothy Vernon's dowry to her new husband, John Manners.

On the Saturday before the first Monday in August, four wells are dressed in the village. Although wells were dressed even at the turn of the 20th century, the present custom dates back only to 1949, when the Bowling Green Well was dressed during Small Dale Wakes. The village has its own particular method for making the colourful screens, section by section, so that the clay does not dry out.

23 ROBIN HOOD

Little Matlock

A family-owned freehouse with stylish accommodation that is popular with both visitors and locals alike.

see page 174

24 YE OLDE BOWLING GREEN INN

Bradwell

An old, historic inn with many period features that also offers six superb, five-star rooms on a B&B basis.

see page 175

25 NEW BATH INN

Bradwell

A friendly pub in a small hamlet that its noted for its friendly clientele and great food and drink.

see page 176

26 POOL CAFÉ

Hathersage

A friendly cafe that sells teas and coffees, light snacks and lunches, and possibly the finest fish and chips in the area!

see page 177

HATHERSAGE

12 miles NE of Buxton off the A625

The name Hathersage comes from the Old English for 'Haefer's ridge' - probably a reference to the line of gritstone edges of which the moorland slopes of **Stanage Edge**, overlooking the town to the east, is the largest. It is surrounded by spectacular tors, such as Higgar Tor, and the ancient fortress at Carl Wark. Several of the edges were quarried for millstones for grinding corn and metals.

It is difficult to know whether to classify Hathersage as a large village or a small town. In either event, it is a pleasant place with interesting literary connections. Charlotte Brontë stayed at Hathersage vicarage in 1845, and the village itself appears as 'Norton' in her novel *Jane Eyre*. The name Eyre was probably gleaned from the monuments to the prominent local landowners with this surname, which can be seen in the village churchyard. The Eyre

Grave of Little John, Hathersage

family has been associated with this area for over 800 years. Legend has it that the family were given their name by William the Conqueror. During the Battle of Hastings, so it is said, William was knocked from his horse and, wearing his now battered helmet, found it difficult to breathe. A Norman, Truelove, saw the King's distress and helped him take the helmet off and get back on his horse. In gratitude the King said that from thenceforth Truelove would be known as 'Air' for helping the King to breathe.

Later the King learned that Air had lost most of a leg in the battle, and made arrangements for Air and his family to be cared for and granted land in this part of Derbyshire. The name became corrupted to Eyre over the years, and the family's coat of arms shows a shield on top of which is a single armoured leg. The 15th century head of the family, Robert Eyre, lived at Highlow Hall. Within sight of this Hall he built seven houses, one for each of his seven sons. **North Lees** was one, which Charlotte Brontë took as a model for Rochester's house, Thornfield Hall. It is one of the finest Elizabethan buildings in the region - a tall square tower with a long wing adjoining and the grounds are open to the public. Another was **Moorseats**, where Charlotte Brontë stayed on holiday and used as the inspiration for Moor House in *Jane Eyre*.

St Michael's Parish Church is said to date from 1381, though it

has been much altered and extended over the years. There are brasses of the Eyre family, and an Eyre family chapel once stood on the north side of the chancel, on the other side of the tomb to Robert Eyre, dating from 1459. In the churchyard lie the reputed remains of **Little John**, Robin Hood's renowned companion. Whether or not the legend is to be believed, it is worth mentioning that when the grave was opened in the 1780s, a 32-inch thighbone was discovered. This would certainly indicate that the owner was well over seven feet tall. The whole area surrounding Hathersage has features with such names as Robin Hood's Cave, Hood Valley, Hood Brook and Robin Hood's Moss.

Until the late 18th century Hathersage was a small agricultural village with cottage industries making brass buttons and wire, until in 1750 a Henry Cocker started the Atlas Works, a mill for making wire. By the early 19th century it had become a centre for the manufacture of needles and pins. Though water power was used initially for the mills, by the mid-19th century smoke from the industrial steam engines enveloped the village. The fragments of dust and steel dispersed in the process of sharpening the needles destroyed the lungs of the workers, reducing their life expectancy to 30 years. There was also a paper mill, with the paper being used to wrap the needles and pins. The last mill here closed in 1902, as needle making moved to Sheffield, but

several of the mills still stand, including the Atlas Works.

Highlow Hall is a fine, battlemented manor built in the 1500s by the Eyre family. It features an attractive gateway and a stone dovecote. It is said to be haunted by a ghost known as The White Lady, thought to be the older sister of the wife of Nicholas Eyre, founder of the Eyre family. Nicholas had promised to marry her, but instead jilted her in favour of her younger sister. She was so humiliated she killed herself.

EAST EDGES OF THE DARK PEAK

FROGGATT

5 miles N of Bakewell off the B6054

This neat village sits below the gritstone escarpment known as **Froggatt Edge**. Nearby **Stoke Hall**, situated high above the Derwent Valley, was built in 1757 for Revd John Simpson and was later leased to Robert Arkwright, son of Sir Richard Arkwright, who lived here while he managed the Lumsford Mill at Bakewell. The Hall is now a hotel and restaurant, but remains home to a ghost, said to have been haunting the building for well over 100 years. The ghost is claimed to be that of a maid at the Hall who, while pining for a soldier fighting overseas, was brutally murdered. Her employers at the Hall were so shocked by this that they built a memorial to her in

27 MILLSTONE COUNTRY INN

Hathersage

A former coaching inn that combines sophistication with traditional values, and offers fine dining, pub grub, drink, and en suite accommodation.

see page 178

25

Froggatt Edge

28 THE EATING HOUSE

Calver Bridge

The perfect place for a lunch or snack, sitting within the ever-popular Derbyshire Craft Centre at Calver Bridge.

🍴 see page 177

possible, to prevent the spread of the disease. Many of the graves were left unmarked, but at Curbar the **Cundy Graves** (dating from 1632) can be seen on the moors above the village. They are named after the Cundy family, who farmed nearby. Below the Wesleyan Reform Church there are other graves.

Missionaries have trained at **Cliffe College,** since 1883. It is now a theological college and conference centre, offering degrees in many aspects of theology, and is sponsored by the Methodist Church. Interesting older features of the village include a circular pinfold or stock compound on top of Pinfold Hill, where stray animals were kept until claimed by their owners. There is also a covered well and circular trough, and an unusual village lock-up with a conical roof. The coarse gritstone ridge of **Curbar Edge,** which shelters the village, is popular with rock climbers.

the front garden. However, the memorial was seen to move not long after it had been erected, and so it was rebuilt in a quiet corner of the estate, where it remains undisturbed.

CURBAR

5 miles NE of Bakewell off the A623

Curbar is a hillside village very close to Calver. It grew up around the crossing point of the River Derwent on the old turnpike road.

Although it is Eyam that is famous as the Plague Village, many communities suffered greatly at the hands of this terrible disease. Curbar was no different, though the plague visited it 30 years before it came to Eyam. During the height of the infection bodies were interred away from the centre of the village, and usually as quickly as

CALVER

4 miles NE of Bakewell off the A623

Recorded as Calvoure in the *Domesday Book*, evidence of an early Anglo-Saxon settlement was found when skeletons were discovered in limestone rock in 1860. It is a pleasant, stone-built village, situated by the River Derwent, with a pleasing 18th century bridge.

Calver is home to one of the most sinister buildings known to television viewers with long memories. The handsome, though austere, **Georgian Cotton Mill,** which is now converted into luxury flats, was the infamous Colditz Castle of the television series of that name. It was built between 1803 and 1804 by Arkwright to replace a mill built in the 1780s.

BASLOW

4 miles NE of Bakewell off the A619

Standing at the northern gates to Chatsworth, Baslow has, for centuries, been closely linked with the affairs of the Cavendish family. The village has three distinct parts – Bridge End, the oldest part around the church, Over End, a residential area to the north of the village and Nether End, next to the Chatsworth Estate. The village is unusual in having thatched cottages rather than the more traditional tile, slate or gritstone shingled roofs. Though most houses in the area were thatched, they are much less common today and give the village a very distinctive air. The village **Church of St Anne** dates partly from the 15th century, with later

Old Tollhouse, Baslow

additions. It was heavily restored in 1852 and 1853 by the then Duke of Devonshire. It is beautifully situated by the River Derwent, and has a squat broach spire that dominates the village. One of the clock faces on the church is very unusual. It was added to commemorate Queen Victoria's Diamond Jubilee in 1897, and it is well worth a second glance. It has 'Victoria' and '1897' around the edge of the clock face in place of numerals - the idea of a local man, Lieutenant-Colonel E. M. Wrench. The fragment of an ancient Saxon cross shaft can also be found in the porch. Inside the church another unusual feature is preserved: a whip that was used to drive stray dogs out of the church during services in the 17th and 18th centuries. Some people claim it was also used to waken people who fell asleep during a service and snored.

Baslow sits beneath its own Peakland 'edge', which provides fine views across the Derwent Valley towards Chatsworth House. From the **Eagle Stone,** a 6 metre high block of gritstone on Baslow Edge, to the north of the village, there are wonderful views. Climbing to the top of this isolated rock was a test for every young Baslow man before he married. It is here that the same Lieutenant-Colonel Wrench who had the unusual clock face installed, erected the **Wellington Monument** in 1866 to celebrate the Duke's victory at Waterloo and to counterbalance the monument to Nelson on Birchen Edge not far away. It is in the form of a ten-feet-high cross.

29 AVANT GARDE OF BASLOW

Baslow

A wonderful shop full of stylish and well designed furnishings and furniture that would grace any interior.

see page 179

30 THE DEVONSHIRE ARMS HOTEL

Baslow

A superb hotel with 12 beautiful en suite rooms, fine dining and a great range of real ales for you to enjoy.

see page 180

31 THE JOLLY SAILOR

Macclesfield

A friendly and warm town pub that you should seek out for its food and drink as well as its five guest bedrooms.

 see page 181

32 DOLPHIN INN

Macclesfield

A favourite with locals and visitors alike. It serves good food at lunchtime, plus a wide range of drinks, including three real ales.

see page 182

33 PUSS IN BOOTS

Macclesfield

A cosy yet spacious pub near the centre of Macclesfield with a canal-side beer garden, serving good food and drink.

see page 182

Baslow has two very fine bridges over the Derwent. The **Old Bridge**, which is near the church, was built in 1603. It is the only bridge across the Derwent which has never been destroyed by floods. It replaced a wooden bridge, and one of the tasks of able-bodied men in the village at one time was to guard this bridge in case its weight limits were exceeded. The watch house still exists, and it has an entrance which is only 3-and-a-half feet high. It also used to offer shelter to tramps and beggars. The **Devonshire Bridge** was built just after the First World War, and carries most of the traffic across the river nowadays.

THE CHESHIRE PEAK DISTRICT

MACCLESFIELD

Nestling below the hills of the High Peak, Macclesfield was once an important silk manufacturing town.

Charles Roe built the first silk mill here, beside the River Bollin, in 1743 and for more than a century-and-a-half, Macclesfield was known as *the* silk town. It's appropriate, then, that Macclesfield can boast the country's only **Silk Museum** where visitors are given a lively introduction to all aspects of the silk industry, from cocoon to loom. Originally the Macclesfield School of Art, built in 1877 to train designers for the silk industry, the museum has an award-winning audio-visual presentation, fascinating exhibitions on the Silk Road across Asia, silk cultivation, fashion and other uses of silk. A shop dedicated to silk offers a range of attractive and unusual gifts – scarves, ties, silk cards and woven pictures along with inexpensive gifts for children.

The silk theme continues at nearby **Paradise Mill**. Built in the 1820s, it is now a working museum demonstrating silk weaving on 26 restored jacquard hand looms. Exhibitions and restored workshops and living rooms capture the working conditions and lives of mill workers in the 1930s. It is also possible to buy locally-made silk products here. Within the town's **Heritage Centre** is another silk museum, which has some interesting displays on Macclesfield's rich and exciting past, (the town was occupied for five days by Scottish troops during the Jacobite Rebellion of 1745, for example). The Hertiage Centre is housed within a former Sunday School which was built in 1813 and finally closed in 1970.

In pre-Saxon times, Macclesfield was known as "Hameston" – the homestead on the rock, and on that rock is set the church founded by King Edward I and Queen Eleanor - the **Parish Church of St Michael and All Angels**. From the modern town, a walk to the church involves climbing a gruelling flight of 108 steps. The core of the church is 14th century, but it was extended in the 1890s. The Legh Chapel within it dates from 1442, when Pierz Legh, who fought at Agincourt and was killed at the Siege of Meaux, was interred within it. Another chapel contains the famous Legh Pardon brass, which recalls the medieval practice of selling pardons for past sins, and even for those not yet committed. The inscription on the brass records that, in return for saying five Paternosters and five Aves, the Legh family received a pardon for 26,000 years and 26 days.

One of the Macclesfield area's most famous sons is **Charles Frederick Tunnicliffe**, the celebrated bird and wild-life artist, who was born at the nearby village of Langley in 1901. He studied at the Macclesfield School of Art and first came to public attention with his illustrations for Henry Williamson's *Tarka the Otter* in 1927. A collection of Tunnicliffe's striking paintings can be seen at the **West Park Museum** on the northwest edge of the town. This purpose-built museum, founded in 1898 by the Brocklehurst family, also includes exhibits of ancient Egyptian artifacts, as well as fine and decorative arts.

Much less well-known is **William Buckley** who was born in Macclesfield around 1780 and later became a soldier. He took part in a mutiny at Gibraltar against the Rock's commanding officer, the Duke of York, father-to-be of Queen Victoria. The mutiny failed and Buckley was transported to Australia. There he escaped into the outback and became the leader of an aboriginal tribe who took this giant of a man, some 6 feet 6 inches tall, as the reincarnation of a dead chief. For 32 years Buckley never saw a white man or heard a word of English. When the explorer John Bateman, on his way to found what is now Melbourne, discovered him, Buckley had virtually forgotten his mother tongue. He was pardoned, given a pension and was killed in an accident at Hobart at the age of 76.

AROUND MACCLESFIELD

PRESTBURY

3 miles N of Macclesfield off the A538

A regular winner of the Best Kept Village title, Prestbury is a charming village where a tree-lined High Street runs down to a bridge over the River Bollin. Ancient stocks stand against the church wall, and old coaching inns and black and white buildings mingle with the mellow red brick work of later Georgian houses. The **Parish Church of St Peter**, dating from the 13th century, still maintains a tradition which began in 1577. Every autumn and winter evening at 8pm a curfew bell is rung, with the number of chimes corresponding to the date of the month. Close by is a building

34 JASPERS

Macclesfield

A friendly eating place that serves good, honest food at value-for-money prices. Check it out!

🍴 see page 183

35 THE RISING SUN INN

Rainow

A picturesque inn with a fine reputation for its great food, cooked on the premsies by Lee, one of the managers and a professional chef.

🍴 see page 183

36 ADLINGTON HALL

Adlington

A superb historic house with interesting original features and a delightful garden.

 see *page 184*

37 VALE INN

Bollington

A handsome, award-winning inn that serves good food and drink, and has a beer garden sloping down to the village cricket pitch.

 see *page 185*

38 COFFEE TAVERN

Pott Shrigley

A superb licensed restaurant and coffee shop in a small village that also sells locally-made craft items.

 see *page 185*

known as the **Norman Chapel** with a striking frontage carved with the characteristic Norman zig-zags and beaked heads. Even older are the carved fragments of an 8th century Saxon cross, preserved under glass in the graveyard. Opposite the church is a remarkable magpie timber-framed house which is now a bank but used to be the vicarage. During the Commonwealth, the rightful incumbent was debarred from preaching in the church by the Puritans. Undaunted, the priest addressed his parishioners from the tiny balcony of his vicarage.

Charles Edward Stuart's Jacobite army passed through the village in late November 1745 on its way south to London. Four or five regiments marched through, followed by the prince and his bodyguard. An eyewitness described him as being a 'very handsome person of a man', in Highland dress, with a blue waistcoat trimmed in silver and wearing a blue Highland bonnet.

ADLINGTON

4 miles N of Macclesfield off the A523

Adlington boasts a fine old house, **Adlington Hall,** which has been the home of the Legh family since 1315 and is now one of the county's most popular attractions. Quadrangular in shape, this magnificent manor house has two distinctive styles of architecture: black and white half-timbered buildings on two sides, later Georgian additions in warm red brick on the others. There is

much to see as you tour the hall, with beautifully polished wooden floors and lovely antique furnishings, enhancing the air of elegance and grandeur. The Great Hall is a breathtaking sight, a vast room of lofty proportions that set off perfectly the exquisitely painted walls. The beautifully preserved 17th century organ here has responded to the touch of many maestros, none more famous than George Frederick Handel who visited the hall in the 1740s.

It wasn't long after Handel's visit to Cheshire that the county was gripped by a mania for building canals, a passion that has left Cheshire with a uniquely complex network of these environmentally friendly waterways.

BOLLINGTON

4 miles NE of Macclesfield on the B5091

In its 19th century heyday, there were 13 cotton mills working away at Bollington, a little town perched on the foothills of the High Peak. Two of the largest mills, the Clarence and the Adelphi, still stand, although now adapted to other purposes. The Victorian shops and cottages around Water Street and the High Street recall those busy days. A striking feature of the town is the splendid 20-arched viaduct which once carried the railway over the River Dean. It is now part of the **Middlewood Way,** a ten mile, traffic-free country trail which follows a scenic route from Macclesfield to Marple. The Way is open to walkers, cyclists and horse riders and during the season cycles are available for hire, complete with child seats if required. Just as remarkable as the viaduct, although in a different way, is **White Nancy.** This sugar-loaf shaped, whitewashed round tower stands on Kerridge Hill, more than 900 feet above sea level. It was erected in 1817 to commemorate the Battle of Waterloo and offers sweeping views in all directions.

SUTTON

2 miles S of Macclesfield off the A523

This small village, close to the Macclesfield Canal, is honoured by scholars as the birthplace of **Raphael Holinshed**, whose famous *Chronicles of England, Scotland & Ireland* (1577) provided the source material for no fewer than 14 of Shakespeare's plays. As well as drawing heavily on the facts in the Chronicles, the playwright wasn't above plagiarising some of Holinshed's happier turns of phrase. The **Parish Church of St George** was built in 1822 as a chapel attached to St Peter's Church in Prestbury. In 1835 it became a parish church in its own right.

BOSLEY

6 miles S of Macclesfield on the A523

To the east of Bosley town centre is the **Macclesfield Canal,** one of the highest waterways in England, running for much of its length at more than 500 feet above sea level. Thomas Telford was the surveyor of the 26-mile long route, opened in 1831, which links the Trent & Mersey and the Peak Forest canals. Between Macclesfield and Congleton, the canal descends over 100 feet in a spectacular series of 12 locks at Bosley, before crossing the River Dane via Telford's handsome iron viaduct.

Other unusual features of this superbly engineered canal are the two "roving bridges" south of Congleton. These swing from one bank to the other where the towpath changes sides and so enabled horses to cross over without having to unhitch the tow-rope.

The red-brick **Parish Church of St Mary** was a chapel of St Peter's in Prestbury before becoming Bosley's parish church in 1883. It dated originally from the 15th century, and the present tower was built in the 16th century.

39 SUTTON HALL

Sutton

A magnificent hotel situated at the heart of 14 acres of grounds, offering wonderful accommodation, great food and cask-conditioned ales.

see page 186

40 THE HANGING GATE INN

Higher Sutton

A real 'olde worlde' inn with spectacular views of the Peak District, a warm friendly welcome and great food and drink.

see page 187

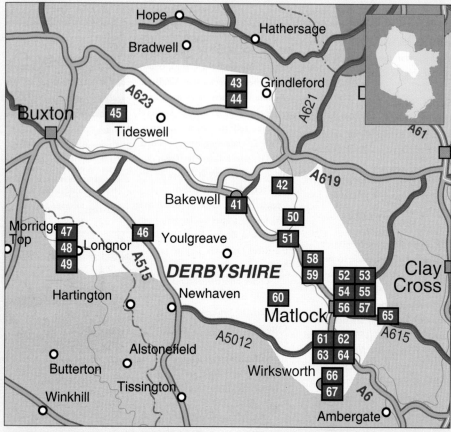

Bakewell, Matlock and the White Peak

Matlock Bath

This region of the Derbyshire Dales, sometimes also known as the Central Peak and occupying the central area of the Peak District National Park between the two major towns of Ashbourne and Buxton, is less wild and isolated than the remote High Peak area. It is more intensely farmed, and sheep and cattle dot the fields, which are separated by dry stone walls. The limestone plateau of the White Peak was laid down in a tropical sea over 300 million years ago, along with the fossilized remains of countless tiny sea creatures. The two main rivers, the Wye and the Derwent, which both have their source farther north, are, in this region, at a more gentle stage of their course. Over the centuries, the fast-flowing waters were harnessed to provide power to drive the mills situated on the riverbanks; any walk taken along these riverbanks will not only give the opportunity to discover a wide range of plant and animal life, but also provide the opportunity to see the remains of buildings that once played an important part in the economy of north Derbyshire.

The town of Bakewell lies in the White Peak and, although to the northeast of the town lie the eastern edges of the Dark Peak, most of its surrounding villages are in the White Peak. It is the only town in the Peak District National Park.

Magpie Mine, Sheldon

33

BAKEWELL

The annual Bakewell Show, held every summer at the beginning of August, started in 1819 and has gone on to become one of the foremost agricultural shows in the country. Across the River Wye stands the enormous Agricultural and Business Centre, where the livestock market takes place.

Bakewell, the only town in the Peak District National Park, dominates the area. Close to it are two of the most magnificent stately homes in Britain, Chatsworth House and Haddon Hall. The vast Chatsworth estate straddles the River Derwent east of Bakewell, but the influence of the Cavendish family extends much further and few villages in the surrounding area have escaped. Haddon Hall is the home of the Manners family, and is considered to be one of the best manor houses in England to have survived from the Middle Ages.

The only true town in the Peak District National Park, Bakewell attracts many day-trippers, walkers and campers as well as locals who come to take advantage of its many amenities. The beautiful medieval five-arched bridge spanning the River Wye is still in use today as the main crossing-point for traffic.

It is mentioned in the *Domesday Book* as 'Badequella', meaning 'bath

well', and indeed 12 hot iron-bearing springs used to rise in and around the town. It enjoys a picturesque setting among well-wooded hills, and while it only has 4,000 inhabitants, it is nevertheless generally acknowledged as the capital of the Peak District National Park. Its situation has always made it the ideal place for a settlement and, as well as being home to the Romans, an Iron Age fort has been discovered close by.

Bakewell was founded in AD924, and though it is famous for its Bakewell puddings, its name has nothing to do with baking. However, for most people it is a dessert that has made the name of Bakewell so famous, but please remember it is referred to locally as a *pudding* and most definitely not as a tart! Its invention is said to have been an accident when what was supposed to have been a strawberry tart turned into something altogether different. The cooking mishap took place in the kitchens of the Rutland Arms Hotel, which was built in 1804 on the site of an old coaching inn called the White. Mrs Greaves, the mistress, instructed the cook to prepare strawberry tart and the cook, instead of stirring the egg mixture into the pastry, spread it on top of the jam. The result was so successful that a Mrs Wilson, wife of a tallow chandler, saw the possibility of making the puddings for sale and obtained the so-called recipe and commenced in a business of her own. Several

Five-Arched Bridge, Bakewell

34

businesses in the town claim to have the original recipe.

Although it's a delightful tale, it is known that similar puddings were being made in the area from about the 16th century onwards. Lady Dorothy Vernon of Haddon Hall (whose famous elopement took place in 1563) is said to have been fond of them. Some people claim that they actually found their way to Derbyshire from France. The likeliest explanation of their origin is that they started as a type of 'transparent' pudding, popular in the 18th century, in which a layer of fruit or jam was covered with a mixture of sugar, butter and eggs and then baked. These puddings were usually baked in a dish without pastry. Eliza Acton's recipe for Bakewell pudding without pastry first appeared in 1845 in 'Modern Cookery'. By 1861 Mrs Beeton's recipe had a puff pastry case. Almonds were not used in the original Bakewell pudding, although either almond essence or ground almonds feature in most modern recipes.

The novelist Jane Austen reputedly stayed at the Rutland Arms in 1811 and it featured in her book *Pride and Prejudice*, while Bakewell itself is said to appear as the town of Lambton, and Pemberley is Chatsworth House. However, in the TV adaptation, Lyme Park in Cheshire and Sudbury Hall south of Ashbourne stood in for Pemberley.

The market town for this whole central area of the Peak District, markets were held here

well before the granting of a charter in 1330. Monday is now Bakewell's market day and the cattle market, one of the largest in Derbyshire, is an important part of the area's farming life.

The large parish **Church of All Saints** was founded in Saxon times, as revealed by the ancient preaching crosses and stonework. Its graceful spire, with its octagonal tower, can be seen for miles around. One of the few places in Derbyshire in the *Domesday Book* to record two priests and a church, the churchyard and church itself contain a wonderful variety of headstones and coffin slabs and, near the porch, a most unusual cross. Over 1,200 years old, it stands an impressive eight feet high. However, its carvers hedged their bets when it came to which gods to worship. On one side it depicts the Crucifixion, on the other are the Norse gods Odin and Loki.

The west front of the church is still essentially Norman. Most of the eastern end , plus the south transept and the chancel, date from the 13th century. The decorative font is early 14th century, as are the chancel stalls, which have interesting misericords. The Vernon Chapel to the east end of the south aisle has impressive monuments to 'The King of the Peak', Sir George Vernon of Haddon Hall, who died in 1567, and also to Sir John Manners, who died in 1584, and his wife Dorothy Vernon - these latter two feature in one of the great romantic legends of the Peak District. Behind the church are the

Traditionally well-dressing flourished in the town in the 18th century, when Bakewell had aspirations to become a fashionable spa. However, the recent revival dates back only to the 1970s, when the British Legion - with the help of the well-dressers of Ashford in the Water - dressed the warm well at Bath House. Today, all five wells are dressed on the last Saturday in June.

St John's Hospital Almshouses, founded in 1709 for the 'deserving poor' of the town.

Behind the church is the lovely **Old House Museum**, housed in a building on Cunningham Place which dates back to 1534. It is thought to be the oldest house in Bakewell, and was originally built as a parsonage. It later became the home of the tithe collector for the local Gell family. This beautiful building escaped demolition and was lovingly restored from 1959 onwards by the Bakewell Historical Society and now displays its original wattle and daub interior walls. It was extended during the early 17th century and, at one time, the building was converted into tenements by the industrialist Richard Arkwright for his mill-workers at Lumford. Now established as a folk museum, it houses a fascinating collection of rural bygones.

The town is full of delightful, mellow stone buildings, many of which date from the early 17th century and are still in use today. The **Old Town Hall** dates from 1790, and is now a shop. It is famous as the scene of the **Bakewell Riots**, which took place in 1796. The Lord Lieutenant of Derbyshire, the Duke of Devonshire, was about to conduct a ballot to see which of the able-bodied men in the town would serve in the local militia, raised due to the great alarm throughout the country on account of the French Revolution. Derbyshire was asked to send 560 men, of which 100

were to come from the High Peak. A rumour circulated that Derbyshire was being asked to send more than its fair share of men for training, and local unrest grew.

To begin with about 40 men, most of them lead miners, marched into Bakewell armed with the tools of their trade - picks and shovels. They assembled at the town hall and announced that they would destroy the ballot papers on the day when the next sitting of the magistrates at the local quarter sessions court took place. The men then made their way to an inn and started drinking.

On the day of the sitting, many men made their way into the town from the surrounding villages. They entered the court, grabbed the papers from the magistrates and threw them on a bonfire. By now an unruly crowd had congregated, armed with clubs, picks and spades. To the dismay of the protest organisers, they started looting, and many Bakewell people volunteered as special constables to put the riots down. However, the magistrates called in the county cavalry instead, and they soon quelled the rioters. Six men were sent to prison, and the damage to the town, in today's terms, ran into many thousands of pounds.

The National Park and Bakewell Visitor Centre is housed in the late 17th century **Market Hall**. Few buildings remain from the days when Bakewell was a minor spa town, but the **Bath House**, on Bath Street, is one such building. Built in 1697 for the Duke of Rutland, it contained a large bath which was filled with the spa water and kept at a constant temperature of 59 degrees Fahrenheit. The **Castle Inn**, dating from the 16th century, sits by the medieval bridge.

There is little evidence of industry in the town, which is not very surprising considering Bakewell is surrounded by farming country, but the remnants of **Lumford Mill** can still be seen. Originally built in 1778 by Sir Richard Arkwright as a cotton spinning mill, over 300 hands, mainly women and children, were employed here. Badly damaged by fire in 1868, the Mill has been rebuilt and it is used as offices today. Here can also be found a very fine example of a low-parapeted packhorse bridge across the Wye, dating from 1664. **Holme Hall** to the north of town dates from 1626. This Jacobean hall faces the water-meadows of the Wye.

NORTH OF BAKEWELL

EDENSOR

2 miles E of Bakewell off the B6012

This model village (the name is pronounced Ensor) was built by the 6th Duke of Devonshire between 1838 and 1842, after the original village was demolished because it spoilt the view from **Chatsworth House**. Unable to decide on a specific design for the buildings, as suggested by the architect Paxton (who also designed his gardens),

the Duke had the cottages and houses in the new village built in a fascinating variety of styles. **St Peter's Church** was rebuilt to the designs of Sir George Gilbert Scott in 1867, though some fabric from an earlier building was incorporated. Inside the church is a brass to John Beaton, a servant of Mary, Queen of Scots.

In the churchyard is buried the late President John F. Kennedy's sister Kathleen (known as "Kick"), who had married the Marquis of Hartington, heir to the 10th Duke of Devonshire, in 1944. Kathleen's mother, Rose Kennedy, objected to the marriage, as the Marquis was a Protestant. When the marquis was killed by a German sniper four months later, Rose saw it as divine retribution. She later became engaged to the 8th Earl Fitzwilliam, and both of them were killed in 1948 in an airplane crash in France.

The original village of Edensor lay nearer to the gates of Chatsworth House. Only Park Cottage remains there now.

42 CHATSWORTH HOUSE

nr Edensor
Magnificent stately home containing a wealth of art treasures including furniture and porcelain.

 see page 189

St Peter's Church, Edensor

37

To the south of the village of Hassop is Hassop Station, built in 1863, to serve the Duke of Devonshire at Chatsworth House and not for the convenience of the villagers. Now situated on the nine-mile-long Monsal Trail, which follows the former course of the old Midland Railway from Bakewell to just east of Buxton, the station building is now a bookshop.

PILSLEY

2 miles NE of Bakewell off the A619

There are two villages in Derbyshire called Pilsley, the other one being in northeast Derbyshire near Chesterfield. This one is a relatively new village created by the Duke of Devonshire after he had demolished Chatsworth village to make way for his mansion house and estate. It is now the estate workers who help the villagers dress four wells to coincide with the village fair in mid-July, a custom revived in 1968. The Shire Horse Stud Farm, built by the 9th Duke of Devonshire in 1910, has been converted into a variety of craft workshops and a farm shop.

HASSOP

3 miles N of Bakewell off the B6001

This little village is dominated by its fine Roman Catholic **Church of All Saints,** which dates from 1818. It was built by the Eyre family who, as well as being devout Catholics, also owned some 20 manors in the area. Hidden behind a high wall is one of the Eyre manor houses, **Hassop Hall**. Dating from the 17th century, the Hall

was garrisoned for the King by Thomas Eyre during the Civil War and it remained in the family until the mid-19th century when there were a series of contested wills. The Hall is now a private hotel and restaurant and it is said to contain a former lead mine shaft under a manhole cover in its cellars.

GREAT LONGSTONE

3 miles NW of Bakewell off the B6465

This attractive stone built Peak District village nestling below the five mile long Longstone Edge, which rises to 1300 feet at Bleak Low. **Longstone Hall**, built in 1747 of red brick, was the home of the Wright family (who now live at Eyam Hall). The present Hall replaced a much larger Elizabethan building which is said to have been similar in style, but bigger, than the present Eyam Hall. **St Giles Parish Church** dates originally from the 13th century, and has a particularly fine roof, with moulded beams, that dates from the 15th century. In the nave is a plaque placed to commemorate the work of Dr Edward Buxton who, in the 1820s and aged 73 years, treated the whole village against an outbreak of typhus.

Thornbridge Hall sits close by and dates from the Georgian period, though it was altered considerably in 1871. It is now a conference centre.

STONEY MIDDLETON

4 miles N of Bakewell off the A623

This village, known simply as "Stoney" locally, is certainly well

Village Cross, Great Longstone

named as, particularly in this part of **Middleton Dale**, great walls of limestone rise up from the valley floor. Further up the Dale there are also many disused limestone quarries as well as the remains of some lead mines. Not all industry has vanished from the area, as this is the home of nearly three-quarters of the country's fluorspar industry. Another relic from the past also survives - a shoe and boot-making company operates from the village and is housed in a former corn mill.

An ancient village, the Romans built a bath here, and it is mentioned in the *Domesday Book* as Midletune. It is thought that the place originated when a motte and bailey castle was built on **Castle Hill**, but was abandoned in the 14th century due to the Black Death. The unusual octagonal **St Martin's Parish Church** of 1759 replaced a smaller one, destroyed by fire, of which the tower still survives. It was built by Joan Eyre in thanksgiving for the safe return of her husband from the field of the Battle of Agincourt in the 15th century. It is said that she actually built the church at a place where she and her husband-to-be met and courted in secret, as her family did not approve of him. Stoney Middleton has preserved its village identity and character and also partakes in the custom of well-dressing, when two wells around The Nook are dressed in late July/ early August.

Middleton Hall dates originally from about 1600, but was much altered by the Denman family in the 19th century. The most famous Denman was a lawyer who became Lord Chief Justice of England in 1832.

Stoney Middleton was one of the villages whose villagers, admiring the resolve of the villagers of Eyam during the plague of 1665-1666, left food and clothing out for them on the edge of Eyam.

EYAM

5 miles N of Bakewell off the B6521

Pronounced 'Eem', this village will forever be known as the **Plague Village**. In 1665, a local tailor, George Vicars, received a bundle of plague-infected clothing from London. Within a short time the infection had spread and the terrified inhabitants prepared to flee the village. However, the local rector, William Mompesson, and his predecessor Thomas Stanley persuaded the villagers to stay put and, thanks to his intervention, most neighbouring villages escaped the disease. Eyam was quarantined for over a year, relying on outside help for supplies of food which were left on the village boundary. Out of a total of 350 inhabitants, only 83 survived. Whole families were wiped out, and there were no formal funerals. People were buried close to where they died without ceremony. At Riley Farm, the farmer's wife buried her husband and six children within eight days. The **Riley Graves**, as they are called nowadays, are still there.

An open-air service is held

Higher up the dale from the village of Stoney Middleton is the dramatically named Lover's Leap. In 1762, a jilted girl, Hannah Badderley, tried to jump to her death by leaping from a high rock. Her voluminous skirts, however, were caught on some brambles and she hung from the ledge before gently rolling down into a sawpit and escaping serious injury.

43 STABLES AT EYAM

Eyam
A superb tearoom and restaurant that is fast gaining a fine reputation for its good food and its amazing value for money.

see page 190

Eyam Parish Church

44 EYAM MUSEUM

Eyam

Learn the full story behind this village, once devasted by plague.

 see page 189

each August at Cucklet Delf to commemorate the villagers' brave self-sacrifice, and the well-dressings are also a thanksgiving for the pureness of the water. Taking place on the last Sunday in August, known as Plague Sunday, this also commemorates the climax of the plague and the death of the rector's wife, Catherine Mompesson.

The village itself is quite large and self-contained, and typical of a mining and quarrying settlement. For all its plague associations, it is said that it was the first village in England to have a public water system. In the 16th century a series of troughs were placed throughout the village, with water being brought to them by pipes. An interesting place to stroll around, there are many information plaques documenting events where they took place. **Eyam Museum** tells the story of the heroic sacrifice and the **Parish Church of St Lawrence** dates partly from the 12th century and restored in the 19th century, houses an excellent exhibition of Eyam's history,

including Mompesson's own chair and the plague register. Also inside the Church are two ancient coffin lids; the top of one of the lids is known as St Helen's Cross. Born in what is now Turkey, she is said to have found a fragment of the cross on which Jesus was crucified. In the churchyard is the best-preserved Saxon cross to be found in the Peak District, along with an unusual sundial which dates from 1775. There is also a memorial to Catherine Mompesson and Thomas Stanley.

The home of the Wright family for over 300 years, **Eyam Hall** is a wonderful, unspoilt 17th century manor house that is now open to the public. As well as touring the house and seeing the impressive stone-flagged hall, tapestry room and the magnificent tester bed, there is also a café and gift shop. The Eyam Hall Crafts Centre, housed in the farm building, contains several individual units which specialise in a variety of unusual and skilfully-fashioned crafts.

A mile or two north of the village is **Eyam Moor**, where there are cairns and stone circles.

GRINDLEFORD

6 miles N of Bakewell off the A625

This is one of the smallest of the Peak District villages. The ruins of ancient **Padley Manor House**, found alongside the track bed of the old railway line, are all that remain of the home of the Fitzherberts, a Roman Catholic family. It was from here, in 1588, that two priests, Robert Ludlam and Nicholas Garlick were taken, in the 16th century, and sentenced to death in Derby, by hanging, drawing and quartering. The then owner of the house, Thomas Fitzherbert, died in the Tower of London three years later while his brother died at Fleet Prison in 1598. There is a pilgrimage each year in July to **Padley Chapel** to commemorate two of the Catholic martyrs. The chapel is on the upper floor of the former Padley Manor gatehouse (which later became a barn), and was created in 1933. Across from Padley Chapel is **Brunt's Barn**, a conservation centre founded in 1981 in memory of Harry Brunt, a local man who helped found the Peak District National Park.

ASHFORD IN THE WATER

1 mile NW of Bakewell off the A6

Not exactly in the water, but certainly on the River Wye, Ashford is another candidate for Derbyshire's prettiest village. It developed around a ford that spanned the river and was once an important crossing place on the ancient Portway. Originally a medieval packhorse bridge, **Sheep Wash Bridge** crosses the Wye, with overhanging willows framing its low arches. It is one of three bridges in the village, and a favourite with artists. There is a small enclosure to one side that provides a clue to its name, as this is still occasionally used for its original purpose - crowds gather to witness sheep being washed in the

river to clean their fleece before they are shorn. The lambs would be penned within the enclosure and the ewes would be thrown in the water at the other side. Seeing their offspring, they would swim across, their wool getting a good wash as they went.

So-called Black Marble, or Ashford Marble, actually a highly polished grey limestone from quarries near the village, was quarried nearby for some considerable time, and particularly during the Victorian era when it was fashionable to have decorative items and fire surrounds made from the stone. It was also exported all over the world. Within the village there was once a thriving cottage industry inlaying Black Marble with coloured marbles, shells and glass. Another industry was candle making, and the house

Padley Chapel, Grindleford

To the northwest of the village of Grindleford is the Longshaw Country Park, some 1,500 acres of open moorland, woodland and the impressive Padley Gorge. Originally a grouse shooting estate owned by the Dukes of Rutland, the land was acquired by the National Trust in the 1970s. At the heart of the country park is Longshaw Lodge, the Duke's former shooting lodge.

41

Ashford is perhaps most famous for its six beautifully executed well-dressings, which are held annually on Trinity Sunday in late May or early June. After a break of many years the custom of well-dressing was briefly revived at Sheepwash Well in 1930, though this revival petered out until the 1950s when the well-dressings became an annual custom once more. Rather than adhering strictly to the custom of depicting scenes from the Bible, the well-dressers of Ashford have depicted such unusual themes as a willow pattern to celebrate the Chinese Year of the Dog, and have also paid tribute to the Land Girls of the First World War.

that now stands on the site of the factory is called The Candle House. It stands in Greaves Lane, "greaves" being the unusable dregs of melted tallow.

The great limestone **Parish Church of the Holy Trinity** was largely rebuilt in 1871 but retained the base of a 13th century tower and a 14th century north arcade. A fine Ashford Marble table is on show as well as a tablet to the memory of Henry Watson, the founder of the marble works who was also an authority on the geology of the area. Several of the pillars within the church are made of the rare Duke's Red marble, which is only found in the mine at Lathkill Dale owned by the Duke of Devonshire. The church also boasts a Norman tympanum, complete with Tree of Life, lion and hog, over the south door. Hanging from the roof of Ashford's church are the remains of four 'virgin's crantses' - paper garlands carried at the funerals of unmarried village girls. One of them dates from 1747.

Near the village is **Churchdale Hall**, which dates from the 18th century and is part of the vast Chatsworth estate. It was also the home, until his death in 1950, of the 10th Duke of Devonshire who never resided at Chatsworth. To the south of Ashford is another manor House, **Ashford Hall** overlooking a picturesque lake formed by the River Wye. Built by the Dukes of Devonshire in 1785 to a design by Joseph Pickford of Derby, it was occupied by them for a time, but

then sold in the early 1950s. It now belongs to the Olivier family. **Thornbridge Hall** dates from 1781, but was extensively refurbished in Victorian times. It has been a teacher training college and a conference centre but is now a private residence once more.

The village also has a pleasant range of mainly 18th century cottages, and a former tithe barn.

MONSAL HEAD
3 miles NW of Bakewell off the B6465

Monsal Head is a renowned, and deservedly so, beauty spot from which there are tremendous views - particularly over **Monsal Dale**, through which the River Wye flows.

WARDLOW
6 miles NW of Bakewell off the B6465

At a crossroads near Wardlow, the body of Anthony Lingard (who had earlier been hanged at Derby) was publicly gibbeted in 1815 for the murder of a local widow. The body was placed in a cage and hung from the gibbet, a sight which drew an enormous crowd - so large that the local lay-preacher at Tideswell found himself preaching to virtually empty pews. Determined not to waste this opportunity to speak to so large a congregation, he made his way to the gibbet and gave his sermon there.

LITTON
6 miles NW of Bakewell off the A623

Situated in the Wye Valley, Litton is a typical example of a Peak District limestone village, and sits at a height of 1,000 feet above sea level. Though the oldest house dates from 1639 - many of the buildings have date stones - most date from the mid-18th century, a time of prosperity for the area when the local lead mining industry was booming. As well as the typical architecture of the Peak District, the ancient patterns of the small, stone-walled fields can also still be seen here. The village green still has an ancient market cross, as well as the old village stocks.

The young workers at **Litton Mill**, unlike those at nearby Cressbrook Mill, experienced very harsh conditions, especially when the mill was owned by Ellis Needham & Co. The mill still stands beside the Wye Mill stream, and is said to be haunted by the ghosts of the orphans who were exploited as cheap labour. Litton was the birthplace, in 1628, of **William Bagshawe**, who earned the title the "Apostle of the Peak" (see also Chapel-en-le-Frith).

Litton

CRESSBROOK

5 miles NW of Bakewell off the B6465

Clinging to the slopes of the Wye Valley, the village cottages of Cressbrook are found in terraces amongst the ash woodland. The handsome **Cressbrook Mill**, built in 1815, was closed down in 1965, and is now being converted into flats. The apprentice house, used to house the pauper children from London and elsewhere who worked long hours in the mill, also exists. The owner of the Mill, William Newton, known as the "Minstral of the Peak" because he wrote

poetry, saw that the apprentices were treated well (see also Tideswell). The stretch of the River Wye between Cressbrook and Litton mills is known as Water-Cum-Jolly Dale. Cressbrook's well-dressing takes place during the first week in June.

TIDESWELL

8 miles NW of Bakewell off the B6049

One of the largest villages in the area, Tideswell takes its name from a Saxon chieftain called Tidi, which may explain why it is known locally as "Tidza". Over 900 feet above sea level, the surrounding countryside offers many opportunities to wander, stroll, or take a leisurely (or energetic) hike through some varied and impressive scenery.

The village is one of the most ancient in the Peak District, and was granted its market charter in 1251. This was where the Great Courts of the Royal Forest of Peak met during the reign of Edward I, and some of buildings in the village

43

St John the Baptist Church, Tideswell

> •
>
> *Two and a half miles north of the village of Tideswell, at Tideslow, is a Neolithic barrow measuring 132 feet in diameter, one of the largest in England.*
>
> •

may have foundations going back to that time.

Known as the 'Cathedral of the Peak', the magnificent 14th century **Parish Church of St John the Baptist** has a wealth of splendid features, and is one of the grandest parish churches in Derbyshire. It was funded from local wool and from the lead mining industry, as Tideswell at one time was one of the major mining villages in the Peak District. The tower is impressive, the windows are beautiful and there is a fine collection of brasses inside. The 'Minstrel of the Peak', William Newton, is buried in the churchyard (see also Cresbrook). **Eccles Hall**, overlooking the Market Place, was built in 1724 and became the home of the headmaster of the Grammar School in 1878.

By the 14th century the village was a flourishing centre for the local wool trade. Today it is home to a number of craftspeople working in buildings converted from other uses. The excellence of their work is apparent, not only in the items they make, but also in the splendid well-dressing they help to arrange annually on the Saturday nearest St John the Baptist's Day, 24th June.

PEAK FOREST

11 miles NW of Bakewell off the A623

High on the White Peak plateau, the village of Peak Forest takes its name from the fact that it once stood at the centre of the Royal Forest of the Peak. The village grew from an earlier settlement called Dam, a hamlet which still exists. The **Parish Church of King Charles the Martyr** speaks of the fierce independence of the village inhabitants, and is one of the few in England dedicated to someone who was never a saint, but who was, nevertheless, revered by many. It was built in 1657 by the wife of the 2nd Earl of Devonshire, during a time when there was a ban on building churches. The church that stands today on the site of the former chapel was built in 1878.

A quirk of ecclesiastical law ensured – up until early in the 19th century – that the village was outside the jurisdiction of the bishop. Thus it was not subject to the laws regarding posting the banns before marriage; hence it became known as 'the Gretna Green of the Peak'. If one or other of the couple has lived in the village for 15 days prior to the ceremony, to this day they can still be married in the church without banns being read.

At Chamber Farm, rebuilt in the 18th century, the Forest courts were held, attended by some 20 foresters whose job it was to maintain the special laws of the area.

Within walking distance of Peak Forest is the 'bottomless' pit of **Eldon Hole**. Once thought to be the Devil's own entrance to Hell, stories abound in which various people were lowered down on increasingly longer pieces of rope. One man, called Charles Cotton, was lowered down on a rope which was reputed to be a mile long but even he never reached the bottom. Another was lowered down and when raised was found to be unconscious, dying soon afterwards.. Potholers, who view the hole as no more than a practice run, maintain that it is, in fact, 'only' 180 feet deep.

TADDINGTON

5 miles E of Buxton off the A6

Now lying just off the main Bakewell to Buxton road, Taddington was one of the first places to be bypassed. A small village and one of the highest in England at 1,100 feet, the cottages here are simple but the **Parish Church of St Michael and All Angels** is well worth looking at. Like many in the Peak District, it was rebuilt in the 14th century with money gained from the then-booming woollen and lead industries in the area. In1891 it was considerably restored.

Taddington Hall, one of the smaller of the Peak District manor houses, dates back to the 16th century though much of the building seen today was constructed in the 18th century. As with all good halls, Taddington has its share of ghost stories. One in particular concerns two brothers. The pair ran a hessian factory from the Hall and one day they quarrelled. The next day one of the brothers, named Isaac, was found dead in the cellar. The other brother was found guilty of the act. It is said that Isaac has been heard wandering around the passages of the Hall from time to time. The other ghost is of a drunken farmer who fell from his horse on his way home from Bakewell Market. Intriguingly, it was the farmer's ghost that revealed to his wife that he was dead before she knew about it.

MILLERS DALE

7 miles NE of Buxton off the B6049

The hamlet takes its name from one of several charming and compact dales that lie along the River Wye and provide excellent walking. The nearby nature reserve occupies land that was originally a limestone

Up on Taddington Moor can be found Five Wells tumulus, at 1,400 feet, the highest megalithic tomb in England. The harsh moorland weather has eroded the earth away to reveal two limestone slabs, the burial chambers of 12 people. Flint tools and scraps of pottery were also found in the chambers.

Five Wells Tumulus, Taddington

Wormhill

Superb self-catering accommodation within a historic country house that has all the amenities for a perfect holiday

 see page 191

•

On the pretty, sloping village green in Wormhill there is an ornate memorial erected in 1895 to James Brindley (see also Tunstead), the civil engineer who was responsible for the Bridgewater Canal. This memorial is the centrepiece for the village's well-dressings at the end of August every year.

•

quarry, which was last used in 1971. This tiny settlement, situated in the narrow valley of the River Wye, began life as late as the 1860s when it was built to provide housing for the workers building the London to Manchester railway. All this has now gone but the dramatic **Monsal Dale Viaduct** (built in the 1860s to carry the railway line) remains and is now used by walkers taking the Monsal Trail. It has stone piers and a wrought iron superstructure. There is another viaduct to the north, built in 1905, to cope with increased traffic on the line.

The disused railway has been converted to a track for walkers, cyclists, horse riders and less active people, including wheelchair users. Between Blackwell and Monsal Head the trail follows the deep limestone valley of the River Wye for eight-and-a-half miles. It is unsuitable for cycling and wheelchairs at its western half, with rocky diversions around tunnels. Level access is available from Miller's Dale Station, for half-a-mile west or two miles east.

The **Parish Church of St Anne's** is on a hillside, and is modern, dating from 1879. It was designed by H. Cockbain.

WORMHILL

4 miles E of Buxton off the A6

The pretty farming hamlet of Wormhill was recorded in the *Domesday Book* and was a much more important settlement in the past. In Norman times it was one of the administrative centres of the Royal Forest of the Peak.

The parish church of St Margaret was largely rebuilt in 1864, though it retains its medieval tower. **Wormhill Hall**, built by the Bagshawe family in 1697, is a stone mansion (privately owned) which can be seen on the approach to the village from the Wye valley.

TUNSTEAD

3 miles E of Buxton off the A6

High in the hills above the valley of the River Wye, Tunstead is a small hamlet with a very famous son in James Brindley, born here in 1716. Known as the father of the canal system, Brindley never learned to read or write but became a millwright in 1742. His skills in engineering brought him to the attention of the Duke of Bridgewater, who commissioned Brindley to build the Bridgwater Canal to carry coal between Manchester and Worsley. Brindley went on to construct many more canals throughout Britain.

Tunstead Quarry, in Great Rocks Dale, is said to be the largest limestone quarry in Europe. Quarrying originally took place on the western slopes of the dale, but in 1978 quarrying also began on the eastern slopes.

KING STERNDALE

2 miles SE of Buxton off the A6

King Sterndale is a charming limestone hamlet high above Ashwood Dale. The cosy **Christ Church Parish Church** was built in 1847 in Gothic style, to a design by Bonomi, though it looks much older. Inside the church there is a memorial to Miss Ellen Hawkins of the neighbouring village of Cowdale, founder of the church. Other memorials include those to the Pickford family, such as the one commemorating William Pickford, a judge who later became Lord Sterndale, Master of the Rolls.

SOUTH AND WEST OF BAKEWELL

SHELDON

3 miles W of Bakewell off the A6

Situated 1,000 feet up on the limestone plateau, Sheldon was mentioned in the *Domesday Book* as Scheldhaun. However, its heyday was in the 18th and 19th centuries, when black marble was mined here, as it was at nearby Ashford in the Water. However, due to a lack of water to power the many manufacturing processes, it was not as successful as its neighbour.

Magpie Mine, to the south of the village, produced lead for over 300 years, only closing down in 1924. This important site of industrial archaeology has been preserved, from the Cornish-style chimney stack, engine house and dynamite cabin right down to the more recent corrugated iron-roofed buildings. Now owned by the Peak District Mines Historical Society, guided parties are taken round to see the techniques used by the miners.

The village itself is chiefly a single row of mainly 18th century cottages lining the main street. The 19th century **Parish Church of St Michael and All Angels**, with some notable features, is well worth a visit. Prehistoric monuments litter the limestone plateau above the village and, from Sheldon numerous footpaths lead through the surrounding countryside to Monyash, Flagg and Monsal Dale.

FLAGG

5 miles W of Bakewell off the A515

Flagg is an ancient village which was founded by the Vikings. The characteristic ridges and furrows of the medieval open fields, enclosed by stone walls in the 18th and 19th centuries, have been preserved in the farmland around Flagg. During the period of enclosure, hundreds of miles of stone walls were built, dividing the land into geometric patterns. Most of this can still be seen today, all over the Peak District, and is one of the particular features of the area. The Elizabethan manor house, **Flagg**

Magpie Mine, Sheldon

47

The Flagg point-to-point horse races on Flagg Moor, which were founded in the early 20th century, take place every year on Easter Monday. The course is two miles long with 20 birch fences, with the horses travelling round the circuit.

To the north of the village of Chelmorton, some 1,440 feet up on Chelmorton Low there is a Bronze Age tumulus and also the source of an unusually named stream, the Illy Willy Water, which flows through the village. The oldest part of the village lies near the top of this hill following the course of the stream, and curiously, the village church and inn now seem to be at the end of a cul-de-sac.

Hall, now known as Flagg Hall Farm, is visible from the main road, and is well worth seeing, although it is not open to the public. It was once owned by the Dale and Flynne families.

CHELMORTON

7 miles W of Bakewell off the A5270

The second highest village in the county, the remains of the narrow strips of land that were allotted to each cottage in medieval times can still be seen. Outside these strips lay the common land and then the parish boundary. Beyond the boundary can be seen the regular fields that were laid out after the first enclosures of 1809. The layout of the village is unchanged probably since Saxon times. It is a single street, with farms at intervals along the street.

The **Parish Church of St John the Baptist** dates partly from the 13h century, though there have been changes and additions over the years. In the south porch there is a small collection of grave slabs.

MONYASH

5 miles W of Bakewell off the B5055

Monyash was recorded in the *Domesday Book* as Maneis, thought to derive from 'many ash trees'. It is a picturesque village clustered around the village green, and at one time had many Quaker families living there. Farming and tourism are its main industries now but it was once at the centre of the Peak District's lead mining industry (from medieval times to

the end of the 19th century) and had its own Barmote Court (one of the oldest industrial courts in the country). Its market charter was granted in 1340 and the old market cross still stands on the village green. Due to its isolated position, Monyash had, for many years, to support itself and this led to a great many industries within the village. As far back as prehistoric times there was a flint-tool 'factory' here and, as well as mining, candle-making and rope-making, mere-building was a village speciality.

The **Parish Church of St Leonard** was founded in 1178, though it has been much altered and added to over the years. It's parish chest is still preserved as one of its greatest treasures. It is ten-feet long and thought to date from ther13th century, when it was used to store the silver vessels and the robes worn during mass.

Today, Monyash, which is situated at the start of **Lathkill Dale**, is busy during the season with walkers keen to discover the surrounding countryside. Lathkill Dale is a road-free beauty spot with ash and elm woods that was designated a National Nature Reserve in 1972. The **River Lathkill**, like others in the limestone area of the Peak District, disappears underground for parts of its course. In this case the river rises, in winter, from a large cave above Monyash, known as Lathkill Head Cave. In summer, the river emerges further downstream at Over Haddon.

POMEROY

7 miles W of Bakewell on the A515

Pomeroy is a charming hamlet with some lovely buildings, some dating back to medieval times. Parts of the Duke of York Inn date back to the early 1400s. The chestnut tree in the car park was planted in the 1900s by the then Prince of Wales, later King Edward VIII, on an occasion when he was visiting the area with Sir Thomas Pomeroy.

EARL STERNDALE

7 miles W of Bakewell off the A515

At the less well-known northern end of Dove Valley, Earl Sterndale is close to the limestone peaks of Hitter Hill and High Wheeldon, where there is Fox Hole Cave, which has been a shelter for people since Stone Age times. Over 1,100 feet above sea level, it is surrounded by lovely farmland. A number of the farmsteads are called 'granges', a relic of the Middle Ages when the granges were where monks of the local Abbey lived. The **Parish Church of St Michael**, built in the early 19th century, was the only church in Derbyshire to suffer a direct hit from a Second World War bomb. It was refurbished and restored in 1952, and retains a Saxon font.

The village inn, the Quiet Woman, has a sign showing a headless woman, with the words 'Soft words turneth away wrath'. It is supposedly of a previous landlord's nagging wife, known as 'Chattering Charteris', whose husband cut off her head.

CROWDECOTE

8 miles W of Bakewell off the B5053

Crowdecote is situated in the deep limestone valley of the River Dove, just on the border with Staffordshire. The limestone reef knolls of the upper part of the valley can be clearly seen from vantage points near the village. Seen as hills, such as **Chrome Hill** and **Parkhouse Hill**, they are as close to peaks as they get in the Peak District. Over 350 million years ago, these knolls were actually coral reefs within a shallow, warm sea - hard to believe, but perhaps not so puzzling when one remembers that much of this landscape has been formed by the action of water. The stone bridge over the River Dove, built in 1709 to replace an earlier wooden one, was a crossing point for the old packhorse route. The nearby Packhorse Inn dating back to 1723 was used by traders when this was the main road to Leek and Buxton.

LONGNOR

8 miles W of Bakewell off the B5053

Situated in Staffordshire, yet still in the heart of the Peak District, on a ridge between the River Manifold and the River Dove, Longnor, with its old gritstone houses stands between the browns of the Dark Peak country and the bright greens of the limestone White Peak landscape. It was once the meeting point of several packhorse routes, and because of this became an important market town and the

46 BULL I' TH' THORN

Hurdlow

A lovely old inn dating from the 15th century that offers the very best in accommodation, food and drink, as well as a rare breeds farm!

see page 192

47 HORSESHOE INN

Longnor

A historic pub in the Peak District that combines olde worlde charm, real ales and great food.

see page 193

48 MERRIL GROVE COTTAGES

Longnor

Three superb four star self catering cottages on a farm, with stunning views all round.

see page 192

49 YE OLDE CHESHIRE CHEESE INN

Longnor

A traditional English inn that is warm and welcoming. It served great food and drink, and its entertainment will pleasantly surprise you!

🍴 *see page 194*

centre of a prosperous farming community. Its **Market Hall** was built in 1873, and outside the hall there is a posting of the market charges of the time. **Longnor Craft Centre** now occupies the beautifully restored building. The village also has some fascinating narrow flagged passages, which seem to go nowhere but suddenly emerge among some beautiful scenery. The town's prosperity declined with the onset of the agricultural depression, and there was an accompanying fall in the population. However, this decline has in recent years been reversed. Longnor is now a conservation area and has attracted a good many craftspeople. The cobbled **Market Square** is one of the oldest in England, dating back to medieval times.

Though the late 18th century **Church of St Bartholomew** is grim and plain, it sits on the foundations of a Norman building, and the font of this building is still within. The churchyard has an interesting gravestone. The epitaph tells the tale of the life of William Billinge, who was born in 1679, and died in 1791. This means that he died in his 112th year. As a soldier Billinge served under Rooke at Gibraltar and Marlborough at Ramilles. After being sent home wounded, he recovered to take part in defending the King in the Jacobite Uprisings of 1715 and 1745. The village was the location for the filming of the TV series *Peak Practice* and fans of the series will easily spot Dr Tom's House,

The Beeches Surgery, The Black Swan (actually the real-life Horsehoe Inn, the oldest in the village) and other familiar buildings.

On the first Thursday after the first Sunday in September, the annual 'Wakes Races', or 'Longnor Sports', takes place in the village. They go back to 1904, and are held at Waterhouse Farm.

OVER HADDON
1½ miles SW of Bakewell off the B5055

A former lead mining centre, Over Haddon is a picturesque village at the top of the steep side of the Lathkill valley. A typical rural settlement of the limestone plateau, it was at the centre of a gold rush in the 1850s when iron pyrites ('fools' gold') was found. The village is now visited by walkers as it lies on the **Lathkill Dale Trail** which follows the River Lathkill up the valley to beyond Monyash. Along the riverbank can be found many remains, some more hidden than others, of the area's lead mining industry. There is an old engine house at **Mandale Mine** that was built in 1847 and further upstream from the mine are the stone pillars of an aqueduct, built in 1840, which carried water down to the engine house. Downstream from the village is the first National Nature Reserve established in the Peak District in 1972. Set mainly in an ash and elm wood, the reserve is home to many varieties of shrubs.

BEELEY
3 miles SE of Bakewell off the B6012

This is another estate village to the

great Chatsworth House which lies to the north. However, although much of the village was built for the 6th Duke of Devonshire by Paxton, there are some older buildings here including an early 17th century Hall (now a private farm) with stone mullioned and transomed windows, and Beeley Hill Top, a gabled 16th century house. The **Parish Church of St Anne** dates originally from the 14th century, though it was much restored in the 19th century. It contains memorials to the Cavendish family, and has parish registers going back to 1538. There is a tradition that, when marriages take place, the bride and groom must not enter the churchyard by the west gate, and must pay a token sum, after the ceremony, to leave by the east gate. A sad but true story is of a young girl who was on her way to be married at the church but died before she reached it.

To the west of Beeley a small road climbs up onto Beeley Moor and here, along a concessionary path from Hell Bank, can be found **Hob Hurst's House**. Local folklore tells that this was the home of a goblin but it is just one of 30 or so Bronze Age barrows to be found on the moor.

ROWSLEY

4 miles SE of Bakewell off the A6

The older part of this small village, at the confluence of the Rivers Wye and Derwent, lies between the two rivers, while to the east is the 'railway village' around the former Midland railway station, now

occupied by an engineering works. The two areas are quite distinct. The old part has gritstone cottages and farmhouses, while the newer part is clearly Victorian. The most impressive building in Rowsley is the Peacock Hotel. It was built in 1652 by John Stevenson, founder in 1636 of the Lady Manners School in Bakewell and private secretary to Lady Manners, mother of the 8th Earl of Rutland. It is aptly named as, above the entrance, there is a carved stone peacock. It was at one time a dower house of nearby **Haddon Hall** and the peacock is actually part of the family crest of the Manners family, whose descendants still live in the hall. It lies to the west of the village, and is reckoned to be the most perfect house to survive from the Middle Ages in England. It goes back to at least to the 12th century, when it was a fortified manor house built by the Avenell family. It next passed by marriage to the de Vernons and then, in the early 16th century, to the Manners family. In the early 17th century it lay empty, but in 1920s it was restored by the 9th Duke of Rutland.

The **Parish Church of St Katherine** dates from 1855, and contains the fine chest tomb of Lady Catherine Manners, first wife of the 7th Duke of Rutland, who died in 1859.

On the banks of the River Wye lies **Caudwell's Mill**, a unique Grade II listed historic roller flour mill. A mill has stood on this site for at least 400 years. The present mill was built in 1874, powered by water from the River Wye, and was run as

50 THE OLD SMITHY

Beeley

A traditional village shop/cafe within an old village smithy that sells local agricultural produce and has a great reputation for its breakfasts, lunches and snacks.

🍴 🏛 *see page 195*

51 EAST LODGE HOTEL AND RESTAURANT

Rowsley

A superior hotel in a rural setting that only offers the very best in hospitality and fine food.

🛏 🍴 *see page 196*

a family business for over a century up until 1978. Since then the Mill has undergone extensive restoration by a group of dedicated volunteers and, using machinery that was installed at the beginning of this century, the mill is once again producing wholemeal flour. Other mill buildings on the site have been converted to house a variety of craft workshops, shops and a restaurant.

On Chatsworth Road near the terminus of the Peak Rail line, **Peak Village** is an extensive factory outlet shopping centre offering over 26 factory outlets selling a range of ladies' and men's fashion, sports and outdoor wear, home furnishings, jewellery, toys and books, and eateries. Also on-site is the charming **Toys of Yesteryear** exhibition and collectors shop. The impressive displays feature over 6,000 toys dating from the early 1900s right up until the 1970s, including a model of the 'Chitty Chitty Bang Bang' car.

MATLOCK

Matlock is the county town of Derbyshire, and much of the southeastern Peakland area around the town lies outside the boundaries of the National Park. However, the towns, villages and much of the surrounding countryside have plenty of the typical Peak District characteristics. Matlock and its various satellite settlements provide the focus and, after a period of decline, this essentially Victorian town is, once again, a busy and bustling place with plenty to offer the visitor. There are also some fine views over the Lower Derwent Valley from its well planned vantage points.

Matlock lies right on the divide between the gritstone of the Dark Peak and the limestone of the White Peak. Though the hilltops are often windswept and bleak, the numerous dales, cut deep into the limestone, provide a lush and green haven for all manner of wild and plant life. Several of the rivers are famous for their trout, particularly the Lathkill, which was greatly favoured by the keen angler and writer Sir Izaak Walton.

Matlock is a bustling town nestling in the lower valley of the River Derwent, and is a busy tourist

Hall Leys Park, Matlock

centre bordering the Peak District National Park. There are actually eight Matlocks which make up the town, along with several other hamlets. Most have simply been engulfed and have lost their identity as the town grew, but **Matlock Bath**, the site of the spa, still maintains some individuality.

Matlock itself is famed as, at one time, having the steepest gradient (a 1-in-5½) tramway in the world. It ran between the railway station and the hydro of John Smedley, and so steep was it that a cable beneath the road connected the two trams - one going uphill and one going downhill. It was also the only tram system in the Peak District. Opened in 1893, the tramcars ran until 1927 and the depot can still be seen at the top of Bank Road. The old ticket office and waiting room at Matlock station have been taken over by the **Peak Rail Society** and here can be found not only their shop, but also exhibitions explaining the history and aims of the society. The Peak Rail has its southernmost terminus just a few minutes walk from the mainline station.

Peak Rail is a rebuilt, refurbished and now preserved railway running between Matlock Riverside station (just a five-minute walk from the mainline station at Matlock) through the charming rural station of Darley Dale to the terminus at Rowsley South. In future it is hoped that the line can be extended to Bakewell, four miles to the northwest. Run entirely by volunteers, this lovely old line

operates on different days throughout the year - please telephone for details. The full journey (one way) takes just 20 minutes, and passengers can alight to enjoy the picnic area at the entrance to Rowsley South Station, or the exhibition coach at Darley Dale platform (please ring for opening times) to learn about the history of the reopening of the line. The restaurant car offers Saturday evening meals, Sunday lunches and afternoon teas. Special events are held throughout the year, and engine-driving courses can be taken - the perfect gift for the steam enthusiast!

The **Parish Church of St Giles** still has fragments of masonry dating from its foundation in the 13th century, and its tower, in the perpendicular style, dates from the 16th century. However, most of the medieval church was destroyed in the 18th century during alterations, and in 1859 the chancel was completely rebuilt. Inside the church can be seen, behind glass, a faded and preserved funeral garland or 'virgin crantse', though the church has others in storage. These were once common all over Derbyshire, and were bell-shaped, decorated with rosettes and ribbons and usually containing a personal item. They were made in memory of a deceased young girl of the parish. At her funeral the garland was carried by the dead girl's friends and, after the service, it would be suspended from the church rafters above the pew she had normally occupied.

52 DUKE OF WELLINGTON RESIDENTIAL COUNTRY INN

Matlock
A great pub with fully en suite accommodation that makes the perfect base from which to explore Derbyshire and the Peak District.

‖ ⊨ see page 197

53 COUNTRY COTTAGE RESTAURANT

Matlock
A restaurant in a historic building that has great food, great wine, and an ambience that owes much to the original features it has retained.

‖ see page 197

54 THE HORSESHOE

Matlock
A pub that is renowned for its great family-friendly atmosphere, its drink and its beautifully cooked and presented food

‖ see page 198

High up on the hill behind the town is the brooding ruin of **Riber Castle**, which sits 850 feet above sea level. The castle was built between 1862 and 1868 and is often linked with the McCaig folly which overlooks Oban on the west coast of Scotland. The castle's creator, John Smedley, built it as his new home. He was a local hosiery manufacturer who became interested in the hydropathic qualities of Matlock, and drew up the designs for the building himself. Lavishly decorated inside, Smedley constructed his own gas-producing plant to provide lighting for the castle and it even had its own well.

Following the death of first Smedley and then his wife, the castle was sold and for a number of years it was a boys' school. During the Second World War, the school having closed, the castle was used as a food store before it was left to become a ruined shell. Now it is being converted into luxury flats.

A fairly new attraction to the area is **Matlock Farm Park**, set in 600 acres of working farm and providing a great day out for all the family. The Park is home to a wide variety of animals including llamas, red deer, donkeys and peacocks which children can feed.

To the west of Matlock, down a no-through road, can be found one of Derbyshire's few Grade I listed buildings, the secluded and well-hidden **Snitterton Hall**. Little is known of the history of this fine Elizabethan manor house, though it is believed to have been built by John Milward around the same time that he purchased half the manor of Snitterton.

On the once busy old road between Matlock and Cromford, in an area known as Starkholmes, The White Lion Inn was formerly called The Buddles Inn, after the habit of locals who would sit in the barn adjacent and 'buddle' - the old word for washing lead.

NORTH OF MATLOCK

DARLEY DALE

2 miles NW of Matlock off the A6

This straggling village along the main road north from Matlock dates only from the 19th century, and was created out of several smaller settlements, three of them being Darley Bridge, Darley Hillside and South Darley. Indeed, Darley is mentioned in the *Domesday Book* as 'Derelie', showing that the name at least is ancient . The all encompassing 'Darley Dale' was either devised by the commercially-minded railway company at work in the area or by the romantically-inclined vicar of the parish. Darley Dale makes up one of three stops on the Matlock-to-Rowsley South Peak Rail line.

One of the most unassuming heroines of this part of Derbyshire must be Lady Louisa Whitworth. She was the second wife of Sir Joseph Whitworth, the famous Victorian engineer whose name is associated with the Great Exhibition of 1851 and who invented the screw thread. Sir

Joseph made a fortune manufacturing, amongst other items, machine tools, munitions and nuts and bolts. Following his death in 1887, Lady Louisa brought sweeping changes to the lifestyle of the local poor and needy. She allowed the grounds of her home, Stancliffe Hall, to be used for school outings and events. In 1889, the Whitworth Cottage Hospital was opened under her auspices.

The **Whitworth Institute** was opened in 1890, bringing to the community a wide range of facilities including a swimming pool (the first heated pool in Britain), an assembly hall, a natural history museum and a library. At a time when a woman was required to take a secondary role in society, Lady Louisa was determined to credit her late husband with these changes, which so benefited Darley Dale. Lady Whitworth died in France in 1896, and is buried next to her husband at the **Parish Church of St Helen**, in the hamlet of Churchtown. The church as we see it today dates from at least the 12th century, and has the tomb of Sir John de Darley dating from 1322. It also contains two fine examples of Burne-Jones stained glass windows.

The churchyard is home to the **Darley Yew**, reputed to be 2,000 years old, and one of the oldest living trees in Britain, with a girth of 33 feet. The yew predates the Norman origins of the church and may be older than the Saxon fragments found here during the last century. Another tree can be seen at the top of **Oker Hill**. This is a lobe sycamore, and an unusual tale is attached to it. It seems that two brothers planted sycamore trees at the same time. One tree flourished, just as the brother who planted it did, while the other one died, just like the other brother, who died soon after. Wordsworth was so inspired by this evocative story that he wrote a poem about it (see also Wensley).

Darley Yew

Much of the stone used for local buildings came from nearby Stancliffe Quarry, which also supplied stone for the Thames Embankment and Hyde Park Corner in London, and the Walker Art Gallery in Liverpool. To the north of the 15th century **Darley Bridge**, which carries the road to Winster over the River Derwent, are the remains of **Mill Close Mine**. This was the largest and most productive lead mine in Derbyshire until 1938, when flooding caused it to be abandoned.

Darley Dale has an extensive park which is very pretty in all

58 THE RED HOUSE COUNTRY HOTEL & RESTAURANT

Darley Dale

An elegant hotel with an unstuffy atmosphere and great views out over the River Derwent.

see page 200

59 TALL TREES COFFEE SHOP & RESTAURANT

Two Dales

A smart, stylish coffee shop and restaurant , within a garden centre, that sells wonderfully cooked food at reasonable prices.

see page 201

Near to Stanton in Peak, the Rowtor Rocks contain caves, which were carved out in the 17th century. Not only was the living space made from the rock, but tables, chairs and alcoves were also made to create a cosy retreat for the local vicar, Rev Thomas Eyre. Prior to these home improvements, the caves were reputedly used by the Druids, who did not believe in such creature comforts (see also Birchover).

seasons. Another of this small village's attractions is **Red House Carriage Museum**, a working carriage museum featuring some fine examples of traditional horse-drawn vehicles and equipment. One of the finest collections in the country, it consists of nearly 40 carriages, including one of the very few surviving Hansom cabs, a stage coach, Royal Mail coach, Park Drag and many other private and commercial vehicles. Carriage rides are available, making regular trips through the countryside to places such as Chatsworth and Haddon Hall, and the carriages and horses can be hired for special occasions.

STANTON IN PEAK

5 miles NW of Matlock off the B5056

This is a typical Peak District village, with numerous alleyways and courtyards off its main street. A quick glance at the village cottages and the visitor will soon notice the initials WPT that appear above most of the doorways. The initials are those of William Pole Thornhill, the owner of Stanton Hall, which stands near the church and is still home to his descendents. There are some fine 17th and 18th century cottages, one of which, Holly House, has some of its windows still blocked since the window tax of 1697. The village pub, The Flying Childers, is named after one of the 4th Duke of Devonshire's most successful racehorses.

The gritstone landscape of **Stanton Moor**, which rises to some 1,096 feet and overlooks the village, is encircled by footpaths and is a popular walking area. There are also several interesting features on the moorland. The folly, **Earl Grey's Tower**, was built in 1832 to commemorate the reform of Parliament. There is also an ancient stone circle dating from the Bronze Age and with over 70 burial mounds. Known as the **Nine Ladies**, the stone circle has a solitary boulder nearby called the King's Stone. Legend has it that one Sunday nine women and a fiddler came up onto the moor to dance and, for their act of sacrilege, they were turned to stone.

ALPORT

5½ miles NW of Matlock on a minor road off the B5056

This is an ancient village, much older than its delightful houses of the 17th to 19th centuries would at first suggest. Considered by many as one of Derbyshire's prettiest villages, it stands at the confluence of the Bradford and Lathkill Rivers. The Lathkill cascades down through the village in a series of

Nine Ladies, Stanton in Peak

weirs to meet the Bradford coming down from Youlgreave. Named after the portway road which ran through the settlement, the Saxon inhabitants added the prefix 'al', which itself means old.

The surrounding countryside, a lead mining area, was owned by the Duke of Rutland and, by the end of the 18th century, the industry was struggling. In order to prevent the mines filling up with water, the Duke had a 4½ mile sough (underground drainage canal) built to run the water off into the River Derwent. Begun in 1766, this project took 21 years to complete and, in an attempt to recover some of the construction costs, a levy was put on any ore being taken from below a certain level.

Sometime after completion of the project, in 1881, the **River Bradford** disappeared underground for several years. As with other rivers in this limestone landscape, it had channelled a route out underground, only this time it was taking the route of the sough to the River Derwent. After sealing the chasm through which the river had joined up with Hillcar Sough, it was restored to the above-ground landscape.

Among Alport's many fine houses, **Monk's Hall** (private) is one of the best, dating from the late 16th or early 17th century and probably, at one time, was connected to a monastic grange. Another is **Harthill Hall Farm**, a gabled 17th century yeoman's farmhouse with stone mullioned and transomed windows.

YOULGREAVE

6 miles NW of Matlock on a minor road off the B5056

This straggling village can also be spelled Youlgrave, and to confuse matters further, it is known locally as Pommy. It lies in Bradford Dale, and was once one of the centres of the Derbyshire lead mining industry. In fact, fluorspar and calcite are still extracted from some of the old mines. The **Parish Church of All Saints,** one of the most beautiful churches in Derbyshire, contains some parts of the original Saxon building though its ancient font is, unfortunately, upturned and used as a sundial. Inside, the working font is Norman and still retains its stoup for holding the Holy Water. It is well worth taking the time to have a look at, as it is the only such font in England. The Church also contains a small tomb with an equally small alabaster effigy; dated 1488, it is a memorial to Thomas Cockayne, who was killed in a brawl when only in his teens. A fine alabaster panel in the north aisle, dated 1492, depicts the Virgin with Robert Gylbert, his wife and seventeen children. There is a glorious Burne-Jones stained-glass window, which was added in 1870, when Norman Shaw very sensitively restored the church.

Well Dressing, Youlgreave

The origin of the local name 'Pommy' for Youlgreave is not known, but some say that it got this unusual name after a pig joined the village band and was heard playing 'Pom pom pom' down the village street. However colourful this derivation, the name more likely stems from the time of the Napoleonic Wars when French prisoners were brought to the area to work.

Further up the village's main street is **Thimble Hall**, the smallest market hall in the Peak District. Typical of the White Peak area of Derbyshire, the Hall dates from 1656 and there are also some rather grand Georgian houses to be found in the village. Nearby the old shop built in 1887 for the local Co-operative Society is now a youth hostel. It featured in the film of DH Lawrence's *The Virgin and the Gypsy*, much of which was filmed in the village. Standing opposite is the **Conduit Head**, a gritstone water tank that has the unofficial name of The Fountain. Built by the village's own water company in 1829, it supplied fresh soft water to all those who paid an annual fee of sixpence. In celebration of their new, clean water supply, the villagers held their first well-dressing in 1829. Today, Youlgreave dresses its wells for the Saturday nearest to St John the Baptist's Day (24th June). Such is the standard of the work that the villagers, all amateurs, are in great demand for advice and help.

The Rivers Lathkill and Bradford are almost unique in Britain in that they both flow entirely through limestone country

and their water quality, while being able to support crayfish, is also responsible for the formation of the unusual mineral tufa. **Lathkill Dale**, which can really only be experienced by walking along the path by the banks of the quiet river, is noted for its solitude and, consequently, there is an abundance of wildlife in and around the riverbank meadows. The upper valley is a National Nature Reserve; those who are lucky enough may even spot a kingfisher or two. One of the country's purest rivers, the Lathkill is famed for the range of aquatic life that it supports as well as being a popular trout river. Renowned for many centuries, it was Izaak Walton who said of the Lathkill, back in 1676, 'the purest and most transparent stream that I ever yet saw, either at home or abroad; and breeds, 'tis said, the reddest and best Trouts in England.'

Two or three miles to the west of the village is the Bronze Age **Arbor Low**, sometimes referred to as the 'Stonehenge of the Peak District'. About 250 feet in diameter, the central plateau is encircled by a ditch, which lies within a high circular bank. On the plateau is a stone circle of limestone blocks, with a group of four stones in the centre cove. There are a total of 47 stones each weighing no less than eight tonnes, and a further three stones in the

Arbor Low

centre. Probably used as an observatory and also a religious site, it is not known whether the stones, which have been placed in pairs, ever stood upright. There is no archaeological evidence to suggest that they did. Gaps in the outer bank, to the northwest and southeast, could have been entrances and exits for religious ceremonies.

Arbor Low dates to the Early Bronze Age period, and there is much evidence in the dales along the River Lathkill that they were inhabited at that time. Nearby there is a large barrow known as **Gib Hill**, which stands at around 16 feet. When it was excavated a stone cist was discovered, containing a clay urn and burned human bones. This circular mound to the south of the stone circle, offers some protection against the weather and it is from this that Arbor Low got its name – 'sheltered heap'.

The Danes also occupied land here and their legacy is the name Lathkill, a Norse word meaning 'narrow valley with a barn'. For several centuries the valley was alive with the lead mining industry that was a mainstay of the economy of much of northern Derbyshire, and any walk along the riverbanks will reveal remains from those workings as well as from limestone quarries.

MIDDLETON BY YOULGREAVE

7 miles NW of Matlock on a minor road east of the A515

Thomas Bateman, the local squire, rebuilt the entire village in the 1820s, though it is still picturesque and quiet. Just outside the village is **Lomberdale Hall**, once the home of Thomas Bateman who, in the 19th century, was responsible for the excavation of some 500 barrows in the Peak District over a 20 year period. It is said that he managed to reveal four in one single day! Many of the artefacts he unearthed can be seen in Sheffield Museum. The village lies in the valley of the River Bradford, at the point where it becomes Middleton Dale, and is unusual among villages in this area of the Peak District in that it has a large number of trees.

WENSLEY

2½ miles W of Matlock off the B5057

Derbyshire, like Yorkshire, has a Wensley and a Wensleydale, though the Derbyshire dale does not produce cheese. Lying just within the boundaries of the National Park, this quiet village does not feature on many tourist-favoured routes through the area, and as a result provides a peaceful and pleasant alternative to many other villages.

BIRCHOVER

4 miles W of Matlock off the B5056

Birchover's name means 'the ridge where the birch trees grow'. Its main street meanders gently up from the unusual outcrops of **Rowtor Rocks** at the foot of the village, heading up towards neighbouring Stanton Moor. The village was once home to father-and-son amateur antiquarians J C and J P Heathcote, who systematically investigated the

●

Wensley Dale can be easily accessed from the village of Wensley and offers the opportunity for a charming walk. On the very edge of a limestone plateau, the valley is dry and its gently sloping grassed banks make a change from the dramatic limestone gorges nearby. Just down the Dale from Wensley is Oker Hill, the summit of which provides magnificent views over both Wensley and Darley Dale (see also Darley Dale)

●

barrows and monuments on Stanton Moor and kept a detailed and fascinating private museum in the old village post office in the main street. The Heathcote collection is now in Sheffield's Weston Park Museum.

The strange Rocks of Rowtor, behind The Druid Inn, are said to have been used for Druidical rites. (see also Stanton in Peak) The Reverend Thomas Eyre, who died in 1717, was fascinated by these rocks and built the strange collection of steps, rooms and seats which have been carved out of the gritstone rocks on the summit of the outcrop. It is said that the reverend would take his friends there to admire the view across the valley below - a view, which nowadays is obscured by trees. Prehistoric cup-and-ring marks have been discovered on the rocks and several rocking stones can be moved by the application of a shoulder. One of these, weighing about 50 tons, could once be rocked easily by hand, but in 1799 fourteen young men decided to remove it for a bit of a lark. However when they put it back, they couldn't get the balance right.

Thomas Eyre lived at the Old Vicarage in the village below Rowtor Rocks, and also restored the lovely little church known as the Jesus Chapel or **Rowtor Chapel**. The chapel had been demoted to the village cheese shop, and it now features, among fragments of Norman work, unusual carvings and some

wonderful decorative features, including modern stained glass by the artist Brian Clarke, who lived at the vicarage for a time during the 1970s.

The equally strange outcrops of **Robin Hood's Stride** (also known as 'Mock beggar's Hall') and **Cratcliff Tor** can be found nearby. A medieval hermit's cave, complete with crucifix, can be seen at the foot of Cratcliff Tor, hidden behind an ancient yew tree. Also in the vicinity is **Nine Stones**, a Bronze Age monument, though only four stones are now visible.

WINSTER

4 miles W of Matlock off the B5056

This attractive gritstone village was once a lead mining centre and market town, the last mine at Mill Close, two miles to the northeast, closing down in 1938. Today it is a conservation village, with a pleasant high street and some fine late 18th century houses. Less splendid than the surrounding houses, but no less interesting, are the *ginnels* - little alleyways - which run off the main street. The name 'Winster' is a corruption of 'Wysterne', the name under which it appears in the *Domesday Book*. It is thought to mean 'Wyn's thorn tree', though who Wyn is no one knows. The most impressive building here, however, must be the **Market House**, owned by the National Trust and found at the top of the main street. The Trust's first purchase in Derbyshire (in 1906) was the rugged, two-storey Market

House. The lower portion, with its built-up arches, is over 500 years old, while the upper portion was added on in the 18th century, and rebuilt in 1905 using old materials. The house is open to the public and acts as an information centre and shop for the Trust.

Within the Burton Institute, Winster's village hall, is a more modern attraction, the **Winster Millennium Tapestry**. It took six years to make, and involved the whole village. For a payment of 25p, villagers could get their name woven into it.

The **Ore House** at Winster is the best preserved ore house left in the Peak District. Up to 50 years ago miners used it to lodge lead ore in safety over night. It had a chute at the back for depositing the lead ore and a vaulted roof for security. The ore house has been preserved by the Peak Park Authority.

Winster Hall, built in 1628 by Francis Moore, a local businessman, has, like all good manor houses, its own ghost, which haunts the grounds. The ghost, in the form of a 'white lady', is said to be that of a daughter from the Hall, who fell in love with one of the coachmen. Her parents were

horrified at her choice of husband and vowed to find a more suitable partner. However, before such a match could be made the girl and her lover climbed to the top of the Hall and jumped, together, to their deaths.

The **Bank House** is another building with a gruesome tale attached to it. It was built around 1580, and was occupied in the early 19th century by the local doctor, William Cuddie. The owner of nearby Oddo House, William Brittlebank, was visiting in 1821, and murdered Cuddie. He then fled, and a reward of £100 (a vast sum in those days) was offered for his capture, but he was never heard of again.

The **Parish Church of St John** stands on the site of an ancient chapel built by the Ferrers family, who was given the manor soon after the Conquest. The nave was built in 1833, tacked on to a tower of 1721, which itself was

60 BLAKELOW COTTAGES

Winster

Superb self catering accommodation on a farm that offers you the delights of the countryside combined with modern amenities.

⊨ see page 201

Market House, Winster

The annual Shrove Tuesday Pancake Race in Winster, from the Crown Inn to the Market House, is a much-anticipated event that is taken seriously in the village. Small frying pans are issued to the men, women and children, it is an open event, and the pancakes are specially made with an emphasis on durability rather than taste.

added to the original Norman building. It has a curfew bell which still rings at 8 pm every evening.

Finally, although Morris dancing is traditionally associated with the Cotswold area, two of the best known and most often played tunes, The Winster Gallop and Blue-eyed Stranger, originate from the village. Collected many years ago by Cecil Sharpe, a legend in the world of Morris dancing, they were rediscovered in the 1960s. The Winster Morris men traditionally dance through the village at the beginning of Wakes Week, in June, finishing, as all good Morris dances do, at one of the local pubs.

ELTON

5 miles W of Matlock off the B5056

Situated at over 900 feet above sea level, the village lies on a fault which actually follows the main street. To the north is limestone and to the south is gritstone. The contrast of the vegetation, - the lime-loving flowers and ash trees on one side with a scattering of oak trees on the other, is very marked. The village has the reputation of being the coldest in Derbyshire, as, as high as it is, it has no shelter from north winds. The two very different stones can also be seen in the buildings of the village, some of limestone, some of gritstone, though many are built using a combination of the two materials.

To the north of the village, on Harthill Moor, is **Castle Ring**, an Iron Age hill fort behind Harthill Moor Farm. The landscape is dominated by Robin Hood's Stride,

a natural gritstone crag, which was thought to have been used for ancient fertility rites. At twilight it looks like a large house, giving it its alternative name, 'Mock Beggars Hall'. It is popular with visitors and rock climbers and is now covered with modern rock carvings and graffiti. Nearby, to the north, is the stone circle called **Nine Stone Close** or the Grey Ladies. It is the only circle in the Peak District that still has large standing stones although the stones are not on the same scale as those at Arbor Low. There were originally nine stones, but only four now remain. A fifth stone is now a gatepost in the wall to the south of the circle.

SOUTH OF MATLOCK

MATLOCK BATH

1 mile S of Matlock off the A6

It is not known whether the Romans discovered the hot springs here, but by the late 17th century the waters were being used for medicinal purposes and the Old Bath Hotel was built. Like many other spa towns, it was not until the late 18th century, when Europe was in turmoil and the wealthy couldn't travel abroad, that Matlock Bath reached its peak. As well as offering cures for many of the ills of the day, Matlock Bath and the surrounding area had much to offer the visitor and, by 1818, it was being described as a favourite summer resort. The spa town was compared to Switzerland by Byron and it has also been much admired by the Scottish philosopher, Dr Thomas Chalmers, and Ruskin, who stayed at the New Bath Hotel in 1829. Many famous people have visited the town, including the young Victoria before she succeeded to the throne.

A new turnpike road built in 1818, and the coming of the railways in 1849, brought Matlock Bath within easy reach, at small cost, to many more people and it became a popular destination for day excursions. Today, it is still essentially a holiday resort and manages to possess an air of Victorian charm left over from the days when the Victorians descended on the town looking for a 'cure'.

One of the great attractions of the town is **The Aquarium**, which occupies what was once the old Matlock Bath Hydro that was established in 1833. The original splendour of the Bath Hydro can still be seen, in the fine stone staircase and also in the thermal pool which now is without its roof. The pool, maintained at a constant temperature of 68 degrees Fahrenheit, was where the rheumatic patients would come to immerse themselves in the waters and relieve their symptoms. Today the pool is home to a large collection of Large Mirror, Common and Koi carp, while the upstairs consulting rooms now house tanks full of native, tropical and marine fish.

Down by the riverbank and housed in the old Pavilion can be found the **Peak District Mining Museum and Temple Mine**. Opened in 1978 and run by the Peak District Mines Historical Society, the Museum tells the story of lead mining in the surrounding area from as far back as Roman times to the 20th century. As well as the more usual displays of artefacts and implements used by the miners over the years, one of the Museum's most popular features are the climbing shafts and tunnels which allow the whole family to get a real feel for the life of a working lead miner. The Museum also houses a huge engine, dating from 1819, which was recovered from a mine near Winster. A unique survivor in Britain, the engine used water instead of steam to provide it with pressure. Adjacent to the Museum can be found the restored workings of Temple Mine.

Masson Mills are on the Derby Road, half a mile south of the town centre. They were built in 1783 by Sir William Arkwright, and

61 TEMPLE HOTEL & RESTAURANT

Matlock Bath

A truly historic hotel with great views over the Derwent Valley, and good quality food and drink.

see page 202

62 THE PRINCESS VICTORIA

Matlock Bath

A fine old inn that is famous for its real ales and the quality of its food, which is home-cooked on the premises to perfection.

see page 201

Matlock Bath

63 THE PEAK DISTRICT MINING MUSEUM

Matlock Bath

An exciting insight into the world of the Derbyshire Mines.

 see page 203

64 HEIGHTS OF ABRAHAM

Matlock Bath

Overlooking the spa town, this country park with its spectacular views, makes an ideal day out .

 see page 203

continued in use right up until 1991. Now the building houses a magnificent working museum dedicated to the cotton spinning industry, as well as a retail village.

Being a relatively new town, Matlock Bath has no ancient place of worship, but the **Parish Church of the Holy Trinity** is a fine early Victorian edifice which was built in 1842 and enlarged in 1873/74 to accommodate the growing congregation. Of greater architectural merit is, however, the **Chapel of St John the Baptist**, found on the road between Matlock and Matlock Bath and built into a cliff. Built in 1897, it was designed by architect Guy Dawber to be a chapel-of-ease for those finding it difficult to attend St Giles in Matlock, but it also became a place of worship for those who preferred a High Church service.

Though on the edge of the splendid countryside of the Peak District National Park, Matlock Bath is surrounded by equally beautiful scenery. Found in the Victorian Railway Station buildings is the **Whistlestop Countryside Centre**, which aims to inform and educate the public on the wildlife of the county as well as manage wildlife conservation. Set up by the Derbyshire Wildlife Trust in 1989, and run by volunteers, the centre has an interesting and informative exhibition and a gift shop. There is also a 'demonstration wildlife garden', set up in the year 2000, which highlights the many plants that can be incorporated into an ordinary garden to attract wildlife.

Many of the staff of the countryside centre are qualified to lead a range of environmental activities.

High Tor is a spectacular 390 feet high limestone cliff that towers above Matlock Bath, giving wonderful views of the town and its environs. Nothing beats a walk on High Tor Grounds., where there are 60 acres of nature trails to wander around, while, far below, the River Derwent appears like a silver thread through the gorge. A popular viewing point for Victorian visitors to the town, today rock climbers practise their skills on the precipitous crags. For those a little less energetic, a relatively steady walk to the top is amply rewarded by the magnificent views over the town and surrounding area.

On the opposite side of the valley are the beautiful wooded slopes of Masson Hill, the southern face of which has become known as the **Heights of Abraham**. This particular name was chosen after the inhabitants of Matlock had shown great enthusiasm for General Wolfe's victory in Quebec in 1759. This part of the Derwent valley was seen to resemble the gorge of the St Lawrence River and the original Heights of Abraham lying a mile north of Quebec. Today it is a well-known viewing point, reached on foot or, more easily, by cable car. The Heights of Abraham have a long history. For many years the slope was mined for lead but, in 1780, it was first developed as a pleasure garden and since then trees and shrubs have been planted to make it a pleasing attraction for those visiting the town. In 1812, the **Great Rutland Cavern**, on the slope, was opened to the public, a new experience for tourists of the time, and it was visited by many including the Grand Duke Michael of Russia and Princess Victoria. Formerly, it was known as the Nestor Mine., but its name was changed to honour the Duke of Rutland, who lived in nearby Haddon Hall. It has, in its time, been lit by candles, gas and now electricity. A recent innovation was a *son et lumiere* show in the Roman Hall area of the cavern. Following the success of the opening of the Great Rutland Cavern, the **Great Masson Cavern** was opened in 1844. It is basically an old lead mine that broke into a natural cavern, and visitors are encouraged to carry old lamps and candles for illumination to give an idea of what the cavern would have looked like to the miners of long ago. The **Prospect Tower** was built by redundant lead miners. It still provides a bird's eye view over Derbyshire. The Heights of Abraham are today as popular as ever and provide all the amenities of a good country park.

Life in a Lens, opened in 2001, is a museum of popular photography set in a beautiful renovated Victorian house. Displays include cameras of all ages, toy and novelty cameras, postcards and much more. The Victorian teashop is the latest attraction, opened in 2005.

Matlock Bath Illumination and Venetian Nights started in Victorian times, when residents illuminated the place with fairy lights. They are now firmly part of the tourism year, and are held annually from the end of August to the end of October.

LEA

4 miles SE of Matlock off the A615

Lea Gardens offer a rare collection of rhododendrons, azaleas, alpines and conifers in a superb woodland setting. This unique collection including kalmias and other plants of interest has been introduced from all over the world to this area in the heart of Derbyshire. The gardens provide a stunning visual display to enthral the whole family. Covering an area of some four acres, the site is set on the remains of a mediaeval millstone quarry and includes a lovely rock garden with dwarf conifers, alpines, heathers and spring bulbs. A mile of walks takes visitors through a blaze of spring colour.

TANSLEY

1 mile SE of Matlock on the A615

This tiny and picturesque village has an 18th century mill, **Tansley Wood Mill** and some good 18th century houses including Knoll House with an impressive carved doorway. It is well worth a visit by keen gardeners for its four garden centres and two horticultural nurseries.

The **Parish Church of Holy Trinity** dates from 1839-40, and was built of local stone. At that time, the village was within the

To the south of the town centre in Matlock Bath is a model village with a difference; Gulliver's Kingdom theme park (one of three such parks in Britain) makes a great day out for all the family. Set on the side of a wooded hill, each terrace is individually themed with styles including Fantasy Terrace, Lilliput Land, Little Switzerland and Bourbon Street. There are plenty of fun rides, a monorail, water slides and other diversions, as well as a café and restaurant.

65 SCOTLAND NURSERIES GARDEN CENTRE, RESTAURANT & CHOCOLATE SHOP

Tansley

A wonderful garden centre that offers everything for the garden, a place to eat wonderful food and to buy chocolate products.

🏛 see page 204

parish of Crich, with the church being four miles away.

HOLLOWAY

4½ miles SE of Matlock off the A6

This tiny village has one famous daughter, Florence Nightingale, who lived here at **Lea Hurst**, a 17th century gabled farmhouse. Named after the Italian city where she was born in 1820, Florence was the second child of Edward William Shore, who later changed his name to Nightingale to take advantage of an inheritance. Nightingale began to alter and enlarge the house in 1825 and he also sold some land to Richard Arkwright so that he could build Willersley Castle, overlooking the River Derwent.

Perhaps the most interesting member of the early Nightingale family was Peter, born in 1736. His nickname was 'Mad Peter' on account of his lifestyle, which consisted of heavy drinking, gambling and horse riding. However, he was an astute businessman and established a lead smelting business and extended an arm of the Cromford Canal.

Florence's father left Lea Hurst to her in his will and, after her courageous work in the dreadful conditions of the Crimean War, she retired to the house and spent the next 50 years writing, specifically on the subject of hospital organisation. Florence died in London in 1910 and the house remained in the family until 1940. Still in private hands, Lea Hurst is occasionally opened to the public.

CROMFORD

2 miles S of Matlock off the A5012

Cromford is a model village known the world over, and it was here, in 1771, that Sir Richard Arkwright started to build **Cromford Mill**, the world's first successful water-powered spinning mill. Though some of the buildings predate Arkwright, he also built a new town round the mill, providing decent housing and other amenities for his workers, such as an inn, shops, a school and a village lock up for miscreants In this respect, Cromford became possibly the first purpose-built industrial town in the world.

Born in Preston, Lancashire in 1732, Arkwright was the inventor of the waterframe, a machine for spinning cotton that was powered by water. The area he had chosen for his mill was perfect: the River Derwent, described by Daniel Defoe as 'a fury of a river',

Cromford Bridge

provided an ample power supply; there was an unorganised but very willing workforce, as the lead mining industry was experiencing a decline, and probably most importantly, Cromford was away from the prying eyes of Arkwright's competitors. In 1792, he commissioned the building of the village church, where he now lies. The mill proved to be a great success and became the model for others both in Britain and abroad, earning Arkwright the accolade 'Father of the Factory System'. His pioneering work and contributions to the great Industrial Age resulted in a knighthood in 1786, and one year later he became High Sheriff of Derbyshire. Cromford Mill and the associated buildings are now an International World Heritage site. Tours of the mill and Cromford village are available throughout the year. Continuing refurbishment and conservation by The Arkwright Society, which bought the site in 1979, ensures that future visitors will be able to follow the fascinating history behind this pioneering establishment. It is sponsored by Derbyshire County Council and the Derbyshire Dales District Council. Within the complex of the mill site there are a range of craft workshops.

The **Cromford Venture Centre** is an ideal base for study visits, holidays, training and self-development courses. It offers self-catering accommodation for parties of up to 24 young people and four staff. It is run by the Arkwright Sociey in association with the Prince's Trust, and is housed in a listed building.

For lovers of waterways, there is an opportunity, at **Cromford Canal,** to wander along the five-mile stretch of towpath to Ambergate. At **Cromford Wharf** there is a warehouse dating back to 1794, a counting house from the same year and a couple of canal cottages. The old **Leawood Pumping Station**, which transferred water from the River Derwent to the Cromford Canal, has been fully restored. Inside, the engine house is a preserved Cornish-type beam engine which is occasionally steamed up. Close by the Pump House is the **Wigwell Aqueduct**, (also known as the Derwent Aqueduct) dating from 1793, which carries the canal high over the River Derwent. It had to be rebuilt when it partially collapsed during construction.

The **High Peak Trail**, which stretches some 17-and-a-half miles up to Dowlow near Buxton, starts at Cromford and follows the trackbed of the Cromford and High Peak Railway. First opened in 1880, the railway was built to connect the Cromford Canal with the Peak Forest Canal. It is somewhat reminiscent of a canal as it has long level sections interspersed with sharp inclines (instead of locks) and many of the stations are known as wharfs. After walking the trail it is not

The 15th century Cromford Bridge has rounded arches on one side and pointed arches on the other. At one time it had a bridge chapel, but now only scant remains are left. Next to the bridge is an 18th century 'fishing temple', with, above its door, the inscription piscatorium sacrum. It was from this bridge, in 1697, so local folklore has it, that a horse and rider took a flying leap from the parapet, plunged into the river 20 feet below and lived to tell the tale.

surprising to learn that its chief engineer was really a canal builder! The railway was finally closed in 1967; the old stations are now car parks and picnic areas and there is an information office in the former Hartington station signal box. Surfaced with clinker rather than limestone, the trail is suitable for walkers, cyclists and horses.

BONSALL

2 miles SW of Matlock off the A5012

In a steep-sided dale beneath Masson Hill, Bonsall was once a famous lead mining centre and many of the fields and meadows around are still littered with the remains of the miners' work. This typical Peak District village has some fine 17th century limestone cottages clustered around its ball-

Gritstone Steps, Bonsall

topped 17th century cross. This is encircled by 13 gritstone steps in the steeply sloping market square. It is also one of the Derbyshire villages which continues the tradition of well-dressing, usually on the last Saturday in July.

Beside the market square cross stands The King's Head inn, dating from the late 17th century and said to be haunted. Another pub in the village reflects the traditional occupations of its residents, as it is called the Barley Mow. Another was called the Pig of Lead but is now a private residence. Above the village centre stands the battlemented **Parish Church of St James**, with its pinnacled tower and spire. Dating originally from ithe 1200s, it has a wonderful clerestory lighting the nave, though the outer walls were substantially rebuilt in 1862-63. From one end of the main street, the road climbs up some 400 feet to the Upper Town which lies just below the rim of the limestone plateau. In order to cope with the steep hill, the village church is split-level.

Bonsall Brook, the power source for many of the textile mills in the village, also supplied power to the original Viyella mill, built in the 1790s by Philip Gell of Hopton Hall. Soon after building the mill, Gell constructed a road from his lead mines in Grangemill to the smelting house at Cromford. Called **Via Gellia** (and in the 19th century known locally as Via Jelly) it was the name of this road, which ran close to the mill, that was changed to 'Viyella' by the owners of the former Hollin Mill when they invented a new brand of hosiery.

The village was at one time a centre of framework knitting, and east of the village cross is an old knitting workshop, with its large windows and outside staircase.

MIDDLETON BY WIRKSWORTH

4 miles SW of Matlock off the A5012

Just north of the village, which is also known as Middleton, lies the **Good Luck Mine**, which is now a lead mining museum. Usually open the first Sunday in the month, this old mine, found on the Via Gellia, is typically narrow and, in places, the roof is low. Not a place for the claustrophobic, it does, however, give an excellent impression of a lead mine. The village also has another mine, where a particularly rare form of limestone is quarried. Hopton Wood marble from here has been used in Westminster Abbey, York Minster and the Houses of Parliament.

The Cromford and High Peak Railway had many inclines, and no less than nine steam-powered winding engines to haul the wagons and engines up them. **Middleton Top Winding Engine**, to the west of the village, was built in 1829, and is the only survivor. On certain days of the year between April and October it can still be seen in action. At **Middleton Top** is a visitor centre that explains the Cromford and High Peak Railway.

WIRKSWORTH

4 miles S of Matlock off the B5023

Nestling in the lush green foothills of the Peak District where north meets south, Wirksworth was once the leading lead-mining town in the Peak District. It is home to the distinctive **Wirksworth Heritage Centre**, housed in a former silk mill, which takes visitors through time from the Romans in Wirksworth to the present day. Quarrying, lead mining and local customs are explored with interactive and fascinating exhibits. One of the town's most interesting sights is the jumble of cottages linked by a maze of tiny lanes on the hillside between The Dale and Greenhill, in particular the area known locally as 'The Puzzle Gardens'.

Babington House dates back to Jacobean Wirksworth. Another former lead merchant's house, **Hopkinsons House**, was restored in 1980 as part of a number of

Almshouses, Wirksworth

66 THE VAULTS

Wirksworth

A great inn that offers comfortable accommodation plus good food and drink, just a short walk from the centre of town.

 see *page 205*

67 THE NATIONAL STONE CENTRE

Wirksworth

A dramatic site in the heart of the Derbyshire Dales is where you will find this wonderful outdoor museum.

 see *page 205*

restoration schemes initiated by the Civic Trust's 'Wirksworth Project'. The ancient **Parish Church of St Mary's** is a fine building dating originally from the 13th century and standing on a site previously occupied by a Saxon and then a Norman church. It sits in a tranquil close bounded by the former (Georgian) grammar school and the Elizabethan **Gell's Almshouses**, named after Sir Philip Gell who founded them in 1584. The church holds one of the oldest stone carvings in the country. Known as the Wirksworth Stone, it is a coffin lid dating from the 8th century, and was found beneath the chancel floor in the 1820s. There are also tombs of the Gell family, local lords of the manor in Tudor times and lead mine owners. The ancient ceremony of 'clypping the church' take place here on the first Sunday after 8th September each year. It is thought to date from pre-Christain times, and consists of the people of the village circling the church and linking hands. Another ceremony is that of well-dressing, which takes place during the last few days of May/first week of June.

The **National Stone Centre** in Porter Lane tells 'the story of stone', with a wealth of exhibits, activities such as gem-panning and fossil-casting, and outdoor trails tailored to introduce topics such as the geology, ecology and history of the dramatic Peak District landscape. Nearby, the 18 inch gauge **Steeple Grange Light Railway Society** runs along a short line over the High Peak Trail

between Steeplehouse Station and Dark Lane Quarry at weekends between May and September. The journey takes 20 minutes. The former quarry is now overgrown with shrubs, trees and a profusion of wildflowers and birds. Power is provided by battery-electric, diesel and petrol locomotives. Passengers are carried in a man rider salvaged from Bevercotes Colliery in Nottinghamshire. Meanwhile, the **Ecclesbourne Valley Railway** runs on a line of track from Wirksworth to Ravenstor. Manned entirely by volunteers, eventually it is hoped to extend the line to Driffield. The original line was laid in 1867 to link Wirksworth with Derby, and finally closed in 1989.

At **North End Mills**, visitors are able to witness hosiery being made as it has been for over half a century; a special viewing area offers an insight into some of the items on sale in the factory shop.

The town has connections with Mary Ann Evans, the author who wrote under the pen name of George Eliot. At the southern end of the town is a cottage known as **Adam Bede Cottage**. This is where Samuel Evans and his wife Elizabeth lived, in real life Mary Ann's aunt and uncle. In the book *Adam Bede,* Wirksworth is called Snowfield, and Samuel and Elizabeth are portrayed as Adam Bede and Dinah Morris. Another literary connection is to be found at the Crown Inn, which Baroness Orczy featured in her novel *Beau Brocade*. Wirksworth was also where D.H. Lawrence's mother came from, and indeed Lawrence lived close to the town at Mountain Cottage for a year with his German born wife.

Carsington Water just outside Wirksworth is one of Britain's newest reservoirs. This 741-acre expanse of water is a beauty spot that has attracted well over a million visitors a year since it was opened by Queen Elizabeth in 1992. It can be reached on foot from Wirksworth along a series of footpaths, and aims to be disabled friendly with wheelchairs available and access to as many attractions as possible. Sailing, windsurfing, fishing and canoeing can be enjoyed here, as well as just quiet strolls or bike rides. The Visitor Centre on the west bank offers visitors the opportunity to learn about all aspects of Severn Trent Water, who own it, and water supplies in general. The reservoir is unusual in that it is not fed by streams and rivers, but by water pumped into it from the River Derwent when the water is high. It can hold up to 7.8 billion gallons of water at any one time.

An impressive exhibit in the courtyard is the Kugel Stone, a massive ball of granite weighing over one tonne, which revolves on a thin film of water under pressure. It can be moved with a touch of the hand! Some half a million trees and shrubs have been planted and are managed to attract wildlife and to enhance the landscape. There are two bird hides and a wildlife centre to help visitors understand the variety of wildlife and observe the birdlife that visits the reservoir. The reservoir is stocked for fishing either from the bank or from boats available for hire. There is a large adventure playground and numerous open spaces for families to relax.

71

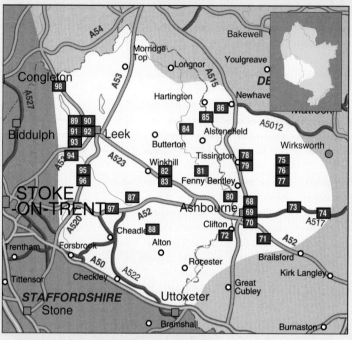

Dovedale and the Staffordshire Moorlands

This area of Derbyshire, which includes a southern section of the Peak District, is probably best known for the beautiful Dovedale. The large car park near Thorpe which gives general access to the dale is often crowded, but there is plenty of room for everyone and the wonderful valley is well worth experiencing. It is also the place to have a go at crossing a river on stepping stones, something that has delighted children for many, many years, though there is a bridge just downstream, which ensures that the crossing can be made with dry feet, particularly when the water level is high.

The River Dove takes its name from the British Gaelic word 'dutho', meaning dark. It is 45 miles long from its source at Axe Edge to the River Derwent, and for much of its length it forms the boundary between Derbyshire and Staffordshire. It is a favourite place for fishermen, and is forever associated with Izaak Walton, who published his famous book, *The Compleat Angler,* in 1653.

He was born in in Stafford, and later moved to London, where he was an ironmonger. He later lived in Farnham, Surrey, but spent a lot of time with his poet friend Charles Cotton at the latter's fishing cottage on the Dove. An old farmhouse, at the head of the Dale, was converted, many years ago, into the well-known and much-loved Izaak Walton Hotel.

Dovedale, however, is not the only dale worth exploring. The River Manifold offers some equally wonderful scenery, as does Ilam. A beautifully preserved estate village, with a well established youth hostel, Ilam is also a popular starting point from which to explore the Manifold Valley.

The ancient custom of well-dressing is almost exclusively confined to the limestone areas of the county. The porous rock, through which rainfall seeps leaving the surface completely dry just a few hours after heavy rainfall, meant that, for the people of these close knit communities, the well or spring was of the utmost importance. If this dried up, the lives of the whole community were at risk. There are plenty of theories as to why well-dressing began or was revived at Tissington. One centres on the purity of the Tissington wells during the Black Death, which swept through the country in the mid-1300s. During this time some 77 of the 100 clergy in Derbyshire died and the surviving villagers simply returned to pagan customs, one of them being well-dressing.

Another plausible theory dates back only as far as the great drought of 1615, when the Tissington wells kept flowing though it was in very short supply everywhere else. Whichever theory is true, one thing is certain: in the last 50 years or so many villages who had not dressed a well for centuries, if ever, are now joining in the colourful tradition.

On the southern edge of the Peak District, the Staffordshire Moorlands certainly rival those of Derbyshire in terms of scenic attraction. The undulating pastures of the moorlands, along with the fresh air and ancient weather-worn crags, make this the ideal place to walk, cycle or trek. It is also an area full of character, with charming scattered villages, historic market towns and a wealth of history. Many of the farms and buildings date back hundreds of years, and the Industrial Revolution also left its mark. The two great reservoirs of Rudyard and Tittesworth, however, built to provide a water supply to the growing industry and population of the Midlands, now offer peaceful havens for a wide variety of plants, animals and birds as well as recreational facilities such as fishing and boating.

68 GALLERY CAFÉ

Ashbourne

Great snacks and meals in a smart, spacious café set above an arts and crafts gallery right in the heart of Ashbourne.

 see page 206

69 THE GREEN MAN ROYAL HOTEL

Ashbourne

An old, elegant coaching inn with good food and drink and 18 fully en suite guest rooms.

 see page 206

70 WHITE HART HOTEL

Ashbourne

A picturesque place with great food and drink and good, old fashioned value-for-money. Five letting rooms are also available.

 see page 205

ASHBOURNE

Ashbourne, the southern gateway to the Peak District National Park, featured in the *Domesday Book* as 'Essiburn', derived from the local stream with its many ash trees. It was originally a small settlement lying on the northern bank of Henmore Brook, which already had a church. It was a 13th century lord of the manor who laid out the new town to the east, around its unusual shaped market place. Many of the town's traders, in order to continue to enjoy the benefits without paying the town's tolls, built themselves houses on the south side of the Brook. The area became known as Compton (or 'Campdene') and it was slowly absorbed into the town. When writing *Adam Bede*, George Eliot based 'Oakbourne' in 'Stonyshire' on the town.

Ashbourne lies on the boundary of the old red sandstone of southern Derbyshire and the limestone which surrounds Dovedale and the White Peak. It is one of Derbyshire's finest old towns, with a wealth of wonderful Georgian architecture. It is a pleasure to visit, with shop-filled streets to potter up and down. The triangular cobbled **Market Square**, in the heart of Ashbourne, was part of the new development begun in the 13th century that shifted the town to the east, away from the church. Weekly markets have been held in the square since 1296, and now take place every Thursday. It was from this market place, once lined with ale houses, that Bonnie Prince Charlie proclaimed his father to be King James III, at the height of the Jacobite Rebellion of 1745. Though the old bull ring no longer exists, the town boasts many fine examples of 18th century architecture as well as some older buildings, notably the **Gingerbread Shop** which is timber framed and probably dates from the 15th century. For many years the building was, curiously, covered over with a mock Tudor front. Traditional Ashbourne gingerbread is said to be made from a recipe that was acquired from French prisoners of war who were kept in the town during the Napoleonic Wars.

Also worthy of a second glance is the **Green Man and Black's Head Royal Hotel**. The inn sign stretches over St John's Street and was put up when the Blackamoor Inn joined with the Green Man in 1825. Though the Blackamoor is no more, the sign remains and it claims to be the longest hotel name in the country. If you look carefully, you will see that the blackamoor's head is smiling on one side and scowling on the other. Of Georgian origin, the amalgamated hotel has played host to James Boswell, Dr Johnson and the young Princess Victoria. Ashbourne was, in fact, one of Dr Johnson's favourite places; he came to the town on several occasions between 1737 and 1784 to visit Dr John Taylor, an old friend. He also visited the hotel so often that he had his own chair with his name on it! The chair can still be seen at the Green Man.

A stroll down Church Street, described by Pevsner as one of the finest streets in Derbyshire, takes the walker past many interesting Georgian houses - including the Grey House, which stands next to the **Grammar School**. Founded by Sir Thomas Cockayne on behalf of Elizabeth I in 1585, the school was visited on its 400th anniversary by the present Queen. Almost opposite the Grey House is **The Mansion**, the late 17th century home of the Reverend Dr John Taylor, oldest friend of Dr Johnson. In 1764, a domed, octagonal drawing room was added to the house, and a new brick façade built facing the street. Next to The Mansion are the **Owfield's Almshouses,** dating from the early 17th century. Next to them, at right angles to the street, are **Pegg's Almshouses**, founded in 1669. Ashbourne also retains many of its narrow alleyways and, in particular, there is Lovatt's Yard where the town lock-up can be seen.

In the **Parish Church of St Oswald,** Ashbourne has one of the most impressive and elegant churches in the country, described by George Eliot as 'the finest mere parish church in England'. James Boswell said that the church was 'one of the largest and most luminous that I have seen in any town of the same size'. St Oswald's stands on the site of a minster church mentioned in the *Domesday Book*, though most of what we

see today dates from rebuilding work in the 13th century. There is a dedication brass in the south transept dated 1241. The south doorway, with its dog-toothed decoration and ribbed moulding, reflects the church's classic early English style. St Oswald's has chapels to its transepts, adding to the spacious feeling that is more reminiscent of a small cathedral than a parish church.

The alabaster tombs and monuments to the Bradbourne and Cockayne families in the north transept chapel are justly famous. Perhaps the best-known monument is that to Penelope Boothby, who died in 1791 at the tender age of five. It is perhaps Thomas Banks, the sculptor's, most famous work, and is in white Carrara marble.

Parish Church of St Oswald, Ashbourne

75

71 SHOULDER OF MUTTON

Osmaston

A traditional pub in a traditional English village that has a great atmosphere and serves wonderful food and drink.

🍴 *see page 207*

72 COCK INN

Clifton

A former coaching inn that believes in all the values of a traditional English pub - good food, good drink and fine English hospitality

🍴 *see page 208*

The figure of the sleeping child is so life-like that it appears that she is only sleeping. Queen Charlotte, wife of George ll, is supposed to have burst into tears when she saw the sculpture at the Royal Academy exhibition. The moving epitaph reads: 'She was in form and intellect most exquisite. The unfortunate parents ventured their all on this frail bark, and the wreck was total.' It is said that Penelope's parents separated at the child's grave and never spoke to each other again. The tower and gracious 212-feet spire of the church were erected between 1330 and 1350, at the crossing of the nave and transepts. To the southeast of the church are the **Spalden Almshouses**, built between 1723 and 1724.

Ashbourne was the birthplace, in 1829, of **Catherine Mumford**, who later married William Booth and helped him found the Salvation Army. There is a bust of her in the War Memorial Gardens. Ashbourne is home, too, to the famous Royal Shrovetide football game played on Shrove Tuesday and Ash Wednesday. The two teams, the 'Up'ards' (those born north of the Henmore Brook) and the 'Down'ards' (those born south of it) begin their match at 2pm behind the Green Man Hotel. The game continues until well into the evening. The two goals are situated three miles apart, along the Brook, on the site of the old mills at Clifton and Sturston. It is rare for more than one goal to be scored in this slow-moving game.

SOUTH AND EAST OF ASHBOURNE

YELDERSLEY

3 miles SE of Ashbourne off the A52

Yeldersley has long been the home of gentlemen farmers and those who love the countryside. This picturesque village offers many scenic delights. **Yeldersley Hall** is a spacious country house, which was built in 1800 for Edmund Evans. It replaced an earlier home some distance away.

OSMASTON

2½ miles SE of Ashbourne off the A52

Osmaston is a sleepy, beautiful village just five minutes' drive from Ashbourne. Neither crowded nor bustling, it offers the visitor a real haven of tranquillity. It is the archetypal English village, with thatched cottages, village green, village pond, pub and church. However - not everything is as it seems - it was built in the 19th century as an estate village to house the workers at the Butterley Iron Works. The manor house, Osmaston Manor, was built in 1849 for Francis Wright, the owner of the ironworks, and was demolished in 1964. The main staircase is now in Wooton Lodge, Staffordshire. The estate at Osmaston today is the location for the annual Osmaston Horse Trials and the Ashbourne Shire Horse Show. The Gothic **Parish Church of St Martin** dates from 1845, and replaced an earlier church of 1606.

BRADLEY

3 miles E of Ashbourne just off the A517

A regular visitor to the Georgian **Bradley Hall** (private) was Dr Johnson, who would visit the Meynell family here when he was staying in Ashbourne with his friend, Dr John Taylor. The Meynells had come to Bradley in 1655 and bought the hall from Sir Andrew Kniveton, who had been ruined by the Civil War.

Opposite the hall stands the rather squat **Parish Church of All Saints**, which is interesting in having a bell turret but no tower on its 14th century nave and chancel. The original wooden bell tower was struck by lightning. There are several memorials to the Meynell family in the church. The base and part of the shaft of a Saxon cross stand in the churchyard. The archway, crossing the formerly gated road between cottages at Moorend, is known locally as 'The Hole in the Wall'. The former village pub had the distinction, common in Derbyshire, of two official names, The Jinglers and the Fox and Hounds. Nearby **Bradley Wood** was given to the people of Ashbourne in 1935 by Captain Fitzherbert Wright.

KIRK IRETON

6 miles NE of Ashbourne off the B5023

Kirk Ireton is a picturesque village, much of it built from locally quarried gritstone. In the hills near Carsington Reservoir, it sits at 700 feet above sea level. Its name means 'church of the irish enclosure', and at one time a Celtic monastery is supposed to have stood here. Much of the village is 17th century and one of the oldest buildings is the Barley Mow Inn. When decimalisation was introduced in 1971, the 87-year-old landlady refused to accept the new money. The Barley Mow was one of the last places in the country to go decimal. The **Parish Church of the Holy Trinity** is partly Norman, with 14th century additions. There is an interesting custom observed here at weddings known as 'roping for weddings', when children would stretch a rope across the road as the bride and broom leave the church. They can only pass if they pay a toll.

KNIVETON

3 miles NE of Ashbourne on the B5035

This tiny village of grey stone houses lies close to Carsington Reservoir, sheltered in a dip in the hills. Its little **Parish Church of St Michael** has a 13th century tower, a Norman doorway, a 13th century font, small lancet windows, battlements and a short spire. The medieval glass in the chancel depicts the arms of the family of Kniveton. Sir Andrew Kniveton became so impoverished through his loyalty to Charles I that he had to sell most of the family estates. A huge sycamore tree and an ancient yew stand in the churchyard. The yew has grooves in its bark, said to have been made by archers sharpening their arrows.

Just north of the village is the Bronze Age burial mound at

73 THE BLACK HORSE INN

Hulland Ward

A quite exceptional traditional English inn with rooms to let, and a great reputation for its real ales and beautifully cooked food.

🍽 ⊨ see page 209

74 TIGER INN

Turnditch

An olde worlde inn that marries tradition with high standards of service and outstanding value for money.

🍽 see page 210

75 RED LION INN

Hognaston

An inn with a great denotation for its accommodation, food and drink, set within a picturesque village.

 see page 211

76 KNOCKERDOWN FARM

Ashbourne

Superior self-catering country cottages within a complex that includes a swimming pool, restaurant, and other amenities.

 see page 211

77 MAIN SAIL RESTAURANT

Carsington Water Visitors Centre

A stylish restaurant right on the water's edge with a commitment to good food prepared and beautifully cooked from local produce.

 see page 212

Wigber Low which has revealed some important remains from the village's past.

HOGNASTON

4 miles NE of Ashbourne off the B5035

The picturesque village of Hognaston stands on a hillside overlooked by **Hognaston Winn**, which rises to 1,000 feet. It has been in existence for at least 1,000 years and there is evidence of medieval field structures and where long demolished houses once stood. It used to be a busy place in coaching days when the London to Manchester coaches passed through. The **Parish Church of St Bartholomew**, dating back to the 12th century, has some extraordinary Norman carvings over the doorway in the tympanum, and an early Norman font. Two of the bells date back to the 13th century. The clock and three of the other bells were a gift from John Smith and Sons, the famous Derby clock-makers as a memorial to John Smith who lived in the village. The village lies close to **Carsington Water**, Britain's newest reservoir, owned by Severn Trent Water. Opened by the Queen in 1992, it draws its water from the River Derwent, and the surrounding area is able to support a whole host of wildlife. One controversial resident is the American ruddy duck. Once unknown outside wildlife reserves, the duck escaped and, in little over 50 years, the breed has become widespread throughout Europe.

Set in eight acres of picturesque grounds overlooking Carsington Water is the famous **Knockerdown Inn**. The property dates back to the 17th century, and opened as an ale house in 1838, when it was known officially as The Greyhound but was given the affectionate name 'The Nock'. The famous stagecoach 'The Devonshire' used to call here en route from Wirksworth to Ashbourne.

HOPTON

8 miles NE of Ashbourne off the B5035

This village, now by-passed by the main road, is dominated by the Carsington Water reservoir. The land rises to the north of Hopton and here can be found the **Hopton Incline**, once the steepest railway incline in the British Isles. Lying on the **High Peak Railway**, carriages were hauled up using fixed engines on their journey from Cromford to Whaley Bridge. It is now part of the High Peak Trail. The **Sir Philip Gell Almshouses** were built between 1719 and 1722 for two men and two women.

Until 1989 **Hopton Hall** was the home of the Gell family and in particular, the home of Philip Gell, the owner of the Viyella mill at Cromford. Though the actual date of the original building is unknown, the Gell family have been known to have lived in the area since 1208 and they have held the manor of Hopton since the 15th century. The Gell family made their fortune in the nearby limestone quarries and they were also responsible for the construction of the Via Gellia, a road which runs along a valley to the west of Cromford.

BRADBOURNE

4 miles NE of Ashbourne off the A5056

This is an ancient village, standing high on a ridge between the valleys of Bradbourne Brook and Havenhill Dale. Even at the time of the recording of the *Domesday Book* its name, Bradeburne (meaning broad stream) was well established. For more than 300 years the monks at Dunstable Priory grazed their sheep on the land around Bradbourne, and also supplied vicars to the **Parish Church of All Saints**. Essentially Norman, but with some fragments of Saxon work - especially on the north side of the nave where typical long-and-short work is visible. The church's large, unbuttressed west tower is Norman and has an elegantly decorated south door. Most of the rest of this appealing little church dates from the 14th century, but there are some fine modern furnishings which owe much to William Morris' Arts and Crafts movement. Some of the wall paintings date from the 17th and 18th centuries. The church is surrounded by its hilltop churchyard which contains not only the remains of a Saxon cross, dated approx AD 800, but also a scene of the crucifixion. Originally the shaft would have been topped with a cross, originally set up to mark a place where people gathered to worship. This one was found in use as a squeeze stile into a nearby field before being identified and placed in the churchyard. Also in the churchyard is the grave of Nat Gould. Nat was born in 1857, and was a

All Saints Church and Saxon Cross, Bradbourne

journalist who emigrated to Australia. There he worked on the Brisbane Telegraph, where his first fiction appeared. Eventually he returned to England and worked on his uncle's farm opposite the church, and by the time of his death in 1919 he had written 130 horse racing novels.

The **Bradbourne Stone**, dating from ancient times, stands well north of the church,

While in the village it is also worth taking a look at the fine grey stone Elizabethen manor house **Bradbourne Hall** (private), with its three gables and beautiful terraced gardens. **The Old Parsonage**, which has a rather peculiar appearance as it was built in three completely different styles and materials, is also worthy of note.

BRASSINGTON

7 miles NE of Ashbourne off the B5056

This grey stone village, 800 feet above sea level and known to the locals as 'Brass'n', has its past firmly embedded in the lead mining and quarrying traditions of this part of Derbyshire. The hollows and bumps in the green meadows tell of 200 years of underground industry in pursuit of lead, and now lead-tolerant flowers such as mountain pansy, sandwort and orchids flourish here.

Protected from the wind by the limestone plateau that soars some 1,000 feet above sea level, the village sits by strange-shaped rocks, the result of weather erosion, with names like **Rainster Rocks** and **Harborough Rocks**. Stone Age man found snug dwellings amongst these dolomite limestone formations and there is evidence that animals like the sabre-toothed tiger, brown bear, wolf and hyena also found comfort here in the caves. As late as the 18th century, families were still living in the caves. At Rainster Rocks there is evidence of a Roman British settlement, and at Harborough there are the remains of a chambered cairn.

Once standing on the main London to Manchester road, this was once a prosperous village and many of the 17th and 18th century cottages survive from those days. Today's post office used to be the tollhouse on the Loughborough to Brassington road, which became a turnpike in 1738; the Gate Inn stood next to the turnpike gate. Brassington's oldest 'resident' is a relief carving depicting a man with one hand over his heart, which can be seen inside the Norman tower of the **Parish Church of St James**. It may date back to Saxon

times, but most of the rest of the church is Norman, heavily restored by the Victorians. The north aisle dates from Victorian times, but the south aisle dates to about 1200. Nearby is the Wesleyan Reform Chapel, one of the so-called 'Smedley Chapels' built by local millowner, Mr Smedley, in 1852. Smedley was a keen Revivalist and his two other chapels in the village are now the village hall and a private house.

BALLIDON

5 miles N of Ashbourne off the B5056

Ballidon is an almost deserted village, which, some 800 years ago, was a thriving community. All that can be seen today are four rather grand 17th century farms and the **Chapel of All Saints** standing isolated in a field surrounded by old crofts and tofts. It dates originally from the Norman period, but it was so heavily restored in 1882 that most Norman details have been obliterated.

Overshadowed by its gigantic limestone quarry, the legacy of this tiny hamlet's days as a robust medieval village, remain in the numerous earthworks, lynchets and evidence of ridge-and-furrow cultivation in its fields. One-and-a-half miles north is **Minning Low**, one of the most impressive early Bronze Age chambered tombs in Derbyshire.

ALDWARK

9 miles NE of Ashbourne off the B5056

Close to the High Peak Trail, just inside the Peak Park boundary,

Aldwark is one of the most unspoilt villages in Derbyshire. A quiet and tranquil backwater, its name comes from the Saxon for 'Old Fort', meaning that even then it was considered an ancient settlement. The highest recorded population was 97 in 1831, though at this time it was one of the staging posts on the coaching route between Derby and Buxton. A chambered tomb dating from 2000 BC was discovered at **Green Low**, just to the north of the village, which contained pottery, flints and animal bones.

FENNY BENTLEY

2 miles N of Ashbourne off the A515

Fenny Bentley is the first village of the Peak for visitors coming from the south, with its steep hill up into the Peak District and the old railway bridge where the Tissington Trail passes through the village (see also Tissington). The trail is a 13-mile trail for walkers and cyclists from the old Ashbourne Station to The High Peak Trail at Parsley Hay.

Inside the **Parish Church of St Edmund's** can be found the tomb of Thomas Beresford, the local lord of the manor who fought, alongside eight of his 16 sons, at Agincourt. The effigies of Beresford and his wife are surrounded by those of their 21 children - each covered by a shroud as, by the time the tombs were built nobody could remember what they had looked like! It is said that everyone with the surname of Beresford is descended from Thomas and his wife, and the annual meeting of the Beresford Family Society takes place in the village each year. During the Civil War, much of the 14th century church, and its rectory, were destroyed. On returning to his parish after the restoration of Charles II in 1661, the rector resolved to rebuild the rectory, which was all but rubble, and restore the church to its former glory. Both of these he managed. The church was once again heavily restored during Victorian times, when the spire was added to the tower.

The 15th century square tower of the Beresford's fortified manor house is now incorporated into **Cherry Orchard Farm**. It was also the home of Charles Cotton at one time, and is a local landmark that can be seen from the main road.

Fortified Manor, Fenny Bentley

78 BLUEBELL INN AND RESTAURANT

Tissington

A gem of a pub that is renowned throughout the area for its fine food and warm welcome.

see page 213

TISSINGTON

4 miles N of Ashbourne off the A515

Sitting at the foothills of the Pennines, Tissington is most famous for its ancient festival of well-dressing, a ceremony which dates back to 1350 or earlier. Today this takes place on Ascension Day, the 40th day after Easter (usually the middle of May), and draws many crowds who come to see the spectacular folk art created by the local people. The significance of the event in Tissington may have been to commemorate those who survived the ravages of the Black Death when it raged throughout the villages of Derbyshire in the mid-1300s. During this time some 77 of the 100 clergy in Derbyshire died; the surviving villagers simply returned to the pagan custom of well-dressing. Another plausible theory dates back only as far as the great drought of 1615, when the Tissington wells kept flowing though water everywhere was in very short supply. Whichever theory is true, one thing is certain: in the last 50 years or so many villages that had not dressed a well for centuries, if ever, began to take part in this colourful tradition.

A total of six wells are dressed at Tissington - the Hall, the Town, the Yew Tree, the Hands, the Coffin and the Children's Wells. Each depicts a separate scene, usually from the Bible. Visitors should follow the signs in the village or ask at the Old Coach House.

Very much on the tourist route, particularly in the early summer, Tissington has plenty of tea rooms and ice cream shops to satisfy the hot and thirsty visitor, as well as that essential of any picturesque English village - a duck pond. The village itself, though often overlooked in favour of the colourful well-dressings, has some interesting buildings. The **Parish Church of St Mary**, situated on a rise overlooking Tissington, dates originally from Norman times, and is still essentially Norman, even though it was restored in 1854, with many mock Norman features being added. It has an unusual tub-shaped font, which dates back to the original Norman Church. The pulpit too is unusual. Converted from a double-decker type, it once had a set of steps leading out from the priest's stall below.

Tissington

Home of the FitzHerbert family for 500 years, **Tissington Hall** is a distinguished and impressive stately home which was built by Francis FitzHerbert in 1609, though there may be fragments of an earlier building incorporated. During the Civil War, the Fitzherberts were for the king, and the then Fitzherbert was a colonel with the Royalist forces. He used the hall as a garrison for his troops.

The estate consists of 2,405 acres, and the Hall boasts a wealth of original pieces, artwork, furnishings and architectural features tracing the times and tastes of the FitzHerbert family over the centuries. The oak-panelled main hall has the original stone-flagged floor and is dominated by a stunning Gothic fireplace installed in 1757. Here visitors will also find a pair of late 18th century Chippendale bookcases, a rosewood piano and other fine pieces. The Dining Room, originally the old kitchen, is also panelled in oak and has an original Waring & Gillow table with a matching set of 13 chairs. The frieze work was added in the early 1900s. Paintings of country scenes and family portraits adorn the walls. The Library is a repository of over 3,000 books, and is adorned with a frieze depicting a woodland scene. Other fine pieces include a bracket clock made by Jasper Taylor of Holborn in about 1907. The East and West Drawing Rooms can also be visited.

Tissington Hall and Gardens are open to the public on certain afternoons throughout the summer. Please call the Estate Office for details. In addition, the gardens are open on several days for charity including the National Gardens Scheme. Private groups and societies are welcome by written appointment throughout the year.

Well at Tissington

Following the old Ashbourne to Parsley Hay railway line, the **Tissington Trail** is a popular walk which can be combined with other old railway trails in the area, or country lanes, to make an enjoyable circular country walk. The trail passes through some lovely countryside and, having a reasonable surface, it is also popular with cyclists. Along the route can also be found many of the old railway buildings and junction boxes and, in particular, Hartington station, which is now a picnic site with an information centre in the old signal box.

79 TISSINGTON HALL & GARDENS

Tissington

Home to the FitzHerbert family, the hall and gardens are open to the public on selected dates during the year.

 see page 214

83

PARWICH

5 miles N of Ashbourne off the A515

This typical Peak District village is delightful, with stone houses and an 1870s church around the village green. The pronunciation of the name varies, however, with some calling it 'Par-itch' and some 'Par-wich'. Most seem to favour the latter. Conspicuous amongst the stone built houses is **Parwich Hall**, constructed of brick and finished in 1747. The wonderful gardens at the Hall were created at the turn of the 20th century and it remains today a family home, though, over the years it has changed hands on several occasions. The **Parish Church of St Peter** is Victorian, built between 1873 and 1874, though there are some Norman details.

Parwich Moor, above the village, is home to many mysterious Bronze Age circles, which vary in size from 12 to 50 feet in diameter. Though their function is unknown,

it is unlikely that they were used as burial chambers. Close to Parwich is Roystone Grange, an important archaeological site where, to the north of the present farmhouse, the remains of a Roman farmhouse have been excavated. To the south are an old engine house and the remains of the old medieval monastic grange. Both Roystone Grange and Parwich lie on the interesting and informative **Roystone Grange Archaeological Trail,** which starts at Minniglow car park. Some 11 miles long, the circular trail follows, in part, the old railway line that was built to connect the Cromford and the Peak Forest Canals in the 1820s before taking in some of the Tissington Trail.

ALSOP-EN-LE-DALE

5 miles N of Ashbourne off the A515

The old station on the Ashbourne-Buxton line, which once served this tiny hamlet is today a car park on the Tissington Trail. The tranquil hamlet itself is on a narrow lane, east of the main road towards Parwich, just a mile from Dovedale. Alsop-en-le-Dale's **Parish Church of St Michael and all Angels** is Norman, though it was refurbished substantially during Victorian times, when the tower was completely rebuilt. The nave retains Norman features, with impressive double zigzag mouldings in the arches, but the west tower is only imitation Norman, and dates from 1883. One unusual feature, which dominates this small church is its extraordinary 19th century square

Parwich Moor

mock-Gothic pulpit.

Opposite the church is the graceful and slender building known as **Alsop Hall**, constructed in the early 1600s for the Alsop family, who were lords of the manor. Though privately owned, it is worth seeing even for its exterior, as it is built in a handsome pre-classical style with stone-mullioned windows.

Alsop makes a good base for exploring the White Peak and is also convenient for Dovedale. The renowned **Viator's Bridge** at Milldale is a mile to the west, and was immortalised in a scene in Izaak Walton's *The Compleat Angler* in which the character Viator complains to another about the size of the tiny, two-arched packhorse bridge, deeming it 'not two fingers broad'.

Surrounding the village are many Bronze Age burial sites, including **Cross Low** (north of the village), **Nat Low** (north west of the village), **Moat Low** (southwest of the village) and **Green Low** on Alsop Moor.

NEWHAVEN

11 miles N of Ashbourne on the A515

The High Peak Trail crosses Newhaven to link up with the Tissington Trail. This charming village is also along the White Peak tourist route, though it retains a tranquil air.

MAPPLETON

2 miles NW of Ashbourne off the A515

Mappleton can also be spelled Mapleton, as some road signs will testify. It is a village that has been in some form or other since before 1086, when it is recorded in the *Domesday Book*. It is a secluded and charming village of the Dove Valley, with attractive views and a wealth of exciting natural beauty. The extremely small **Parish Church of St Mary** dates from 1751, and is unusual in that it has a dome rather than a tower or a steeple. There has been a church here since at least the reign of Edward I.

THORPE

3 miles NW of Ashbourne off the A515

Thorpe was mentioned in the *Domesday Book* and is one of the few villages in the Peak whose name has Norse origins, for the Danish settlers did not generally penetrate far into this area. It lies at the confluence of the Rivers Manifold and Dove, and is dominated by the conical hill of **Thorpe Cloud**, which guards the entrance to **Dovedale**. Cloud is a corruption of the Old English word 'clud', meaning hill. The summit is a short but stiff climb from any direction, but whichever way you go you are rewarded with panoramic views over Dovedale all the way to Alstonefield, Ilam and the lower Manifold valley. Although the Dale becomes over-crowded at times, there is always plenty of open space to explore on the hill as well as excellent walking. For much of its 45-mile course from Axe Edge to its confluence with the River Trent, the **River Dove** is a walker's river as it is

80 OKEOVER ARMS

Mappleton

A pub that is famous, not only for its great selection of drinks, but for its food, which is famous throughout the area.

see page 215

Mappleton's main claim to fame is its annual New Year's Day charity Bridge Jump, when ten teams of three people paddle down half a mile of the River Dove and then jump off a bridge. The Dove is said to be England's coldest river (and it is New Year's Day!) and is not easily navigable. The bridge is also 30 feet high and after the jump there is a 500-yard sprint to the pub. Hundreds of people come to watch each year.

Close by the River Dove, not far from the village of Thorpe, is a 17th century farmhouse that has been sympathetically transformed into the Izaak Walton Hotel. The delights of trout fishing along this stretch of the river have been much written about, and most famously in Walton's The Compleat Angler. *His fishing house, which he shared with his friend Charles Cotton, is preserved and can be seen in Beresford Dale. At this point along the river there is also a public car park, complete with other amenities. A stroll up Dovedale from this point as far as Milldale will show the beauty of this stretch of the valley to its fullest. The terrain along the river bank is relatively easy for walkers (in many places wheelchairs will have no problem), but after rain it can get quite muddy.*

Thorpe Cloud

mostly inaccessible by car. The steep sided valley, the fast-flowing water and the magnificent white rock formations all give Dovedale a special charm.

Dovedale, however, is only a short section of the valley; above Viator Bridge it becomes **Mill Dale** and further upstream again are **Wolfscote Dale** and **Beresford Dale**. The temptation to provide amenities for visitors, at the expense of the scenery, has been avoided, and the limestone village of Thorpe, clustered around its church, remains unspoilt and unsophisticated. The beautiful little **Parish Church of St Leonard**, with its Norman tower and nave, was built about 1100, with some Saxon work still evident. It has walls of limestone rubble which give the curious impression that the building is leaning outwards. There is a fine tomb of the Millward family (1632) by the altar, showing John Milward, his two daughters

and his two sons. The sundial of 1767 in the churchyard is curious, as it is too high to be read properly. In the porch of the church are some scratch marks, said to have been made by archers in the 14th and 15th centuries, sharpening their arrows before practising archery in the churchyard.

The Victorians delighted in visiting the area. It was praised by such writers as Byron and Tennyson and soon became as popular as Switzerland. However, their enthusiasm for the Dovedale also had a down side. As well as providing donkey rides up the dale, in the late 19th century sycamore trees were planted along its sides. Not native to this area and, in fact, not native to Britain, they overshadow the ash and obscure many of the rock formations that make this such a special place. The National Trust are keeping the trees in check and encouraging the ash to grow. On higher, more windswept ground, the story would have been different as sycamore trees are ideal for providing a natural wind break.

The Victorian **Stepping Stones**, a delight for children, are the first point of interest, though for those who do not want to cross the river at this point there is a foot bridge closer to the car park, below Thorpe Cloud. Further up the dale is the limestone crag known as **Dovedale Castle** and, on the opposite bank, the higher promontory known as **Lover's Leap**, which has to be climbed by a series of steps. The promontory was named after a young woman, who, on hearing that her lover had been killed in the Napoleonic Wars, tried to commit suicide here by jumping. However, her skirts billowed out like a parachute and she survived. The poignant end to the story is that, soon after, she discovered that her lover was very much alive, and on his way home. Other interesting natural features with romantic names found along the way include the **Twelve Apostles**, a series of limestone crags, and the **Tissington Spires**, another limestone outcrop.

ILAM

4 miles NW of Ashbourne off the A52

The village was inhabited in Saxon times and the church still displays some Saxon stonework as well as the tomb of the Saxon saint, Bertram, who lived as a hermit in this area. Now a model village of great charm on the Staffordshire side of the River Dove, Ilam was originally an important settlement

Limestone Crags, Dovedale

belonging to Burton Abbey. Following the Reformation in the 16th century, the estate was broken up and Ilam came into the hands of the Port family. In the early 1800s the family sold the property to Jesse Watts Russell, a wealthy industrialist. He moved the village from its position near Ilam Hall and rebuilt it in its current location in 'Alpine style'. This explains both the Swiss style of the buildings and the surprising distance between them and the village church.

Ilam Hall was originally built by John Port in 1546, and while in the possession of the Ports, both Samuel Johnson and the playwright William Congreve stayed there. Watts Russell bought it in 1820 along with the estate and rebuilt it. As well as building a fine mansion, Watts Russell also spent a great deal

81 THE SOUTH PEAK ESTATE

Ilam

The estate centres around Ham Hall and within its 4,000 acres are popular visitor attractions such as Dovedale.

🏛 *see page 214*

87

Village Cross, Ilam

82 LEEHOUSE FARM

Waterhouses

A four star B&B that offers beautiful, comfortable rooms and hearty, filling breakfasts.

 see page 216

of money refurbishing the village. Obviously devoted to his wife, he had the village hall rebuilt in a romantic Gothic style and, in the centre of the village, he had a cross erected in her memory. In the 1930s most of the hall had been demolished before being bought by Sir Robert McDougall, who presented it to the Youth Hostelling Association in 1934. It remains a youth hostel to this day. The 158 acres of **Ilam Park**, on which the hall stands, is owned and managed by the National Trust,.

The ancient **Parish Church of the Holy Cross**, with its saddleback tower, was largely rebuilt in 1855, and again the Watts Russell family is not forgotten, as there is an enormous mausoleum dominating the north side. Opposite, on the south side, there is a little chapel which was rebuilt in 1618 and contains the shrine of a much-loved Staffordshire saint and 8th century Mercian king, Bertelin, or Bertram.

The chapel became the object of many pilgrimages in medieval times. Another important Saxon item inside the church is the font in the nave, while outside in the churchyard there are several Saxon cross shafts. As with many other churches in Derbyshire, it was the custom for garlands to be hung in the Church on the death of a young girl in the parish. The sad, faded 'virgin crants', referred to by Shakespeare at the death of Ophelia, can still be seen.

In the valley of the River Manifold, a much-used starting point for walks along this beautiful stretch of river, the Manifold disappears underground north of the village in summer, to reappear below Ilam Hall. The village is also the place where the Rivers Manifold and Dove merge. Though Dovedale is, deservedly so, considered the most scenic of the Peak District valleys, the Manifold Valley is very similar and while being marginally less beautiful it is often much less crowded. The two rivers rise close together, on Axe Edge, and for much of their course follow a parallel path, so it is fitting that they should come together eventually.

WATERHOUSES

6 miles NW of Ashbourne off the A523

Between here and Hulme End, the Leek and Manifold Valley Light Railway, a picturesque narrow-gauge (2' 6") line, used to follow the valleys of the Manifold and the Hamps, crisscrossing the latter on little bridges. Sadly, trains no longer run but its track bed has been made into the **Hamps-Manifold Track**, a marvellous walk which is ideal for small children and people in wheelchairs, since its surface is level and tarred throughout its eight miles. The Track can be reached from car parks at Hulme End, Waterhouses, Weags Bridge near Grindon, and Wetton.

The **River Hamps** is similar to the River Manifold and, indeed, other rivers which pass over limestone plateaux, in that it disappears underground for some of its course. In the case of the Hamps, it disappears at Waterhouses and reappears again near Ilam before merging with the River Manifold.

WATERFALL

7 miles NW of Ashbourne off the A523

The tiny village of Waterfall is on the Staffordshire moors. It gets its name from the way that the River Hamps disappears underground through crevices in the ground. It was once the starting point of the Manifold Valley Light Railway, a narrow gauge railway from the main Leek-Ashbourne railway line, via Wetton to Hume End. The line has since been removed and now the track is the Manifold Trail, a well used tourist trail for walkers and cyclists.

The **Parish Church of St James and St Bartholomew** is originally Norman but was largely rebuilt in the 19th century. However, the Norman chancel has been retained.

GRINDON

7 miles NW of Ashbourne off the B5053

This unique moorland hill village stands over 1,000 feet above sea level and overlooks the beautiful Manifold Valley. Recorded in the *Domesday Book* as Grendon, meaning green hill, 'an ancient manor in the 20th year of the reign of William the Conqueror', Grindon is reputed to have been visited by Bonnie Prince Charlie on his way to Derby. It was once a staging post on the packhorse route from Ecton Hill and had the most productive copper mine in the country, where many of the local people would have worked. The local pub, the Cavalier, was possibly named after Bonny Prince Charlie.

The splendid isolation in which this village stands is confirmed by a look around the churchyard. The names on the epitaphs and graves reflect the close-knit nature of the communities. The Salt family, for instance, are to be seen everywhere, followed closely by the Stubbs, Cantrells, Hambletons and, to a lesser extent, the Mycocks.

WETTON

7 miles NW of Ashbourne between the B5053 and the A515

Wetton Mill, which closed down in the 19th century, has been sympathetically converted by the National Trust into a café, a very welcome sight for those walking the **Manifold Valley Trail**. There is also a car park here for the less energetic and a picnic area for

83 RED LION INN

Waterfall

A truly charming pub with a welcoming, warm atmosphere, real ales and beautifully cooked and presented food.

see page 217

The Parish Church of All Saints in Grindon, dating from 1848/1849, is sometimes called the 'cathedral of the moors', Outside the church entrance there is a Rindle Stone. This records that: 'The Lord of the Manor of Grindon established his right to this rindle at Stafford Assizes on March 17th 1872'. A rindle is a brook which runs only in wet weather, a common phenomenon in these parts. In the church can also be found a memorial to six RAF men who were killed in 1947 when their Halifax aircraft crash-landed during a blizzard on Grindon Moor. They were trying to parachute in food packages to the surrounding villages, which had been totally cut off by the excessive snowfall.

Thor's Cave

84 PADDOCK HOUSE FARM HOLIDAY COTTAGES

Alstonefield, Ashbourne

Five well appointed self-catering cottages, set amid beautiful scenery, offer an ideal base for exploring the area.

see page 216

those who would rather cater for themselves. Much of the hillside either side of the track also belongs to the National Trust and is a splendid place for walks.

Below the mill can be found the ominous-sounding **Thor's Cave**, situated some 360 feet above the River Manifold. Though the cave is not deep, the entrance is huge, some 60 feet high, and the stiff climb up is well worth the effort for the spectacular views, all framed by the great natural stone arch. The acoustics, too, are interesting, and conversations can easily be carried out with people far below. Ancient bones and implements have been found here dating back 10,000 years. The openings at the bottom of the crag on which the cave sits are known as **Radcliffe Stables** and are said to have been used by a Jacobite as a hiding place after Bonnie Prince Charlie had retreated from Derby.

The **Parish Church of St Margaret** is partly 14th century, though most of it dates from around 1820. In the churchyard is the grave of Samuel Carrington, who, along with Thomas Bateman of Youlgreave, found evidence that Thor's Cave was occupied in ancient times. Carrington also

excavated the fields close to Wetton, where he was schoolmaster in the mid 1800s, and found an abandoned village, though neither he nor his friend Bateman could put an age to the settlement.

On **Wetton Low** are many burial mounds, some of which contained bones dating back at least to 1600 BC. **Ecton Hill** is covered in the remains of old lead mines worked by the Duke of Devonshire. His profits from the mine were used to build the Crescent at Buxton.

ALSTONEFIELD

7 miles NW of Ashbourne off the A515

This ancient village, situated between the Manifold and the Dove valleys, lies at the crossroads of several old packhorse routes and even had its own market charter granted in 1308. The market ceased in 1500 but the annual cattle sales continued right up until the beginning of the 20th century. At nearby **Hope** is a village pond which is said never to dry up. The hamlet was also the site of England's first co-operative cheese factory, which produced a variety of Derby cheese.

Its geographical location has helped to maintain the charm of Alstonefield. There has been no invasion by the canal or railway builders (it lies at 900 feet above sea level) and it is still two miles from the nearest classified road. One hundred and fifty years ago Alstonefield was at the centre of a huge parish which covered all the land between the two rivers. There has been a church here since at least AD 892, when a visit by St Oswald is recorded, but the earliest known parts of the large **Parish Church of St Peter** are the Norman doorway and chancel arch of 1100. It was added to in the 15th century and restored in Victorian times. There is also plenty of 17th century woodwork and a double-decker pulpit dated 1637. Izaak Walton's friend, Charles Cotton, and his family, lived at nearby Beresford Hall, now unfortunately no more, but their elaborate pew, with the Cotton coat-of-arms, is still in the church.

The village also retains its ancient **Tithe Barn**, found behind the late 16th century rectory. The internal exposed wattle and daub wall and the spiral stone staircase may, however, have been part of an earlier building.

ECTON

9½ miles NW of Ashbourne off the B5054

The tiny hamlet of Ecton, close to Hulme End, was once the site of great activity. The copper mines here were owned by the Duke of Devonshire and it is generally accepted that the profits from the ore extraction paid for his building of The Crescent at Buxton. One of the mines, Deep Ecton, to the north of **Ecton Hill** was, at nearly 1,400 feet, one of the deepest in Europe. Work had ceased in the mines by 1900 but, so impervious was the surrounding limestone that the workings took several years to flood, though now they are under water.

WARSLOW

9 miles NW of Ashbourne off the B5054

Situated opposite Wetton on the other side of the River Manifold, the village is one of the main access points to this dramatic section of the Manifold Valley. Lying below the gritstone moorlands, this was an estate village for the eccentric Crewe family, who lived at Calke Abbey in south Derbyshire. The **Parish Church of St Lawrence** is a handsome building of 1820, and was formerly dedicated to St James.

HULME END

9 miles NW of Ashbourne on the B5054

This is the ideal place from which to explore the **Manifold Valley**. From here to Ilam, the River Manifold runs southwards through a deep, twisting limestone cleft, between steep and wooded banks. For much of its dramatic course the Manifold disappears underground in dry weather through swallow holes, which is typical of a river in a limestone area.

The village also lays at the terminus of the narrow gauge **Leek and Manifold Valley Light Railway**, which opened in 1904. Already aware of the tourism possibilities of the Peak District by the beginning of the 20th century, the other reason for constructing the railway was to transport coal and other raw materials to the surrounding settlements. The line, however, was unable to pay its way, particularly after the creamery at

Beresford Dale

85 WOLFSCOTE GRANGE COTTAGES

Hartington

Luxurious self-catering accommodation in olde worlde cottages with up-to-date amenities.

 see page 218

Ecton, just a mile south of Hulme End, closed in 1933. The following year the railway ceased operation. The tracks were taken up and, if it had not been turned into a semi-long distance footpath, the route of the railway might have been lost forever.

Considering that the buildings at Hulme End station were constructed using materials that were not designed to withstand the test of time, chiefly corrugated iron and wood, it is surprising to find that two of the three survive. Though the station, along with the railway, closed in 1934, the sheds are still in use today.

HARTINGTON

10 miles NW of Ashbourne on the B5054

This charming limestone village was granted a market charter in 1203 and it is likely that its spacious market place was once the village green. **Hartington Hall**, built in the 17th century and enlarged in the 19th century, is typical of many Peak District manor houses and a fine example of a Derbyshire yeoman's house and farm. It is thought that Bonny Prince Charlie stayed there on his way to Derby. It became a youth hostel in 1934, and is the oldest such youth hostel in the Peak District. The village is also the home to the only cheese factory remaining in Derbyshire. From the dairy, not far from the village pond, veined, plain or flavoured Stilton is still made and can be bought at the dairy shop.

The **Parish Church of St Giles** stands above the market square, and has a fine perpendicular tower. Up until 1848, it was divided into two churches, as the south transept was used for worship by the people of the nearby hamlet of Biggin.

The village is very much on the tourist route and, though popular, has retained much of its village appeal. As well as the famous cheese shop, there are two old coaching inns left over from the days when this was an important market centre. One of these goes by the rather unusual name of The Charles Cotton, named after the friend of Izaak Walton. Situated in the valley of the River Dove, Hartington is an excellent place from which to explore both the Dove and the Manifold valleys. To the south lies **Beresford Dale**, the upper valley of the River Dove and every bit as pretty as its more famous neighbour, Dovedale. It was immortalised by Izaak Walton and Charles Cotton when *The Compleat Angler* was published in 1653.

MAYFIELD

2½ miles SW of Ashbourne on the A5032

Mayfield is a large village on the edge of Ashbourne, divided into Upper Mayfield and Middle Mayfield. Though it is so close to Ashbourne, it actually lies in Staffordshire, as the border runs west of the village. Mayfield was originally a Saxon village, dating back over a thousand years and listed in the *Domesday Book* as Mavreveldt. The first Norman church was probably built about 1125 during the reign of Henry I, and the present **Parish Church of St John the Baptist** illustrates the progressive styles of architecture since that date, with a 14th century chancel and a 16th century tower. In the churchyard there is an original Saxon cross. The ballad writer, Thomas Moore, lived at Moore Cottage, formerly Stancliffe Farm. His young daughter, Olivia, is buried in the local churchyard, her slate tombstone reading 'Olivia Byron Moore, died March 18, 1815'. Moore was friendly with Lord Byron, who visited him here.

On 7th December 1745 Bonnie Prince Charlie and his army passed through Mayfield on their retreat from Derby, terrorising the local populace. They shot the innkeeper at Hanging Bridge as well as a Mr Humphrey Brown, who refused to hand over his horse to them. Many of the terrified villagers locked themselves in the church. The soldiers fired shots through the door and the bullet holes can still be seen in the woodwork of the

west door. Legend has it that many of the rebels were caught and hung from gibbets on the old packhorse bridge, whose 500-year-old grey stone arches can still be seen, even though the bridge has been rebuilt.

There is however a road out of the village, leading to the main Leek highway, marked on the Ordnance Survey map as "Gallowstree Lane", suggesting that those to be hung went their way via the bridge and Gallowstree Lane to Gallowstree Hill. Today it is a pleasant walk rewarded by a lovely view down the Dove Valley.

Mayfield Mill has been producing textiles for 200 years. The first mention of a mill occurs in 1291, when Mayfield , including its mill, belonged to the Priory of Tutbury. By 1793 there had been various owners of the site, which now included two corn mills, a leather mill and two fulling mills. Textiles were first produced in 1795. In 1806 the interior of the building and all its machinery was destroyed in a fire. The mill was eventually rebuilt with a cast iron framework and brick vaulted ceilings, as can still be seen today.

The spinning of cotton continued in Mayfield until 1934 when it was sold to William Tatton and Company who used the mill to process silk.

CAULDON

8 miles SE of Leek off the A52

This was the site of the quarry from which wagons travelled, down a railway track, to Froghall Wharf.

86 BIGGIN HALL COUNTRY HOUSE HOTEL

Biggin-by-Hartington

A superb country house hotel that combines luxurious surroundings, informality and affordable prices.

🛏 see page 219

87 FOX AND GOOSE

Foxt

A stunning inn with wonderful views out over Staffordshire countryside that is well worth seeking out for its great food and range of drinks.

🍴 see page 220

88 YE OLDE STAR INN

Cotton

A family-run free house which has a great reputation for its food and drink among locals and visitors alike.

🍴 see page 221

89 THE WHITE LION

Leek

A superb, food-orientated inn that is famous throughout the area for its commitment to high quality and fresh, organic produce in its dishes.

🍽 see page 222

90 THE BLACK SWAN

Leek

A picturesque, whitewashed town pub in the heart of town with an atmosphere al of its own, plus great food and drink.

🍽 see page 223

91 THE ABBEY INN

Leek

A delightful 17th century inn close to the Peak District national Park that not only serves good food and drink, but has first class accommodation as well.

🍽 🛏 see page 224

94

LEEK

15 miles NW of Ashbourne on the A523

Known as the 'Queen of the Moorlands', this is an attractive textile centre on the banks of the River Churnet. It was here that French Huguenots settled, after fleeing from religious oppression, and established the silk industry that thrived due to the abundance of soft water coming off the nearby moorland. Until the 19th century, this was a domestic industry with the workshops on the top storeys of the houses. Many examples of these 'top shops' have survived to this day. Leek also became an important dyeing town, particularly after the death of Prince Albert, when 'Raven Black' was popularised by Queen Victoria, who remained in mourning for her beloved husband for many years.

William Morris, founder of the Arts and Crafts movement, lived and worked in Leek for many months between 1875 and 1878. Much of his time here was spent investigating new techniques of dyeing but he also revived the use of traditional dyes. His influence can be seen not only in the art here but also in the architecture. **All Saints Church,** built in the 1880s, has some fine stained glass designed by him. The imposing brick-built Nicholson Institute holds exhibitions on the wonderful and intricate work of the famous Leek School of Embroidery that was founded by Lady Wardle in the 1870s. A replica of the Bayeux Tapestry, now on display in the

Museum of Reading was first displayed here in 1886. Elizabeth Wardle, along with thirty-five members of the Leek Embroidery Society and other embroiderers from the surrounding area completed it in just over a year. Each embroiderer stitched her name beneath her completed panel.

Leek is an ancient borough, granted its charter in 1214, and was a thriving market centre, rivalling Macclesfield and Congleton. **The Butter Cross,** which now stands in the **Market Place,** was originally erected near the junction of Sheep Market and Stanley Street by the Joliffe family in 1671. Every road coming into the town seems to converge on the old cobbled Market Place and the road to the west leads down to the church. Dedicated to Edward the Confessor (the full name is the **Parish Church of St Edward's and All Saints**), the original church was burnt down in 1297 and rebuilt some 20 years later, though the building is now largely 17th century. The timber roof of the nave is well worth a second look and is the church's pride and joy. It is boasted that each of the cross beams was hewn from a separate oak tree and, in the west part of the nave, an enormous 18th century gallery rises up, tier on tier, giving the impression of a theatre's dress circle.

Although much has been altered inside the church, most notably in 1865 when G.E. Street rebuilt the chancel, reredos, sanctuary, pulpit and stalls, there still remains one interesting original artefact to see - a wooden chair. Traditionally this is believed to have been a ducking stool for scolds, which was used in the nearby River Churnet. Outside, in the churchyard, can be found a curious inscription on a gravestone: 'James Robinson interred February the 28th 1788 Aged 438'! To the north side of the church is an area still known locally as 'Petty France', which holds the graves of many Napoleonic prisoners of war who lived nearby.

Another building worthy of a second glance is the imposing **Nicholson Institute**, mentioned earlier, with its copper dome. Completed in 1884 and funded by the local industrialist Joshua Nicholson, the Institute offered the people of Leek an opportunity to learn and expand their cultural horizons. Many of the great Victorian literary giants, including George Bernard Shaw and Mark Twain, came here to admire the building. The town's **War Memorial**, built in Portland stone and with a clock tower, has a dedication to the youngest Nicholson son, who was killed in the First World War. Leek was the home of James Brindley, the 18th-century engineer who built much of the early canal network. A water-powered corn mill built by him in 1752 (on the stite of an earlier mill) in Mill Street, has been restored and now houses the **Brindley Water Museum** (known as Brindley Mill), which is devoted to his life and work. Visitors can

see corn being ground and see displays of millwrighting skills. Leek has a traditional outdoor market every Wednesday, a craft and antiques market on Saturday and an indoor 'butter market' on Wednesday, Friday and Saturday.

The **River Churnet**, though little known outside Staffordshire, has a wealth of scenery and industrial archaeology. It is easily accessible to walkers and its valley deserves better recognition. The river rises to the west of Leek in rugged gritstone country, but for most of its length it flows through softer, red sandstone countryside in a valley that was carved out during the Ice Age. Though there are few footpaths directly adjacent to the riverbank, most of the valley can be walked close to the river using a combination of canal towpaths and former railway tracks.

Four miles to the north of Leek on the A53 rise the dark, jagged gritstone outcrops of **The Roaches**, **Ramshaw Rocks** and **Hen Cloud**. Roaches is a corruption of the French word 'roches' or rocks and

92 DEN ENGEL BELGIAN BAR AND RESTAURANT AND EL 4 GATS TAPAS BAR

Leek

A stylish, modern and well-known Belgian bar serving not only a range of great Belgian beers, but good food with a Belgian touch as well. Soon it will also be serving tapas!

see page 225

Saxon Cross, Leek

93 THE COFFEE CLIQUE

Leek

A coffee shop with a contemporary feel about it that serves a wide range of hot and cold beverages plus some seriously good food.

see page 226

94 THE GARDEN HOUSE

Cheddleton

Comfortable bed and breakfast accommodation in a modern house that offers superb amenities at down to earth prices.

see page 227

95 CASTRO'S RESTAURANT AND LOUNGE

Cheddleton

A smart, stylish restaurant beside the Caldon Canal specialising in authentic Latin American cuisine.

see page 228

the name was reputedly given by Napoleonic prisoners. 'Cloud' is a local word used for high hills. Just below The Roaches there is a delightful stretch of water, **Tittesworth Reservoir**, which is extremely popular with trout fishermen. It has some trails, a visitor centre with an interactive exhibition, a restaurant and a gift shop.

At Winkhill is the **Blackbrook Zoological Park**, which is open all year, and which has rare birds, insects, reptiles and unusual animals. **Kiddies Kingdom,** in Cross Mill Street, is an indoor play area for children, just right for children's parties and days out.

RUDYARD

2 miles NW of Leek off the A523

In fond memory of the place where they first met in 1863, Mr and Mrs Kipling named their famous son, born in 1865, after this village. The nearby two-mile-long **Rudyard Lake** was built in 1831 by John Rennie to feed the Cauldon canal. With steeply wooded banks, the lake is now a leisure centre with facilities for picnicking, walking, fishing and sailing. Along the west shore is also a section of the **Staffordshire Way**, the long distance footpath which runs from Mow Cop to **Kinver Edge**, near Stourbridge. This is a sandstone

The Roaches

ridge covered in woodland and heath, and with several famous rock houses which were inhabited until the 1950s.

Back in Victorian days, Rudyard was a popular lakeside resort which developed after the construction of the North Staffordshire Railway in 1845. The **Rudyard Lake Steam Railway** uses miniature narrow gauge steam trains to give a three-mile return trip along the side of the reservoir. Its popularity became so great that, on one particular day in 1877, over 20,000 people came here to see Captain Webb, the first man to swim the English Channel, swim in the reservoir.

RUSHTON SPENCER

5 miles NW of Leek on the A523

This pleasant, moorland village nestles under the distinctive hill called the **Cloud** (from the Old English 'clud', meaning rock) and is the ideal starting point for a walk to the summit. Parts of it are owned by the National Trust. It is also well known for its lonely church, the **'Chapel in the Wilderness'**, dedicated to St Lawrence and originally built of wood in the 14th century. It served both Rushton Spencer and neighbouring Rushton James. It has been almost rebuilt in stone.

FLASH

7 miles N of Leek off the A53

At over 1,518 feet above sea level, Flash is said to be the highest village in England. At one time cock fighting was popular here, and it continued long after it had been made illegal. **Three Shires Head** is a local beauty spot where the three counties of Derbyshire, Cheshire and Staffordshire meet. The village was also noted, at one time, for the production of counterfeit money, which earned the nickname 'flash' from its place of origin.

96 THE HOLLYBUSH INN

Denford

An old, canal-side inn with a friendly atmosphere that harks back to former times, while at the same time offering the modern concepts of value for money and efficient service.

see page 229

97 RAILWAY INN

Froghall

A fine old inn with a 'railway feel' dating from the 19th century that has five superb guest rooms, as well as good food and drink.

see page 230

98 KNOT INN

Rushton Spencer

A friendly, stylish inn in a small village between Leek and Macclesfield with a fine reputation for its food, drink and warm welcome.

see page 231

97

The Trent Valley

In the valley of the River Trent, which runs through the southern part of the county of Derbyshire, can be found many splendid stately homes, including Kedleston Hall and the eccentric Calke Abbey. The scenery affords ample opportunities to enjoy pleasant walks. This chapter also includes the western side of the region known as Erewash.

Derbyshire was at the forefront of modern thinking at the beginning of the Industrial Revolution. The chief inheritor of this legacy was Derby, and the city is still a busy industrial centre, home to engineering companies as well as a university and a cathedral. It is one of England's more recent cities, having been granted city status as late as 1977. However, it is a historic place, full of places to visit. And though the county is called Derbyshire, the city is not the country town. This honour goes to Matlock, where the city council meets.

Truly an area of hidden places, the Trent Valley has many gems worth visiting, such as the picturesque villages of Church Gresley and Castle Gresley, the welcoming centres of Melbourne and Hartshorne, quiet Repton on the River Trent itself and the 'border' town of Swadlincote.

ACCOMMODATION

FOOD & DRINK

PLACES OF INTEREST

DERBY

Essentially a commercial and industrial city, Derby's position, historically and geographically, has ensured that it has remained one of the most important and interesting cities in the East Midlands. Consequently, there is much for the visitor to see, whether from an architectural or historical point of view. There are, however, two things that most people, whether they have been to the city before or not, know of Derby: **Rolls-Royce** and Royal Crown Derby porcelain. When, in 1904, Sir Henry Royce and the Hon C S Rolls joined forces, and subsequently built the first Rolls-Royce (a Silver Ghost) at Derby in 1906, they built much more than just a motor car - they built a legend. Considered by many to be the best cars in the world, it is often said that the noisiest moving part in any Rolls-Royce is the dashboard clock! It is now owned by BMW of Germany, though the aero engine division (also based in Derby, but an entirely separate company), is a joint venture between BMW and Rolls Royce itself.

The home of **Royal Crown Derby** porcelain, any visit to the city would not be complete without a trip to the factory and its museum and shop on Ormaston Road. The guided tours offer an intriguing insight into the high level of skill required to create the delicate flower petals, hand-gild the plates and hand paint the Derby Dwarves. The museum houses the most comprehensive collection of Derby Porcelain to be seen anywhere in the world, including 18th century figurines, many interpretations of the Japanese designs for which the company is famous, the delicate 'Eggshell' China by French Art Director Desire Leroy, and examples of the Crown Derby ware commissioned for the restaurants of the *Titanic*.

There has been a church on the site of the city's **Cathedral of All Saints** since at least AD 943. It possesses a fine 16th century tower, the second highest perpendicular tower in England, and the oldest ring of ten bells in the country. Before 1927 it was the Parish Church of All Saints, the main church for Derby, but in that year was raised to cathedral status. In the early 18th century the nave and chancel was in a ruinous state, so they were rebuilt between 1723 and 1725 to the designs of James Gibbs. Inside is a beautiful wrought-iron screen by Robert Bakewell and, among the splendid monuments, is the tomb of Bess of Hardwick Hall, who died in 1607. In the late 1960s and early 1970s the building was extended eastwards and the retrochoir, baldacchino and sacristy were added, along with the screen. Only five minutes walk from the cathedral, the beautifully restored medieval **St Mary's Chapel on the Bridge** is one of only six surviving bridge chapels still in use. There is some medieval stained glass in one of the windows. In 1588 three Catholic priests, Nicholas Garlick,

Derby

Journey back in time to the early 18th century and learn about the industrial heritage of Derby.

 see page 232

St Mary's Chapel on the Bridge, Derby

100 DERBY MUSEUMS AND ART GALLERY

Derby

A fascinating museum and art gallery, housing collections of porcelain, paintings, archaelogy, geology and wildlife.

 see *page 232*

Richard Simpson and Robert Ludlum (the 'Padley Martyrs') were hung drawn and quartered, and their remains hung from the chapel entrance. The bridge itself is 18th century, and straddles the River Derwent.

One of Derby's most interesting museums is **Pickford's House**, situated on the city's finest Georgian street, Friar Gate, at number 41. This Grade I listed building was erected in 1770 by the architect Joseph Pickford as a combined family home and place of work. Pickford House differs from the majority of grand stately homes in that it does not have a wealth of priceless furniture or works of art. Instead, visitors are able to gain a true insight into everyday upper middle-class life. The kitchen and servants' quarters have been re-created showing the conditions they worked under during the 1830s. Pickford House is the epitome of a late-Georgian professional man's residence. There is an exciting programme of

temporary exhibitions, as well as other displays which deal with the history of the Friargate area and the importance of Joseph Pickford as a Midlands architect. One special feature of Pickford House is the excellent collection of costumes, some dating back to the mid-1700s. A period 18th century garden is also laid out at the rear of the house, and there are toy theatres from the Frank Bradley collection.

Just a short walk from Pickford House is the **Derby Industrial Museum**, housed in an old silk mill. The mill preceded Richard Arkwright's first cotton mill by over 50 years, but was badly damaged by fire in 1910 and had to be substantially rebuilt. However, it still gives a good idea of Lombe's original mill and tower.

Since 1915 Derby has been involved with the manufacture of engines, and the whole of the ground floor galleries are devoted to the Rolls-Royce aero engine collection, illustrating the importance played by the industry in the city's history. There are also model aircraft sectioned engines which demonstrate how aircraft fly. A specially designed annexe houses a complete RB211 turbo-fan engine, a model which powered the Boeing 757 and Tupolev Tu204 aircraft. On the first floor of the building there is an introduction to other Derbyshire industries, with displays on lead and coal mining, iron founding, limestone quarrying, ceramics and brick making. There is also a railway engineering gallery complete with a signal box, and displays on the growth of the railways in Derby since the 1840s. The railway industry has played a large part in the life of the city, and along with Rolls Royce, British Rail Engineering Ltd (BREL) is one of its largest employers

The **City Museum and Art Gallery** in the Strand is also well worth visiting. Opened in 1879, it is the oldest of Derby's museums and the displays include natural history, archaeology and social history. Derbyshire wildlife and geology feature in an exciting series of natural settings and hands-on exhibits. One section of the museum is devoted to a Military Gallery which tells of Derby's regiments over the years. The walk-in First World War trench scene captures the experience of a night at the front. The Bonnie Prince Charlie room commemorates Derby's role in the 1745 uprising.

A ground floor gallery houses the city's superb, and internationally important, collection of fine Royal Crown Derby porcelain, manufactured in the city from the mid-18th century. The collection is displayed in a new, Lottery-funded gallery, complete with a colourful database of the collection. The museum is also home to a collection of portraits, landscapes, scientific and industrial scenes by the local painter Joseph Wright, ARA. On the second floor of the Museum are temporary exhibition galleries. These change every three or four weeks and cover not only the museum's own collection but also travelling exhibitions.

The Derby Gaol is situated in the depths of the original dungeons of the Derbyshire County Gaol, dating back to 1756. It offers a reminder of the city's grisly past. It includes a debtor's cell and a condemned cell, and was the site of the last hanging, drawing and quartering in the country, which took place after England's last revolution, the Pentrich Rebellion, in 1817. Three men were sentenced to the grizzly form of execution, while thirteen others were send to a penal colony in Australia. The Gaol is open on Tuesday, Thursday and Sunday, and has conducted tours.

Parks in the city include **Allestree Park** on Duffield Road, **Derby Arboretum** and **Markeaton Park**. The ancient custom of well-dressing, more commonly associated with the villages and towns of northern Derbyshire and the Peak District, has found expression here in Derby (in Chester Green, at Mansfield Street Chapel) since 1982, on the Saturday before the late Spring Bank Holiday (Whitsun).

AROUND DERBY

DARLEY ABBEY

2 miles N of Derby off the A6

Darley Abbey is a tranquil village of delightfully restored mill cottages, built in rows or around squares. The Augustinian **Abbey of St Mary** was founded by Robert Ferrers, second Earl of Derby, around 1140 and grew to become the most powerful abbey in Derbyshire and possibly in the whole of the East Midlands. In

Pride Park Stadium, the home of Derby County Football Club, was officially opened in 1997, by Her Majesty the Queen. Visitors can take a 'behind the scenes' look at 'the Rams' new sporting arena. A guided tour includes visits to the director's box, corporate areas, crowd control centre and even the police cells. But the high point for any football fan has to be emerging from the players' tunnel on to the pitch.

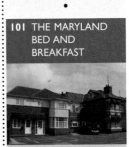

101 THE MARYLAND BED AND BREAKFAST

Alvaston

A bed and breakfast establishment on the outskirts of Derby that makes a perfect base from which to explore all the attractions of the area.

see page 232

As its name suggests, Breadsall Priory stands on the site of an Augustinian Priory founded in the 13th century. The only part of the original building extant is an arch in the basement. Most of what stands today dates back to the Jacobean period, with many early 19th century additions and embellishments. Breadsall Priory was home to Erasmus Darwin in his later years. A poet, physician and philosopher, he is better known as grandfather of Charles Darwin. Born in 1731, he died in Breadsall in 1802, and there is a memorial to him in All Saints Church. The Priory is now a private hotel with golf course.

1538 the Abbey was surrendered to the crown as part of the Dissolution of the Monasteries. Sadly, few monasteries could have been so completely obliterated, and what is now known as The Abbey pub is the only building remaining. The layout is of a simple medieval hall house and is thought to have been used as the Abbey's guest house for travellers and pilgrims during the 13th century. During renovation, 12th century pottery was unearthed.

Darley Park, on the river Derwent, was landscaped by William Evans and has attractive flower beds, shrubberies and lawns. It once had a hall, built in 1727 but now demolished, that for 120 years was the home of the Evans family who built the cotton mill by the river in 1783.

The mill area is quite a large complex. The oldest parts, east mill, middle mill and west mill, are five-storeyed and brick built. There is also a finishing house which has three storeys and sash windows, and an octagonal toll house in the mill yard. The Evans family built the red brick houses, still evident in the village, for the mill workers. They were typical paternalistic employers, providing subsidised rents, coal, blankets in cold weather and even arranging burials and memorials for their workers.

The **Parish Church of St Matthew** was built in the early 19th century, with a chancel added between 1885 and 1901. It is an elegant building in Gothic style, and contains monuments to the Evans family.

BREADSALL
3 miles N of Derby off the A6

Breadsall began life as a small hamlet clustered around its Norman church. It is now known primarily as a residential suburb of Derby, with new estates around the original centre. **The Parish Church of All Saints** possesses one of the most elegant steeples in the country, dating from the early 1400s. The south doorway is Norman and the tower and chancel date back to the 1200s. The church was burnt down by suffragettes in 1914 and carefully restored over the next two years. Inside there is a touching pieta from the late 1300s. This beautiful alabaster depiction of the Virgin Mary with the crucified Christ lying across her knees, was found under the floor of the church after another fire, and was restored to its present position by W D Caroe.

Opposite the west end of the church can be found **The Old Hall**, which has been part of village life for over 600 years. It was originally the manor house when the village was divided into the wards of Overhall and Netherhall. In later years it has been employed as a school, farmhouse, hunting box, public house, shop, joiner's shop and post office. It currently serves as a parish hall and is used by various village organisations.

MACKWORTH
2 miles NW of Derby off the A52

Standing alone in a field to the east of the village is the **Parish Church** of All Saints, dating mainly from the 14th century. Although its position is unusual, it is well worth taking a look inside to see the wealth of ancient and modern alabaster carving that it holds. A ruined 15th century gatehouse in the village is sometimes referred to as **Mackworth Castle**, but it may have been the gatehouse of Mackworth Hall, a mansion which was never built.

KIRK LANGLEY
4 miles NW of Derby on the A52

Kirk Langley village has some fine 18th century stone houses, a mid-17th century gabled red brick rectory, an old village school and a church. The **Parish Church of St Michael** is early 14th century, built on the site of an older Saxon church. There are monuments to the Meynell and Pole families, including a memorial to Hugo Frances Meynell, 'who was deprived of his life in a collision of carriages' in Clay Cross tunnel. Another one commemorates William Meynell, who was killed in the 19th century when leading the Turks against the Russians on the river Danube. The only pub is the Bluebell at Langley Common.

KEDLESTON
4 miles NW of Derby off the A52

Kedleston Hall has been the family seat of the Curzon family since the 12th century and, until it was taken over by the National Trust, it had the longest continuous male line in Derbyshire and one of the longest in the country. Nothing

remains of the original medieval structure and little is known about it other than details recorded in a survey of 1657 which state that one of the doorways was over 500 years old and that there was also a large hall and a buttery.

The present elegant mansion was built between 1759 and 1765 to designs by Robert Adam and it remains one of the finest examples of his work. The façade represents an impressive Roman temple with six tall columns supporting a portico, and a double-armed stone stairway leading to the entrance. Inside, the elegant and extravagant Marble Hall is a massive open space, dominated by 20 pink alabaster Corinthian columns around a white marble inlaid floor, with an intricate plasterwork ceiling above. As well as the design for the

102 BLUEBELL INN

Kirk Langley

Combining olde worlde charm with modern standards of service, this inn offers great food and drink at value-for-money prices.

see page 233

103 BLACK COW

Dalbury Lees

A picturesque pub by a village green that will impress you with its range of drinks and its wholesome home cooking

see page 233

Kedleston Hall

house and the three-arched bridge across the lake, it is likely that Robert Adam had a hand in designing the 820-acre parkland in the Serpentine style. The three-mile Long Walk was created in 1776. Edwin Lutyens designed the sunken rose garden.

Since taking over the property, the National Trust has embarked on a major restoration programme and many of the stately home's rooms have been beautifully furnished with contemporary pieces; modern photographs of the family can be seen mingled with priceless paintings and other treasures such as Blue John vases. Along with the house itself and the park with its lakes, there are the boat house and fishing pavilion to explore.

One member of the family, George Nathaniel Curzon, was the Viceroy of India from 1899 to 1905. When he returned to England he brought back numerous works of art, carvings and ivories that can be seen on display in the **Indian Museum**. Though he was out in India for some time, George would not have missed his family home, as Government House in Calcutta is a copy of Kedleston Hall. Once back in England, George did not have much time to enjoy his lands: he became a member of Lloyd George's inner War Cabinet, which met over 500 times during the First World War.

The nearby **All Saints Church**, in the ownership of the Churches Conservation Trust, is the only part of the old village that was allowed to remain when the rest was moved in 1765 to make way for the landscaped park around the Hall. It dates from the 12th century, and is of an unusual design for Derbyshire in that it is cruciform in shape and the tower is placed in the centre. Inside are Curzon monuments dating from 1275 to the present day, some designed by Adam. The only brass in the church is to Richard Curzon, who died in 1496. Perhaps the most magnificent tomb is of Mary, wife of George Curzon, Viceroy of India. It was built within a magnificent memorial chapel by her husband between 1907 and 1913, and is of white marble. The church has an unusual east-facing sundial. Because of its orientation, the dial only catches the sun between the hours of 6am and 11am. The hour lines are parallel with each other, with half hour lines in between. The gnomon is in the form of a letter "T", the top bar of which casts a shadow across the dial. The inscription above the dial is "WEE SHALL", which cryptically links to sundial (soon die all) to make a sombre

All Saints Church, Kedleston

message. This is reinforced by the carvings on top of the dial, showing a skull between two hour glasses.

BRAILSFORD

8 miles NW of Derby on the A52

Brailsford is a pretty, red-brick village bisected by the A52. It is mentioned in the *Domesday Book* as having a priest and 'half a church'. This referred to the fact that it was shared by the hamlet of Ednaston, to the north. The owner then was the Saxon, Elfin, who appears to have managed to retain his lordship after the Conquest. The carved Saxon cross in the churchyard of the **Parish Church of All Saints** parish church dates from Elfin's time. The church itself is an interesting building of the 11th and 12th centuries, with much Norman work and an ashlar-faced diagonally buttressed tower.

EDNASTON

7 miles NW of Derby off the A52

This is an ancient manor which was recorded, in the Domesday Survey of 1086, as being in the ownership of Henry de Ferrers of Duffield Castle. The present manor house, **Ednaston Manor** on Brailsford Brook was built to designs by Sir Edwin Lutyens between 1912 and 1914 . Unfortunately it is not open to the public.

LONG LANE

6 miles NW of Derby off the A52

Long Lane village is truly a hidden place, not found on most maps. It is south of the A52, and can be

reached by heading for the village of Lees and then following the sign for Long Lane. It is set on the old Roman road bearing the same name and is not much more than a cluster of cottages, a school, a church and a pub. **The Three Horseshoes** in Long Lane dates back to 1750, when it was a grain store where ale was brewed for the adjacent blacksmith's. Unusually, the property is owned by the village itself. The **Parish Church of Christ Church** dates from the 1860s.

LONGFORD

8 miles W of Derby well south of the A515

Truly a hidden place, Longford lies very much off the beaten track, but it is well worth finding as the village has the distinction of being the home of the first cheese factory in England. Opened on the 4th May in 1870, its first manager bore the memorable name Cornelius Schermerhorn. Derbyshire, with its excellent rail and canal links, made the county an ideal centre for the mass production of cheeses for foreign markets.

Longford Hall is a late medieval house, renovated by Pickford in 1762 and restored after a bad fire in 1942. It was the family seat, first of the Longford family and then the Cokes. The Longfords settled here in the 12th century and the church, which is close to the hall, was built then. The **Parish Church of St Chad,** surrounded by magnificent lime trees, still retains many Norman parts, though the tower was added in the 15th century. There are some fine

104 CULLAND MOUNT FARM

Brailsford

Superb self-catering accommodation on a working farm that offers the very best in comfort and convenience.

 see page 233

At Mugginton, near Brailsford, can be found Halter Devil Chapel, now part of a farm and built, so legend has it, in 1723 by a reformed drinker who once tried to halter a cow in the mistaken belief that it was his horse. In his stupor the farmer, Francis Browen, saw the horns and thought he had haltered the Devil. He is said to have built the chapel in repentance. The Parish Church of All Saints at Muggington dates originally from Norman times, though there have been alterations and additions since. In the churchyard is a yew tree said to be over 1,000 years old.

105 CAVENDISH ARMS

Doveridge

A well-appointed inn in a quiet village that is full of character, and where good food and drink is available.

🍴 see page 234

•

Norbury Manor, next to the church in Norbury, is a Grade I listed building. The original medieval manor house is still attached to a later hall. It was the seat of the Fitzherbert family from medieval times. Now owned by the National trust, it is open to the public by appointment only.

•

monuments to both the Cokes and the Longfords. The village is the home of the Longford Mummers, who keep alive the old English tradition of 'mumming', where people blacked up and wore masks and bizarre costumes to present plays. The masks were so that people would not recognise the identity of the players. If a player was recognised, the play's magical qualities would be spoiled.

NORBURY

14 miles W of Derby off the B5033

Norbury lies on the River Dove and was recorded in the *Domesday Book* as Norberre or Nordberie, the 'norther' defence on the Dove. The mainly 14th and 15th century **Parish Church of St Mary and St Barlok** is definitely worth a visit, as it houses the alabaster tombs of the 15th century FitzHerberts, one of the oldest families in Derbyshire. It is probable that the family contributed much towards the church building over the years. Those familiar with the works of George Eliot will feel much at home in this part of the county. The characters Adam and Seth from her famous novel *Adam Bede* were based on her father, Robert Evans, and his brother, and many scenes from the book are set in this village. Members of Eliot's family are buried in the churchyard.

DOVERIDGE

15 miles W of Derby off the A50

As its name suggests, this village is situated on the banks of the River Dove and, although there is a fair

amount of modern housing, Doveridge still retains a rural atmosphere. The village boasts the **Parish Church of St Cuthbert**, dating essentially from the 13th century. It contains memorials to the Canvendish family. In the churchyard is a 1,200 year old yew tree that is reputed to be one of the oldest and largest in Derbyshire.

BOYLESTONE

10 miles W of Derby off the A515

This isolated village sits amid gently rolling countryside south of Ashbourne. The **Parish Church of St John the Baptist** is famous for an incident during the Civil War. Two hundred Royalist troops spent the night in the local church on their way to Wingfield Manor. Rather foolishly they set no watch, and in the morning found themselves surrounded by Cromwell's men. The Royalists surrendered, were disarmed, and quietly filed out of the building.

The church itself is mainly 14th century, and has an unusual pyramidal roof. The unusual tower dates from 1846, and was added after a fire

CHURCH BROUGHTON

10 miles W of Derby off the A50

Church Broughton is a quiet village which was, until the early part of the 20th century, part of the Duke of Devonshire's Derbyshire estates. It is now mainly a commuter village for nearby towns. The **Parish Church of St Michael** dates back to the early 14th century. It has a large west tower with Victorian pinnacles and big gargoyles, and is topped with a small spire. The **Old Hall** (private) in Hall Lane is a 16th century timber framed building.

SUTTON-ON-THE-HILL

8 miles W of Derby off the A516

Despite its name, this is a sheltered spot, with the church standing above the village on the hill. The **Parish Church of St Michael** has a 14th century tower with a spire that was rebuilt in 1841. A few other parts are 14th century, but mostly the church was rebuilt in 1863. It contains an unusual monument to Judith Sleigh, who died in 1634. It is a standing coffin with handles carved in black stone. Cricket fans will take special pleasure in visiting Sutton-on-the-Hill, as it was the family home of G. M. and R. H. R. Buckston, both of whom captained the Derbyshire cricket team.

SUDBURY

12 miles W of Derby off the A50

This is the estate village to **Sudbury Hall**, home of a branch of the Vernon family who lived at Haddon Hall. It was built in the late 17th century by George Vernon in red brick and gifted to the National Trust in 1967. A splendid example of a house of Charles II's time, inside Sudbury Hall contains elaborate plasterwork and murals throughout, wood carvings by Grinling Gibbons, and some fine examples of mythological paintings

Sudbury

by Laguerre. The beautiful staircase of the Main Hall featured in the BBC's *Pride and Predudice*. Of particular interest is the **Museum of Childhood,** which is situated in the servants' wing and provides a fascinating insight into the lives of children down the ages. Displays range from a wealthy family's nursery and an Edwardian schoolroom to a 'chimney climb' and coal tunnel for the adventurous. The formal gardens and meadows lead to the tree-fringed lake. Wildlife abounds, including kestrels, grey herons, grass snakes, dragonflies, newts, frogs, toads, little and tawny owls and woodpeckers. Special events are held throughout the year.

Next to the hall is the **Parish Church of All Saints**, which was recorded in the *Domesday Book*, and has been extensively restored in later years. The east window, made in Germany in 1850, was donated by Queen Victoria and Prince Albert.

106 BOARS HEAD HOTEL

Sudbury

A superb country hotel that has luxurious comfortable rooms, an informal atmosphere and great food and drink.

 see page 235

107

107 THE YARD CAFÉ BAR & RESTAURANT

Swadlincote

A stylish, modern bar/ restaurant in the centre of the town that offers coffee, drinks and some of the best food in the area.

 see page 236

108 NEW INN

Woodville

A traditional village "local" in a traditional English village that serves great food and drink, and has an inviting, welcoming atmosphere.

 see page 237

ETWALL

5 miles SW of Derby off the A516

This charming place has a fine range of Georgian buildings including some almshouses known as the **Port Hospital Almshouses,** built by Sir John Port, the founder of nearby Repton College. The almshouses, fronted by wrought iron gates made by Robert Bakewell of Derby, were rebuilt in 1681 and recently restored again. Until the 1960s, almsmen and women wore special hats or bonnets and a dark blue cloak with a silver clasp.

The original site of **Etwall Hall**, where Sir John lived, is now the site of a large comprehensive school, which bears his name. For a village that derived its name from 'Eata's Well', it seems strange that Etwall only took up the custom of well-dressing recently and by chance. To mark the centenary of the village primary school, the teachers dressed a token well while the Women's Institute, with the help of people from two villages within the Peak District, dressed the only true well in Etwall, Town Well. This was in 1970 and the event, in mid May, was so successful that it is now an annual occasion and a total of eight wells are decorated.

As there is no long-standing tradition of well-dressing in the village, the themes for the dressings are not the more usual Biblical subjects but have covered a wide range of stories and ideas, including racial unity and the life and times of Sir John Port. Etwall is also the most southerly village to take part in the custom of well-dressing and its position, well below the harsh uplands of Derbyshire's Peak District, has ensured that there is always a good supply of flowers, even though the dressing takes place late in spring.

The **Parish Church of St Helen** has some stonework of the 13th century and earlier, though the building was largely rebuilt in the mid-16th century after a great storm damaged it. It was restored in 1881, and has a monument to Sir Arthur Cochrane, who died in 1954 and was the Clarenceux King of Arms, an officer of the College of Arms who looked after the armorial bearings for the south of England.

HILTON

8 miles SW of Derby off the A5132

Wakelyn Old Hall is an unusual half-timbered house dating from the 17th century. When the Wakelyn family left in 1621, the building became The Bull's Head Inn. It was also, reputedly, one of the places that Mary, Queen of Scots stopped at on her way to Tutbury Castle. The Old Talbot Inn dates back to the 15th century. The old gravel works are now a bird sanctuary and a nature reserve.

SWADLINCOTE

Here at the extreme edge of Derbyshire, well south of the River Trent, Swadlincote shares many characteristics with Staffordshire. Among the town's thriving industries, based on the clay and coal on which it stands, are brickworks and large potteries. The best known was Sharpe's founded in 1821 by Thomas Sharpe for the manufacture of sanitary ware. Work has started on converting the Sharpe buildings into a pottery heritage centre. Historically more a collection of villages, though officially an urban district, it retains a rural feel that is charming and worth exploring.

The **Parish Church of Emmanuelle** was built in 1846, the year Swadlincote became a parish in its own right.

NORTH OF SWADLINCOTE

HARTSHORNE

1 mile NE of Swadlincote off the A514

One of this lovely village's most renowned sons was George Stanhope, who grew up to be a famous preacher, a bold critic and a brave writer during the reign of Queen Anne.

The **Parish Church of St Peter** was rebuilt in 1835, though it retains its 15th century tower and 14th century font. A fine altar tomb shows the alabaster figures of Sir Humphry Dethick of 1599 and his wife, along with relief carvings of their six children. The Dethicks paid long and loyal service to the Royal family of their day - one of the Dethicks went to Cleves to find a fourth wife for Henry VIII. His son Sir William is said to have laid a pall of rich velvet on the coffin of Mary, Queen of Scots.

CALKE

5 miles NE of Swadlincote off the B587

In 1985 the National Trust bought **Calke Abbey**, a large Baroque-style mansion built between 1701 and 1704 on the site of an Augustinian priory founded in 1133. However, it was not until 1989 that the Trust were able to open the house to the public, for this was no ordinary building. Dubbed 'the house that time forgot', since the death of the owner, Sir Vauncy Harpur-Crewe, in 1924, nothing had been altered in the mansion. In fact, the seclusion of the house and also the rather bizarre lifestyle of its inhabitants, had left many rooms and objects untouched for over 100 years. There was even a spectacular 18th century Chinese silk state bed that had never been unpacked.

Today, the Trust has repaired the house and returned all 13,000 items to their original positions so that the Abbey now looks just as it did when it was bought in 1981. The attention to detail has been so great that none of the rooms have been redecorated. Visitors can enjoy the display of silver and trace the route of 18th century servants along the brew house tunnel to the house cellars. The house stands in its own large park with gardens, a chapel and stables that are also open to the public. There are three walled gardens with their glasshouses, a restored orangery, vegetable garden, pheasant aviaries and the summer flower display

109 COFFEE CONCEPT INTERNET CAFÉ

Woodville, Swadlincote

An internet cafe serving great coffee and food including soups, cakes and breakfasts.

see page 239

110 THE THREE HORSESHOES INN

Breedon-on-the-Hill

A completely refurbished village inn that serves the best food in the area, within surroundings that combine tradition with a contemporary feel.

see page 238

Melbourne

One of the best restaurants in the county, which combines the freshest of local produce with imagination and flair to give you a superb eating experience.

see page 240

within the unusual 'auricular' theatre. Calke is home to lots of wildlife including fallow deer, weasels, stoats, barn, little and tawny owls, woodpeckers, common toads, butterflies and beetles.

MELBOURNE

6 miles NE of Swadlincote off the B587

This small town, which gave its name to the rather better-known city in Australia, is a successful market garden centre. A famous son of Melbourne, who started his working life in one of the market gardens, was Thomas Cook, who was born here in 1808. He went on to pioneer personally-conducted tours and gave his name to the famous travel company.

Full of Georgian charm, Melbourne has many fine buildings which include one of the finest Norman churches in the country, the **Parish Church of St Michael and St Mary**. It sits on the site of an earlier Saxon church, and seems rather a grand church for this modest place. However, it is no ordinary parish church. In the 12th century, when the Bishopric of Carlisle was formed, the bishops needed a place of safety for the clergy when Carlisle was being raided by the Scots. So this church was built many miles south at Melbourne and, while Carlisle was subjected to raids and violence, the Bishop retired to Melbourne and continued to carry out his duties. The church was built between 1133 and 1229 and, in 1299, the then Bishop built a palace on land that is now home to Melbourne Hall.

The birthplace of the 19th century statesman Lord Melbourne, and also the home of Lady Caroline Lamb, **Melbourne Hall** is another fine building in this area of Derbyshire. A modest building, the hall was originally built in the 13th century as a rectory for the parish church and lodgings for the Bishop of Carlisle. In 1628 it came into the possession of Sir John Coke who largely rebuilt it. It is now home to Lord and Lady Kerr and their family.

It is surrounded by beautiful gardens, laid out in 1704 with help from Queen Anne's gardeners. The most notable feature is a beautiful wrought-iron birdcage pergola, built in the early 1700s by Robert Bakewell, a local blacksmith from Derby. Bakewell lived in Melbourne

Melbourne

for a time at the house of a widow named Fisher and her daughters. However when one daughter became pregnant, he moved hurriedly to Derby. Unfortunately the house is only open to the public in August, but the splendid and famous formal gardens are open in August and September, and are well worth a visit.

Melbourne Castle was built by the Earl of Lancaster in the early 14th century, and later became a royal castle when it came into the possession of Henry IV. The castle was bought from the crown by the Earl of Huntingdon, who demolished it in 1637. Remnants of it can be seen in Castle Farm by prior appointment. The **Thomas Cook Memorial Cottages** in the High street were built between 1890 and 1891, and still provide accommodation for some of the town's senior citizens.

SWARKESTONE

9 miles NE of Swadlincote off the A5132

Excavations in the village of Swarkestone, at Lowes Farm, led to the discovery that the district was occupied in the Bronze Age and also in Saxon times. This small village has also been, quite literally, a turning point in history. The **Swarkestone Bridge**, with its seven arches and three-quarter-mile long causeway, crosses the River Trent. In 1745, during the second Jacobite Rebellion, the advance guard of Bonnie Prince Charlie reached the bridge and, had they managed to cross it at this point,

they would have faced no other natural barriers on their 120-mile march to London. As it transpired, the army retreated and fled north, Bonnie Prince Charlie managed to escape after the Battle of Culloden and the Jacobite Rebellion was no more.

Legend has it that the original bridge at Swarkestone was built by two daughters of the Harpur family in the early 13th century. The girls were celebrating their joint betrothals when their fiancés were summoned to a barons' meeting across the river. While they were away torrential rain fell, flooding the river, and the two young men drowned as they attempted to ford the raging torrent on their return. The girls built the bridge as a memorial to their lovers. Both girls later died impoverished and unmarried.

The **Parish Church of St James** was so heavily restored between 1874 and 1876 that little now remains of the original church, apart form the southwest tower and

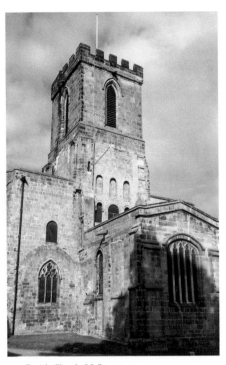

Parish Church, Melbourne

112 IVY HOUSE FARM GUESTHOUSE AND HOLIDAY COTTAGES

Stanton-by-Bridge

A superior and comfortable guest house and five self-catering cottages on a working farm among some of the loveliest scenery in England.

see page 239

Swarkestone Bridge

windows lend the church a light and airy atmosphere. The base of the square tower and the north aisle date from the 1300s; there is also a Georgian east window.

The village chapel (now a private house), unsurprisingly in Chapel Lane, was erected on arches so that it could reach the level of the road, which was higher up than it is today. This was not to everyone's liking: the marks of shots fired on the building can still be seen in the inscription stone set in the front of the building.

the Harpur Chapel. The chapel contains tomb chests of Richard Harpur, who died in 1573, and Sir John Harpur, who died in 1627, and his wife.

BARROW-ON-TRENT

8 miles NE of Swadlincote off the A514

Barrow-on-Trent, as its name tells us, stands between the River Trent and the Trent and Mersey Canal in this rich agricultural part of south Derbyshire. The row of parish cottages, built by parish levy in the 18th century, is an interesting feature of this attractive village. First rented for 30 shillings (£1.50) a year, the parish council still keeps them in a good state of repair.

The **Parish Church of St Wilfrid** is first mentioned in the *Domesday Book*, but the present building, which is approached down a pretty lane which also leads towards the river, dates mainly from the 13th century. The north arcade, with its original columns, is a notable feature. The plain glass

MILTON

5 miles N of Swadlincote off the A514

Milton is a small village, established over 1,500 years ago. It was once owned by the Burdett family, who built the nearby church of St Saviour. The 230-acre **Foremark Water** is a reservoir and nature reserve with footpaths and picnic areas.

BRETBY

2 miles N of Swadlincote off the A50

Now a leafy rural backwater, Bretby was first mentioned in the *Domesday Book* as an agricultural settlement around a green. There was once a castle in this quiet village until it was demolished in the reign of James l, and the stones used to build a mansion house. In the 18th century, that too was demolished and **Bretby Hall** was built in 1813 by Sir Jeffrey Wyatville, the designer of the 19th century extension at Chatsworth House. The hall was once owned by the

Earl of Carnarvon, who sold it to fund his archaeological excavation of the Tutankhamun tomb in Egypt.

REPTON

5 miles N of Swadlincote off the B5008

This village, by the tranquil waters of the River Trent, is steeped in history. The first mention of Repton came in the 7th century when it was established as the capital of the Saxon kingdom of Mercia. A monastery, housing both monks and nuns, was founded here sometime after AD 653 but the building was sacked by the Danes in AD 874. Three Mercian kings were buried here - Merewahl in AD 686, Aethelbald in AD 757 and Wiglaf in AD 839, as well as St Wystan, who was Wiglaf's grandson. He is supposed to have been interred alongside his grandfather. A battle-axe, now on display in the school museum, was excavated a little distance from the church. It had apparently lain undisturbed for well over 1,000 years.

The **Parish Church of St Wystan** is famous for its Anglo-Saxon chancel and crypt, and just how much of the stonework is from the original Saxon abbey is a matter for conjecture. However, it now features many later architectural styles as well. When the chancel and part of the nave were enlarged in 1854, the original Anglo-Saxon columns were moved to the 14th century porch. The crypt claims to be one of the oldest intact Anglo-Saxon buildings in England. The crypt

was rediscovered by chance in 1779 by a workman who was digging a hole for a grave in the chancel floor.

The ancient but restored **Cross**, still at the central crossroads in the village, has been the focal point of life here for centuries and it has also stood at the heart of the Wednesday market. Right up until the late 19th century a Statutes Fair, for the hiring of farm labourers and domestics, was also held here at Michaelmas.

Parts of an Augustinian priory, founded in 1170, are incorporated in the buildings of **Repton College**, itself founded in 1557. Sir John Port had specifically intended the college to be a grammar school for the local poor children of Etwall, Repton and Burnaston. These intentions have somewhat deviated over the passing years and now Repton is one of the foremost public schools in the country. Interestingly, two of its headmasters, Dr Temple and Dr Fisher, went on to become

113 RISING SUN

Willington

A traditional village pub just off the A50 that offers great food and drink within a friendly and relaxing atmosphere.

see page 241

Priory Gateway, Repton

114 THE BARLEY MOW

Church Gresley

A really friendly pub that offers great ales and other drinks, plus entertainment every Friday evening.

see page 241

115 DRUM AND MONKEY

Castle Gresley

A great stopping off place on the A444 which is warm and friendly, and which serves great food and drink.

see page 242

Archbishops of Canterbury, while Dr Ramsey was a pupil at the school under Dr Fisher's guiding light. Film buffs will recognise the 14th century gatehouse and causeway, as they featured in both film versions of the popular story *Goodbye, Mr Chips*.

Just to the west of the village is **Foremark Hall**, built by Robert Adam in 1762 for the Burdett family. It is now a preparatory school for Repton College.

SOUTH OF SWADLINCOTE

CHURCH GRESLEY

2 miles SW of Swadlincote off the A514

This former mining village has a distinguished history dating back to the time of the Augustinian monks who settled here in the 12th century and founded a priory. The village's name, like that of nearby Castle Gresley, recalls the great Gresley family, said to have been the only Derbyshire family to have retained their lands from the time of the *Domesday Book* up until the 20th century.

The **Parish Church of St Mary and St George** has a link with this illustrious past, as the tower and two internal arches are all that remain of the priory church. It became run-down after the Dissolution of the Monasteries, and remained in a sad state of disrepair up until 1872, when a new chancel was built. Remains of the priory have been found, including fragments of painted glass, stone coffins and medieval tiles. An

impressive alabaster monument of 1699 depicts Sir Thomas Gresley, surrounded by arms showing the marriages of his ancestors dating back to the time of William the Conqueror. The church's treasures, though, are the 10 large and wonderfully carved 17th century stalls.

CASTLE GRESLEY

3 miles SW of Swadlincote on the A444

Unfortunately, nothing is left of the castle built by William de Gresley in the mid 14th century which gives this attractive village its name - apart from the grassy mound, or motte, on which it stood, still known as **Castle Knob**.

LINTON

2 miles SW of Swadlincote off the A444

Linton is a charming and restful village, within the National Forest, which is mainly agricultural since the closure of the Coton Park colliery.

ROSLISTON

5 miles SW of Swadlincote off the A444

Rosliston was recorded in the *Domesday Book* as Redlauseton, an Ango-Saxon name meaning 'farm of Hrolf', this Hrolf probably being a Norseman. Rosliston is part of the National Forest and in the **Rosliston Forestry Centre** there are way-marked walks, a wildlife hide and children's play equipment.

The **Parish Church of St Mary the Virgin** is mainly 19th century but the 14th century tower with its broach spire still remains. The interior has a triple chancel arch.

COTON-IN-THE-ELMS

6 miles SW of Swadlincote off the A444

Mentioned in the *Domesday Book* as Cotune, it got its name from the elm trees which bordered every road into the village until they were killed off by Dutch Elm disease in the mid 20th century. The **Parish Church of St Mary** dates from 1846. It replaced an earlier church which stood behind the Shoulder of Mutton pub in the village. The bells from this older church were removed when it was pulled down and hung in the nearby church at Lullington. It is said that when the wind is in the right direction, the villagers of Coton-in-the-Elms can still hear their original bells.

NETHERSEAL

6 miles S of Swadlincote off the A444

Netherseal is a picturesque village on the banks of the river Mease, overlooking Leicestershire. 'Seal' means forested and Netherseal was recorded in the *Domesday Book* as a wooded area on the edge of the Ashby Woulds. It was once a mining community with a two-shaft colliery and several related industries. The mining industry has long gone and the centre of Netherseal village is now a conservation area with many listed buildings, including the 17th century almshouses.

The **Parish Church of St Peter** was built in the 19th century, though it looks much older, and has

some medieval fragments, including the tower. It stands on the site of an earlier church dating from the 13th century. Sir Nigel Gresley, who designed the famous Mallard locomotive, is buried in the churchyard.

DONISTHORPE

3 miles SE of Swadlincote off the A444

Donisthorpe is a famous old mining village right on the Derbyshire-Leicestershire border. The River Mease, which marks the border, runs right through it. Its inhabitants are justly proud of the village's industrial and historical heritage. The old colliery, the pit railway and the old British Rail line closed down by the 1960s. Left behind is a proud history and a tranquillity unknown in the days of the mines.

MOIRA

6 miles SE of Swadlincote off the A444

Moira Furnace Museum is based in a 19th century iron blast furnace. There are interactive displays and information on how the furnace worked, and its influence on the local economy and the lives of the workers. Moira is actually just over the border in Leicestershire, and close by is **Conkers**, at the heart of the National Forest. It is a mix of indoor and outdoor experiences where you can watch the effect the four seasons have on a forest. There are over 1,000 interactive exhibits.

116 SHOULDER OF MUTTON

Coton-in-the-Elms

A friendly, inviting village pub that offers the very best in food and drink, and is sure to give you a warm welcome.

see page 242

117 ROBIN HOOD INN & GLADES RESTAURANT

Overseal

A wonderful pub and restaurant that has a great atmosphere and the feel of a traditional English village local.

see page 243

118 SHOULDER OF MUTTON

Oakthorpe

A delightful pub that is popular with visitors and locals alike, and which serves good, honest pub food at affordable prices.

see page 244

The Amber Valley and Erewash

This area encompasses the Amber Valley and the eastern part of the area known as Erewash. These two regions cover the eastern and south eastern parts of Derbyshire respectively. The Rivers Amber, Derwent and Trent run through this part of the county. Though the scenery is perhaps less dramatic than the popular Peak District, in which most of north Derbyshire lies, there are still ample opportunities to enjoy pleasant drives and walks.

The southeast area of Derbyshire has been heavily influenced by the two towns of Derby and Nottingham, just over the border. Originally small farming communities, many of the villages expanded at the time of the Industrial Revolution and they can, in many cases, be characterised by unflattering rows of workers' cottages. And while a lot of the area did not escape from the growth of Derby and Nottingham, there are still some interesting and unique buildings to be found in this corner of of the county, as well as several attractive villages, such as Ockbrook, where what is known as the Moravian Settlement was founded in 1750. The Moravians, a Christian sect, originally came from Germany, and greatly influenced John Wesley. However, unlike the area to the west, there are no great stately mansions, except for one, Elvaston Castle, which, along with its extensive grounds, is an interesting and delightful place to explore. The ruined Dale Abbey is another of the region's attractions, founded here by Augustinian monks in the 13th century.

ACCOMMODATION

FOOD & DRINK

PLACES OF INTEREST

ALFRETON

This historic town dates back to Saxon times and, despite local legends to the contrary, Alfred the Great was not immortalised in the naming of the place, nor, as legend tells us, did he live in a house on what is now King Street. Instead the town belonged to a Saxon nobleman called Alfred, and was named 'Aelfredingtune', which, in the *Domesday Book*, is recorded as 'Elstretune'.

This attractive former coal mining town stands on a hill close to the Nottinghamshire border, and benefited from the philanthropy of Robert Watchorn, a pit boy made good, who emigrated to America and became Commissioner of Immigration in the early 19th century. He amassed a fortune, much of which was used to rebuild the southern part of the town. Along the charming High Street can be found the George Hotel, a fine Georgian building that looks down the length of the street. There are also a number of other 18th century stone built houses. The **Parish Church of St Martin** is large, and dates originally from the 13th century. The south arcade is 14th century, and the north arcade was rebuilt in 1868. Its impressive fine western tower dates from the 15th century, and rises from an earlier base.

In King Street there is a **House of Confinement**, or lock-up, which was built in 1820 to house lawbreakers and drunkards. The close confines of the prison, with its two cells, minute windows and thick outer walls, must have been a very effective deterrent.

The market at Alfreton was granted, in 1251, to Robert de Latham and Thomas de Chaworth, to be held on a Monday, together with a fair for three days at the Feast of St Margaret. There is still a bustling market and Afreton attracts visitors from a wide radius to its busy town centre. The **Alfreton Heritage Centre** in Rodgers Lane is housed in an old chapel with the municipal cemetery, and has occasional displays and exhibitions about the town's history.

AROUND ALFRETON

SOUTH NORMANTON

2 miles east of Alfreton off the B6109

Normanton, meaning the farm of the north men or 'Northwegans' was a small holding belonging to William Peveril at the time of the *Domesday Book*. Now a large, busy industrial village, it grew from a largely agricultural settlement which also had some tanning and framework knitting industries and small scale coal mining. The village was transformed after the opening of 'A Winning' colliery in 1871 and 'B Winning' in 1875, by the Blackwell Colliery Company. By the 1880s 'A Winning' had the largest output of coal in Derbyshire and employed around 500 men. Terraced houses were built to accommodate the growing population, which doubled in the ten years from 1871 to 1881. Like many Victorian industrialists, the

Among the many splendid old buildings in Alfreton, the most impressive is Alfreton Hall, the centrepiece of an attractive public park. In soft mellow stone, the Hall was built around 1730, with 19th century additions. Owned until fairly recently by the Palmer-Morewood family, owners of the local coal mines, it is now used as an Arts and Adult Education Centre. The park is quite extensive, boasting its own cricket ground and a horse-riding track around its perimeters.

119 SITWELL ARMS

Morton

A picturesque pub, in an equally picturesque village, that is famed for its good food and drink and its warm welcome.

🍴 see page 245

Blackwell Colliery Company took a paternalistic attitude to its workforce, providing a reading room, library, tennis courts and playing fields, as well as a cottage hospital. South Normanton Colliery closed in 1952, B Winning in 1964 and A Winning in 1969. In February 1937 the South Normanton Mining Disaster killed eight miners due to an underground explosion.

The present population is around 8,000. Despite the unemployment caused by the closing of the coal mines, the community spirit, typical of mining villages, continues. Jedediah Strutt, who, along with Rickard Arkwright, founded the Derbyshire cotton industry, was born in the village 1726. The village centre, around the old market place, has moved to a new market area and housing covers the site of Strutt's birthplace. New industries have taken over with the expansion of industrial estates

around the village.

The **Parish Church of St Michael** dates from around the 13th century but most of the present building is 19th century. It contains a monument to a Robert Ravel who lived at the nearby Carnfield Hall, an early 17th century stone mansion built by the Revell family.

OAKERTHORPE

1 mile W of Alfreton off the B6013

At **Oakerthorpe Nature Reserve**, subsidence from the Oakerthorpe coal mine has created a marshy area, which is now a nature reserve managed by Derbyshire Wildlife Trust.

SOUTH WINGFIELD

2 miles W of Alfreton on the B5053

Above the village, on the rise of a hill, stand the graceful ruins of the 15th century **Wingfield Manor**, owned by English Heritage. Built by Ralph Lord Cromwell, Lord Treasurer of England, in the 1440s, the manor house was used as Mary, Queen of Scots' prison on two separate occasions in 1569 and 1584 when she was held under the care of the Earl of Shrewsbury. The local squire, Anthony Babington, attempted to rescue the queen and lead her to safety but the plot failed and, instead, led to them both being beheaded. One of the less well-known of Derbyshire's many manor houses and mansions, the history and architectural interest provided by the ruins make it one of the more fascinating places to visit in the area.

Wingfield Manor

A wander around the remains reveals the large banqueting hall with its unusual oriel window and a crypt which was probably used to store food and wine. Whatever its use, it is a particularly fine example and rivals a similar structure at Fountains Abbey. High up in the tower can also be seen a single archer's slit, built the opposite way round so that only one archer was needed to defend the whole tower. The ruins have been used as a location for a number of film and TV productions, including *Peak Practice* and Zeffirelli's *Jane Eyre*.

East of the village is the **Parish Church of All Saints**, which dates originally from the 13th century. At the same time as building Wingfield Manor, Cromwell refurbished the church and built a new tower, while at the same time preserving the arcades on both sides of the nave.

CRICH

6 miles W of Alfreton off the A6

Probably best known as the village of Cardale in the TV series *Peak Practice*, Crich (pronounced 'Cry-ch' and meaning 'hilltop'), with its church and market cross, is also the home of the **Crich Tramway Village**. Referring to itself intriguingly as 'the museum that's a mile long', it offers a wonderful opportunity to enjoy a tram ride along a Victorian street. The signposts, stone flags and gas lamps are all original and come from such diverse places as Liverpool, Oldham and Leeds. Today, in many

towns and cities, trams are making a come-back, but here the museum gives visitors the opportunity to view tramways of the past. As well as those shuttling up and down the mile-long scenic route, there is an exhibition, which contains not only trams but much more besides, including some wonderfully colourful fairground organs. Throughout the year the museum holds many special events and, with their policy of no hidden extras, this is a great place to take all the family for a fun day out. Started in 1959, it now has over 50 trams, with a third of them being in full working order. It stands on the site of a quarry that was owned by the great engineer, George Stephenson, who also owned the railway that carried the stone down the steep incline to his lime kilns alongside the Cromford Canal.

This large, straggling village, which retains its medieval market cross, was also a flourishing knitting centre at one time, and the telltale 18th century cottages with their long upper windows can still be seen. The **Parish Church of St Mary**, with its tall spire, dates originally from Norman times, but is now mostly 14th century. It sits on a hilltop, and has a built-in stone lectern, which, though common in Derbyshire, is rare elsewhere in the country.

WHATSTANDWELL

4 miles W of Alfreton off the A6

This tiny village, of which it has been said 'the loveliness of the English countryside is always here,'

120 CRICH TRAMWAY VILLAGE

Crich

Ride on beautifully restored trams through the re-created period streets and into spectacular countryside.

🏛 see page 244

•

Above the quarry is Crich Stand, a local landmark that looks rather like a lighthouse. In fact this is the village war memorial for the Sherwood Foresters, erected in 1923. It stands almost 1,000 feet above sea level and from its viewing gallery, on a clear day, it is said that seven counties can be seen. A lantern is lit in the tower at night and the regiment still holds an annual pilgrimage to the tower on the first Sunday in July.

•

Built in the late 19th century, the Parish Church of St Anne in Ambergate was a gift to the village from the Johnson family of the Ambergate Wire Works. Inside the church there is a marble figure depicting an angel protecting a child from a serpent. This was sculpted by a Belgian sculptor, the son of refugees who came to England during the First World War. He is reputed to have been sculptor to the King of Belgium, and he had originally intended the sculpture for his own church in that country.

was once owned by the monks of Darley Abbey and nestles in the valley of the River Derwent. To the south and on the west bank of the Derwent are the **Shining Cliff Woods**, and along the steep lanes lie grey stone cottages and farmhouses, built of stone from local quarries, which merge gently into the background of woods and cliff. Florence Nightingale knew and loved the village, and took a keen interest in its people. Ellen MacArthur, the round-the-world yachtswoman, was brought up in the village.

FRITCHLEY

3 miles SW of Alfreton off the A610

This quiet hamlet was, during the 19th and early 20th centuries, an important meeting place for Quakers, and a flourishing community survives today. The simple, brick-built **Meeting House** of 1897, is in the centre of the village. Here also can be seen the remains of a pre-Stephenson tramway that was built at the end of the 18th century to carry stone to the lime kilns at Bull Bridge.

AMBERGATE

6 miles SW of Alfreton off the A6

Ambergate stands where the River Amber joins the Derwent, and is on the route of the National Heritage Way, a 55-mile walk along the Derwent valley. The village itself is surrounded by deciduous woodland, including the fine Shining Cliff Woods (see Whatstandwell) , an important refuge for wildlife. Before 1840

and the building of Ambergate station for the North Midland Railway in 1840, there was no village here at all, though there was a tollhouse for the recently constructed turnpike road, opened in 1817. The railway, road and canal here are all squeezed into the tight river valley, and the railway station, standing 100 feet above the road, had a triangular layout of platforms, due to the configuration of the lines. It was an important junction, and in its heyday employed over 50 men. Now there is just one platform.

SWANWICK

2 miles S of Alfreton off the A38

Swanwick is an old Derbyshire village, which grew into a thriving industrial centre over the 18th and 19th centuries. Coal mining and stocking manufacture had provided work for centuries, but it was the arrival of the Butterley Company, the largest coal, iron and engineering concern in the East Midlands in the late 18th century that changed the face of Swanwick. Despite the fact that it has lost much of its original industries, Swanwick has doubled its size to around 5,000 during the 20th century, no doubt due to its easy access to the motorway and the large towns and cities nearby. The **Parish Church of St Andrew**, a substantial and attractive stone building, was completed in 1860, with the tower being added 43 years later.

RIDDINGS

2 miles S of Alfreton on the B6016

Riddings was first recorded in the

12th century as Ryddynges, meaning a clearing in the grove. Now a tranquil village, Riddings has twice been the scene of important discoveries. In the mid-1700s, 800 precious Roman coins were uncovered here. The second time was in the mid-1800s, when James Oakes, a colliery proprietor and ironmaster, discovered a mysterious liquid flowing in one of his coal mines. He called in the assistance of his brother-in-law, Sir Lyon Playfair, one of the most brilliant practical scientists of his day. Playfair found the liquid to be petroleum, then a product with no commercial value, although it had been known as *naphtha*, 'salt of the earth', from Biblical times.

Playfair summoned the help of his Scottish friend, James Young, who, soon after he came to Riddings, approached Playfair in dismay to show him that the oil was in a thick, contaminated condition. Playfair recognised at once the presence of paraffin, and instructed Young to extract enough paraffin to make two candles - the first paraffin-wax candles ever produced.

With one candle in his left hand and the other in his right, Playfair illuminated a lecture he gave at the Royal Institution. From these small beginnings date the enormous petroleum industry and the rich trade in paraffin and its by-products. Young, known thereafter as Paraffin Young, earned himself a fortune, and when the knowledge of his work spread about, a worldwide search for petroleum began.

RIPLEY

Ripley is an industrial town, mentioned in the *Domesday Book* as Ripelie. Once a typical small market town, Ripley expanded dramatically during the Industrial Revolution when great use was made of the iron, clay and coal deposits found nearby. The town's Butterley ironworks, founded in 1792 by a group of men which included renowned engineer Benjamin Outram, created the arched roof for London's St Pancras station. Outram's even more famous son Sir James enjoyed an illustrious career that saw him claimed Bayard of India, and earned him a resting place in Westminster Abbey.

AROUND RIPLEY

PENTRICH

1 mile N of Ripley off the A38

Mentioned in the *Domesday Book* as Pentric, this hilltop village with its brownstone gabled houses is very charming. Its sturdy church is approached via a picturesque flight of 48 steps. The **Parish Church of St Matthew** lies above the village, close to a Saxon Cross. It dates back to the 12th century, with much rebuilding and alterations being carried out in the 15th century. A striking stained-glass War Memorial window created in 1916 depicts the warrior saints of England and France and a figure of St Michael.

Pentrich is famous as the site of the last revolution in England, which took place here in June 1817.

121 LATTE LOUNGE

Ripley

A stylish, modern place with a fine reputation for its food, drink and accommodation, right in the heart of Ripley.

see page 244

Near to Ripley town is the Midland Railway Centre, which is a railway complex and museum to delight railway buffs or families looking for a diverting day out. There are working steam trains running along a line from Butterley to Riddings, through a 35-acre country park which provides the habitat for an abundance of wildlife from herons to foxes, as well as picnic areas for visitors. You can see a Victorian railwayman's church, the 'Tin Tabernacle', rescued from the railway village of Westhouses. There is a working signal box, a collection of locomotives and farm and industrial machinery. As well as a model railway there is the Butterley Park Miniature Railway, a 3.5-inch and 5-inch gauge line with a circuit of approximately one sixth of a mile. The line is fully signalled using miniature examples of traditional railway signals controlled from a miniature Midland Railway signal box. The museum is open every weekend throughout the year, and most school holidays.

121

Butterley Railway Centre, Ripley

122 EAGLE TAVERN

Heage

A friendly, family run pub that combines the best of service with good food and drink and value-for-money

 see page 246

123 SPANKER INN

Nether Heage

A traditional English inn that serves real ales and which has a great reputation for its beautifully cooked meals.

see page 246

A small band of half-starved weavers, labourers and stockingers - no more than 200 or 300 men - met and marched towards Nottingham, where they expected to meet up with more men before marching on London. However, the uprising was soon quelled, with a resultant trial of 50 of the insurgents in Derby that lasted 10 days. The men were accused of high treason, and a few were pardoned, 11 sent to Australia for life and three to Australia for 14 years. Three of the men, however, were executed at Derby Gaol. The poet Shelley witnessed the scene and described the despair of the relatives and the disturbance of the crowd as the men were beheaded. So restless and angry was the crowd watching the executions that the executioners were masked and their names kept secret. The execution block is still to be seen in Derby Prison. The 1821 census recorded a decrease of a third in the population of the parish because the Duke of Devonshire's agents destroyed many of the houses after the insurrection.

LOWER HARTSHAY
2 miles W of Ripley off the A610

Lower Hartshay sits on what was Ryknield Street, an important Roman military and trade route from the Fosse Way in Gloucestershire to the north. The line of Ryknield Street through Ripley, Pentrich and Lower Hartshay can still be seen and makes a pleasant walk with splendid views. Lower Hartshay was still on a main route for traffic until the 1970s. Now by-passed by the major trunk roads, it is a pleasant and tranquil backwater.

HEAGE
1 mile W of Ripley on the B6013

Heage, from the Anglo-Saxon word 'heegge', meaning 'high', was on the ancient packhorse route from Derby to Chesterfield, and the old turnpike road passed through here. The village has no obvious centre and is scattered along the roads and lanes interspersed with some small estates of modern housing. The main occupation for centuries was farming and coal mining. In fact, Morley Park has been worked for coal and ironstone since 1372, and the remains of bell-pits were discovered during recent open cast mining. On Morley Park are the remains of two cold blast coke iron furnaces built by Francis Hurt in 1780 and the Mold Brothers in 1818. The older furnace was probably the first of its kind in Derbyshire. Other local industries included framework knitting and weaving.

The **Parish Church of St Luke** was originally constructed of wood, and during a great storm in June 1545 it was destroyed. It was then rebuilt in stone in 1661, and subsequently enlarged in 1836. The oldest domestic building in the village is Heage Hall Farm, once the home of a branch of the Pole family. Crowtrees Farm was built in 1450 with three good cruck beams and was refurbished in 1712. An interesting feature of the village is its postbox, on the wall of the post office. It is one of the few in the country bearing the name of Edward Vll, who abdicated in 1936.

Heage Windmill is situated west of the village between Heage and Nether Heage. It is a Grade II listed tower mill and the only one in Derbyshire to retain its six sails, fan tail and machinery. Standing on the brow of a hill, overlooking Nether Heage, it is built of local sandstone and is over two hundred years old. It has been restored to full working order and is open to the public at weekends and bank holidays.

DENBY

2 miles S of Ripley off the A38

Denby was mentioned in the *Domesday Book* as Denebi, which

Hot Air Balloons over Heage

means village of the Danes. Ryknield Street, a Roman road, runs through the village.

Denby Pottery, to the north of the village, is one of the biggest attractions in Derbyshire, and has a fascinating history. Derbyshire has a long tradition of stoneware pottery, closely associated with the natural clay deposits of the county. When a seam of clay was discovered in Denby in 1806 while constructing a road, a local man, William Borne, recognised its quality, and thus Denby Pottery was born. Production of salt-glazed pottery began in 1809, with Bourne's son Joseph in charge. Soon the company was known world-wide for its containers and stoneware bottles. Soon the company diversified into kitchen and

124 DENBY VISITOR CENTRE

Denby

An interesting day out can be found here with tours of the factory and a selection of retail options.

🏛 see page 247

125 THE PANTHEON RESTAURANT AND BAR

Codnor

A restaurant/bar with letting rooms within a well-known golf course that offers the very best in hospitality, food and drink.

🍴 🛏 see page 247

tableware By the 1930s, classic ranges such as Imperial Blue orient ware, which was brown, had established the company as one of the premier stoneware potteries in the world, introducing its 'oven to tableware' in the 1970s.

The business took on a new lease of life when the visitor centre was added, and it now welcomes nearly 300,000 visitors a year. The site offers a chance to see the latest in ceramic technology, and at the factory shop, seconds and discounts start at 20 per cent off the RRP. The cookery emporium offers cookery demonstrations and has in stock over 3,000 kitchen gadgets, supplies and equipment. There are tours on offer as well, including a full tour of the pottery or the craftsmen's workshop tour. A factory shop for Dartington Crystal can also be found at this superb attraction.

As well as pottery, coal and iron have made Denby famous, though the village itself remains largely unspoilt. A mile from the pottery visitor centre, in Denby's

Codnor Castle

oldest part, is the little **Parish Church of St Mary**, set amid a lovely churchyard filled with trees. The church's round arches and pillars date from the late 12th century, while the chancel with its sedilia, piscina and aumbry is from the 14th century. The altar table is 17th century, while the tower, spire, porch and eight-sided font are from the 20th century.

One of Denby's most famous sons was **John Flamsteed**, born here in 1646. A poor boy, he went on to become the first Astronomer-Royal at the then new observatory at Greenwich. Benjamin Outram, the railway engineer was also born here.

CODNOR
2 miles SE of Ripley on the A610

Codnor is mentioned in the *Domesday Book* as Cotenovre, and was given to Wiliam Peveril, William the Conqueror's illegitimate son. The surrounding fields and woods make it easy to forget the coal and iron which made this part of Derbyshire famous. Once it was a great park of nearly 2,000 acres, the centrepiece being the mighty **Codnor Castle**, the scant ruins of which still stand. It was the home of the influential de Grey family, the most famous member being Richard de Grey, who was one of Henry III's loyal barons. Edward II visited another Richard de Grey here after fighting the rebels at Burton-on-Trent. Yet another was sent by Henry V to bring Hotspur's son from Scotland, while Henry de Grey the last of them, busied himself with alchemy in a vain attempt to change base metals into gold.

In 1496, on the death of Henry, the castle passed to Sir John Zouch, a relative by marriage. The de Greys built their castle with two courts, four enormous round towers and a great gateway, but by the time the Zouch family sold it in the mid 1600s it was already beginning to decay. All that survives today is a length of the boundary wall from the upper court, parts of the dividing wall and the defending towers, as well as the odd doorway, window and fireplace.

HEANOR

3 miles SE of Ripley off the A608

Heanor sits close to the Nottinghamshire border, with, a mile across the valley, the town of Eastwood, birthplace of D.H. Lawrence. Its hub is the market place, where the annual fair is held, as well as a twice-weekly market, which takes place on Fridays and Saturdays. Away from the bustle of the market are the **Memorial Gardens**. This peaceful setting always promises a magnificent spread of floral arrangements, herbaceous borders and shrubberies. Near the park is **Shanakeil House**, built in the early 1900s form Dr E.V. Eaves.

Coal mining was once the dominant industry, but since all the pits have closed, the scarred landscape has been reclaimed and restored. To the south of Heanor is the **Shipley Country Park**, on the estate of the now-demolished Shipley Hall. In addition to its magnificent lake, the country park boasts over 600 acres of beautiful countryside, which should keep even the most enthusiastic walker busy. Well known as both an educational and holiday centre, there are facilities for horse riding, cycling and fishing. This medieval estate was mentioned in the *Domesday Book* and, under the Miller-Mundy family it became a centre for farming and coal mining production during the 18th century. Restoration over the years has transformed former railways into wooded paths, reservoirs into peaceful lakes, and has re-established the once-flowering meadows and rolling hills, which had been destroyed by the colliery pits. Here also can be found the American Adventure, a busy theme park with over a hundred thrill rides, gun fights, special events and boat trips on the lake.

The River Erewash passes through the area at Langley Mill and visitors are able to enjoy the restored boats, which travel to and from the 200-year-old canal basin.

The ancient **Parish Church of St Lawrence** dates back to the 12th century, though little of the old church remains after rebuilding in 1868. The 15th century tower is still intact.

BELPER

Belper is a small, attractive market town eight miles north of Derby. In 1740, the population of Belper was around 500. It grew rapidly at

The longest tramway in the world once ran through Heanor. Starting at Upper Parliament Street in Nottingham, it ran for eleven miles and terminated at Ripley. Known as the 'Ripley Rattler', D.H. Lawrence knew it well, and even wrote a short story, Tickets Please, *about it. It was reckoned to be the most dangerous tramway in Britain, as it was single track, with passing places. As the trams swung into the passing places passengers were thrown about. Accidents were a regular occurrence, and one tram even got stuck under a bridge. On one occasion, a double-decker tram ran into a wall and catapulted some passengers into a graveyard.*

126 BLACK SWAN

Belper

An old pub in the heart of Belper that has recently been taken over and refurbished an exceptionally high standard.

see page 248

127 THE RAILWAY

Belper

A superb pub in the heart of Belper that is family run, making for a warm, friendly atmosphere and value for money.

see page 249

the beginning of the 19th century due to the industrial development of cotton mills. However the origins of the town go back much further than the Industrial Revolution. It was mentioned in the *Domesday Book* as 'Beau Repaire', the beautiful retreat; in 1964 the remains of a Roman kiln were found here. Its football team is called 'The Nailers', for the nail makers who worked here when the area was part of the Royal Forest.

Now famous for its cotton mills, the town is situated alongside the **River Derwent** on the floor of the valley. In 1776, Jedediah Strutt, the wheelwright son of a South Normanton farmer, set up one of the earliest water-powered cotton mills here to harness the natural powers of the river. With the river providing power and fuel coming from the nearby South Derbyshire coalfield, the valley has a good claim to be one of the cradles of the Industrial Revolution. Earlier, in 1771, Strutt had gone into profitable partnership with Richard Arkwright to establish the world's first water-powered cotton mill at Cromford. In 1780 another mill was built at Milford. When the partnership with Arkwright was dissolved, Strutt and his son William retained the North Mill at Belper. Great benefactors of the town for 150 years, the Strutt family provided housing, work, education and even food from the model farms they established in the surrounding countryside.

Over 200 years later the mills are still standing, as well as some

unique mill-workers' cottages. The **Derwent Valley Visitor Centre** tells the story of the cotton industry and the great influence the Strutt family had on the town. It also tells of Samuel Slater, Strutt's apprentice, who emigrated to America in 1789, built a mill, and became the father of the American cotton industry. The centre is housed in the oldest surviving mill, the two-storey **North Mill** at Bridgefoot, near the magnificent crescent-shaped weir in the Derwent and the town's main bridge. Built in 1876, it has cast-iron columns and beams, and hollow tile floors which provided a warm-air central heating system. The massive, neighbouring redbrick **East Mill** was constructed in 1912, but now is largely empty. A Jubilee Tower in terracotta was erected on the site in 1897 to mark Queen Victoria's 60th anniversary on the throne. Train travellers through Belper can admire George Stephenson's mile-long cutting, walled in gritstone throughout and spanned by no fewer than ten bridges. When completed in 1840 it was considered an engineering wonder of its day.

The **Chapel of St John the Baptist** in The Butts was the chapel of the original village of Belper. It consists of nave and chancel only, and dates from 1634. The **Parish Church of St Peter** with its pinnacled west tower dates from 1824. It contains a monument to George Brettle, who built **George Brettle's Warehouse** in Chapel Street, a distinctive and elegant

Derwent Valley

128 TRAVELLER'S ERST

Kilburn

A superb establishment that offers a great range of real ales to discerning lovers of the traditional English pub.

🍴 see page 250

129 HUNTER ARMS

Kilburn

A great pub that has regained its former glory, and now serves great food and drink to local and visitor alike.

🍴 see page 250

130 THE RAILWAY

Shottle

A pub that is renowned for the quality of its food, its great selection of drinks and its family-friendly atmosphere.

🍴 see page 251

building in the classical style.

The River Gardens were established in 1905 and today they are a pleasant place for a stroll among the beautifully tended gardens. Rowing boats can be hired for a trip along the Derwent. The gardens are a favourite with the film industry, having been used in Ken Russell's *Women in Love*, as well as television's *Sounding Brass* and *In the Shadow of the Noose*. The riverside walk through the meadows is particularly rich in bird life.

AROUND BELPER

FARNAH GREEN

1 mile W of Belper on the A517

Farnah Green is a charming hamlet on the outskirts of Belper. It has no shops but has a pleasant old country pub which serves food.

SHOTTLE

2 miles W of Belper off the A517

Shottle is a picturesque hamlet of a few farms, houses, the **Parish Church of St Lawrence**, and a chapel, surrounded by little lanes and footpaths. Unlike most of the surrounding villages it appears little changed since the 19th century. Shottle was the birthplace of Samuel Slater, the apprentice to Jedediah Strutt, who left Belper for the USA and built the first water powered cotton mill there. He is credited as the father of the Industrial Revolution in the USA and his original Slater Mill at Pawtucket is now a museum.

IDRIDGEHAY

10 miles NW of Derby off the B5023

This pleasant village is called

131 KING WILLIAM IV

Milford

A superb olde worlde pub that offers real ale, a range of light snacks, and comfortable, affordable B&B accommodation.

 see page 250

132 SPOTTED COW

Holbrook

A traditional pub that offers olde worlde charm, great food, good drink and B&B accommodation - all at competitive prices.

see page 252

'Ithersee' by the locals and it lies in the valley of the River Ecclesbourne. Formerly a working rural village, it is now purely residential. Part of the village is a conservation area including the half-timbered building, **South Sitch.** The date above the door, 1621, may refer to alterations carried out to a much older building. The apparent Elizabethan mansion, **Alton Manor**, was in fact built by Sir George Gilbert Scott in 1846, when he moved from Darley Dale because of the coming of the railway. The **Parish Church of St James** was built in the early 1840s and consecrated in 1845.

MILFORD

1 mile S of Belper off the A6

Milford was a quiet hamlet until the cotton mills came. The village's first cotton mill was built by Richard Arkwright and Jedediah Strutt using stone transported from nearby Hopping Hill. It was only a year later that their partnership dissolved and both industrialists went their separate ways to forge individual empires. Housing, some of which still stands, was built for the workforce. Although most of the mill buildings are now gone, those that remain are used by small businesses.

HOLBROOK

2 miles S of Belper off the A6

The Saxon name for Holbrook was Hale Broc meaning Badger Hill. The ancient Roman Portway (which the Romans surfaced with coal) runs through the village and one of the toll houses for the turnpike road still stands in the village. In the early 1960s two Roman kilns were discovered here. Holbrook was once a busy industrial village well known for framework knitters, who supplied stockings for royalty. It is now a pleasant place, with some attractive old houses, serving mainly as a commuter area for the nearby towns of Belper and Derby.

The **Parish Church of St Michael** was built in 1761 as a private chapel to Holbrook Hall. It was rebuilt as the parish church in 1841, but still retains the elegant classical lines of its predecessor. Holbrook Hall was built in 1681 although it looks later, and is now a residential home for the elderly.

DUFFIELD

2 miles S of Belper off the A6

This ancient village is a charming place, with Georgian houses and cottages lining the banks of the River Ecclesbourne. For such a cosy place, it seems odd that the **Parish Church of St Alkmund** is situated in isolation down by the river. However, as it stands on the site of a Saxon one, it is thought that the river was used to baptise converts. The saint to whom it is dedicated was a Northumbrian prince who was murdered in AD 800 at nearby Derby by bodyguards supposed to be protecting him. They were sent by King Eardulf, who was trying to claim the Northumbrian throne. Alkmund's sarcophagus is now in a Derby museum.

The church has a 14th century east tower with a recessed spire. It was much restored in the 19th century. Inside the Church there is an impressive monument dating from 1600, dedicated to Anthony Bradshaw, his two wives and their 20 children. He had 23 children in all, with the 22nd being called 'Penultima'. Bradshaw was a barrister and the deputy steward of Duffield Firth, a former hunting forest between Duffield and Wirksworth. His great nephew went on to officiate over the court, which called for the execution of Charles I.

Duffield Hall is situated at the southern edge of the village. It is an Elizabethan building, enlarged in 1870 and once used as a girls boarding school. It is now the head quarters of the Derbyshire Building Society.

ILKESTON

With a population of just over 37,000, Ilkeston is the third largest town in Derbyshire. It received its royal charter for a market and fair in 1252, and both have continued to the present day. The **Charter Fair**, held in October each year, is one of the oldest and largest in Europe. The history of the town, however, goes back to when it was an Anglo-Saxon hilltop settlement known as Tilchestune.

Once a mining and lace-making centre, Ilkeston's history is told in the **Erewash Museum**, housed in a fine Georgian house with Victorian extensions on the High Street. It was a family home and then part of a school before becoming a Museum in the 1980s.

Many original features survive including a restored Edwardian kitchen and wash house. The garden has unrivalled views across the Erewash Valley. Other fine examples of elegant 18th century houses can be found in East Street while, in Wharncliffe Road, there are period houses with art nouveau features.

Ilkeston commands fine, wide views from the hillside above the valley of the **Erewash**, which here bounds the county. The **Parish Church of St Mary** has undergone many changes since it was first erected in the 1200s. It is particularly notable for its window tracery, especially in the six windows in the older part of the church. A former tower and elegant spire were destroyed by storm in 1714. The tower only was rebuilt, to be succeeded by another on the old foundations in 1855. This tower was then moved westwards in 1907, at which time the nave was doubled in length. One intriguing feature it has retained throughout all these changes is its 13th century archway. The organ is also distinguished, in that it originally came from a London church and is known to have been played by the great Mendelssohn himself.

AROUND ILKESTON

MAPPERLEY

2 miles NW of Ilkeston off the A609

This historic village was first granted a market charter in 1267 and, though its old church was demolished due to mining

• Also in the village of *Duffield is a large mound, all that remains of Duffield Castle which was ransacked and burnt to the ground in 1266. However, excavations show that it must have been a massive building, with a large keep whose walls were over 16 feet thick. Following the Battle of Hastings in 1066, William the Conqueror rewarded Henry de Ferrers, one of his chief supporters, by giving him great areas of land. Controlling his estates from Tutbury Castle in Staffordshire, Henry built a motte and bailey castle here in around 1080 and installed his son Engenulph. The de Ferrers estates passed peacefully from father to son for nearly 200 years until they were inherited by Robert de Ferrers in 1254. Only 15 years of age at that time, by the age of 27 he had managed to ruin the family name and lose the estate and titles. The two-acre site on which the Castle stood is owned by the National Trust. The interesting relics that were excavated here between 1886 and 1957 can be seen in Derby Museum.*

•

The Nutbrook Trail for cyclists and walkers follows the old Stanton to Shipley mineral railway line more or less, parallel to the canal, from Long Eaton to Heanor. It is part of the Sustrans network of cycle ways and is very popular with both recreational users and commuters. The railway trail and the canal towpath can create a circular walk between West Hallam and Stanton Bridge. The Nutbrook Trail received grant aid from East Midlands Arts for three sculptures, which drew their inspiration from the social and industrial heritage of the Erewash Valley. The three sculptures represent vegetation found along the trail- Birch, Campion and Vetch and the collection is entitled 'Wild Weeds'.

•

subsidence, the modern church has some interesting stained glass windows. In the heart of Derbyshire mining country, any stroll from the village centre will take the walker past industrial remains.

To the south of Mapperley is the former branch line of the Midland Railway, which served Mapperley Colliery, as well as the old raised track which is all that remains of an old tramway, which ran from the Blue Fly Shaft of West Hallam Pit to the **Nutbrook Canal** further east. The canal, which opened in 1796, carried coal from the pits at Shipley to the ironworks at Stanton and beyond. Only just over four miles long, the canal had some 13 locks but it fell into disuse after the Second World War and much of it has now been filled in.

To the northeast of the village is the family-orientated **American Adventure Theme Park**, which has fairground rides, free fall flights and all the fun of the fair, with an American twist.

WEST HALLAM

2 miles W of Ilkeston off the A609

West Hallam stands on a hilltop. Its **Parish Church of St Wilfrid**, set between the great expanse of **West Hallam Hall** and the rectory, is approached via a lovely avenue of limes. The church is over 700 years old and has a very handsome tower, with a blue clock with gilt hands and figures. The rector's garden has a glorious lime tree, and looks out over the valley to a great windmill

with its arms still working as they have done since Georgian times.

The Powtrell family were historically important to the village of West Hallam, and their former home was offered as a hiding place for fugitive priests during the 16th century. One priest taken at the house was condemned to death, but after long imprisonment his sentence was commuted to banishment. Another priest, sentenced for celebrating mass at West Hallam Hall, was sent to prison and later died there. On a stone on the chancel floor of the village church is an engraved portrait of Thomas Powtrell in armour, dating from the 15th century. A magnificent canopied tomb depicts Walter Powtrell, who died in 1598, and his wife Cassandra. He wears richly decorated armour, she a gown of many folds. Around them are depicted their seven children.

One of the premier attractions in the area, **The Bottle Kiln** is a handsome and impressive brick built former working pottery, now home to a contemporary arts and crafts centre. Visitors can take a leisurely look at exhibitions (changing throughout the year) of both British studio ceramics and contemporary painting in the European tradition. Two shops filled with jewellery, cards, gifts, objects d'art, soft furnishings and house wares with an accent on style, design and originality can also be found here. At the Buttery Café, visitors can enjoy a wide choice of freshly prepared and hearty food, along with a tasty selection of teas, coffees and cakes. Visitors can also take their meals in the tranquil Japanese tea garden on fine days.

West Hallam has a well-dressing ceremony each year, normally held during the second week of July.

HORSLEY

6 miles W of Ilkeston on the A609

Horsley is a charming little village with a population of around 500. It has a main street lined with mature trees and a village green. The **Parish Church of St Clement and St James** is a real gem dating back to the 13th century with later additions. It has a broach spire and mid-15th century battlements and a pretty porch with a medieval crucifix. The interior is much restored but there are some scraps of ancient glass in one window.

The village pillar box is one of the most unusual in England, as it is made of stone. The village also has three wells, called Blanche, Sophie and Rosamund. They were given to the village in 1824 by the local vicar, Reverend Sitwell.

MORLEY

4 miles SW of Ilkeston off the A608

Morley is essentially a rural village with working farms around it. There are four parts to the village, Brackley Gate and the Croft, the Smithy and Brick Kiln Lane, Almshouse Lane and Church Lane.

Brackley Gates has some disused quarries and marvellous views to the north. It is now a wildlife reserve owned by the

Derbyshire Wildlife Trust. The Croft has a cluster of 17th and 18th century cottages. The 17th century **Almshouses** in Almshouse Lane were originally provided by Jacinth Sitwell, then Lord of the Manor of Morley for 'six poor, lame or impotent men'.

The **Parish Church of St Matthew** has a Norman nave, with the tower, chancel and north chapel being late 14th/early 15th century. It is perhaps best known for its magnificent stained glass windows dating from medieval times. Originally in the Abbey Refectory at Dale, the windows were acquired by Sir Henry Sacheverell in 1539. There are monuments and brasses to important local families like the Sacheverell's and the Sitwell's, including one to John Sacheverell, who died at Bosworth Field in 1485, and the beautifully carved tomb chest of Henry Sacheverell, who died in 1558 and his beautiful wife Katherine Babington, who died in 1553.

DALE ABBEY

3 miles SW of Ilkeston off the A6096

The village takes its name from the now-ruined abbey that was founded here by Augustinian monks in the 13th century. Beginning life in a very humble manner, local legend has it that a Derbyshire baker had a vision of the Virgin Mary, which told him to come to Dale Abbey and live the life of a hermit. He accordingly came to the area in 1130, carved himself a niche in the sandstone and devoted himself to the way of the hermit. The owner

Dale Abbey Ruins

To the north of the village of Dale Abbey is the Cat and Fiddle Windmill, built in the 18th century and a fine example of the oldest type of mill. The stone roundhouse is capped with a box-like wooden structure which houses the machinery and which is fitted onto an upright post around which it can rotate to catch the wind.

of the land, Ralph FitzGeremunde, discovered the baker and was so impressed by the man's devotion that he bestowed on him the land and tithe rights to his mill in Borrowash. In about 1200 the Augustinian canons founded **Dale Abbey** on the site, which lasted until the Dissolution of the monasteries in 1538.

The sandstone cave and the romantic ruined 40-feet-high window archway (all that now remains of the original Dale Abbey) are popular attractions locally and a walk around the village is both an interesting and pleasurable experience. Nearby **Hermit's Wood** is an ancient area of woodland with beech, ash, oak and lime trees. It is wonderful at any time of year, but particularly in the spring when the woodland floor is covered with a carpet of bluebells.

The **Parish Church of All Saints**, which dates back to the mid-12th century, must be the only church in England, which shares its roof with a farm. The church has a pulpit that dates from 1634 and the whole interior appears rather crammed with its box pews and open benches. The farmhouse was once possibly used as an infirmary for the Abbey and then as an inn. The adjoining door was blocked up in the 1820s to prevent swift transition from salvation to damnation.

STANLEY

3 miles SW of Ilkeston off the A609

Stanley is a pleasant little rural village, whose main industry was coal mining until the closure of Stanley colliery in 1959.

The Parish Church of St Andrew dates originally from the 12th century, though all that remains of this Norman building nowadays is the south door. Some of the buttresses and a small lancet date from the mid 1200s. The font dates back to the 1300s, and the pulpit from the 17th century. A brass tablet on the floor by the pulpit is dedicated to Sir John Bentley of Breadsall, who was buried here 20 years before the Civil War.

STANTON BY DALE

2 miles S of Ilkeston off the A6096

Stanton by Dale is mentioned in the *Domesday Book* and derives its name from the nearby stone quarries. The houses in the village are mainly 18th and 19th century brick or stone, built to house the workers of the Stanton Ironworks, which still continues to provide employment as Stanton PLC. The village pump, erected in 1897 to commemorate Queen Victoria's jubilee, had fallen into a sad state of dilapidation. It is now repaired, completely renovated and returned to its original green and gold. The **Parish Church of St Michael and All Angels** is 13th century in origin but there is a fine modern stained glass window depicting Stanton Ironworks. The **Middlemore Almshouses** were built to accommodate 'eight poor people'.

SANDIACRE

4 miles S of Ilkeston off the B5010

Sandiacre is situated on the border with Nottinghamshire. Although it has been all but incorporated into the ever-expanding Nottingham conurbation, it maintains many village features including the picturesque 14th century **Parish Church of St Giles**, situated up a narrow lane at the top of a hill. In the churchyard, four stones commemorate the remarkable Charlton family. One was an MP as far back as 1318. Sir Richard was slain on Bosworth field. Sir Thomas was Speaker in 1453. Edward was a commissioner in the Civil War.

RISLEY

4 miles S of Ilkeston on the B5010

This small village has become a quiet backwater now that the main Derby to Nottingham A52 road bypasses it to the south. Apart from ribbon building along the former main road, Risley consists of no more than a small group of old buildings, but they are unique and well worth a visit. In 1593, Sir Michael Willoughby started to rebuild the **Parish Church of All Saints**. Although small, even by the standards of the day, it is charming and essentially Gothic in style. In the same year his wife

Stanton by Dale

founded a school and, although none of the original school houses exist, those seen today date from the early 18th century and were constructed by a trust founded by the family. The central school building is a perfect example of the Queen Anne style and acted as both the school and school house, with the boarders sleeping in the garrets. The trustees still maintain this wonderful building, along with the Latin School of 1724, the English School of 1753 and another School House built in 1771.

Nothing now remains of the original Risley Hall, home of the Willoughbys, except an Elizabethan gateway. The present one dates from the late 17th century. The 12-acre **Risley Hall Gardens** are open to the public.

---

135 ALL SAINTS CHURCH

Dale Abbey

Little altered since 1650, this fascinating little church has some interesting features and still holds regular services.

see page 254

133

Historical research has discovered that Ockbrook may have been a pagan religious site well before The Parish Church of All Saints' Church. It became the parish church in the mid 1500s and its most interesting features include a Saxon font, the 12th century tower, some fine windows and the oak chancel screen dating from around 1520.

OCKBROOK

4 miles SW of Ilkeston off the A52

This quiet village close to, but hidden from, the busy main road between Derby and Nottingham, is well worth a visit. The old part of Ockbrook was established by Occa, an Anglo-Saxon, around the 6th century. The village is unusual in that, in the mid-18th century, a Moravian Settlement was founded here by the Moravian Church in about 1750. The settlement has several fine buildings, including **The Manse**, built in 1822, and the handsome **Moravian Chapel**. Within the settlement there is also a girls' boarding school.

This is farming country and many of the ancient hedgerows remain, sustaining all manner of wildlife that has disappeared from many other areas. Several old farm buildings also remain, including an impressive 17th century timber-framed building at Church Farm. Little but the ground floor however, remains of **Ockbrook Windmill**, one of only 10 windmill sites extant in Derbyshire.

BORROWASH

6 miles SW of Ilkeston off the A6005

Close to the River Derwent, this once quiet place, separated from its neighbour, Ockbrook, by the main Derby to Nottingham road, has developed into a commuter village. Pronounced 'borrow-ash', the village has lost its railway station and canal, which was filled in during the early 1960s. P H Currey designed the small redbrick **Parish Church of St Stephen** in 1899. The interior features a low, 18th century ironwork chancel screen, believed to be the work of Robert Bakewell of Derby. The communion rail is said to have come from the 18th century **Hopwell Hall**.

SPONDON

5 miles SW of Ilkeston on the A6096

This village, with many Georgian brick houses, is now almost engulfed by Derby, but the older parts can still be picked out. The **Parish Church of St Werburgh**, damaged by fire in 1340, was completely rebuilt and has also undergone restoration work in 1826 and again in the 1890s. Nearby is **Locko Park**, the privately owned ancestral home of the Drury-Lowe family since 1747, when it was purchased from the Gilberts by John Lowe. In 1790 it passed to William Drury, who changed his name to Drury-Lowe. The present hall was built by Francis Smith in the mid 1700s, and since then it has been given an Italian appearance. Today, the hall houses one of the largest private collections of Italian paintings in Britain. The chapel is earlier than the hall, having been built in 1669. Way back in medieval times a leper hospital stood here, and indeed the word 'Locko' comes from the Old French 'loques', meaning rags.

BREASTON

5 miles S of Ilkeston on the A6005

On the southern borders of the county, close to Nottinghamshire and Leicestershire, Breaston occupies the flat countryside near the point where the River Derwent joins the River Trent. The mainly 13th century **Parish Church of St Michael** boasts the 'Boy of Breaston' - a small, chubby-faced child, immortalised in the 13th century by the mason of the nave arches. He has smiled down on worshippers and visitors for the past seven centuries. The story has it that this boy would come in and watch the masons at work while the church was being built. The master mason decided to make the child part of the church, so that he could always have a good view of it.

The now drained **Derby Canal** passed through the village at one time. The basin where the narrowboats were turned can still be seen.

DRAYCOTT

7 miles S of Ilkeston on the A6005

Having strong connections with the Nottingham lace trade, Draycott's **Victoria Mill** was built in 1888 and established as one of the most important lace factories in the world. The four-storey building, with its green-capped ornamental clock tower, still dominates the Draycott skyline though it is now the home of an electrical component manufacturer. **Draycott House**, designed by Joseph Pickford, was built in 1781. It remains a private residence.

ELVASTON

8 miles SW of Ilkeston on the B5010

Elvaston is gathered around the edge of the **Elvaston Castle** estate, one time home of the Earls of Harrington. The magnificent Gothic castle seen today replaced a 17th century brick and gabled manor house, parts of which can be seen on the end of the south front. Designed by James Wyatt, the castle was finished in the early 19th century but, unfortunately, the 3rd Earl died in 1829 and had little time to enjoy his new home. It is now owned by Derbyshire County Council.

It is, perhaps, the grounds, which make Elvaston Castle famous. They were originally laid out and designed for the 4th Earl by William Barron. Barron, who was born in Berwickshire in 1805, started work in 1830 on what, at first, appeared to be an impossible task. The 4th Earl wanted a garden 'second to none', but the land available, which had never been landscaped, was flat, water-logged and uninspiring with just two avenues of trees and a walled kitchen garden (but no greenhouses or hot houses). First draining the land, Barron then planted trees to offer shelter to more tender plants. From there the project grew.

In order to stock the gardens, Barron began a programme of propagation of rarer tree species and, along with the tree-planting methods he developed specially to deal with Elvaston's problems, his fame spread. The gardens became a showcase of rare and interesting trees, many to be found nowhere else in Britain. Barron continued to work for the 5th Earl, but resigned

Coffins had to be carried to neighbouring Church Wilne for burial up until the early 1800s, as there was no burial ground at Breaston until that time. For this reason the footpath over the fields of Wilne continues to be known by villagers as the 'Coffin Walk'.

135

Trent and Mersey Canal, Shardlow

136 THE NAVIGATION INN

Shardlow

A pub which sits close to the Shardlow Marina and which serves good ale and great food.

see page 255

provide details.

The **Parish Church of St Bartholomew** dates from the 13th century, with later additions. There is a monument to the 3rd Earl of Harrington, who brought the Golden Gates to Elvaston, dating from 1829. It was the work of the Venetian Antonio Canova, and one of only three in England.

SHARDLOW

9 miles SW of Ilkeston off the A6

in 1865 to live in nearby Borrowash and set up his own nursery. Now owned by Derby County Council, the gardens, after years of neglect, have been completely restored and the delights of the formal gardens, with their fine topiary, the avenues and the kitchen garden can be enjoyed by all visitors to the grounds, which are now a Country Park.

As well as fine formal gardens and the walled kitchen garden, there are gentle woodland walks and, of course, the man-made lake. However, no visit to Elvaston would be complete without a walk down to the **Golden Gates**. Erected in 1819 at the southern end of the formal gardens, the gates were brought from the Palace of Versailles by the 3rd Earl of Harrington. Little is known of the gates' history, but they remain a fine monument and are the symbol of Elvaston. Around the courtyard of the castle can be found a restaurant as well as an information centre and well-stocked gift shop. All manner of activities take place from the castle, which can

Shardlow is located just within the Derbyshire border. There was a settlement here at the time of the *Domesday Book*, when the area belonged to the Abbey of Chester and the village was known as Serdelov. Shardlow was once an important port on the River Trent and a horse drawn ferry was used to cross the river. This was replaced in 1760 by a toll bridge and the stone giving the toll charges can still be seen on the roadside approaching the modern Cavendish Bridge. This replaced the old bridge, which collapsed in 1947.

After 1777, when the **Trent and Mersey Canal** was opened, Shardlow became a canal port, one of only a few in the country. With Liverpool, Hull and Bristol now linked by water, the warehouses here were quickly filled with heavy goods of all descriptions that could be carried at half the cost of road transport and with greater safety. Many of the homes of the canal carriers and their warehouses survive to this day and the port is now a modern marina, linked to the

River Trent, and filled with all manner of pleasure barges.

Many of the old cottages in Shardlow were swept away by 1960s development but some were saved when much of the canal side was designated a conservation area in 1978. There are still some fine houses remaining that were built by the wealthy canal merchants. **Broughton House**, built in the early part of the 19th century is just one example. The **Shardlow Heritage Centre** is housed in the earliest of the old canal warehouses, the Old Salt Warehouse, and has exhibitions and displays about Shardlow's heyday as a canal port. The outstanding **Shardlow Marina** covers 46 acres, of which the Marina itself covers 12 acres, set in beautiful rolling countryside. The marina has moorings for up to 365 boats, with berths available for up to 70-feet narrow and wide-beam boats.

The **Parish Church of St James**, though it looks much older, dates only from 1838, and sits on land given to the village by the Sutton Family of Shardlow hall.

ASTON-ON-TRENT

9 miles S of Ilkeston off the A50

Aston stands on the River Trent, marking the border between Derbyshire and Leicestershire. Aston's **Parish Church of All Saints** is mainly Norman, though there is plenty of evidence of Saxon masonry, notably in the northeast corner of the nave. There is an octagonal font dating from the 1200s inside the church, and a

moving, early 15th century alabaster tomb chest of a husband and wife holding hands, she with a small dog at her feet.

Aston Hall dates from 1753; much enlarged over the centuries, it was originally a fine Georgian mansion with no fewer than five bays and central Venetian windows. Ashton Lodge stands close to the heart of the village and was once the home of the Bowden family, who were lace makers. The main part of the house was dismantled and transported to the United States, while the rest was converted into flats.

CASTLE DONINGTON

10 miles S of Ilkeston off the A50

Castle Donington (pronounced Dunington) is just over the Leicestershire border on a hill above the Trent River. The castle from which Castle Donington takes its name is now merely a mound on the northern edge of the village. It was built in the 11th or 12th century, demolished in 1216, rebuilt later that century and was finally demolished in 1595. The oldest part of the **Parish Church of St Edward, King and Martyr**, dates back to 1200 but it was probably built on the site of an older Saxon church. The spire, rising to a height of 160 feet, is a landmark for miles around.

A 17th century stone farmhouse in the centre of Castle Donington is now a museum tracing its fascinating history. **Donington Park Museum,** on the edge of the racing circuit, boasts

137 MALT SHOVEL INN

Aston-on-Trent

An olde worlde pub in a picturesque village that offers good food and drink and a warm welcome.

see page 254

Castle Donington

138 THE CROSS KEYS

Castle Donington

A friendly village pub close to Castle Donington Race Circuit and East Midlands Airport that is noted for its real ales.

see page 255

the Grand Prix collection of more than 130 vehicles from motor racing history, most in working order. Vehicles on show include Ascari's Ferrari, Jim Clark's Lotus 23 and Nigel Mansell's Williams.

Close to the village stands **Nottingham East Midlands Airport**, originally a Royal Air Force base. It was purchased in the 1960s and soon became the main airport for the nearby conurbations of Derby, Nottingham and Leicester.

LONG EATON

7 miles SE of Ilkeston off the A52

Long Eaton, straddling the Derbyshire and Nottinghamshire border, has a history that goes back earlier than the 7th century. Lying close by the River Trent, the name came from the Anglo-Saxon 'Aitone' meaning town by the water. Visited by the Romans and settled by the Danes, the medieval village remained undisturbed for centuries. A national census of 1801 recorded that only some 504 people lived here.

The **Parish Church of St Lawrence**, according to local legend, dates from the time of King Canute, though it is more likely to be Norman in origin. At one time it was only a 'chapel of ease' for the main parish church in Sawley, but in 1868, when the church was largely rebuilt, it became a parish church in its own right.

It was the **Industrial Revolution** that transformed Long Eaton from a small market town into a boom town by the mid-19th century. The arrival of the railway in 1847 triggered the expansion, and the hosiery and lace making factories, escaping the restrictive practices in nearby Nottingham, brought employment for many and wealth for some. By the 1870s the population was recorded at over 3,000, doubling over the following 10 years. In 1915 construction began on the National Shell Filling Factory sited just over a mile away from Long Eaton's ancient market place. A staggering 19 million large shells were filled to aid the war effort, and it was not until there had been some 19 explosions at the plant, the worst with a death toll of 140, that the operation ceased.

The lace industry, forever associated with this area, gave way to furniture, narrow fabrics and electrical wiring manufacture which reflected the interests and activities of a stream of entrepreneurs drawn to the town. The most famous of these men was Ernest Tehra Hooley - lace maker, property dealer, builder, benefactor and company director. Hooley was responsible for the flotation of such well-known names as Dunlop, Raleigh, Humber and Bovril before he went bankrupt.

SAWLEY

8 miles SE of Ilkeston off the B6540

Situated close to the county border with both Nottinghamshire and Leicestershire, Sawley is an attractive village standing on the banks of the River Trent. Over 1,000 years ago a small collective of monks boated down the Trent from Repton to the green meadows of Sawley, where they built the **Parish Church of All Saints**. Much of the church we see today is 14th century, with a 15th century tower and spire and much 15th century timbering. The chancel arch is Saxon. The interior boasts an impressive group of monuments, a 600-year-old font, a 500-year-old screen, a Jacobean pulpit and 17th century altar table.

In the late 1400s the Bothes (or Booths) settled at Sawley in a house of which some of the timbers remain in the cellars of **Bothe**

Village Pump, Sawley

Hall, near the church. Sawley's most noted son was John Clifford. Born here in 1836, he became one of the most powerful voices of nonconformity, known as 'the greatest Free Churchman of his day'.

Sawley Marina, with over 600 moorings, has been described as the 'most sophisticated ' marina on the inland waterways network, sitting as it does at the junction of four cruising routes. You can cruise from here all the way to the North Sea.

139 JOLLY SAILOR

Hemington

A superb village pub that combines olde worlde charm with a modern, airy feel, and which serves great food and drink.

see page 256

Derbyshire Coal Mines

This area of northeast Derbyshire centres around Chesterfield. This was the heart of the county's coal mining area, and many of the towns and villages reflect the prosperity the mines brought in Victorian times. Sadly, the vast majority of the collieries are now closed, and visitors today will be surprised at the wealth of history and fine architecture to be seen throughout the region. Geologically this area makes up one of Derbyshire's four distinct regions, with sandy coal east of Derby and

Chesterfield and a band of magnesium limestone around Bolsover and Whitwell.

Sometimes overlooked, this part of the county is well worth exploring, and there are many new and interesting sights and attractions to discover. The ancient custom of well-dressing is just as popular and well-executed here as elsewhere in the county, plus there are curiosities such as a 'castle that isn't a castle despite its battlements, a church clock that has 63 minutes in an hour and an Italian-style garden in the grounds owned by a famous English family', according to the North East Derbyshire District Council. The area boasts two exceptional Norman churches, at Steetley (near Creswell) and Ault Hucknall.

Despite the fact that many of the places in and around Chesterfield only date from the Industrial Revolution, the area is rich in history. From medieval times this has been an area of trade, and the weekly markets were an important part of the local economy. Though some have been lost over the years, most of these traditional centres and meeting-places remain.

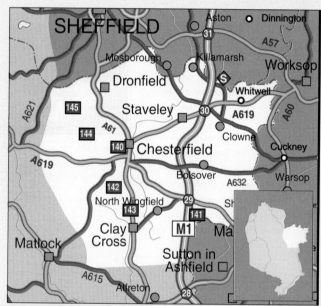

CHESTERFIELD

This friendly, bustling town on the edge of the **Peak District National Park** grew up around its open-air market, which was established over 800 years ago and claims to be England's largest. As the town lies at the crossroads of the country, the hub of trade routes from all points of the compass, the town's claim seems easily justified. Life in Chesterfield has revolved around this market since the town's earliest days. It was earning royal revenue in 1165, as the Sheriff of Derbyshire recorded in the Pipe Rolls and, in that year, the market earned the princely sum of £1 2s 7d for the Crown. The Pipe Roll of 1182 also mentions a fair in Chesterfield. Such fairs were large markets, usually lasting for several days, and drawing traders and buyers from a much wider area. Chesterfield's formal charter, however, was not granted until 1204, but this charter made the town one of the first eight free boroughs in the country. They escaped redevelopment in the 1970s, are as popular as ever and are held every Monday, Friday and Saturday, with a flea market each Thursday.

The town centre has been conserved for future generations by a far-sighted council, and many buildings have been saved, including the Victorian **Market Hall** built in 1857. The traditional cobbled paving was restored in the Market Place, and New Square was given a complete facelift. There are several Tudor buildings in the heart of Chesterfield, most notably the former Peacock inn which is now home to the **Peacock Heritage Centre** - built in 1500 for the wealthy Revell family, who later moved to Carnfield Hall near Alfreton. The black-and-white timbering in Knifesmithgate, however, was built only in the 1930s to resemble the famous rows in Chester.

Visitors to the town are drawn to a peculiarly graceful spire, reaching high into the skyline. Twisting and leaning, it is totally confusing to the eye. Recognised as one of Chesterfield's landmarks, the **Parish Church of St Mary and All Saints,** with its crooked spire, has dominated the skyline for so long that local folk have ceased to notice its unusual shape. Superstition surrounds it but, sadly, the real story of its unusual appearance has been lost over the years. The truth probably lies in the wake of the Black Death during the 14th century, when the people of Chesterfield were building their beautiful new church and awe-inspiring steeple.

140 COUNTY BAR AND RESTAURANT

Chesterfield

A lively, stylish bar/restaurant in the centre of Chesterfield that has a reputation even beyond the town itself.

see page 257

Crooked Spire of St Mary and All Saints

Chesterfield owes much of its prosperity during the industrial age to the great railway engineer George Stephenson. His home, Tapton House, lies just outside the town and it was to here that he retired and carried out his experiments in horticulture. Buried in Holy Trinity Church, where one of the windows was created in his memory, his death, in 1848, was announced by one local newspaper with the headline 'Inventor of Straight Cucumber Dies'.

Many must have fallen to the plague and, among them, skilled craftsmen who knew how to season wood.

The survivors built the spire out of green timber, which, over the years, has distorted under the heavy lead covering. However, some stories say it was the Devil who, pausing for a rest during one of his flights, clung to the spire for a moment or two. Incense from the church drifted upwards and the Devil sneezed, causing the spire to twist out of shape.

This magnificent spire rises to 228 feet and leans 9 feet 4 inches from the true, and is still moving. It is eight-sided, but the herringbone pattern of the lead slates trick the eye into seeing 16 sides from the ground. The spire is open most Bank Holidays and at advertised times; the church, the largest in Derbyshire, is open all year, Monday to Saturday 9am to 5pm (9am to 3pm January and February), and Sundays at service times only.

Opposite the church is **Chesterfield Museum and Art Gallery**, home to exhibitions depicting the story of the town, from the arrival of the Romans to the first days of the market town, the industry of the 18th century and the coming of the 'father of the railways', George Stephenson. The Art Gallery displays paintings by local artists such as Joseph Syddall (who lived at nearby Whittington).

In the heart of Chesterfield, **The Spread Eagle** stands opposite the new shopping mall in Beetwell Street. The premises date back some 400 years and once had stables to the rear - the archway where the carriages and carts used to pull in can still be seen. Once upon a time prisoners would be held in the cellars here when the police station cells were full. The old police station used to stand across the road, in what is now the library, and an underground tunnel linked the two buildings. The fine **Queen's Park** has delighted locals and visitors alike since it was opened in Victorian times. There are gardens, a boating lake, children's play area, and occasionally it is used for county cricket.

Perhaps surprisingly, Chesterfield is home to one of the earliest canals in the country, the **Chesterfield Canal**. After seeing the success of the Bridgewater Canal in 1763, the businessmen of Chesterfield, which was at the start

Chesterfield Market

of its rapid expansion, looked to link the town with the River Trent via Worksop and Retford in Nottinghamshire. Construction work began in 1771, just a year before its builder, James Brindley, died while surveying the Cauldon Canal. The biggest engineering project along the length of the new canal was the Norwood Tunnel, which took four years to build. The tunnel was officially opened on 9th May 1775. It was 2,884 yards long, 9 feet 3 inches wide and 12 feet high. The entire canal was officially opened in 1777.

The most famous item carried on the canal was stone to rebuild the Houses of Parliament in the 1840s. The stone was loaded into canal boats at Dog Kennels Bridge, carried to West Stockwith, and transferred to Trent sloops for the journey to Westminster, via the Humber, North Sea and the Thames. In October 1907 the roof of Norwood Tunnel collapsed, cutting the canal in two. Coal cargoes from Shireoaks colliery continued until the Second World War, but after that there was little boat traffic apart from brick cargoes from the kilns at Walkeringham. All the working boats on the Chesterfield Canal were horse-drawn until, by 1962, virtually all the boat traffic had gone. The whole length of the canal is in the process of restoration and is open to walkers and, though some sections border onto busy roads, much of the waterway runs through quiet and secluded countryside. The

Chesterfield

Chesterfield Canal Trust runs boat trips on the canal, and one of the boats has wheelchair access.

Finally, although the custom of tap-dressing took place in Chesterfield in the 19th century, it was not until 1991 that the tradition, this time of well-dressing, was revived. Initially with help from local experts from Holymoorside, the Chesterfield dressers are developing their own styles and customs and, while the well-

Despite the growth of Chesterfield, Whittington has managed, on the whole, to retain its village centre, though one of its best buildings (apart from Revolution House), Manor Farm, was demolished in the 1970s. However, the farm's barns still survive and can be found to the west of the Parish Church of St Bartholomew, built in 1896 after the previous church, which itself replaced the original Norman church in 1865, was burnt down.

dressing at the Peacock Centre takes its inspiration from buildings, their colleagues at St Mary and All Saints Church follow the theme of the stained glass windows within the church.

AROUND CHESTERFIELD

SHEEPBRIDGE
3 miles N of Chesterfield off the A61

Dunstan Hall, below Newbold Moor, was built in the 17th century and extended in the 18th century. In an excellent parkland setting, the Gothic style park railings mirror the Gothic revival details that were added to the hall in 1826.

WHITTINGTON
3 miles NE of Chesterfield off the B6052/A61

During the 17th century, **Revolution House**, a tiny cottage with thatched roof, flower border and charming garden gate, was part of an alehouse called the Cock and Pynot ('pynot' being the local dialect word for magpie). It was here, in 1688, that three local noblemen - the Earl of Devonshire, the Earl of Danby and John D'Arcy - met to plan the events which led to the overthrow of James II in favour of his daughter Mary and her husband, William of Orange. The Glorious Revolution took place later in the same year, and it was in the year of its 250th anniversary that this modest house was turned into a museum. Both the 100th and the 200th anniversary of the revolution were keenly celebrated here.

Revolution House is now open to the public and features period furnishings and a changing programme of exhibitions on local themes. A video relates the story of the revolution and the role which the house played in those fraught and dangerous days.

ECKINGTON
6 miles NE of Chesterfield off the A616

This large, sprawling village built of local Derbyshire stone, lies close to the Yorkshire county border. The name Eckington is of Saxon origin, meaning the township of Ecca. In medieval times it was a small but important settlement, whose main occupations were farming and then mining. Since the decline of coal mining in the late 20th century, several light industries have become established and much farmland has been lost.

The **Parish Church of St Peter and St Paul** dates from 1100 and still retains the original Norman doorway. In a field at the back of the church, near the river, stands the Priest's Well where the parish priest used to draw water, as did the travelling people who used the field as a camp until the 1930s.

The Sitwell family had their home, **Renishaw Hall**, close by, situated midway between Eckington and neighbouring Renishaw. It was built by George Sitwell in 1625 after he had re-established his fortune with the success of the Renishaw Iron Works. The massive house was greatly transformed under the first baronet, Sir Sitwell Sitwell, and in the grounds can be found the world's most northerly vineyard. The Sitwell family and, in particular, Dame Edith, Sir Sacheverell and Sir Osbert, have, over the years, become famous for their literary leanings - perhaps there is something in the wine that promotes success in this field!

The Hall is also said to be haunted by a number of ghosts. In particular there is the little boy in pink, known as the kissing ghost because it seems that this is just what he likes to do to any guests at the Hall. The grounds of the village rectory, a handsome late-Georgian building, are also worth a second glance. Though not laid out by the Reverend Christopher Alderson, he set about improving them in the late 18th century. A magazine of the time said that the Reverend 'was so renowned as a garden improver that he was employed at Windsor aswell'.

Renishaw Hall

RENISHAW
6 miles NE of Chesterfield off the A616

The village lies close to the Sitwell family home and was the site of the family ironworks, which helped to re-establish their fortune.

STAVELEY
4 miles NE of Chesterfield off the A619

Staveley lies to the south of the great **Staveley Iron Works** and has its fair share of large 20th century housing estates. However, this is not altogether a modern village and has some fine earlier structures, including the **Parish Church of St John the Baptist**, dating originally from the 13th century. In the north aisle is a rare example of a medieval Easter Sepulchre. The name of Frecheville is one that crops up from time to time in this part of Derbyshire, and the church has a selection of tombs and monuments to the family. As well as the tomb-chest of Peter Frecheville, dating from around 1480, there is also an early 16th century monument to Piers Frecheville. In the Frecheville Chapel is a memorial to Christina Frecheville, who died in childbirth in 1653. Another fine building in the village is **Staveley Hall**, built in 1604 and now the District Council Offices.

BARLBOROUGH
7 miles NE of Chesterfield off the A619

Lying close to the county borders with both Nottinghamshire and Yorkshire, this village still retains its manor house. Lying just north of the village centre, **Barlborough Hall** (private) was built in 1584 by

The custom of well-dressing in Barlborough was started anew in 1975 when the Young Wives' Group produced a modest picture to dress the village well for St James' Day (25 July). From such humble beginnings, well-dressing in Barlborough is now an annual event that coincides with the church flower festival.

Lord Justice Francis Rodes to plans drawn up by the designer of Hardwick Hall, Robert Smythson. Those who visit both houses will notice the strong resemblance. As well as building houses, Rodes was also one of the judges at the trial of Mary, Queen of Scots. The Hall is supposed to be haunted by a grey lady, said to be the ghost of a bride who received the news of her groom's death as she was on her way to the village church. Barlborough Hall should not be confused with **Barlborough Old Hall**: this is an easy mistake to make as Barlborough Old Hall is actually the younger of the two! Built in 1618, as the date stone over the front door states, the Old Hall is of a large H-plan design and has mullioned windows.

Although there is a lot of new development, particularly around Barlborough Links, the village also boasts some fine old stone houses with pantile roofs. The **Parish Church of St James** dates from the beginning of the 13th century, though it was heavily restored in 1899. Among the medieval work extant is the four-bay north arcade. The church contains the effigy of a grieving woman, said to be Lady Furnival, who died in 1395. The monument was probably brought here from Worksop, where she is buried.

The **Market Cross**, which stands in the High Street, bears testimony to the fact that this was an important place at one time - a centre of trade for the surrounding area.

CLOWNE
7½ miles NE of Chesterfield off the A616

This small town has grown up around the county's coal mining industry though, away from the centre, the part-Norman **Parish Church of St John the Baptist** can still be seen. The village is now mainly residential, but retains its own identity and sense of community. It is well known locally for its dazzling Christmas lights display.

CRESWELL
9 miles E of Chesterfield on the A616

Once a sleepy hamlet nestling amid peaceful farming country, the character of Creswell was irreversibly changed at the end of the 19th century. It was then that Creswell Colliery was opened, and now the village is one of the biggest in the county. There is also a village within a village here as, between 1896 and 1900 a model village of houses and cottages was built around a green. The **Model Village** was built by the Bolsover and Creswell Colliery Company in 1896 to house the workforce at the Creswell Colliery, and everybody who lived on the Model worked in the coal mine. It remained as housing for miners until the mid 1980s when they were let on the open market. The houses were neglected, repairs were not done and the area became run down. Now with the help of a lottery grant, the central park has been almost restored to its original Victorian state with newly planted trees and shrubs, seating and play areas. Many of the houses around the green have been restored and renovated and more will be restored in the next phase. The restored Model Village is an excellent example of Victorian social housing for working families.

Lying close to the Derbyshire-Nottinghamshire border, the limestone gorge of the **Creswell Crags** is well worth seeing. Formed thousands of years ago by river erosion which cut through the limestone, this rock, which is porous and subject to erosion underground as well as on the surface, contributed to the forming of natural chambers. The subterranean movement of water created a vast network of caves, which were subsequently exposed. Used by Neanderthal man as shelters while out hunting, tours can be taken from the visitor centre, where there is also a display of artefacts found in the area. Testimony to the artistry of the later inhabitants of these caves was the discovery of a bone carved with the head of a horse, which is about 12,000 years old, and can now be seen in the British Museum. The largest cavern, Church Hole Cave, extends some 170 feet into the side of the gorge; it was here that hand tools were found.

Steetley Chapel

WHALEY

8 miles E of Chesterfield off the A632

The **Whaley Thorns Heritage Centre**, situated in a disused school, tells the story of human activity in the area from the Stone Age to the present day. In particular there are displays illustrating the history of coal mining in this region of Derbyshire and, since the decline of the industry, the efforts that have been made to restore the area to its natural state.

BOLSOVER

7 miles E of Chesterfield off the A632

The approach to Bolsover from the north and east is dominated by the splendid, sandstone structure of **Bolsover Castle**, which sits high on a limestone ridge. A castle has stood here since the 12th century, though the present building is a fairytale 'folly' built for Sir Charles Cavendish during the early 1600s on the site of a ruined castle. By the mid-18th century much of the building had been reduced to the ruins seen today, though thankfully the splendid keep has withstood the test of time.

Pevsner remarked that not many large houses in England occupy such an impressive position

Not far from the village of Cresswell and close to the county border with Nottinghamshire is Steetley Chapel, or the Chapel of All Saints, thought by many to be the most perfect specimen of Norman architecture in Britain. Whether this is so or not, the elaborate chapel, no more than 52 feet long by 15 feet wide, has a rare and unique beauty. Having lain derelict for many years after being desecrated during the Commonwealth, the Chapel of All Saints was restored in the 1880s and at this time some of the wonderful carvings to be seen in the porchway were re-created. Luckily much of the interior remains intact, having survived the test of time. It remains a mystery as to why such a small building should be given such elaborate decoration in the mid-12th century.

Bolsover Castle

The town of Bolsover is industrial, dominated for many years by coal mining, and at one time famous for the manufacture of buckles. The Hudson Bay public house across the road from the castle recalls in its name the fact that it was originally built by Peter Fidler, a Bolsover man, who was a distinguished surveyor with the Hudson Bay Company in Canada during the 18th century. A Peter Fidler Society exists in Canada to this day. Bolsover's oldest public house is probably The White Swan, and is said to have served as the moot hall from the Middle Ages to the early 19th century. Bolsover was granted its market charter by Henry III in 1225.

as Bolsover Castle, as it stands on the brow of a hill overlooking the valley of the River Rother and Doe Lea. The first castle at Bolsover was built by William Peveril, illegitimate son of William the Conqueror, as part of his vast Derbyshire estates. Nothing remains of that Norman building. Now owned by English Heritage, visitors can explore the Little Castle, or Keep, which is decorated in an elaborate Jacobean celebration with wonderful fireplaces, panelling and wall paintings. The series of remarkable rooms includes the Vaulted Hall, the Pillar Room, the Star Chamber, the Elysium and the Heaven Room. Sir Charles' son, William, was responsible for the eastern range of buildings known as the Riding School, an impressive indoor area built in the 17th century, and the roofless but still impressive western terrace. The ruins of the state apartments are also here to be discovered. The whole building later descended to the Dukes of Portland, and it remains a strangely impressive place. However it is threatened by its industrial

surroundings. The legacy of centuries of coal mining beneath its walls is subsidence.

Naturally, the **Parish Church of St Mary's** in Bolsover holds many monuments to the Cavendish family, but it seems amazing that the church has survived when its recent history is revealed. Dating from the 13th century, the church's monuments include two magnificent tombs to Charles Cavendish, who died in 1617, and Henry Cavendish, who died in 1727. Destroyed by fire in 1897, except for the Cavendish Chapel, St Mary's was rebuilt, only to be damaged again by fire in 1960. It has since been restored. Buried in the churchyard are John Smythson and Huntingdon Smythson, the 17th century architects probably responsible for the design of the rebuilt Bolsover Castle.

SCARCLIFFE

8 miles E of Chesterfield off the B6417

Scarcliffe, recorded as Scardeclif in the *Domesday Book*, takes its name from the escarpment of magnesium limestone on which the village stands. It was settled in Roman times evidenced by the collection of Roman coins found near the village in 1876. The **Parish Church of St Leonard** is Norman and contains a magnificent monument of a woman holding a child in her arms. Dating from the 12th or 13th century, the effigy is probably that of Constantia de Frecheville, who died in 1175. Known in Scarcliffe as Lady Constantia, a bell is tolled in her memory around Christmas. During the industrial revolution, coal mining was the main industry and the Lancashire, Derbyshire and East Coast Railway cut through the previously agricultural land. It included a tunnel between Scarcliffe and Bolsover. The Langwith Colliery closed in 1978 and the railway has long gone.

Poulter Country Park, created from the old colliery spoil heaps, provides scenic walks with excellent views of the surrounding countryside.

HEATH
5 miles SE of Chesterfield off the A617

To the north of Heath, overlooking the M1, are the ruins of what was one of the grandest mansions in Derbyshire, **Sutton Scarsdale Hall**. Built in 1724 for the 4th Earl of Scarsdale, to the designs of Francis Smith, the stonework of the previous Tudor manor house was completely hidden behind the Baroque splendour of the new hall. The magnificent Italian plasterwork can now be seen at the Philadelphia Museum in Pennsylvania, and demolition of the back of the house has revealed some Tudor brickwork. At the beginning of the 20th century Sutton Scarsdale was owned by a descendent of Sir Richard Arkwright, the famous industrialist. It is this gentleman that D H Lawrence is supposed to have chosen as the inspiration for his character of Sir Clifford Chatterley in the novel *Lady Chatterley's Lover*. The hall is supposed to have many ghosts.

Also close to Heath is the National Trust-owned **Stainsby Mill**, which at one time belonged to the Hardwick Estate. With its machinery now restored to illustrate the workings of a 19th century water-powered corn mill, Stainsby is well worth a visit. Though there has been a mill here since medieval times, the buildings seen today date from 1849 when the then new machinery was first fitted. The large (17-feet) cast-iron waterwheel, which, because of its particular design, is known as a high breast shot, not only provided power to turn the millstones but also for lifting sacks, cleaning the grain and sieving the flour. Open between the end of March and the end of October, visitors can watch the operations from a viewing gallery.

AULT HUCKNALL
6 miles SE of Chesterfield off the A617

The strange name of this village probably means 'Hucca's high nook of land', and this pleasant place, standing on a ridge close to the Nottinghamshire border, is home to

The Parish Church of All Saints in Heath dates from 1853. In the porch are two coffin slabs dating from the 11th or 12th centuries. They were found at the old church, the scant remains of which are about a quarter of a mile away.

Old Church Ruins, Heath

141 HARDWICK INN

Hardwick Park

One of England's oldest and most historic inns that served well kept real ales and good, honest food at affordable prices.

 see page 258

St John the Baptist Church, Ault Hucknall

the magnificent Tudor house, **Hardwick Hall**. 'More glass than wall', it is one of Derbyshire's Big Three stately homes alongside Chatsworth and Haddon, all three glorious monuments to the great land-owning families who played so great a role in shaping the history of the county. Set in rolling parkland, the house, with its glittering tiers of windows and crowned turrets, offers quite a spellbinding sight. Inside, the silence of the chambers strewn with rush matting, combined with the simplicity of the white-washed walls, gives a feeling of almost overwhelming peace. The letters E S can be seen carved in stone on the outside of the house: E S, or Elizabeth of Shrewsbury, was perhaps better known as Bess of Hardwick. This larger-than-life figure had attachments with many places in Derbyshire, and the story of her life makes fascinating reading.

She was born in the manor house at Hardwick in 1520. The house stood only a little distance from the present-day hall and was then not much more than a farmhouse. The young Bess married her neighbour's son, Robert Barlow, when she was only 12. When her young husband, himself only 14, died a few months later she naturally inherited a great deal of property. Some 15 years later she married Sir William Cavendish and, when he died in 1557, she was bequeathed his entire fortune. By this time she was the richest woman in England, save for one, Queen Elizabeth.

The Gallery at Hardwick Hall, with its gorgeous lavender-hued tapestries, has, in pride of place, a portrait of this formidable woman. It depicts a personage who could be mistaken for Queen Elizabeth, and indeed they were both forceful, independently-minded women. Bess began the building of the house in 1590, towards the end of her life and after her fourth lucrative marriage to George Talbot, sixth Earl of Shrewsbury. It stands as a monument to her wealth and good taste, and is justly famous for its magnificent needlework and tapestries, carved fireplaces and friezes, which are considered as among the finest in Britain. She died in 1608, and now lies within Derby Cathedral.

Though Bess is the first person that springs to mind with regard to Hardwick Hall, it was the 6th Duke of Devonshire who was responsible for the hall's antiquarian atmosphere. He inherited the property in 1811 and, as well as promoting the legend that Mary,

Queen of Scots stayed here, he filled the house with furniture, paintings and tapestries from his other houses and from Chatsworth in particular.

As well as viewing the hall, there are some wonderful grounds to explore. To the south are the formal gardens, laid out in the 19th century and separated by long walks lined with yew. One area has been planted as a Tudor herb garden and is stocked with both culinary and medicinal plants used at that time. Down in the southeast corner of the garden is the small Elizabethan banqueting hall, used as a smoking room by the 6th Duke's orchestra, as they were not allowed to smoke in the hall itself. There is also, to the back of the house, a lake and lime avenue. Owned by the National Trust, Hardwick Hall is a must for any visitor to Derbyshire and is certainly a place not to be missed. The parkland, which overlooks the valley of the Doe Lea as well as the M1, is home to an impressive herd of Longhorn cattle among the stag-headed oaks. The ruins of Hardwick Old Hall (English Heritage) also stand in the grounds, and are the remains of Bess's former Tudor mansion.

The **Parish Church of St John the Baptist**, situated on a back lane, is one of the finest in Derbyshire. Overlooking Hardwick Hall's beautiful parklands, with the square towers of Bess of Hardwick's great house in the distance, the battlemented church exterior does not prepare visitors for its dark, mysterious interior,

which reveals the church's much earlier origins. Though dating originally from Saxon times, there are many Norman features, including the north arcade, nave and the narrow arches holding up the rare crossing tower. There is more Norman work in the plain capitals of the north arcade.

There are several interesting tombs in the church, such as the large and detailed wall monument just below the east window to the first Countess of Devonshire, dating from 1627. On the floor in front is a simple black slab commemorating the influential and renowned philosopher, Thomas Hobbes - author of *The Leviathan* and *De Mirabilibus Pecci: Concerning the Wonders of the Peak* (the latter being one of the first accounts of the Seven Wonders of the Peak) - who died at Hardwick. A much simpler table in the north aisle commemorates Robert Hackett, a keeper of Hardwick Park who died n 1703. It reads: 'Long has he chas'd/The red and fallow deer/ But death's cold dart/At last has fix'd him here.'

WINSICK
2 miles S of Chesterfield off the A617

This charming hamlet is just a short drive from the centre of Chesterfield but retains a tranquil rural feel.

WINGERWORTH
3 miles S of Chesterfield off the A61

The village was settled in Anglo-Saxon times, and is recorded in the *Domesday Book*, as a community of

142 HUNLOKE ARMS

Wingerworth

A great inn with a fine reputation for food that sits in a village just off the A61 south of Chesterfield.

see page 259

Tibshelf has one strange claim to fame - England's very first inland oil well was sunk here. There had been coal mines here for over 650 years until the last two pits, Long Pit and Bottom Pit, closed 70 years ago. In 1891 over 2,000 men were employed in the village mines.

fourteen households. It expanded after the Middle Ages although until the 20th century the population never exceeded 500. The Hunlokes were the dominant family in Wingerworth from the reign of Queen Elizabeth I until 1920, acquiring nine-tenths of the land in the parish and becoming lords of the manor. The grand mansion of Wingerworth Hall, which they built in the early 18th century, was demolished in the 1920s. Olave, Lady Baden-Powell, first Chief Guide, was born here in 1889. The **Parish Church of all Saints**, although it retains some Norman and 13th century work, has had many additions. A tower was added around 1500 and a substantial extension in 1963.

GRASSMOOR

3 miles S of Chesterfield on the B6038

Originally named Gresmore ('Grey Copse') according to parish records of 1568, the main employment in the village was for many years coal mining, at Grassmoor Colliery. The first shaft was sunk in 1846 and officially opened in 1880. It closed 90 years later in 1970. The site of the colliery is now a country park and the start of a pleasant walk called the **Five Pits Trail**, a popular trail running between Grassmoor and Tibshelf, with eight miles of traffic-free walking and cycling. Originally created in 1971, the paths have been recently re-surfaced. There are many picnic sites along the way past the sites of the old pits, along the line of some of the old railways. Almost all traces of the pits have disappeared, although the head gear remains at Holmewood Pit.

PILSLEY

5 miles S of Chesterfield off the B6014

The Herb Garden in Pilsley, featured on the BBC TV programme *Country Gardens*, is one of the foremost gardens in the country. Consisting of four display gardens, the largest is the Mixed Herb Garden, boasting an impressive established parterre. The remaining three gardens are the Physic, the Lavender and the Pot Pourri, each with its own special theme and housing many rare and unusual species. Areas of native flowers and wild spring bulbs can be enjoyed from March to September. On the grounds there is also a lovely tea room serving such delicacies as lavender cake, rosemary fruit slice and cheese and herb scones. The **Parish Church of St Mary** dates from 1873, and was designed by local architect S. Rollinson.

TIBSHELF

6 miles S of Chesterfield on the B6014

Stretching from here north, to Grassmoor, the **Five Pits Trail** is a scenic route which passes the old collieries at Tibshelf, Pilsley, Alameda, Williamthorpe and Grassmoor. At first the idea of exploring these old coal workings may not appeal, but since their reclamation by Derbyshire County Council this is now an interesting and entertaining seven-mile walk. Suitable for walkers, cyclists and horse riders, the trail is lovely, and offers some splendid views.

With the closure of the pits, which had been largely developed since the middle of the 19th century, the land had fallen into disuse. With the help of the Countryside Ranger Service, Derbyshire County Council manages the trail together with a great deal of support from local groups who have contributed much time and effort to bring this land back to life. The clearing of paths and the addition of plantations, ponds and meadows has ensured that many species of wildlife have been encouraged to return here. Wild plants to look out for include the bush vetch, meadowsweet and the corn poppy. At one time these lovely wild flowers could be seen in abundance in many of Derbyshire's fields and hedgerows.

The **Parish Church of St John the Baptist** has been much restored over the centuries but it still retains an impressive 14th century tower.

CLAY CROSS

5 miles S of Chesterfield off the A61

This busy market town, situated on a high ridge, is largely a product of the Industrial Revolution. It developed after coal was discovered in the area, when George Stephenson was building a railway tunnel. It grew from a small farming community into an industrial town dominated by the Clay Cross Company. The Company also provided schools, churches and housing. An

impressive monument consisting of two large wheels with the inscription "In memory of all North East Derbyshire miners who lost their lives working to keep the home fires burning and the wheels of industry turning", takes pride of place in the High Street. The **Parish Church of St Bartholomew** dates from 1851, though it looks much older. The land on which it stands was gifted to the church by George Stephenson and Company. In 1972 the town earned the title "the Republic of Clay Cross", when left wing councillors, including David and Graham Skinner, both related to Dennis Skinner, MP for Bolsover, would not implement the terms of the Tory Housing Finance Act. The Clay Cross Rebels, as they became known, refused to put up council house rents by £1 a week. After a bitter dispute with the Government, which divided the community, they were surcharged, bankrupted and disqualified from office.

STRETTON

6 miles S of Chesterfield on the A61

Stretton village lies close to **Ogston Resevoir**, which covers an area of over 200 acres and is a favourite place for sailing. The man-made lake is overlooked by the romantic **Ogston Hall**, which dates from the 16th century and was the ancestral home of the Turbutt and Revell families. The house was altered extensively in 1768, and then modernised and 'medievalised' during Victorian times.

143 BATEMAN'S MILL COUNTRY HOTEL & RESTAURANT

Old Tupton

A hotel with a great reputation for its fine food which also has eight comfortable, fully en suite rooms on offer.

see page 260

BRACKENFIELD

7 miles S of Chesterfield off the A615

This village was known as Brackenthwaite in the Middle Ages, a name that means 'clearing in the bracken'. Like Clay Cross, Brackenfield is known today primarily for its proximity to the Ogston Reservoir, created in 1960 by damming the River Amber at the south end of the valley. The site of the former Ogston Mill was submerged under the rising waters. Hidden in the surrounding trees is the ruin of the former **Trinity Chapel**. The church is mentioned in the *Domesday Book*, but was abandoned when the new **Parish Church of the Holy Trinity** was built in 1856. A 15th century screen was removed from the chapel and brought to the new church.

ASHOVER

6 miles SW of Chesterfield off the B6036

Viewed from the southern rocky ridge known as **The Fabric** (apparently because it provided the fabric for much of the local building stone) and with the monolith of **Cocking Tor** in the foreground, Ashover can be seen as a scattered village filling the pleasantly wooded valley of the River Amber. The name of this village means 'ash tree slope' and though there are, indeed, many ash trees in the area, other varieties, including oak and birch, also flourish. Ashover was a flourishing industrial town in the past. As well as lead mining, which dated back to Roman times, there was nail making, lace, ropes, stocking weaving and malting. The ropes were said to be the longest and strongest in the country.

One part of the village is called the Rattle because of the sound of the looms rattling in the making of stockings. The industries, with the exception of quarrying and fluorspar have all died out and the work is now chiefly farming. Ashover lies just outside the boundary of the Peak District National Park but it still captures the typical character of a Peak village. At the heart of the largest parish in northeast Derbyshire, the village is chiefly constructed from limestone and gritstone, which were both quarried locally. The ruined shell of **Eastwood Hall**, once a large fortified Elizabethan manor house, also lies in the village. Owned, over the years, by several prominent Derbyshire families, including the Willoughbys, the house was blown up by the Roundheads during the Civil War. The Crispin Inn, next to the

Eastwood Hall Ruins, Ashover

154

church, claims to date from the time of Agincourt, 1415. However, it is far more likely that, like many other buildings in the parish, it dates from the 17th century. The inn's name reflects one of Ashover's traditional trades: St Crispin is the patron saint of shoemakers and cobblers.

The **Parish Church of All Saints,** with its 15th century tower, houses the alabaster tomb of Thomas Babington and his wife, said by many to be the best in Derbyshire. There are also some handsome brasses. What is surprising is the lead-lined Norman font, described by Pevsner as 'the most important Norman font in the country'. It is the only lead-lined font in an area that is so well known for its mining.

HOLYMOORSIDE

3 miles SW of Chesterfield off the A619

Surrounded by the attractive moorland of Beeley Moor and Eastmoor, and lying in the picturesque valley of the River Hipper, this scattered village has grown into a popular residential area for the nearby towns and cities. The custom of well-dressing in the village was revived in 1979 after a gap of about 80 years. Two wells are dressed, a large one and a smaller one for children, on the Wednesday before the late summer Bank Holiday in August.

The dressers follow the tradition of Barlow, where only flowers and leaves are used and not wool, seed and shells, though they do not stick to biblical themes. In

1990 the well-dressing depicted a scene commemorating the 50th anniversary of the Battle of Britain, one of their most spectacular dressings to date which resulted in photographs the national press.

The **Stone Edge Cupola**, in a remote spot beside the B5057, is Britain's oldest free-standing chimney. Dating from 1770, it is a testimony to the lead mining industry that survived here until the 19th century.

OLD BRAMPTON

3½ miles W of Chesterfield off the A619

Situated on a quiet road above a wooded valley, Brampton retains both its medieval church and its manor hall from the 16th century. The mainly 13th century **Parish Church of Saints Peter and Paul** is of interest for its battlemented walls, short octagonal spire and Norman doorway and window. Also worthy of note is the large cruck barn, probably the largest in Derbyshire, to be found at **Frith Hall Farmhouse.**

CUTTHORPE

4 miles W of Chesterfield off the B6050

Before the Second World War the well-dressings in this village, which take place on the third Friday in July, had no religious links. After the war the custom died out, but was revived again by three people from nearby Barlow, in 1978. The three dressed wells are blessed during a service of thanksgiving for the pure water.

Near the village are the three **Linacre Reservoirs**, set in an area

144 THREE MERRY LADS

Cutthorpe

An open, friendly pub that sells six real ales and has a fine reputation for its beautifully cooked and presented food.

see page 261

West of the village, Barlow Woodseats are not as uncomfortable as they sound for this is the name of an irregular gabled 16th century house, also called Woodseats Hall (private), which has a cruck barn in its grounds. It is home to the Mower family - Arthur Mower was the agent to the Barlow family in the 16th century, and kept a truly remarkable diary from 1555 to 1610. All 52 volumes are now kept in the British Museum. He records the death of Bess of Hardwick in 1608, recalling her as 'a great purchaser and getter together of much goods' and notes that she 'builded Chattesworth, Hardwick and Owlcotes'.

145 THE ANGEL INN

Holmesfield

A fine inn with a great reputation for its food. It is popular with both tourists and locals alike.

see page 261

of 200 acres within the attractively wooded Linacre Valley. Built between 1855 and 1904, until recently they supplied water to Chesterfield. Today the area is home to many species of fish, waterfowl, mammals and plant life, and is considered one of the most important ecological sites in the area. There are very pleasant walks, nature trails and fishing, and a scenic picnic area.

BARLOW

3 miles NW of Chesterfield on the B6051

Over a century ago, there were at least 14 coal mines and as many open cast sites in and around Barlow. Now the mining industry has gone completely, though it helped, over the years, to shape the village. It is mentioned in the *Domesday Book*, and was the home of Robert Barlow, the first of Bess of Hardwick's four husbands. Although situated outside the limestone area, Barlow has been dressing its main well for longer than most. It is not known for certain when the custom began in the village, though it is known that, like Tissington, the well here provided water throughout the drought of 1615; this may have marked the start of this colourful practice.

Another theory suggests that the tradition in Barlow could date back to the days of Elizabeth I's reign, as the church register of 1572 states that the festival of St Lawrence was celebrated. Whatever the origins of the well-dressings in the village, it is known that they

have continued, unbroken even through two World Wars, throughout living memory. The wells are dressed during the second week of August every year.

For those interested in Norman churches, the **Parish Church of St Lawrence** will be prove fascinating. It may appear to be Victorian, but this was the work of enthusiastic remodelling in the 1860s. The interior reveals the true Norman features - the doorways leading from the nave and the short chancel - and there is also a fine alabaster slab in memory of Robert Barley, who died in 1467, and his wife. (The village was originally known as Barley, and the family took their name from it, later changing it to Barlow.) Bess's husband Robert Barlow is also buried here.

HOLMESFIELD

4 miles NW of Chesterfield off the B6054

Holmesfield is an attractive village with its own flavour and rural tranquillity. The **Parish Church of St Swithin** was built in 1826 on the highest point of the village, giving spectacular views both north and south.

DRONFIELD

5 miles NW of Chesterfield off the A61

An important market town which has since developed industrially, there are some fine 17th and 18th century buildings in the town's conservation area. The **Peel Monument** dates from 1854, and commemorates Sir Robert Peel. **The Cottage**, close to the monument, dates from the 16th century, and is reputed to have been owned by Lord Byron, though he never visited it. The **Parish Church of St John the Baptist** has a fine perpendicular tower, though much of it is 14th century. South of the church is a fine **Cruck Barn**. **The Hall** is also worthy of a second glance as it has an attractive balustrade and a fine Queen Anne façade. In front of the early 18th century **Manor House**, now the home of the town library, is a highly elaborate **Town Cross**, erected to commemorate the repeal of the Corn Laws in 1846.

The prosperity of Dronfield in the early years of the Industrial Revolution was such that an unexpectedly large number of mansions were built in and around the town. Of those that remain today, **Chiverton House**, built in 1712, and **Rose Hill**, dating from 1719, are worthy of note.

To the east of the town can be seen a large group of 19th century coke ovens, once a common sight in this part of Derbyshire. The 48 seen here, arranged in two groups, were part of the Summerley Colliery complex; the tall engine house also survives.

Accommodation, Food & Drink and Places of Interest

The establishments featured in this section includes hotels, inns, guest houses, bed & breakfasts, restaurants, cafes, tea and coffee shops, tourist attractions and places to visit. Each establishment has an entry number which can be used to identify its location at the beginning of the relevant county chapter. This section is ordered by county and the page number in the column to to right indicates the first establishment in each county.

In addition full details of all these establishments and many others can be found on the Travel Publishing website - www.travelpublishing.co.uk. This website has a comprehensive database ocovering the whole of Britain and Ireland.

ACCOMMODATION

8	The New Soldier Dick, Furness Vale
15	The Old Nag's Head, Edale
16	The Rambler Country House Hotel, Edale
17	Causeway House, Castleton
19	Woodroffe Arms, Hope
20	Ye Derwent Hotel, Bamford
21	Ladybower Inn, Bamford
23	Robin Hood, Little Matlock
24	Ye Olde Bowling Green Inn, Bradwell
27	Millstone Country Inn, Hathersage
30	The Devonshire Arms Hotel, Baslow
31	The Jolly Sailor, Macclesfield
39	Sutton Hall, Sutton
45	Hargate Hall, Wormhill
46	Bull I'th' Thorn, Hurdlow
48	Merril Grove Cottages, Longnor
51	East Lodge Hotel & Restaurant, Rowsley
52	Duke of Wellington Country Inn, Matlock
55	Glendon Guest House, Matlock
56	Bradley House Hotel, Matlock
57	The White Lion Inn, Matlock
58	The Red House Country Hotel & Restaurant, Darley Dale
60	Blakelow Cottages, Winster
61	Temple Hotel, Matlock Bath
66	The Vaults, Wirksworth
69	The Green Man Royal Hotel, Ashbourne
70	White Hart Hotel, Ashbourne
73	The Black Horse Inn, Hulland Ward
75	Red Lion Inn, Hognaston
76	Knockerdown Farm, Carsington Water
78	Bluebell Inn & Restaurant, Tissington
82	Leehouse Farm, Waterhouses
84	Paddock House Farm Holiday Cottages, Alstonefield
85	Wolfscote Grange Cottages, Hartington
86	Biggin Hall Country House Hotel, Biggin-by-Hartington
91	The Abbey Inn, Leek
94	The Garden House, Cheddleton
97	Railway Inn, Froghall
101	The Maryland Bed and Breakfast, Alvaston
104	Culland Mount Farm, Brailsford
106	Boars Head Hotel, Sudbury
112	Ivy House Farm Guesthouse & Holiday Cottages, Stanton-by-Bridge
117	Robin Hood Inn & Glades Restaurant, Overseal
121	Latte Lounge, Ripley
125	The Pantheon Restaurant & Bar, Codnor
131	King William IV, Milford
132	Spotted Cow, Holbrook
133	Horsley Lodge, Horsley
143	Bateman's Mill Country Hotel & Restaurant, Old Tupton

FOOD & DRINK

1	White Lion, Buxton
2	Café Nats and the George, Buxton
3	The Kings Head, Buxton
4	The Old Sun Inn, Buxton
5	The Café @ The Green Pavilion, Buxton
6	The Hydro Café Tea Rooms, Buxton
8	The New Soldier Dick, Furness Vale
9	The Masons Arms, New Mills
10	The Duke of York, Romiley
11	Royal Oak Inn, Glossop
12	The Rainbow Bistro, Glossop
13	The Old Glove Works, Glossop
14	The Chieftain, Hadfield
15	The Old Nag's Head, Edale
16	The Rambler Country House Hotel, Edale
19	Woodroffe Arms, Hope
20	Ye Derwent Hotel, Bamford
21	Ladybower Inn, Bamford
22	The Castle Inn, Bolsterstone Village
23	Robin Hood, Little Matlock
24	Ye Olde Bowling Green Inn, Bradwell
25	New Bath Inn, Bradwell
26	Pool Café, Hathersage
27	Millstone Country Inn, Hathersage
28	The Eating House, Calver Bridge
30	The Devonshire Arms Hotel, Baslow
31	The Jolly Sailor, Macclesfield
32	Dolphin Inn, Macclesfield
33	Puss In Boots, Macclesfield
34	Jaspers, Macclesfield
35	The Rising Sun Inn, Rainow
37	Vale Inn, Bollington
38	Coffee Tavern, Pott Shrigley
39	Sutton Hall, Sutton
40	The Hanging Gate Inn, Higher Sutton
41	Farmers Feast, Bakewell
43	The Stables at Eyam, Eyam
46	Bull I'th' Thorn, Hurdlow
47	Horseshoe Inn, Longnor
49	Ye Olde Cheshire Cheese Inn, Longnor
50	The Old Smithy, Beeley
51	East Lodge Hotel & Restaurant, Rowsley
52	Duke of Wellington Residential Country Inn, Matlock
53	Country Cottage Restaurant, Matlock
54	The Horseshoe, Matlock
57	The White Lion Inn, Matlock
58	The Red House Country Hotel & Restaurant, Darley Dale
59	Tall Trees Coffee Shop & Restaurant, Two Dales
61	Temple Hotel & Restaurant, Matlock Bath
62	The Princess Victoria, Matlock Bath
65	Scotland Nurseries Garden Centre, Tansley

FOOD & DRINK

66	The Vaults, Wirksworth
68	Gallery Café, Ashbourne
69	The Green Man Royal Hotel, Ashbourne
70	White Hart Hotel, Ashbourne
71	Shoulder of Mutton, Osmaston
72	Cock Inn, Clifton
73	The Black Horse Inn, Hulland Ward
74	Tiger Inn, Turnditch
75	Red Lion Inn, Hognaston
77	Main Sail Restaurant, Carsington Water
78	Bluebell Inn & Restaurant, Tissington
80	Okeover Arms, Mappleton
83	Red Lion Inn, Waterfall
87	Fox and Goose, Foxt
88	Ye Olde Star Inn, Cotton
89	The White Lion , Leek
90	The Black Swan, Leek
91	The Abbey Inn, Leek
92	Den Engel Belgian Bar and Restaurant and El 4 Gats Tapas Bar, Leek
93	The Coffee Clique, Leek
95	Castro's Restaurant and Lounge, Cheddleton
96	The Hollybush Inn, Denford
97	Railway Inn, Froghall
98	Knot Inn, Rushton Spenser
102	Bluebell Inn , Kirk Langley
103	Black Cow, Dalbury Lees
105	Cavendish Arms, Doveridge
106	Boars Head Hotel, Sudbury
107	The Yard Café Bar & Restaurant, Swadlincote
108	New Inn, Woodville
109	Coffee Concept Internet Café, Woodville
110	The Three Horseshoes Inn, Breedon-on-the-Hill
111	Bay Tree Restaurant, Melbourne
113	Rising Sun, Willington
114	The Barley Mow, Church Gresley
115	Drum & Monkey, Castle Gresley
116	Shoulder of Mutton, Coton-in-the-Elms
117	Robin Hood Inn & Glades Restaurant, Overseal
118	Shoulder of Mutton, Oakthorpe
119	Sitwell Arms, Morton
121	Latte Lounge, Ripley
122	Eagle Tavern, Heage
123	Spanker Inn, Nether Heage
125	The Pantheon Restaurant & Bar, Codnor
126	Black Swan, Belper
127	The Railway, Belper
128	Traveller's Rest, Kilburn
129	Hunter Arms, Kilburn
130	The Railway, Shottle
131	King William IV, Milford
132	Spotted Cow, Holbrook
133	Horsley Lodge, Horsley
134	Three Horseshoes, Morley
136	The Navigation Inn, Shardlow

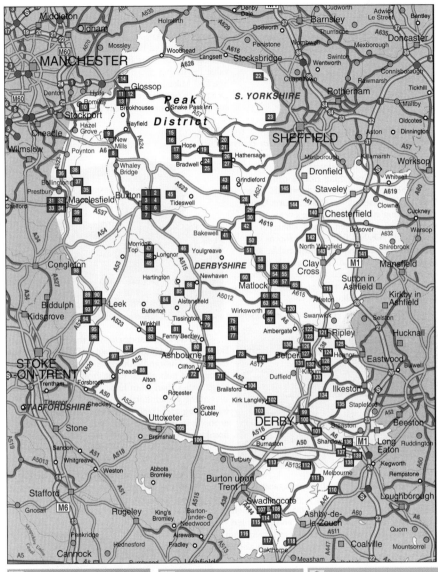

159

CAFÉ NATS AND THE GEORGE

Café Nats: 9/11 Market street,
Buxton, Derbyshire SK17 6JY
☎ 01298 23969
The George: The Square, Buxton,
Derbyshire SK17 6AZ
☎ 01298 24711

These two well known and well respected premises are in the heart of Buxton, and are well worth seeking out for their friendly atmosphere and great value for money. Both are owned and managed by Sue and Mike Jordan, who take a great pride in the two places popularity and the down-to-earth, competitive prices they offer to locals and visitors alike.

Café Nats is open Monday to Saturday from 10am to 10pm and 10am to 3pm on Sunday (closed on bank holidays). Here you can enjoy a drink, a snack or a full meal in surroundings that marry the traditional with the contemporary. Everything from a drink and light snack to a hearty meal is available. The Café is a member of the Peak Cuisine Group, and booking is advisable in the evenings. All the produce is sourced locally wherever possible. It also has five en suite rooms on offer, and all are cosy and comfortable, and available all year round. This makes it the perfect base from which to explore the Peak District National Park and the beautiful county of Derbyshire as well.

The George stands close to the famous Buxton Opera House, and parts of it date back to the 1600s. George Washington once stayed here, though the pub got its name from one of the kings rather than from him. The interior is everything a traditional pub should be - warm, welcoming and cosy. Traditional features such as exposed stone, low ceilings and handsome, open fireplaces combine with modern standards of service to create a pub that is well worth seeking out.

It has six real ales on offer at any one time, most coming from micro-breweries, and they are ever changing, the regular is Pale Rider. So make sure to visit more than once if you're a fan! The pub is also in the Good Beer Guide, and is open all day and every day. It sells good, honest English food that is immaculately cooked and presented. During the week, at lunchtimes, it is served until 3pm, and at weekends until 4pm. You can also eat in the evenings by prior arrangement. At least twice a week there is regular live entertainment, and you should ring for details.

This is a lively and cheerful pub that values tradition while still being committed to modern standards. The regulars (and there are many of them!) will offer you a very warm welcome. So come on in and enjoy a refreshing pint, or, if you're driving, a soct drink while chatting to the locals. You won't be disappointed!

2 WHITE LION

Spring Gardens, Buxton,
Derbyshire SK17 6BZ
☎ 01298 23099

The **White Lion** in Buxton is one of those pubs which you want to come back to again and again. It sits in the heart of Buxton, within a pedestrian precinct, and is close to all the town's amenities, including the famous Opera House. Parts of the building, which is of old, warm brick, dates back to 1661, and at one time it was a coaching inn. So there is the perfect mix of history, tradition and modern standards of service to make it the ideal place to enjoy a quiet drink if you're sightseeing, shopping or heading for a show.

The interior is equally as attractive, and continues the traditional theme. There are three bars, including one with pool tables, football table and wide-screen satellite TV for watching sports. The Tap Room is cosy and comfortable, while still having a spacious feel to it. There are two real ales available - Marston's Pedigree and Bitter, and they are kept immaculately by Ann Smith, who owns the place. Plus there is a great selection of beers, lagers, cider, spirits, wines and soft drinks.

Ann has been here since 1996, and she is determined to not only maintain the reputation of what is surely one of Buxton's finest pubs, but enhance it even further. She extends a warm welcome to old friends, and invites you to become a new friend by visiting her establishment and enjoying its wonderful ambience and great hospitality!

3 THE KINGS HEAD

Market Place, Buxton,
Derbyshire SK17 6EJ
☎ 01298 27719

The Kings Head in Buxton is a real find - a gem of a pub that sits in the market place of Buxton, one of the most historic towns in England. However, all is not what it seems here, for the pub was once a parsonage, and the elegant lines of the old building, with its bow windows, give a hint of its past purpose. Photographs and panels inside the pub explain its history. In charge is local man Wayne Mosley, who has been here nine years, and in that timer has created a pub that is friendly, welcoming and warm.

He keeps an excellent cellar of real ales, and there are normally two on offer - Marstons Bitter and Marston's Pedigree, with an occasional guest ale. Food is served from 12 noon to 9pm Monday to Saturday and 12 noon to 7pm on Sunday, and you can choose from the specials board or off

a menu. There is a separate Sunday carvery, and you are advised to book. The pub runs its own "curry club", and there are at least 12 different kinds offered each day. Plus Wednesday evening is steak evening, when you get a free pint of beer with your meal.

All credit cards with the exception of Diners and American Express are accepted, and there is occasional entertainment. There is a patio to the rear and a terrace to the side and front. The King's Head is disabled-friendly.

161

4 THE OLD SUN INN

33 High Street, Buxton,
Derbyshire SK17 6HA
☎ 01298 23452

Close to Buxton's market place stands a traditional inn that reflects the real warmth and character of the traditional English pub - **The Old Sun Inn**. It dates back over 400 years, and was once one of the main coaching inns in the town. With its whitewashed walls and window boxes, the exterior is charming and colourful, and here you can sit at a table in the evening and enjoy a perfect pint.

This is a pub that values its customers, and offers them six carefully kept real ales, including Marston's Bitter, Marston's Pedigree, Burton Bitter, Old Empire IPA, Banks and a rotating guest ale. Plus the food is exceptional. It is all home-cooked on the premises, and you can chose from the daily specials board or the menu. There are also sandwiches and light bites. Favourites here include the steak and stout pie, 10 oz gammon

steaks, juicy entrecote steaks and so much more to set your taste buds dancing! The dining room is non smoking.

Serving times are Monday to Friday 12 - 2.30pm and on Saturday and Sunday 12 - 4pm. In the evenings the times are 6.30pm - 9.30pm Monday to Thursday, 6.30pm - 10pm Friday and Saturday and 5.30pm - 8pm on Sunday. You are advised to book at weekends. The premises can be pre booked for visitors to the theatre in the evenings, and you should ring for details. Children are welcome up until 7pm, and credit cards are accepted, apart from Diners and American Express.

5 THE CAFÉ @ THE GREEN PAVILION

4 Terrace Road, Buxton,
Derbyshire SK17 6AW
☎ 01298 77480

Situated right in the heart of Buxton, the **Café @ The Green Pavilion** is the place to go for lunches, snacks, teas and morning coffee. It is open seven days a week from 8am to 5pm in winter and 7am to 6pm in summer. It is non smoking, and can seat 16 in complete comfort. The vast majority of the food, including the meals, snacks and baking, is home

made from local ingredients, ensuring freshness and flavour. The service is friendly and efficient, and the prices are always reasonable.

6 THE HYDRO CAFÉ TEA ROOMS

75 Spring Gardens, Buxton,
Derbyshire SK17 6BP
☎ 01298 79065

If you're looking for a place to eat, or just have a refreshing cup of tea or coffee, then **The Hydro Café Tea Rooms** is the place for you. It is almost an institution in Buxton, and well patronised by visitors and locals alike. The reasons aren't hard to find - quick friendly service, quality food at affordable prices and a warm, inviting atmosphere. It is open seven days a week, and you can choose from a

printed menu or a specials board. You'll find everything from breakfasts to full cream teas, and from paninis to salads. Don't miss it!

Buxton Road, Furness Vale, High Peak,
Derbyshire SK23 7PH
☎ 01663 743868
Mobile: 07977 234581
e-mail: maz@thenewsoldierdick.co.uk
or info@thenewsoldierdick.co.uk
⊞ www.thenewsoldierdick.co.uk

Without a doubt, **The New Soldier Dick** is the place in which to drink and dine in Derbyshire's High Peak district. It has earned an enviable reputation for its good food, its great selection of drinks and its comfortable, affordable accommodation. It is situated in Furness Vale, close to the A6, north of Whaley Bridge and south of New Mills.

This is an immaculately kept inn - the exterior is whitewashed, with hanging baskets, which present a pleasing display of colour in the summer months, and the interior has warm colours, warm wood and an atmosphere that is friendly and welcoming - what more could anyone want?

It is open all day every day, and offers three real ales - Marston's Pedigree, Jennings Cumberland Ale and a rotating guest ale. The food is famous throughout the area, and people flock to sample the magnificent cuisine. Head Chef Adrian Walsh has over ten years experience, and chooses only the finest and freshest of local produce wherever possible for his dishes. The spacious, no-smoking restaurant seats 38, and you are advised to book at weekends.

You can choose from printed menus or from a seasonally changing specials board. Dishes include such things as peppered sirloin and served with a mixed peppercorn sauce, chicken supreme, cheese and onion pie and possibly the best fish and chips you will ever taste. On Sunday roasts are added to the menu.

Food is served every day except Monday. From Tuesday to Saturday the times are from 12 noon until 3pm and from 6pm until 9pm. On Sunday it is 12 noon until 5pm. On the last Wednesday of each month there is a themed evening, for which booking is essential.

The New Soldier Dick also offers

accommodation, making this the ideal base from which to explore the Peak District. It has six superb, fully en suite rooms which are available all year round - two double, three twin and a single. You can book them on B&B basis. The New Soldier Dick is a friendly place where no one stands on ceremony. Once a week - either on Friday of Saturday evening - there is live jazz, and on Wednesday evenings there is traditional jazz. You should ring for details. Children are most welcome, and all credit cards with the exception of Diners and American Express are accepted. The restaurant and bar are disabled friendly, though you should phone about the accommodation.

7 BUXTON MUSEUM AND ART GALLERY

Terrace Road, Buxton,
Derbyshire SK17 6DA
☎ 01298 24658 Fax: 01298 79394
e-mail: buxton.museum@derbyshire.gov.uk
🌐 www.derbyshire.gov.uk

Explore the Wonders of the Peak through seven time zones. Discover when sharks swam in warm 'Derbyshire' seas; when lions and sabre tooth cats terrorised mastodons. Meet the Roman Legionaries, and the scientists unravelling the history of Earth. An audio tour, 'Time Moves On', helps to enhance your visit. For art lovers, enjoy intricate Ashford Black Marble inlay and Blue John ornaments, and a regular programme of exhibitions, featuring work by national and local artists, photographers and craftworkers. Activities for all the family accompany the exhibitions.

10 THE DUKE OF YORK

Stockport Road, Romiley,
Stockport SK6 3AN
☎ 0161 430 2806
e-mail: duke.of.york@btconnect.com
🌐 www.thedukeofyork.net

The **Duke of York** is a fine old inn on the banks of the Peak Forest Canal. It was originally a coaching inn, and now serves some of the best food and drink in the area. Landlord Jim Grindrod is also the chef, and is proud of the inn's traditional cuisine, which attracts

people from the whole area. He is also proud of the six real ales he serves, all beautifully kept. It is open all day, every day, with food being served from 12 noon to 2.30pm and 5pm to 10pm (except Sunday).

9 THE MASONS ARMS

High Street, New Mills, High Peak,
Derbyshire SK22 4BR
☎ 01663 744292

If it's a real, good, old-fashioned English pub you are looking for, then look no further than **The Masons Arms** in New Mills. It looks very picturesque, with its whitewashed walls, bow window and shutters. It dates back to 1838, and was once three cottages that have been converted into a warm, friendly place where traditional English hospitality still holds sway.

The place is popular with visitors and locals alike, and here you can relax and enjoy convivial times over a glass or two of real ale. In charge is mine host Vic Chappell, who keeps an immaculate cellar of three real ales - Robinson's Unicorn, Hatter's Dark Mild and a rotating ale. The well stocked bar also sells a great range

of beers, lagers, cider, wine, spirits, liqueurs and soft drinks. The interior is cosy and warm in winter and cool in summer, and there is always an inviting atmosphere.

There is occasional entertainment, and you should phone for details. Off road parking is available in a large car park, and there is also outdoor seating for those hot summer days!

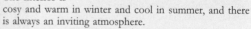

11 ROYAL OAK INN

Sheffield Road, Glossop,
Derbyshire SK13 8QY
☎ 01457 856879

The **Royal Oak Inn** is an outstanding inn situated right on the A57 on the outskirts of Glossop. It is a former coaching inn with stables and smithy. The building is of old, mellow stone, pleasantly proportioned and with ivy growing up its walls. The A57 is also known as the "Snake Road", as it leads to the famous "Snake Pass, which reaches a height of 1,680 feet and is one of the oldest turnpike roads in Derbyshire. It started at the Royal Oak, which was built in 1818 on the site of an old farm by the Duke of Norfolk. Joshua Shepley, son of a local farmer, was the first landlord.

The interior is warm and welcoming, with comfortable seating, glowing wood fittings, an open fireplace for the winter months and beamed ceilings. This is the place to enjoy a relaxing drink as you explore the marvellous Peak District. In fact, the inn is sometimes known as the "Gateway to the Peak".

Mine hosts are Jackie and Richard Madden, who between them have over 30 years experience in the licensed trade. They've been here over two years, and have continued to build on the inn's reputation for fine hospitality, good company, good drink and great food. It is open all day, every day, except for Mondays in winter, when it opens at 6pm.

The bar offers two regular real ales - Greene King PIPA and Ruddles County, plus there are occasional guest ales. Of course, there is also a great selection of other beers, lagers, cider, spirits, wines and soft drinks should you be driving.

Food is served from Wednesday to Saturday each week from 12 noon to 8pm, and from 12 noon to 6pm on Sundays. Everything is cooked on the premises by Jackie, who uses good, wholesome local produce. You can choose from the menu or the specials board. Starters include such dishes as prawn cocktail, garlic mushrooms or spicy potato wedges. For the main dish, you can choose such things as roast of the day, juicy steaks, steak and ale pie, home made lasagne, and so on. Everything is keenly priced and cooked to perfection. You can dine in the non-smoking restaurant, which seats 24, in the lounge, or outside in the summer months.

Children are very welcome until 8 pm, and all credit cards (except American Express and Diners) are accepted. Every Tuesday evening from 9.30pm there is a quiz, and on the second Thursday of each month a live band ("Dr Jelly") performs from 9pm. There is plenty of off road parking, plus there is a beer garden, and seating at the front of the inn.

12 THE RAINBOW BISTRO

The Basement, 14 High Street East,
Glossop, Derbyshire SK13 8DA
☎ 01457 865990

If you're looking for good food, great coffee and tea, and a place to recharge your batteries while exploring the Peak District National Park, then head for the **Rainbow Bistro** in Glossop. It can be easily found, tucked away in a quiet corner of the town, yet still close to all the amenities, and with a large car park to its rear.

Owner Alison McLeod took over here in August 2006, and has built on the restaurant's fine reputation. So much so that it has been getting 'rave reviews' for the quality and style of its cooking, and people are coming from miles away just to eat here. The interior is intimate, cosy and stylish, with good use being made of exposed brick, wooden floors, beams and polished wood tables and chairs. But for all its intimacy, it is also spacious, and there is plenty of room to stretch your legs and relax!

Alison has been a chef for over 20 years (including a stint as chef on the QE2!) so, as you would imagine, the food here is outstanding. The lunchtime menu has such favourites as hot and cold sandwiches, filled baguettes, jacket potatoes and omelettes (which are one of her most popular dishes). The evening menu includes such starters as Ceasar salad, filo prawns and soup of the day, while the main dishes include juicy steaks with all the trimmings, pork loin fillet, chicken chasseur, grilled salmon steak, mussels in a white wine and onion sauce, stilton and vegetable crumble, red pepper en croute, and so on. But even if it's just a refreshing cup of tea or coffee you're after, you will be made more than welcome!

Alison uses only the finest and freshest of local produce wherever possible, so you know you are getting food that has been prepared with imagination, flair and much thought. The bistro is non-smoking, and can seat up to 40 people in absolute comfort. Opening times are 10.30am to 2.30pm from Tuesday to Saturday, and 6pm to 9pm on evenings from Wednesday to Saturday. The premises are licensed, so you can enjoy a glass of wine with your meal.

Children are very welcome, and high chairs are available. All credit and debit cards with the exception of American Express and Diners Club are accepted. The bistro is disabled-friendly, as it is all on the one level.

So while in Glossop, make your way to the Rainbow Bistro and enjoy its great food and its warm, friendly atmosphere. You won't be disappointed!

166

Riverside Mill, George Street, Glossop,
Derbyshire SK13 8AY
☎ 01457 858432
e-mail: anybody@thegloveworks.co.
🌐 www.thegloveworks.co.uk

Just a few hundred yards from Glossop's main street, next to the river, is one of the best inns in the whole area - **The Old Glove Works**. This freehouse is located within a former mill, and its old brickwork, hanging baskets and high windows give it a jaunty air. The interior is equally attractive, with exposed brick, dark walls, warm, mellow wood and well-stocked bar.

Mine hosts are the husband and wife team of Sharon and Russell Dalton, who have been here since 1998, creating in that time a fine establishment that is popular with both locals and visitors alike. They are ably assisted in their efforts by a very popular member of staff - their English Mastiff, Boddington! At the rear is a patio area where you can relax over a welcoming drink during the summer months, and there is an equally attractive terraced area at the front which adds to the pleasing ambience of the place.

The inn is open from mid-Thursday until Sunday each week, and the spacious bar offers no less than six real ales, which are kept in tip-top condition. The two regulars come from the Copper Dragon and Howard Town

breweries, plus four rotating ales, one of which is always from a micro-brewery. So good is the ale that the inn has won an award from a national publican's magazine and has an entry in the Good beer Guide.

Russell is the chef, and wherever possible he uses only fresh local produce in his dishes. Food is served on Thursday and Friday from 12 noon until 2pm and on Saturday and Sunday from 12 noon until 3pm. 'Hot beef Fridays' take place every Friday evening from 5.30pm until 6.30pm, and there is a curry evening every Thursday from 5pm until 9pm. You can choose from six curries one being a

vegetarian option). If your party is over four, you are best to book for all meals. Thursday evening is a 'pling what you bring' evening, when you are invited to bring along a musical instrument (or just yourself if you want to sing!) for a musical jamming session that is always enjoyable. Every Friday and Saturday from 9.15pm there is an 'over 25s' disco. All major sporting events are shown on big screen TV (over 25s only).

All credit cards are accepted with the exception of Diners Club, and there is ample parking space.

Green Lane, Hadfield,
Derbyshire SK13 2DT
☎ 01457 86023
e-mail: jen-alan@hotmail.co.uk

Renowned as the real life "Royston Vasey", home to the hit TV series *The League of Gentlemen*, Hadfield sits off the A628 Manchester to Barnsley road. Here you will find **The Chieftain**, a superb pub that, since June 2006, has been managed by Jenny and Alan Hazlehurst, who have over 26 years experience in the licensing trade in places such as Yorkshire, Leicestershire, Nottinghamshire and so on.

This is an attractive looking, modern pub that has a real buzz about it since Jenny and Alan took over. It's exterior looks trim and attractive, with hanging baskets in the summer months, bow windows and an overall feeling of warmth. The open-plan interior is equally as attractive, and this, coupled with the warm welcome you will always get, makes it one of the friendliest pubs in the area. It is popular with both locals and visitors alike, and is the perfect place to have a quiet, relaxing drink or a beautifully cooked meal or snack.

It is open all day, every day, for some

of the best ales in the village. Four real ales are on offer, Hydes Bitter, Hydes Dark Mild and two top brewery guest ales each month. All are kept in immaculate condition. Other fine drinks, of course, are also available, such as beer, lager, cider, spirits, wines, liqueurs and, should you be driving, soft drinks.

Food is served from Monday to Thursday between 12 noon and 2pm and 5.30pm and 8.15pm. On Friday, Saturday and Sunday food times are 12 noon to 8.15pm. The dishes are all home-cooked on the premises by Jenny, using local produce wherever possible. There is a daily specials board, or you can choose of the printed menu. A popular dish in this pub is lamb shank, which Jenny cooks to perfection, and among the snacks, the filled baguettes are to die for! Every Sunday roasts are added to the menu, though you are wel advised to book in advance, so popular are they.

Thursday night is quiz night, and on Saturday evenings there is live music from 9pm. All credit cards, with the exception of Diners and American Express, are accepted, and children are most welcome. There are two superb beer gardens and plenty of off-road parking.

To find The Chieftain, turn south off the A628, and just before you reach Dinting Viaduct, turn left onto the road signposted for Hadfield and Longendale Trail. After a short distance, turn left again onto Green Lane. A short distance along it is the pub.

Grindsbrook, Booth, Edale, Hope valley,
Derbyshire S33 7ZD
☎ 01433 670291
e-mail: malkfrance@cbits.net
🌐 www.peakdistrictonline.co.uk

At the start of the Pennine Way Walk in Edale is
The Old Nag's Head, one of the most
picturesque inns in the whole area. With its mix of
old stone, bay windows and tubs of bright
flowers, this family-owned inn was built in 1577,
and is renowned as one of the "100 great pubs of
England".

It has been the centre of the community
for many years, and is loved by visitors and
locals alike as a place to enjoy a quiet drink, a
chat to friends old and new, and great food.
The interior is equally as impressive as the
exterior. Original fittings have been retained,
such as the huge open fire, bare stone walls,
low beamed ceilings and comfortable
furniture. It looks warm and inviting, and
indeed it is renowned as one of the
friendliest pubs in the county.

The inn boasts excellent hand-pulled ales,
good home-cooked food, and even
accommodation in a self-catering cottage.
There are four real ales on offer, the regular

one being Nags 1577, which is specially brewed for the pub. The other three are rotating guest
ales. They are kept in tip top condition by
mine host Malcolm France and his wife Sarah,
who have been in the trade for over 17 years,
on and off. In addition., there is a fine range
of other drinks, including wines, spirits, beers,
lagers and soft drinks if you're driving. It is
open all day, every day except during the
winter months, when it closes on Monday and
Tuesday.

Food is available whenever the inn is
open, and is served between 12 noon and
9.45pm. Malcolm is the cook, and over ninety
per cent of the produce he uses is sourced
locally, so you know you are in for a meal that
is made from only the finest and most

flavoursome ingredients! You can choose from
a comprehensive menu or a changing specials
board. Why not try the 8 oz Cumberland
sausage, or Edale gammon, which are
specialities of the house? Or you could try
their steak and stout pie, burgers, fish and
chips (with mushy peas!) or lasagne Verdi with
salad and garlic bread. The prices are
reasonable, and the portions are hearty!

In addition, the inn offers a self-catering
cottage to discerning holidaymakers. It sleeps
up to four people, and children and pets are
welcome. Please phone for details. It would
make the ideal base from which to explore the
area.

16 THE RAMBLER COUNTRY HOUSE HOTEL

Edale, Hope Valley, Derbyshire S33 7ZA
☎ 01433 670268
e-mail: therambler@darbiere.co.uk
🌐 www.therambler.co.uk

The **Rambler Country House Hotel** is situated in Edale, a pretty village that also gives its name to the valley nestling between Mam Tor, Lose Hill and Kinder. It makes the perfect base from which to explore an area that lends itself to many outdoor activities, such as walking, golf, fishing, hang-gliding, cycling and so on. If you want a holiday that is less energetic, it is also a place where you can relax in absolute comfort, far from the bustle of modern life.

When you arrive at the three-star Rambler Country House Hotel you will be struck by the superb and inviting décor, the warm, friendly feel of the place and the attentive staff who are there to look after your every need.

The accommodation consists of nine beautifully furnished and decorated upstairs rooms, each one fully en suite and each one spacious while still being cosy and welcoming. All have tea/coffee making facilities, television, hair dryer and direct dial telephone. Doubles, twins and singles are available, with each ensuring a good night's sleep.

Food is important at the Rambler Country House Hotel, as people from all over have already discovered. The chefs have created many dishes that combine fresh produce with imagination and flare, and you are guaranteed hearty portions at excellent prices. Starters include home made soup, prawn salad and grilled goats cheese, while for the main course you can choose from such dishes as juicy Aberdeen Angus steak with stilton or cheddar and chips and salads, pan fried chicken breast with a rustic mash, lamb shank slowly baked and coated in a rich red currant and rosemary sauce, and served with stilton and broccoli.

The bar serves up to four real ales, all rotating, plus the usual range of beers, lager, wines, spirits and soft drinks. This is the place in which to relax over a drink or two while discussing the day's adventures.

The hotel is open all day, every day in the summer, and closed on Wednesdays and Thursdays in winter. Food is served between opening time up until 9.30pm daily, and you are advised to book at weekends. The no-smoking restaurant seats up to 45 people in absolute comfort. Children are most welcome, and both the eating and drinking areas are disabled friendly, though you should phone about the accommodation.

This is a hotel that places great emphasis on comfort, a warm welcome and outstanding value for money. If you visit, you are sure to agree.

17 CAUSEWAY HOUSE

Back Street, Castleton, Hope Valley,
Derbyshire S33 8WE
☎ 01433 623291
e-mail: steynberg@btinternet.com

Causeway House is situated in Castleton, which is overlooked by the ruins of the famous Peveril Castle. It offers outstanding bed and breakfast accommodation in an area of the Peak District that is renowned for its scenery, history and heritage, and would make a fine base from which to explore it all.

The house is built of old, warm stone, and has a pleasing, well-proportioned look, with a garden to the front that is a riot of colour and greenery in the summer months. It is owned and run by Janet and Nick Steynberg, who have created one of the finest B&B establishments in Derbyshire since they took over in May 2006. People return to it again and again because of its value for money, its friendly service and its comfortable rooms. It offers four fully en suite rooms that are beautifully furnished and decorated. There are two double/family rooms, a single and a

twin, with one of the rooms having a four-poster bed.

A hearty English breakfast is included in the tariff, or a lighter Continental breakfast if required. You can ever order vegetarian or gluten-free. Breakfast times are flexible, but are usually between 8am and 9am. The establishment is non-smoking, and children are most welcome. This is a place that, once visited, you'll want to come back to again and again, as other people do. It is friendly, unstuffy and welcoming, and both Janet and Nick have a wealth of information about places round about to visit and explore.

18 TREAK CLIFF CAVERN

Castleton, Hope Valley,
Derbyshire S33 8WP
☎ 01433 620571
e-mail: treakcliff@bluejohnstone.com
🌐 www.bluejohnstone.com

Treak Cliff Cavern is an underground wonderland of stalactites, stalagmites, rocks, minerals and fossils. It is also home to Blue John Stone, a rare form of fluorite with beautiful colours. Popular as an ornamental stone and mined for 300 years, one of the largest pieces ever found, called The Pillar, is still in situ. The Blue John Stone in Treak Cliff Cavern can be seen all around the walls and roof of the Witch's Cave. The guided tour takes you deeper underground to see multi coloured flowstone adorning the walls of Aladdin's Cave, and further on you can experience the wonder of the stalactites and stalagmites in Fairyland and the Dream Cave. The most famous formation is 'The Stork', standing on one leg.

People of all ages can enjoy a visit to Treak Cliff Cavern (guided tours take about 40 minutes), and also experience special events held at certain times during the year. 'Polish your own' Blue John Stone is an activity usually available during most of the school holidays. Other events include an Easter Egg Hunt and. prior to Christmas. 'Carols By Candlelight' in the cavern.

19 WOODROFFE ARMS

I Castleton Road, Hope,
Derbyshire S33 6SB
☎ 01433 620351

Hope is a charming, picturesque village lying nine miles northeast of Buxton and it is here that you will find the **Woodroffe Arms**. Parts of it date back over 400 years, and this, combined with modern concepts such as great service and value for money, make it a popular place for locals and visitors alike.

It has five rooms on offer, each one comfortable and fully en suite, making this an ideal base from which to explore Derbyshire. The tariff includes a full, hearty English breakfast, just right to set you up for a day exploring the area. It is open all day, every day in summer, (from 4pm until closing time on Monday), and from 4pm until closing time Monday to Thursday, and all day Friday, Saturday and Sunday in the winter months. There are always at least three real ales on tap with Timothy Taylor Landlord and John Smith's Cask being the regulars.

It serves good, honest, wholesome pub food that is cooked on the premises using only the finest local produce and you can choose from a menu or a daily specials board. A curry night is held midweek (ring for details). The no-smoking dining room seats up to 30.

Children are most welcome, and all credit cards are accepted. There is occasional live entertainment on Friday or Saturday evenings and the bar and dining areas are disabled friendly.

20 YE DERWENT HOTEL

Main Road, Bamford, Hope Valley,
Derbyshire S33 0AY
☎ Mobile: 07971955252

Ye Derwent Hotel is an exceedingly attractive inn situated on the A6013 within the charming old village of Bamford, and close to Ladybower Reservoir. Mine hosts Julie and John Wilson have recently taken over here, and have already established it as one of the best inns of its kind in the area. It boasts ten exceedingly comfortable rooms, most of which are fully en suite. Each one is furnished and decorated to a high standard, ensuring that your stay here is as enjoyable as possible. It makes the perfect place for an overnight dinner, B&B stay, B&B only, or as a base from which to explore an area that is rich in scenery, history and heritage.

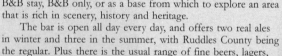

The bar is open all day every day, and offers two real ales in winter and three in the summer, with Ruddles County being the regular. Plus there is the usual range of fine beers, lagers, cider, spirits, wines and soft drinks.

The kitchens have recently been refurbished completely and the outstanding food is served at lunchtimes and evenings, with a reduced menu in the afternoons. Everything is home cooked by Julie from fresh, local produce, and you can make your choice from a blackboard selection.

Children are more than welcome, and the bar and eating areas are disabled friendly. All credit cards with the exception of Diners are accepted. Within the hotel, there are designated no-smoking areas for your comfort.

21 LADYBOWER INN

Bamford, Hope Valley,
Derbyshire S33 0AX
☎ 01433 651241
e-mail: info@ladybower-inn.co.uk
⊕ www.ladybower-inn.co.uk

The **Ladybower Inn** is a charming old inn that overlooks the still waters of the Ladybower Reservoir, built during the Second World War. Under the expert management of Deborah and Stephen, it offers a warm, Derbyshire welcome to old friends and new visitors.

It sits on the A57 Sheffield to Manchester road, and is a free house, serving great food and drink, and offering comfortable accommodation. It has seven en suite rooms and all are spacious, well furnished and beautifully decorated. The surrounding countryside is stunningly beautiful, and the inn makes the perfect base from which to explore it.

The cosy, friendly bar offers four real ales which are Bradfield Blonde (from a local micro brewery), Barnsley Bitter

and two rotating guest ales. Good, home-cooked food is served daily 12noon - 9.30pm and the produce is sourced locally wherever possible, making the dishes tasty and full of flavour. The 30-seat restaurant is spacious and comfortable, though you can eat in the bar or outside. The bar prides itself on its range of wines, so there is sure to be something to your taste.

This is a no-smoking establishment, and the bar and dining areas are disabled friendly, though you should phone about your accommodation requirements.

22 THE CASTLE INN

Bolsterstone Village, Sheffield,
Derbyshire S36 3ZB
☎ 0114 283 7011/8097

The Peak District National Park is truly one of England's most beautiful places, and in it you will find the village of Bolderstone. It is home to an outstanding pub - **The Castle Inn**, managed by Jo and Adrian, who bring a wealth of experience to the job.

The exterior is in warm, local stone, and during the summer months the façade is a riot of colour with hanging baskets. The interior is warm and welcoming, with old wood and contemporary furnishings creating a space that is inviting and cosy in winter and light and airy in summer. This is a genuine village local, and you will be made very welcome.

There are up to three real ales on offer here. Stones Bitter is the regular, and there are two rotating guest ales. Food is served from Monday to Friday between 12 noon and 2pm and 5pm to 8pm, Saturday 12 noon to 8pm, and Sunday 12 noon to 4pm. The Castle Inn employs

professional chefs, so you know the food is great! The no-smoking dining room is comfortable and spacious, and can seat up to 50 people in comfort. You are advised to book on Sundays. The lunchtime specials -with a set price - are very popular, and you can choose from the daily specials or from a blackboard. Friday is fish day, when dishes containing either prawns, salmon, cod or other fish are on offer.

All major credit cards are taken, and Tuesday, Thursday, Saturday and Sunday evenings are quiz nights. Children are very welcome, and there is a small beer garden.

Greaves Lane, Little Matlock,
Derbyshire S6 6BG
☎ 0114 234565
e-mail: robinhoodloxley@virgin.net
⊕ www.robin-hood-loxley.co.uk

The **Robin Hood** is a charming, family run inn that is said to be one of the best in the area. It is situated in the hamlet of Little Matlock, between the villages of Stannington and Loxley. It can be reached by following the excellent directions given on their website, and is worth searching out from whatever direction you are travelling..

The building dates back over 200 years and has links with the Sheffield Flood of 1864, at that time it was known as The Rock. Some time later the name was changed to the present, in keeping with the legend, Robin Hood of Loxley.

Keeley, the daughter of present owners Bridget and Scott Appleyard runs the inn which has two contrasting styles. The tap room with its traditional dark wood and cottage style plaster walls is cosy with an open fire, and welcomes walkers with muddy boots, dogs and bikers. The rotating real ales are from local breweries and also sourced from micro breweries around the country.

The lounge/restaurant with it's stone flagged floor and candle lit tables creates a fresh but warm bistro feel. A selection of wines from around the world are available to accompany the black board menu that offers fresh, traditional food, cooked to order, with a modern slant. The locally sourced fresh produce forms the seasonally changing menu.

Food is served 12pm to 2.30pm and 6pm to 8.30pm Monday to Saturday. Sundays hosts a carvery over three sittings, 1pm, 2.30pm and 4pm, when a choice of four roasts and eleven fresh seasonal vegetables is followed by traditional home-made puddings. It is essential to book in advance.

The new addition to this business is the accommodation giving true meaning to the word inn. There are four en-suite luxury boutique style bedrooms themed around the name of the pub. Each is individually designed and tastefully furnished to a very high standard, with personal touches. There is an enclosed rear patio garden for residents, giving direct access to the accommodation. This has recently been awarded a 4 Star rating and received a Silver Award from the Visit Britain Quality Assurance Scheme.

There are many footpaths and noted walks of historical interest in this area and the surrounding valleys.garden.

Smalldale, Bradwell, Hope Valley,
Derbyshire S33 9JQ
☎ 01433 620450
🌐 www.bowlinggreeninn.co.uk

Ye Olde Bowling Green Inn is one of the most delightful inns in Derbyshire. Tucked away in the picturesque surroundings of Smalldale, it has whitewashed walls, bow windows and hanging baskets of colourful flowers. It is also a historic place, as it is a former coaching inn dating from 1577. The interior is everything that an English pub interior should be - warm, cosy and traditional, with many original features, such as exposed stone walls, low-beamed ceilings, dark wood and open fireplaces. Just the place to enjoy a quiet, relaxing drink as you explore this beautiful part of Derbyshire!

And yet the standards of service are firmly rooted in modern times. It is popular with tourists and visitors alike, and Angela and Glyn, who are mine hosts, are justly proud of the value-for-money-prices they have set. There is a fine range of real ales, including Tetleys and Stones, and weekly changing guest beers all are immaculately kept. Plus, of course, there are beers, lagers, cider, spirits, wines, liqueurs and soft drinks for those driving.

Ye Olde Bowling Green Inn also sells good pub food, and the platefuls are always hearty and filling. Angela is a superb cook, and prepares the food herself. She tries to source as much of the produce she uses locally, so that the dishes are always fresh and full of flavour. Serving times are 12 noon to 2pm and 6pm to 8pm seven days a week. There are two restaurants, (both non smoking) and if you wish to eat on Friday and Saturday evenings or Sunday lunchtime, you are well advised to book. There is a printed menu and a changing specials board that always has tempting dishes such as Thai red chicken curry, pork chops with orange and ginger, lamb chops (using the finest Derbyshire lamb) and juicy fillet steaks cooked to order. Fresh fish delivered daily includes monkfish, seabream, seabass and a popular favourite is the large fresh cod fillet cooked in beer batter.

The inn also offers six fully en suite rooms in a converted barn on a B&B basis, and each one is furnished and decorated to a high standard. They have been given a four star rating by the Automobile Association, so you know you are getting the very best!

All major credit cards are taken, and there is a pool table indoors and a patio and beer garden outside with stunning views.

Stretfield, Bradwell, Hope Valley,
Derbyshire S33 9JT
☎ 01433 620431

The **New Bath inn** is a friendly, family run inn that sits in Stretfield, close to Bradwell on the B6046, between the A6187 and A623. Since January 2005 it has been run by the Flemington family, and they have made it one of the best pubs in the area, popular with both visitors and locals alike.

The building is of local, warm stone, and is well-proportioned and inviting. The interior is equally as attractive, with plenty of wood and natural materials, and has that traditional "village pub" feel that everyone admires nowadays. The Flemingtons - mum Bobbie, daughter Liz and her partner Pete - have worked hard on the pub's reputation, ensuring that it only stocks the best of drink and the best of food.

The pub is open during regular pub hours on week days, and all day on Saturday and Sunday. The bar serves two real ales - Stones Bitter and a rotating guest ale. It als sells a wide range of beers, lagers, cider, spirits, wines, liqueurs and soft drinks should you be driving. Why not enjoy a quiet drink in the bar and chat to the regulars? They're a friendly bunch of people who will make you more than welcome!

The food at the New Bath Inn is outstanding, and represents the very best in traditional pub food, with hearty portions and value-for-money prices. The greatest majority of the produce that goes into the dishes is sourced locally so that it is always fresh and full of flavour. Bobby and Pete are the chefs, and they cook with imagination and flair. It is best to book a table on Saturdays and Sundays, and all week in the summer months, such a high reputation does the place have. Food is served between 12 noon and 2pm and between 6pm and 8.30pm, and from 12 noon until 3pm on Sundays. No food is served on Sunday evening.

You can choose off a printed menu or a specials board. The menu contains such appetising dishes as chicken goujons, juicy steaks, breaded haddock, whole tail scampi, farmhouse chicken, lamb hot pot and five-bean chilli and rice. Vegetarians are catered for, and the desserts are sure to set your mouth watering! Children are most welcome, and there is a children's menu.

The spacious dining area is no-smoking, and there is a separate menu for Sundays, when roasts are very popular. Friday night is quiz night, and there is occasional live music on Saturday nights, and you should ring for details. There is plenty of off road parking and a beer garden.

26 POOL CAFÉ

Oddfellows Road, Hathersage,
Hope Valley, Derbyshire S32 1DU
☎ 01433 651159
e-mail: kevinasmith41@hotmail.com

Situated right next to the Hathersage Lido, the **Pool Café** is the place to go for a cup of coffee or tea, a light snack or a lunch in the area. This child-friendly establishment offers food that is beautifully cooked and presented, using fresh, local produce wherever possible. You can choose from a printed menu or a specials board, with favourites being the full English breakfast, steak pie, broccoli and cheese bake, burgers, baked potatoes with a choice of tasty fillings, home made cottage pie, chilli con carne and a host of other dishes that will satisfy the largest appetite. Portions are generous and prices represent value for money. And take note - the café's fish and chips are reputed to be the best for miles around! An addition to the menu is the popular Sunday lunches, for which you are well advised to book.

Kevin Smith has owned and managed the café for over three years, and in that time has built a reputation that is second to none. The Pool Café seats 40 in absolute comfort, and children are most welcome. It is open every day of the year with the exception of Christmas Day, Boxing Day and New Year's Day. Opening hours are from 8am to 6pm between mid-September and Easter, and 8am to 7.30pm for the rest of the year. There is a takeaway service and the café can also be booked for private functions. Though it isn't licensed, you can BYOB (bring your own bottle!)

28 THE EATING HOUSE

The Derbyshire Craft Centre,
Calver Bridge, Hope Valley,
Derbyshire S32 3XA
☎ 01433 631583

The Eating House at the Derbyshire Craft Centre is a popular destination for both tourists and locals alike. The Craft Centre is located adjacent to the A623 and is open every day of the year except Christmas Day and Boxing Day. It is housed in a building of warm, old stone, and it's interior has a traditional feel combined with contemporary designs and fittings. It is the perfect place to have a delicious meal, snack or cup of coffee if you're visiting the Craft Centre or just passing by. Homemade soups and fresh quiche, baked to their own recipe, help to reflect the

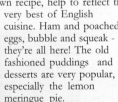

very best of English cuisine. Ham and poached eggs, bubble and squeak - they're all here! The old fashioned puddings and desserts are very popular, especially the lemon meringue pie.

The Eating House is self-service, and the daily dishes are listed on the blackboard. It has seating for 35 inside and a further 15 outside. Children are welcome, and the establishment is disabled-friendly but does not have disabled toilet facilities. There is plenty of off-road parking for customers, and all credit cards are taken with the exception of American express and Diners. The Eating House is non-smoking.

Sheffield Road, Hathersage, Hope Valley,
Derbyshire S32 1DA
☎ 01433 650258
e-mail: jerry@millstoneinn.co.uk
⊕ www.millstoneinn.co.uk

The wild beauty of the Peak District makes a fine setting for the **Millstone Country Inn**, which has unspoilt views across the Hope Valley. A former coaching inn, with parts dating to the 17th century, it now blends all the charms

of a traditional English inn with modern amenities and high standards of service.

It has seven en suite rooms, all of them comfortable and extremely well furnished and decorated. They range in size from singles, through doubles and twins, to family rooms that are spacious yet cosy. People return to it again and again - be they tourists or business people -for its warm, inviting atmosphere and olde worlde feel. Each room has a colour TV, telephone and tea and coffee making facilities. In addition, there is wireless broadband available if requested. All guests are provided with a hearty English breakfast, which will set you up for the day, or something lighter if required.

With its open fire and friendly staff, the bar exudes all that is best about the traditional English inn. It offers five hand-pulled real ales - Timothy Taylor Landlord, Black Sheep and three rotating guest ales(no wonder it has been voted CAMRA pub of the month), plus a wide range of beers, cider, spirits wines and soft drinks should you be driving.

The food at the Millstone is out of this world. You can eat in the bar, or in the recently added Terrace Restaurant. The bar serves traditional pub food that is beautifully cooked and always tasty. Dishes such as homemade pies, fish 'n' chips, juicy sirloin steak, chicken and seafood paella and roasted vegetable lasagne are always available, and represent remarkable value for money. Or there is the unique "pick and mix" sausage menu, where you can choose the kind of sausages you want, the kind of mash and the sauce. There are also daily specials. As an alternative, the Terrace Restaurant offers you fine dining. Here the highest standards of cuisine and service are maintained within an ambience that is at once elegant and sophisticated and yet relaxed and friendly. Special themed food nights are also held both in the bar and the restaurant, where you can experiment with overseas cuisine. Plus there is a good selection of wines, and you are sure to find something that will complement your meal exactly.

Though the Millstone is in a quiet country village, the city of Sheffield with its wonderful shopping, is only a short distance away, as is Chatsworth and all the attractions of the Peak District. The inn is the ideal base from which to explore them all.

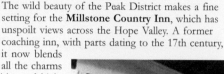

178

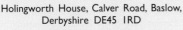

Holingworth House, Calver Road, Baslow,
Derbyshire DE45 1RD
☎ 01246 583888
e-mail: avantgarde@btopenworld.com
🌐 www.avantgarde-of-baslow.co.uk

Avante Garde sells a stylish range of goods for the home and garden, and can be found a short drive from Chatsworth House on the A623. Great attention is paid by the owners, Linda and John Lowen, to design, colour, texture and fitness-for-purpose of the many items in the shop. So committed are they that they scour the UK and Europe looking for the latest trends.

Whether it's mirrors, cushions and throws from Sweden, wicker baskets, vases, artificial flowers, books or gift wraps, there is sure to be something that will catch your eye. So well designed and crafted are the objects that the shop has featured many times in *Country Living*. All the items are displayed on various pieces of furniture such as painted housekeepers' cupboards, painted dressers and old pine chests, accentuating that country look that is so admired nowadays.

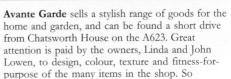

Plus there are many charming items for the garden, for not only do people like to personalise their interiors, they like to do the same to their gardens. French garden furniture, brightly painted bird houses, galvanised planters, sweet pea baskets, metal obelisks and beautiful benches made from old metal bed heads - Avante Garde has got them all. Another section is called "Planted", where seasonal plants, bulbs and herbs are set in beautiful containers.

Just two doors away from Avante Garde is an exciting new venture. Linda has acquired the premises to sell a selection of beautifully crafted furniture, including many original pieces that can be found nowhere else. There are glass fronted cupboards, painted tables and chairs, wardrobes, small occasional tables plus many more pieces that would add grace and elegance to any house interior. There will also be bespoke pieces using original materials. In addition, Linda will also be featuring an extension to her existing ranges of mirrors, lamps and pictures. Everything on display is designed and crafted with style in mind, and you are invited to browse to your heart's content.

Avante Garde of Baslow is a must-visit place for all your gift needs, and you can even buy Christmas gifts and decorations. It sits two miles from Chatsworth House and the market town of Bakewell. It is open seven days a week from 10am to 5pm.

30 THE DEVONSHIRE ARMS HOTEL

Nether End, Baslow,
Derbyshire DE45 1SR
☎ 01246 582551
e-mail: paul@devonshirearmsbaslow.com
🌐 www.devonshirearmsbaslow.com

Built on the site of an old coaching inn, the family-run **Devonshire Arms Hotel** has recently been refurbished to provide twelve en suite rooms to discerning guests. Each room is individually furnished and decorated to an extremely high standard, and represents outstanding value for money. It is set in the Peak District, so is the ideal base from which to explore a beautiful area that is rich in history and heritage. Chatsworth Park, Eyam and Haddon Hall are only a short distance away, as are the picturesque towns of Matlock, Buxton and Ashbourne.

It is managed by Joanne and Paul Kaczmarek, who, between them, have many years experience in the licensing trade, and they have created a hotel that combines charm, friendliness and high standards of service, with great food and drink. The hotel is open all day, every day, and sells four real ales, all beautifully kept. These are Greene King Abbot, Greene King IPA, Directors and a rotating guest ale. Plus there is a wide selection of beers, spirits, wines and soft drinks should you be driving.

Food is important in the Devonshire Arms, and no less than four chefs are employed in the kitchen. You can choose from the daily specials board or the printed menu, which contains such

favourites as garlic mushrooms, smoked cheese chicken, pork fillet and black pudding, home-made vegetable lasagne, tarragon poached salmon, and so much more. If you would rather have a light bite or a snack, you can have Greek salad, red pepper and smoked bacon frittata, omelettes, etc. Plus there is a daily carvery, which is very popular with visitors and locals alike. As much of the produce as possible is sourced locally, ensuring freshness and great flavour.

You can eat in the spacious main lounge, which seats up to 68 people, or in the beautiful, circular Chatsworth Suite, which seats 90 in absolute comfort. Food is served from 12 noon to 8.45pm (8pm in winter), seven days a week. The carvery is available from 12 noon to 2.30pm and from 5.30pm to 8.30pm Monday to Saturday and from 12 noon to 8.30pm on Sunday.

The Chatsworth Suite, with its own bar, is the ideal place for a wedding, party or anniversary celebration. All credit cards are taken with the exception of Diners and American Express, and children are most welcome. Dogs may stay in some rooms for an extra charge, and are welcome in some parts of the bar/restaurant area.

68 Sunderland Street, Macclesfield,
Cheshire SK11 6HN

☎ 01625 422015

e-mail: userlo6499@aol.com

🌐 www.glenandsarah@thejollysailor.co.uk

Close to all the amenities in Macclesfield, such as the bus and railway stations, you will find a gem of a pub, **The Jolly Sailor.** It is a real find, with mine hosts Sarah and Glen Lowe having been here since July 2006. They have made something special out of the pub. It dates from the 19th century, and has a well-proportioned exterior in red brick, with hanging baskets that bring a lot of colour to an already colourful and delightful building.

But being the landlord of the Jolly Sailor is a sort of return home for Glen, whose great-great grandfather was once licensee here, and many of his family were born in and around Sunderland Street. The interior is as delightful as the exterior, with a relaxed, cosy atmosphere Here you can enjoy a quiet drink or a delicious home-cooked meal, with the locals offering a real welcome. In fact, it's one of the most popular pubs in the area, and much visited by visitors and locals alike.

It is open all day, every day for a great range of drinks. It serves one real ale, which is Bass, and also has a wide selection of beers, lager, cider, spirits, wines, liqueurs and, if you're driving, soft drinks. The pub also sells good, honest pub food that is tasty and always beautifully cooked from local produce where possible. There is a fine selection of hot and cold dishes in the winter months, such as hot pot, beef stew and dumplings and so on.

Children are very welcome, and there are no smoking areas to the rear of the premises. Sarah and glen regret, however, that they only take cash - they do not accept credit or debit cards or cheques. There are also five guest rooms (all twin) available, and these can be taken on a bed and breakfast or dinner, bed and breakfast basis. Each room is comfortable, well furnished and pleasantly decorated. The rooms are located on the first floor.

Packed lunches are available on request, and there is live music on Friday evenings from 8 pm, and on alternate Saturdays from 8pm and Sundays from 4pm. Ring for details. Parking is next to the pub, and it has CCTV coverage. The dining and drinking areas downstairs are disabled friendly, though you should ring beforehand about the accommodation.

The Jolly Sailor in Macclesfield is a real find - a cosy town pub that has lost none of its character and warmth while at the same time offering up to date facilities, high standards of service and real value for money. Make it your first stop in Macclesfield!

32 DOLPHIN INN

**76 Windmill street, Macclesfield,
Cheshire SK11 7HS
☎ 01625 616179**

For good food and well-kept ales, you can't beat the **Dolphin Inn** in Windmill Street, a ten-minute walk from the town centre. Here, in this pub which dates to the 19th century, your hosts, Bev and John Lythaby, will make you most welcome. They've been here six years and during that time have turned the inn into one of the best and most popular in town. The exterior is whitewashed and picturesque, and the interior is cosy, warm and trim, as every pub should be, with comfortable seating and carpeted floors.

Food is served at lunchtimes only here, with Beth being the cook. Serving times are 12 noon to 2pm from Monday to Saturday. There is an across the board menu, with most of the produce being sourced locally, so you are assured of freshness and flavour at all times. The speciality of the house is steak pie, which is always piping hot and delicious.

The pub is open every session and all day Sunday with three real ales on offer, Robinson's Unicorn, Hatters and seasonally brewed brewery ale. This is usually Old Tom 8 per cent in the winter months. Plus there is a good range of beers, wines, spirits and soft drinks.

The Dolphin is a real English local, though visitors are always made welcome. There are no-smoking areas and children are allowed if eating. It is regretted that payment is by cash only.

33 PUSS IN BOOTS

**198 Buxton Road, Macclesfield,
Cheshire SK10 1NF
☎ 01625 423261**

Only a short walk from the centre of Macclesfield, and on the borders of the Peak District National Park, you will find a superb small inn called the **Puss in Boots**. It has a fine, well-proportioned exterior of local stone, and dates from the 18th century, when it was a coaching inn. Inside it has warm carpeting, dark, polished wood and comfortable seating. Behind the pub is a canal, with alongside it, a beer garden where you can sit and enjoy a pint. Mine hosts are Wendy and John Pickford, who used to manage the inn between 1986 and 1992, and once again took over in 2003. They serve good beer and equally good food, and take a great pride in the popularity of the inn.

The Puss in Boots is open all day, every day, and sells two real ales, Boddington's and Deuchar's IPA. There is also a good selection of wines, spirits, beers, lager, cider and, if you're driving, soft drinks. Food is served on Wednesday, Thursday and Friday from 12 noon until 3pm and 5.30pm until 8pm. On Saturdays and Sundays food times are 12 noon until 8pm. You

are well advised to book on a Sunday. There is no food served on a Monday or Tuesday. There is a printed menu and a daily changing specials board, which takes advantage of produce that is in season.

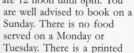

Wednesday evening is curry evening, and you can order a curry and a pint at a special price. On Thursday evening from 8.30pm there is a quiz.. All major credit cards are taken, and children are most welcome

34 JASPERS

71 Park Lane, Macclesfield,
Cheshire SK11 6TX
☎ 01625 421514
e-mail: philx4@hotmail.co.uk

The no-smoking **Jaspers** has had a full refurbishment, and is now one of the best eating places in Macclesfield. It is warm, cosy and inviting, and serves good food that always represents great value for money.

Everything is home made from locally sourced produce where possible. Try its steak, ale  and Guinness pie, its all-day breakfast or its marvellous selection of sandwiches, jacket potatoes, burgers and salads. Everything is delicious and well cooked, and if you visit you're sure to come back again and again!

35 THE RISING SUN INN

Hawkins Lane, Rainow, Macclesfield,
Cheshire SK10 5TL
☎ 01625 424235

The Rising Sun Inn is one of the most picturesque inns in the area, and is adjacent to the B5470 Macclesfield to Whaley Bridge Road, within the Peak District National Park. It dates back over 300 years, and under the management of Cheryl and Darren Sellars, it has regained all of its former popularity with the locals.

It is open all day (and from 6pm on Mondays) for the sale of a wide range of beers, lagers, cider, wines, spirits and soft drinks. It also offers three real ales, which are immaculately kept. These are Young's Bitter and two rotating guest ales. Great food is served Tuesday to Friday from 12 noon to 3pm and 6pm to 9pm, from 12 noon to 9pm on Saturday and from 12 noon to 6pm on Sunday. Darren is a trained chef, and does all the coking, using only the finest and freshest local produce wherever possible. You can choose from a printed menu or a  daily changing specials

board. Darren's specialities are Cumberland sausage, lamb Henry and game pie, and they are all very popular with the locals!

All credit cards are accepted with the exception of American Express and Diners, and children are most welcome. There are no-smoking areas in he pub, and there is also occasional entertainment and themed food nights. Please ring for details. Off road parking is available and there is a beer garden to the rear.

Mill lane, Adlington, Macclesfield,
Cheshire SK10 4LF
☎ 01625 827 595 Fax: 01625 820 797
e-mail: enquiries@adlingtonhall.com
🌐 www.adlingtonhall.com

Adlington Hall, the home of the Leghs of Adlington from 1315 to the present day, was built on the site of a hunting lodge which stood in the Forest of Macclesfield in 1040. The Hall is a manor house, quadrangular in shape, and was at one time surrounded by a moat. Two sides of the courtyard and the east wing were built in 1581 in the typical 'black& white' Cheshire style. The south front and west wing were added between 1749 and 1757 and are built of red brick with a handsome stone portico with four Ionic columns.

Two oak trees, part of the original building, still remain with their roots in the ground and support the east end of the Great Hall, which was built between 1480 and 1505. Between the trees in the Great Hall stands an organ built in the style of 'Father' Bernard Smith (c 1670-80). Handel subsequently played on this instrument and, now fully restored, it is the largest 17th century organ in the country. At the west end of the Great Hall is a very fully developed canopy. This takes the form of a cove or quadrant and is divided into 60 panels containing armorial shields. The windows are on the south side so that the murals which adorn the north and west walls can be seen to advantage. Adlington Hall was a royalist garrison during the Civil War.

Adlington Hall is a great Cheshire garden set in the heart of the Cheshire Plain amidst some of England's finest countryside. The Estate, which is continually evolving, was landscaped in the 'Brownian' style during the 18th century, complete with a ha-ha. Earlier plantings are still in evidence, such as the ancient Lime Avenue dating from 1688 and the Wilderness with its myriad winding paths and open glades, also home to temples, bridges and follies. The large herbaceous border also along the North Drive is packed with interest from spring until late autumn and the woodland border offers exuberant displays of

autumn colour. The path through the laburnum arcade leads into the formal Rose Garden which offers a feast of colour and fragrance all summer long. Pillars and rope swags frame the garden with a gazebo centrepiece providing a tranquil seating area. Carry on through the Rose Garden and you will discover a maze created from English yew.

Other features include rockeries, shrub borders and many fine specimen trees. The Father Tiber water garden, created in 2002, goes from strength to strength and offers a peaceful haven amongst ponds, rills, fountains and a water cascade.

The Hunting Lodge is part of the beautifully converted Georgian Mews adjacent to the black and white East Wing of Adlington Hall. The first floor banqueting suite is approached by a beautiful sweeping staircase (a lift is available if required).

The hunting Lodge is an ideal venue for wedding receptions, banquets, conferences or indeed any social or business occasion. For more information please contact The Hunting Lodge on 01625 827595.

37 VALE INN

Adlington Road, Bollington, Macclesfield,
Cheshire SK10 5JT
☎ 01625 575147
🌐 www.valeinn.co.uk

The handsome, stone-built **Vale Inn** at Bollington dates from the mid 19th century, when it was part of a row of cottages. Now it has absorbed the cottages, and has become one of the most welcoming inns in the whole area. The interior is a mixture of 'olde worlde' and spaciousness, with exposed stone walls, warm wood and a welcoming ambience. It opens every session through the week and all day Saturday and Sunday, selling six real ales. One of them is Vale Ale, brewed locally for the inn, and ever changing guest ales. It was voted Summer Pub of the Season for Macclesfield and East Cheshire in 2006, so well kept are the ales. In addition, it serves a wide range of beers, wines, spirits, lagers and soft drinks, so there is sure to be something to suit everyone.

Food is served from Monday to Friday from 12 noon to 2.30pm and 6pm to 9pm, and on Saturday and Sunday from 12

noon right through until 9 pm. Most of the produce is sourced locally, and the owner, Lee Wainright, gets a lot of his meat from his father, who is a farmer. You are well advised to book on Saturday evening and Sunday lunchtime. The pub has no-smoking areas, and all credit cards with the exception of American Express and Diners are accepted. There is plenty of off road parking, and there are two beer gardens at the back, one sloping down to the village cricket pitch, and the other sheltered by trees.

38 COFFEE TAVERN

Shrigley Road, Pott Shrigley,
Cheshire SK10 5SE
☎ 01625 576370

Pott Shrigley is a small village north of Macclesfield, on a minor road between the A523 and the B5470 that stands right on the edge of the Peak District National Park. Here you will find the excellent **Coffee Tavern**, housed in what was a reading room and library built in 1887 for workers on the nearby Lowther Estate. It's an establishment that is renowned for serving some of the best food - from home-baked cakes scones to full, three course meals - in the area.

All the food is cooked on the premises by Andrew Buffey, son of the owners (who have been here since 1992), and he uses the finest of local produce in the kitchen wherever possible. It seats 33 people in comfort, and is open from 10am to 6pm every day except Tuesday. The tavern is licensed, and it has such a fine reputation that you are well advised to book a table at weekends.

The Coffee Tavern is popular with walkers and cyclists, who enjoy not only the food, but the excellent tea and coffee that is served as well. Not only that - people come from all over the area to sample the delicious cuisine and then pay a visit to the small craft shop upstairs. Here you will find a fascinating collection of craft items, from paintings and jewellery to pottery and cards, all made by local artists and craftspeople.

39 SUTTON HALL

Bullocks Lane, Sutton, Nr Macclesfield,
Cheshire SK11 0HE
☎ 01260 253211
🌐 www.suttonhall.co.uk
www.suttonhallhotel.co.uk
www.suttonhall.com

The outstanding **Sutton Hall** is owned and personally managed by Phyllida and Robert Bradshaw, who have created a hotel, restaurant and inn that is famous throughout the area. It is truly an 'inn of distinction', and sits in 14 acres of lovely grounds. Once the baronial residence of the Sutton family and more recently a convent associated with the diocese of Shrewsbury, it has been converted with great skill, and at great expense, into an establishment that offers the very best in English hospitality.

The fully licensed lounge bar, with its original oak panelling, stained galls, log fires and eye catching decorative features, makes a civilised, atmospheric spot for enjoying a fine range of cask-conditioned ales, wines, spirits (over 40 malts alone!) and freshly squeezed fruit juices. Not only that - a selection of home-cooked food is available every lunchtime and evening. For a more formal occasion, the elegant and spacious dining room offers a regularly changing menu of dishes prepared from the finest and freshest seasonal produce wherever possible.

In the library, which is also used as a function room seating up to 24 people, guests can browse through the books and enjoy a coffee or digestif in front of a huge log fire. While doing so, he or she can admire the Dutton coat-of-arms above the fireplace! During the summer tables are set out on the lawn, which makes an idyllic setting for a drink, meal or afternoon tea.

The hotel has ten magnificent, en suite rooms on offer, reached by an imposing oak staircase. Each one has its own individual charm and character, and the sumptuous four-poster beds add a definite romantic feel. Rooms can be booked on a bed and breakfast or dinner bed and breakfast basis. Moorings can be booked on the nearby canal, and Sutton Hall can arrange fishing, golf and other outdoor activities for its guests.

The hotel is a short drive south from Macclesfield, on the A523. Turn left into Byron's Lane signposted Langley Wincle, and right just before the canal into Bullocks Lane.

40 THE HANGING GATE INN

Meg Lane, Higher Sutton, Nr Macclesfield,
Cheshire SK10 0NG
☎ 01260 252238

The Hanging Gate Inn is a charming, picturesque inn within the village of Higher Sutton, near Macclesfield. It's whitewashed exterior speaks of tradition, and indeed the inn is everything that a traditional English inn should be - cosy, welcoming and offering the very best in food, drink and hospitality. The building, a former farmhouse, dates back to 1621 and is very 'olde worlde'.

It must be one of the leading contenders in the Peak District for having the most spectacular views surrounding it - pastoral scenes of fields and woodland. Mine hosts are Luda and Ian Rottenbury, who took over in August 2006. Since then, they have built on the inn's fine reputation, and created an establishment that is popular with both locals and visitors alike. It is their first venture in running a pub, but Ian has been a chef for over 22 years who once worked in a well-known Cheshire restaurant.

So, as you can imagine, food is very important here. The spacious, no-smoking restaurant seats up to 36 people in absolute comfort, or you can eat in the bar areas. There

is a printed menu or you can choose from the daily-changing specials board. Ian is very particular about the produce he uses, so everything is sourced locally and is organic wherever possible to ensure freshness and maximum flavour. Dishes featuring local game are normally available in season. Food is served Monday to Saturday between 12 noon and 2.30pm and 6.45pm and 9.30pm, and between 12 noon and 3pm and 6.45pm and 9.30pm on Sunday (occasionally all day Sunday).

During the week the inn opens every session, and al day Saturday and Sunday. It boasts two regular real ales, Hyde's Original and Jeckyl's Gold, plus a rotating guest ale.

There is also a fine range of beers, wines, spirits, lagers, cider and soft drinks for those people who are driving.

Children are more than welcome at this friendly inn, and all credit cards with the exception of Diners are accepted. There are occasional wine-tasting evenings, and on special occasions there is live entertainment. You should ring for details before visiting. Off road parking is no problem, and from the outdoor seating and beer garden there are wonderful views of the surrounding countryside. This is an inn that, once visited, you will return to again and again.

**Agricultural Business Centre,
Agricultural Way, Bakewell,
Derbyshire DE45 IAH
☎ 01629 8156768**

The **Farmers Feast Café and Bar** is a real find. Housed in a new, stylish building that is bright and airy, with glass walls, it offers the very best in food and drink in a café-type environment, and is popular not only with the local people, but with farmers visiting the cattle market next door.

It stands off the main A6, south of the centre of Bakewell, and to find it you should look for signs indicating the Agricultural Business Park. It has been owned by David Nuttall since 2003, and is one of the finest places in the area for good food and great drink. Farmers appreciate fresh produce and value-for-money food, and they certainly appreciate the Farmers Feast Café and Bar! It is open seven days a week from 9am to 5pm, and seats 200 in absolute comfort. The interior is bright and spacious, with modern, stylish furniture that speaks of efficiency and friendly service. There are also plenty of parking spaces nearby.

The food here, as you would imagine, is outstanding, with large, healthy portions being the

order of the day. Dishes are itemised on blackboards or signs on the walls, and include such favourites as fish and chips with mushy peas, seafood platter, gammon steaks, sirloin steaks with all the trimmings, an all-day English breakfast and scampi, chips and peas. All the produce used in the kitchen is sourced locally wherever possible, ensuring that it is fresh and always full of flavour. There is very little frozen foodstuffs used here! You can also enjoy a glass of beer or a glass of wine with your meal, and teas, coffees and hot chocolate are available at all times. There is also a children's menu. On weekdays, there is waitress service at your tables after you have ordered your meal. On Monday and Thursday the place is very busy, as these are cattle market days. There are no smoking areas within the Farmer's Feast Café and Bar, and it is regretted that payment is by cash only - credit cards and cheques are not accepted.

Adjacent to the café is a smart licensed bar area that opens at the same times. It offers three keg draught bitters and three draught lagers, and you can either eat and drink here or in the café area.

When you're in the Bakewell area, the Farmer's Feast and Café Bar is the place to go. The service is smart and efficient, the food and drink is excellent, and the whole places represents amazing value for money. So make your way here - you won't be disappointed!

42 CHATSWORTH HOUSE

nr Edensor, Derbyshire DE45 1PP
☎ 01246 565300   Fax: 01246 583536
e-mail: visit@chatsworth.org
🌐 www.chatsworth.org

On the outskirts of the village lies the home of the Dukes of Devonshire. **Chatsworth House**, known as the "Palace of the Peak", is without doubt one of the finest of the great houses in Britain. The origins of the House as a great showpiece must be attributable to the redoubtable Bess of Hardwick, whose marriage into the Cavendish family helped to secure the future of the palace.

Bess's husband, Sir William Cavendish, bought the estate for £600 in 1549. It was Bess who completed the new House after his death. Over the years, the Cavendish fortune continued to pour into Chatsworth, making it an almost unparalleled showcase for art treasures. Every aspect of the fine arts is here, ranging from old masterpieces, furniture, tapestries, porcelain and some magnificent alabaster carvings.

The gardens of this stately home also have some marvellous features, including the

Emperor Fountain, which dominates the Canal Pond and is said to reach a height of 290 feet. There is a maze and a Laburnum Tunnel and, behind the house, the famous Cascades. The overall appearance of the park as it is seen today is chiefly due to the talents of "Capability" Brown, who was first consulted in 1761. However, the name perhaps most strongly associated with Chatsworth is Joseph Paxton. His experiments in glasshouse design led him eventually to his masterpiece, the Crystal Palace, built to house the Great Exhibition of 1851.

44 EYAM MUSEUM

Hawkhill Road, Eyam,
Derbyshire, S32 5QP
☎ 01433 631371
🌐 www.eyam.org

Bubonic plague has been described as the 'most dangerous disease known to mankind' and has killed more souls than all the wars ever fought between all the nations of the world. Known as the Black Death, the Great Plague entered London in the 17th Century and came to Eyam by the most unfortunate of mishaps - carried by fleas festering in a box of cloth brought from the capital for the village tailor. When the box was opened plague fleas were released. Between September 1665 and October 1666 260 people - perhaps a third of the population - met an awful, pained death. Only the intervention of two clergymen ensured that the village survived through the next terrible months. William Mompesson was newly appointed rector of Eyam - and he and his predecessor Thomas Stanley, persuaded the village to enter voluntary quarantine, to bury their own dead and even change their pattern of worship. Some had sent their children away, but most folk stayed in Eyam.

People in the surrounding area, especially the Earl of Devonshire, sent provisions to the people of Eyam so they would not starve, though careful precautions were taken to avoid infection. When the plague finally loosed its terrible grip on the village, it left a population of more than 400 people who, needing to make a living, returned to their traditional task of mining lead in the hills above the village. Smallholdings were tended again, a few sheep and cows helping provide some of the necessities of life. Cottages in the village, emptied by the plague, were filled again, often by grown-up sons and daughters who had once moved away. In this way Eyam prospered again. Visit Eyam Museum to experience the full story.

Eyam Hall Crafts Centre, Church Street,
Eyam, Hope Valley, Derbyshire S32 5QN
☎ 01433 630505
e-mail: dawn.eric@gmail.com

Eyam is famous as being the "Plague Village", and it is here, in the former stables within the grounds of historic Eyam Hall, that you will find **The Stables at Eyam**, one of the best tea rooms and restaurants in the Hope Valley. Owned and managed by Dawn and Eric Boocock and their daughter-in-law Hannah since August 2006, it is fast gaining the kind of reputation that other establishments take years to achieve, and now people come from all over to sample the cuisine. This is their first venture together, but they have a lot of experience in the catering trade.

The exterior is of solid local stone, and speaks of tradition, while the interior is spacious, colourful and has many original features, such as bare stone walls. Here you can relax and enjoy some of the best baking and food in Derbyshire, all cooked and presented to perfection and all representing amazing value for money.

You can choose from a printed menu or a daily specials board, which makes use of fresh local produce in season whenever possible. Everything is home made on the premises, so there is no 'fast food' here! The establishment seats 30 in absolute comfort inside, and 30 outside during the warmer months. The downstairs tearoom (waitress service) is open from Tuesday to Sunday each week from October to July between 10 am and 5.30 am, and is open seven days in August and September. The upstairs restaurant, which again has waitress service, is open on Wednesday, Thursday, Friday and Saturday evenings from 6.30 pm until 9 pm, which is last orders, and Sunday lunchtime from 12 noon to 2.30 pm.

The cuisine is Anglo/Mediterranean, and there are many fine dishes on the menu that combine good, fresh ingredients with imagination and flair. The restaurant is licensed, so you can enjoy a glass of wine with your meal. Children are most welcome, and all credit cards are taken with the exception of Diners. The downstairs tearoom is disabled friendly, but you should phone about the upstairs restaurant.

45 HARGATE HALL

Wormhill, Nr Buxton,
Derbyshire SK17 8TA
☎ 01298 872591
e-mail: info@hargate-hall.co.uk
🌐 www.hargate-hall.co.uk

Set within the lovely Peak District National Park is three-star **Hargate Hall** - a mellow country house that has been converted into 12 self-catering apartments of the highest standard. It is a family-run concern, and Julie and Anthony Knox want to welcome you to a place they are proud of - a place where you can enjoy a holiday that is as peaceful or as action-packed as you want.

Built in 1899, it sits in seven acres of stunning gardens, and boasts twelve self-catering apartments that offer a good level of comfort and amenities, including colour TVs, high-fis, videos and/or DVD players. In some of the larger suites, there are TVs in the bedrooms. All apartments have at least one bathroom, the larger ones having two, and one apartment can sleep up to ten people. The kitchens come with everything from mixing bowls to microwaves, with a dishwasher as standard in some of the larger units. All bed linen is provided, and towels are available at an extra charge of £5 per week.

Electricity is by a £1 slot meter, and the hall is completely non-smoking. There is central heating in all communal areas, with additional individual heating in all of the suites. Some even have open fires with logs and coal freely available. Well-behaved dogs are welcome, if kept on a lead in the communal areas, and there is plenty of off road parking.

The outside facilities are truly exceptional with bikes being available, as well as facilities for football, cricket, boules, croquet and barbecues. Plus there is a terrific adventure playground, and enough space for kids to run around and get rid of excess energy while the adults take it easy!

Inside, there are pleasant areas to chat and read (such as the large hallway, with its comfy

chairs and sofas), plenty of books and magazines and a small video library with videos to play in your rooms. A funhouse contains not just a table tennis table, but a pool table, a huge ball pool, slide and so much more.

Hargate Hall is the perfect place for a long or short stay among some of the most beautiful and rugged scenery in England. Large or small parties can be easily accommodated, and it makes the perfect venue for management training courses, wedding receptions and get togethers. Why not use it as a base from which to explore the area? Buxton is close by, and the conurbations of Manchester and Sheffield are only 90 minutes away by car - perfect for a day's shopping!

46 BULL I' TH' THORN

Ashbourne Road, Hurdlow, Nr Buxton,
Derbyshire SK17 9QQ
☎ 01298 83348
e-mail: amaltby-baker@tiscali.co.uk
⊕ www.bulliththorn.co.uk

The former coaching inn of **Bull I' th' Thorn** dates back to 1472, with parts that may even date back to the 12th century, making it one of the most historic inns in Derbyshire. Today it still retains many of its original features, though it now combines them

with modern standards of service and outstanding value for money. It has three double en suite rooms and these are beautifully furnished and decorated. The whole inn has a warmth that is due in no small part to mine hosts Annette and Graeme Maltby-Baker, who have created a place that is renowned throughout the area for its food and drink. It is open every day with the exception of Mondays, though it opens on bank holiday Mondays. It offers one real ale at the bar - Robinson's Unicorn, as well as a wide array of beers, lagers, wines and spirits.

Food is served 12 noon - 2.30pm and 5.30pm - 8.45pm and all day weekends. Graeme is the chef, and he uses locally sourced, fresh produce wherever possible. There is a menu and a daily specials board. You are well advised to book at weekends. Children are most welcome, and all credit and debit cards, with the exception of American Express and Diners, are accepted. To the rear is a rare breeds farm, which opens in the summer months. There is also a caravanning and camping site (with showers) and occasional medieval evenings are held within the inn itself.

48 MERRIL GROVE COTTAGES

Longnor, Nr Buxton,
Derbyshire SK17 0QY
☎ 01298 83621
e-mail: merrilgrovecottages@gmail.com
⊕ merrilgrovecottages.com

The stone-built **Merril Grove Cottages**, three miles from the village of Longnor, offer some of the best self-catering accommodation in Derbyshire. Rated four star and dating from the 18th century, they are set in 14 acres of countryside, with stunning views in all directions.

There are three cottages on offer - Summerhill, Honeysuckle and Rose, and all have been upgraded to an extremely high standard, with TV, video, CD player, fridge/freezer, dishwasher, microwave, linen, patio area and off road parking. All are non-smoking. They are situated around a walled courtyard next to the original Merril Grove farmhouse.

Rose Cottage boasts two bedrooms, a double and a twin, and has a hallway, lounge/dining room, kitchen and bathroom. Honeysuckle Cottage has a hall, a large double bedroom and a single bedroom, with a

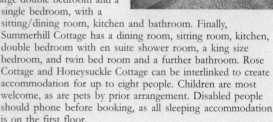

sitting/dining room, kitchen and bathroom. Finally, Summerhill Cottage has a dining room, sitting room, kitchen, double bedroom with en suite shower room, a king size bedroom, and twin bed room and a further bathroom. Rose Cottage and Honeysuckle Cottage can be interlinked to create accommodation for up to eight people. Children are most welcome, as are pets by prior arrangement. Disabled people should phone before booking, as all sleeping accommodation is on the first floor.

Longnor, Derbyshire SK17 0NT
☎ 01298 83262

Longnor is a small, attractive village a short drive west off the A515 Buxton to Ashbourne road. It is home to the **Horseshoe Inn**, a village pub that is full of olde worlde character and tradition. If it seems familiar to you, then this isn't surprising. It featured in the long running TV series *Peak Practice* as the "Black Swan". The building itself - built of old, local stone and covered in ivy, dates back to 1604, and overlooks the market place.

Mine hosts Sam and James Corbishley have been in charge since March 2005, and since then have turned the place into a popular spot for locals to meet and have a drink and for visitors to stop and eat. From Monday to Friday it is open from 5pm, and at weekends (Saturday and Sunday) from 12 noon. It stocks three real ales, all immaculately kept, these being Burton Bitter, Marstons Pedigree and a rotating guest ale. In addition, there is a fine range of beers, lager, cider, spirits, wines, liqueurs and, should you be driving, soft drinks.

Sam is the cook in the Horseshoe Inn, and she combines imagination and flair to produce some of the best pub fare in the area. She insists on only fresh, local produce wherever possible, which means that her food is full of flavour and goodness. Everything, as you would imagine, is home-cooked, and presented beautifully. Serving time are:12 noon to 3pm and 6pm to 8.30pm on Saturday and Sunday. Friday evenings are steak nights, served between 6pm and 9pm. The steaks are juicy and thick, so you are in for a treat if you visit then! Plus you are well advised to book a table for Saturday evenings and Sunday lunchtime, so popular is the food here. You can choose off the printed menu of the specials board. Children are very welcome, and payment is by cash and cheque only. The inn offers no problems to the disabled.

Sam and James will soon be offering superior accommodation at the Horseshoe Inn, so phone them for details. From above the pub Sam also runs a professional beauty and holistic treatment practise, and in addition James leads motor cycle guided tours (leaving from the pub) which explore the rugged beauty of the Peak District. Leaflets are available for both of these.

Sam and James want to welcome you to their inn. It offers superb English hospitality at reasonable prices, plus a charm that will make you want to come back again and again.

49 YE OLDE CHESHIRE CHEESE INN

High Street, Longnor, Buxton,
Derbyshire SK17 0NS
☎ 01298 83218
🌐 www.yeoldecheshirecheeseinn.com

A short drive from Buxton via the A515 and B5053 will take you to one of the quaintest and oldest inns in the Peak District - **Ye Olde Cheshire Cheese Inn**. Built in 1621, the building was a former farmhouse before being opened as an inn in 1706 by the Milward family. It got its name because the family dealt in Cheshire cheeses which it sold all over Derbyshire and Yorkshire.

It is a mellow building in old stone, with hanging baskets and window boxes adding colour in the summer months to an already charming exterior. Inside, it is equally appealing, with low, beamed rooms, warm wood and comfortable furniture. Many prints and nick-nacks hang on the walls. Look out for a photograph of Mrs Thirza Robinson, who was landlady here from 1909 until 1947. She is now reputed to haunt the building!

Mine hosts are Lynn and Chris Stevenson, who have created a place that is popular with visitors and locals alike. It offers two real ales - Robinson's Unicorn and a seasonally changing brewery guest ale, as well as a great selection of beers, wines, spirits and soft drinks if you're driving.

The inn is closed on Mondays, excluding bank holidays when they are open all day. Also open all day on Sunday. Great food is served in the Olde Cheshire Cheese, and you can choose from a specials board or a menu. Everything is home-cooked on the premises, and Lynn, who is a superb cook, sources the produce used in the kitchen locally, wherever possible. The home made steak and ale pie is a popular dish, and on Saturday evenings and Sunday lunchtimes you are well advised to book in advance. Sunday lunch is a carvery - usually pork, beef or gammon, plus as many vegetables and potatoes as you can eat.

By the spring of 2007 there will be four letting rooms available within a converted barn opposite the inn. One will be specially adapted for the disabled, and you should ring for details.

Children are very welcome, and all credit cards, with the exception of American Express and Diners, are accepted. Chris is a professional magician, and can often be seen in the bar up to his tricks, if you ask he will visit your table and astound you with his sleight of hand!

194

Chapel Hill, Beeley, Derbyshire DE4 2NR
☎ 01629 734666

Situated in the lovely old village of Beeley, on the Chatsworth estate, **The Old Smithy** is a village shop with a difference. For not only is it a shop, it is also a licensed café that sells superb food and drink. It can be reached by turning off the main A6 (Bakewell to Matlock road) at Rowsley and taking the B6012, which is signposted to Baslow and Beeley. After about three quarters of a mile, turn right into Beeley village by taking a left turn opposite the pub, and you'll find this shop and café on your right.

It opened in May 2004, and since then has gone from strength to strength. It is owned and run by Helen Grosvenor, who used to run the village pub, and as the name implies, it was once the premises of the village blacksmith. Parts of it date as far back as the 17th century, though now the standards of service and good, old fashioned value for money are a bit more up to date than that!

The shop itself is to the front of the building, where the smithy was once

housed, and the café is to the rear, in an extension. Both shop and café specialise in good, fresh, local agricultural produce, and you are assured of freshness and full flavour should you come here. There are delicious "deli" foods on offer in the shop, such as local cheeses, meats, jams, chutneys and preserves, as well as the day-to-day items all villages need, including daily papers.

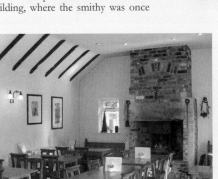

The café seats 40 in absolute comfort, with room for a further 50 on a patio. The décor is an attractive mix of traditional style and modern, clean lines, and here you can eat good, wholesome country produce that is sourced locally. Hearty breakfasts, lunches and snacks are all on offer, and the main-course specials are both delicious and filling. The Sunday lunch is particularly popular, and you are well advised to book in advance. As the café is licensed, you can enjoy a beer or wine with your food, or in fact just relax over a welcoming drink between visiting local attractions.

One of the pluses of The Old Smithy is the warm welcome you are sure to receive from Helen Grosvenor, who has built up a loyal clientele from both near and far by her attention to detail, the quality of what she has to offer and her commitment to keen prices.

The opening hours of the shop are from 8am to 5.30pm, with the café and tearooms opening between 10am and 4pm. Children are very welcome in this no-smoking establishment.

51 | EAST LODGE HOTEL AND RESTAURANT

Rowsley, Matlock, Derbyshire DE4 2EF
☎ 01629 734474
e-mail: info@eastlodge.com
🌐 www.eastlodge.com

A warm, welcoming and friendly atmosphere awaits you when you visit the no-smoking **East Lodge Hotel and Restaurant**. It is set in the truly beautiful Peak District National Park, and is the nearest hotel to Chatsworth House, England's finest stately home.

The experience of staying at East Lodge has been described by guests as timeless, elegant and memorable. It sits in in its own ten acres of peaceful gardens, and has fourteen fully en suite rooms that are delightfully and individually furnished and decorated to the highest possible standards. There are three executive rooms, three superior rooms and six standard rooms, including a ground floor room that has facilities for the disabled, and one that is reputed to be haunted! This is English hospitality at its best, and yet East Lodge is unstuffy and relaxing - just the place to escape the hustle and bustle of modern life. It sits close to the cities of Sheffield, Manchester, Derby, Nottingham and Leicester, and only two hours from London, but is a world away in ambience and character.

The hotel is the only one in in the Peak District with a Gold Award from the Tourist Board, and is the highest rated three star establishment in the area. It has been featured in good hotel guides, and has even won a "most excellent service" award in the recent Condé Nast Johansens hotel awards. For the last seven years the hotel restaurant has won an AA Rosette for its food, with the produce always being fresh and sourced locally. The restaurant itself has an ambience that complements the high standards of cuisine, and friendly service ensures that you can relax and enjoy a unique eating experience. The wine list contains many fine wines, and the attentive staff will be more than pleased to recommend a particular wine for a particular meal.

For a quiet drink, the Garden Room bar is the place to go. It serves a wide range of drinks, and here you can relax and unwind after a hard day exploring the surrounding countryside. In fact, if two people book the special package of a double room for a minimum of two nights with breakfasts and dinner, they get one free entry each to Chatsworth!

The hotel can also hold civil marriage ceremonies, and can organise the perfect reception, meaning that all worries are removed. Details are available on request.

52 DUKE OF WELLINGTON RESIDENTIAL COUNTRY INN

15 Wellington Street, Matlock,
Derbyshire DE4 3GX
☎ 01629 582299
e-mail: dukeatmatlock@aol.com
and fireside taverns@aol.com
🌐 www.dukeofwellingtonmatlock.co.uk

Situated on the A632, a short distance from the centre of Matlock, the **Duke of Wellington Residential Country Inn** is one of the finest pubs in Derbyshire. It has an ambience that is welcoming and friendly, and on Friday, Saturday and Sunday is open all day for the sale of three real ales (Hardy & Hanson's Original, Old Trip and Green King IPA) as well as a great range of beers, lagers, cider, spirits, wine and soft drinks.

The inn also serves superb food, and you can choose from the printed menu or the specials board. All the dishes are cooked on the premises from only the finest and freshest local produce wherever possible. The speciality of the house is the sizzling skillet of steak. Food is served from 12 noon to 2pm and from 5pm to 7pm from Monday to Thursday, and from opening until 7pm the rest of the week.

It has also recently converted some old stables into nine beautifully decorated and furnished en suite rooms for the discerning tourist, five of which are on the ground floor. The tariff is usually room only, but breakfasts are available at a small extra charge by prior arrangement. They are available all year round, and have a three-star rating.

The Duke of Wellington makes the ideal base from which to explore Derbyshire and the Peak District. Matlock is close by, as are Buxton, Chesterfield, Ashbourne and Bakewell, and the cities of Sheffield, Derby and Nottingham are no more than half an hour's drive away.

53 COUNTRY COTTAGE RESTAURANT

69 Matlock Green, Matlock,
Derbyshire DE4 3BT
☎ 01629 584600
e-mail:
enquiries@countrycottagerestaurant.co.uk
🌐 www.countrycottagerestaurant.co.uk

Quarter of a mile from the centre of the historic town of Matlock, on the A615, you will find one of the best restaurants in the area – **Country Cottage Restaurant**, housed within a property that has been traced back to the 1600s when it was originally a saddlery. This warm, yet spacious establishment has stone walls and exposed beams, and combined with the burgundy table linen and sparkling cutlery and tableware, ensures an intimate and memorable eating environment. It is owned and run by Alan and Ruth Baxter, and they pride themselves on the quality of food and service that they offer.

The cuisine is English-French with subtle influences from other parts of the world, and the menu contains such mouth-watering dishes as lamb and black pudding noisettes, medallions of fillet steak, chicken stuffed with sun-dried tomatoes and basil, and paprika scented seabass. Desserts include lemon and lavender panna cotta, St. Clement crème brûlée and a traditional cheese platter with port.

Alan, who is the chef, has trained and work in many prestigious restaurants, and uses produce that is sourced locally wherever possible, ensuring freshness that is apparent in the flavour. The menu changes monthly and can be viewed on their website.

The restaurant seats 20 in comfort, is non-smoking and licensed, so there is sure to be a wine that complements your meal. Children are welcome and can chose from the main menu. **Country Cottage Restaurant** is open every evening except Sunday and Monday. Reservations are advisable.

197

81 Matlock Green, Matlock,
Derbyshire DE4 3BX
☎ 01629 592911
e-mail: matlockhorseshoe@aol.com
🌐 www.matlockhorseshoe.com

The Horseshoe is a family-friendly pub, and one of the best of its kind in the whole of Derbyshire. Here, in this former coaching inn, you and your family can relax in warm, welcoming surroundings, knowing that you are safe and well looked after. It is popular with locals and visitors alike, and people from all over the globe have visited on a regular basis. Mandy and James Hilton, who run the pub, are committed to the highest standards of service, the keenest prices and great quality when it comes to food and drink. It has been recommended in the Senior Citizens Food Guide to Derbyshire for its outstanding commitment to excellence, and has so far received two Cask Marque Awards for the way that its ale is looked after.

The well proportioned building itself is of local stone, and makes a welcoming sight for anyone seeking out a place for great food and drink. It is open all day, every day, and serves between one and three real ales on a rotating basis, including Deuchars, Pale Rider and Charles wells Bombadier. Plus, of course, there is a wide range of beers, lagers, wines, spirits and soft drinks if you're driving.

The food is outstanding. It is served between 12 noon and 2.30pm and 6pm and 9pm every day. There is also a carvery every Sunday between 12 noon and 5pm. You are well advised to book at weekends, as the Horseshoe is the most popular place in the area for family meals. All the produce used in the kitchen is sourced locally, so you know that it is going to be fresh and full of flavour. Mandy is the chef, and everything is beautifully home- cooked on the premises. You can choose from printed menus or from a changing daily specials board.

The Horseshoe also has a popular senior citizens' menu that contains such favourites as cod and chips, steak and ale pie and cottage pie. And the children's menu has all the kids' favourites - chicken nuggets, pizza, fish fingers, burgers and so on.

The no-smoking dining room seats up to 18, though you are free to eat elsewhere in the pub. On Saturday evenings there are live singers from about 9pm, and on Wednesday evenings around 9.30 pm there is a music quiz. Friday night is party night, with either a disco or karaoke and basket meals (ring for details) The inn is disabled friendly, and has plenty of off road parking. There is also a large beer garden and a children's play area.

The Horseshoe is the place to bring the family or to enjoy a quiet meal or a party atmosphere on Friday evenings. Mandy and James look forward to welcoming you to their establishment.

55 GLENDON GUEST HOUSE

Knowleston Place, Matlock,
Derbyshire DE4 3BU
☎ 01629 584732

On the A615, and only a short walk from the centre of Matlock, is the **Glendon Guest House**, owned and run by the husband and wife team of Sylvia and Dennis Elliott. They have been providing top quality bed and breakfast accommodation in these premises for over 30 years, and during that time have created a superb establishment that attracts people back again and again.

It has four extremely comfortable rooms, two of which are fully en suite, and one being a family room. They are both comfortable and well furnished, and the whole B&B has a real "home from home" feel to it. Rooms have wash hand basins, colour TVs, shaver points and tea/coffee making facilities. The building is a grade two listed dwelling house built in 1862, and retains many original features. It has been graded four stars from the AA, so good is the hospitality.

The breakfasts at the Glendon are legendary. Sylvia only uses eggs from her own hens, home-cured bacon, sausages and home-grown tomatoes in season. Breakfast times are flexible, but are usually between 8am and 9am. There is plenty of off road parking, and the premises comply fully with fire regulations.

This is the perfect base from which to explore Derbyshire and the Peak District, and Sylvia and Dennis will offer you a real Derbyshire welcome should you choose to stay here!

56 BRADLEY HOUSE HOTEL

14 Dale Road, Matlock,
Derbyshire DE4 3LT
☎ 01629 582677
e-mail: bradleymatlock@aol.com
🌐 www.bradleyhousehotel.co.uk

With a fine situation right in the heart of Matlock, the **Bradley House Hotel** is a guest house offering superior bed and breakfast to discerning tourists. There are five rooms,

two of which are en suite. There is a real home-from-home atmosphere, and people come back again and again. There is plenty of parking, and all credit cards with the exception of American Express and Diners are accepted. The owners understand sign language, so people with hearing problems are especially welcome.

57 THE WHITE LION INN

195 Starkholmes Road, Matlock,
Derbyshire DE4 5JA
☎ 01629 582511
e-mail: info@whitelionmatlock.co.uk
⊕ www.whitelionmatlock.co.uk

The White Lion Inn is a charming, stone-built inn dating from the 18th century. It sits on a minor road between Matlock Green and Cromford Mill, and is everything that a country pub should be - inviting, friendly and cosy, with an interior that features low, oak beams, dark wood and a flagstoned floor. The wall lighting is subdued, contributing to its 'olde worlde' air, and the dining area is carpeted throughout.

The home-cooked food here is outstanding yet reasonably priced Dishes can be chosen from the menu or from a specials board, where only the finest and freshest of local produce in season is used wherever possible. Food is served from Tuesday to Saturday, 12 - 2pm and 5.30pm to 9pm, (no food Tuesday lunchtime in winter). A traditional Sunday lunch is served 12 - 3pm (with vegetarian options). The inn is closed at Monday

lunchtime, but is open at all other times and serves three to four real ales - Marston's Pedigree and guest ales - plus the usual range of beers, wine, spirits and soft drinks. All major credit cards are accepted, and children are most welcome.

The inn also offers two comfortable guest rooms at affordable prices, a double and a triple. They both have private bathrooms and are delightfully furnished and decorated.

The drinking and dining areas are disabled friendly, but please phone about the accommodation, which is upstairs.

58 THE RED HOUSE COUNTRY HOTEL & RESTAURANT

Old Road, Darley Dale. Matlock,
Derbyshire DE4 2ER
☎ 01629 734854
e-mail:
enquiries@theredhousecountryhotel.co.uk
⊕ www.theredhousecountryhotel.co.uk

The **Red House Country Hotel and Restaurant**, north of Matlock, is set within an acre of grounds, and is housed in a building constructed in 1891 for a Manchester architect. It marries all the elegance and warmth of a bygone age with modern standards of service and great value for money. Its many-gabled, well proportioned front commands superb views down the Derwent Valley which can be appreciated by the many guests who return again and again. It has ten en suite rooms (three on the ground floor), each one individually and comfortably furnished. Two have four-poster beds, and one has an antique French bed. Each one has a TV, direct dial phone and tea/coffee making facilities.

The restaurant has an excellent reputation throughout the area. It is situated within the former drawing room, with views over the gardens and valley. The finest and freshest of produce is used in the kitchens wherever possible, and the cuisine is traditional English with hints of Scotland, the Mediterranean and even further afield. Special winter breaks are on offer at the Red House, and in November and December guests staying for three nights or more are given complimentary tickets to see Chatsworth in all its Christmas splendour. The Red House operates a strict no-smoking policy in all parts of the hotel.

59 TALL TREES COFFEE SHOP & RESTAURANT

Oddford Lane, Two Dales, Matlock,
Derbyshire DE4 2EX
☎ 01629 732932

Housed within the Forest Garden Centre,
off the A6 in Two Dales, the **Tall Trees
Coffee Shop and Restaurant** is the ideal
place for that welcoming cup of tea or
coffee, or a hearty, filling lunch. It is a
charming and stylish establishment with
friendly,
efficient
staff and
down to
earth
prices that
are sure to
please. All
the
produce
used in

the kitchen is sourced locally wherever
possible, and everything is home-cooked to
perfection. If you're in the area, you just
can't afford to miss it!

62 THE PRINCESS VICTORIA

174/176 South Parade, Matlock Bath,
Derbyshire DE4 3NR
☎ 01629 57462

Housed in a building that dates from the
18th century, **The Princess Victoria** is one
of Matlock Bath's finest inns. It has a cosy,
welcoming atmosphere and serves five real
ales and a fine selection of beers, wine and
spirits.

The
upstairs
restaurant
seats 40,
though
you can
eat
throughout
the inn.
The food
is good,

honest pub food, beautifully home-cooked
on the premises from fresh local produce
where possible. It is always tasty and filling,
and represents great value for money.

60 BLAKELOW COTTAGES

Blakelow Farm, Bonsall Lane, Winster,
Matlock, Derbyshire DE4 2PD
☎ 01629 650814
e-mail: blakelawcottages@w3z.co.uk
🌐 www.blakelawcottages.co.uk

Blakelow Cottages are set within eight acres of
superb countryside near Winster, and consist of
three, five-star cottages that offer the very best in
self-catering accommodation. The cottages have
been converted
from old farm
buildings and have well-appointed kitchens, TVs, radios and
CD players, central heating and laundry facilities. Duvets, linen
and towels are provided and there are parking facilities.

Candle Cottage sleeps two in one bedroom, and has a
ground floor sitting/dining room with vaulted ceiling, wooden
floors and wood burning stove. The bathroom is also on the
ground floor, and the galleried double bedroom is on the first
floor. Cranberry Cottage sleeps four in two bedrooms. It has a
spacious sitting room with gritstone fireplace and electric fire,

plus French windows that open out onto a south facing patio.
The dining area window has views across to Chatsworth House.

Christmas Cottage also has two bedrooms and sleeps four.
It boasts a spacious sitting room/dining area, a large gritstone
fireplace and a log burning stove. The open plan kitchen has
French windows that open onto a patio area.

Blakelow Farm is over 200 years old, and all the cottages
have preserved the original character of the farm buildings,
ensuring that you, the discerning customer, has a holiday
experience that is as relaxing or as activity-filled as possible.

61 TEMPLE HOTEL & RESTAURANT

Temple Walk, Matlock Bath,
Derbyshire DE4 3PG
☎ 01629 583911
e-mail: templehotel@btconnect.com
🌐 www.templehotel.co.uk

The **Temple Hotel** is an impressive, white-washed building that stands above the town of Matlock Bath, just south of Matlock itself. Set in two acres of hillside, it enjoys great views out over the Derwent Valley. The hotel dates from about the 1780s and in its time has been visited by Princess Victoria, before she was Queen and by Lord Byron as a guest, both of whom etched writings on the restaurant window. The original pane can now be seen in a display cabinet, with a copy of Byron's unfinished poem.

A warm, friendly and informal feel makes the Temple Hotel one of the most popular establishments of its kind in Derbyshire. The completely non-smoking policy inside the hotel makes a pleasant change and the new owners, from March 2006, have brought a lot of energy to the hotel and are building a great reputation.

There are fourteen fully en suite rooms, ten doubles, two twins, one single and one family. They all have a colour TV, clock/radio, hair dryer, tea and coffee making facilities and telephones. They are available all year round, and can be booked on a bed and breakfast basis.

The Chatsworth Lounge Bar has an atmosphere that speaks of less hurried times, and here you can relax fully over a pint of real ale, mainly sourced from the local area. Plus the wine cellar is sure to have a wine that will complement your meal. During the summer, you can drink outside on the terrace and enjoy the views.

An extensive range of whiskies to suit all tastes is also available in the bar and whisky menus are provided to guide you to the perfect choice. The selection includes many Single Malts, from Scotland, Bourbons from America and even a new Welsh Whisky.

Evening meals, are always home cooked and well-presented. All of the produce in the kitchen is as fresh as can be, and most sourced locally ensuring a great eating experience. The main bar menu has some good English options as well as the more unusual choices offered as the daily specials. They are also happy to cater for special dietary requirements.

The Temple Hotel makes a great base from which to explore the Peak District. The Heights of Abraham and Gulliver's Kingdom are on the doorstep and Chatsworth, Haddon Hall, and Crich Tramway Village are all within an easy drive. There are plenty of local walks to undertake and the surrounding countryside offers routes to suit most abilities. It is also ideal for short summer or winter breaks, as well as for weddings and anniversaries. Business meetings, conferences and seminars can be accommodated in the Panorama Room.

63 THE PEAK DISTRICT MINING MUSEUM 🏛

**The Pavilion, Matlock Bath,
Derbyshire DE4 3NR
☎ 01629 583 834
e-mail: mail@peakmines.co.uk
🌐 www.peakmines.co.uk**

Visit a hands-on museum where you can experience and wonder at the almost forgotten world of a Derbyshire lead miner. For centuries men have toiled underground in cramped and hazardous conditions to earn a meagre living by extracting the mineral *galena*, lead ore.

See the tools they used and the clothes they wore and encounter the problems that the miner overcame - flooding, explosions and roof falls. Experience the maze of twisting tunnels and shafts and observe the advances in technology and the great importance of lead in our modern day lives. Refresh yourself in the cafe and browse in the well-stocked shop. See the magnificent water pressure engine that was rescued from deep down in a local lead mine.

You can find out what "nicking" means and discover for yourself the amazing network of tunnels that exist under your feet and wonder at the crystals glistening in the walls. This two-man, working lead and fluorspar mine will give you an authentic insight into life underground and the tools and equipment involved. Gold! Gold! The magic word in mining. Stand in a real gold strike, then try your hand at panning for "gold" - but you won't get rich quick with the sort of gold that you recover! Don't think that the museum is a dry-as-dust, wet weather activity. The average family will be enthralled by the many hands-on, interactive and novel opportunities.

64 HEIGHTS OF ABRAHAM 🏛

**Matlock Bath, Derbyshire DE4 3PD
☎ 01629 582365 Fax 01629 580279
e-mail: office@heightsofabraham.com
🌐 www.heightsofabraham.com**

Featuring steep rocky gorges, vast caverns, fast running rivers, wide panoramic views and a cable car, it is easy to understand why the Victorian's called Matlock Bath "Little Switzerland"; however, the **Heights of Abraham Country Park and Caverns** overlooks the famous spa town, and provides a unique aspect to a day out or holiday in the Derbyshire Dales and Peak District.

The journey to the summit of the country park is easily made by taking the cable car, adjacent to Matlock Bath railway station and car park. The cable car ticket includes all the attractions in the grounds, as well as the two spectacular underground caverns. Tours throughout the day allow you to experience the exciting underground world within the hillside, with the "miner's tale' in the Great Rutland Cavern Nestus Mine, and the multivision presentation of the "story in the rock" at the Masson Cavern Pavilion.

The sixty-acre country park also features woodland walks, the Owl Maze, the Explorers Challenge, play and picnic areas, Victoria Prospect Tower, plus the High Falls Rocks & Fossils Shop featuring Ichthyosaur remains. When you have worked up an appetite, why not relax with a drink on the terrace and take in the views, or enjoy a snack in the Coffee Shop or a meal in the Woodlanders Restaurant. So next time you are planning a trip to the mountains, remember The Heights of Abraham at Matlock Bath "Little Switzerland" is nearer than you think.

65 SCOTLAND NURSERIES GARDEN CENTRE, RESTAURANT & CHOCOLATE SHOP

Butterly Road, Tansley, Matlock,
Derbyshire DE4 5GF
☎ 01629 583036 (garden centre)
☎ 01629 582349 (restaurant)
e-mail: sales@scotlandnurseries.co.uk
⊕ www.scotlandnurseries.co.uk

Situated on the B6104 one mile east of its junction with the A615 in Tansley is **Scotland Nurseries, Garden Centre, Restaurant & Chocolate Shop**. This is a large complex set above the village that includes a superb garden centre, landscaping supplies, coffee house/restaurant and chocolate shop that offers the best in food and drink.

The business has been family-run since 1986, and offers everything you need for your garden, including trees, shrubs, heathers, alpines, herbaceous perennials, herbs and soft fruit. Set at 1,000ft above sea level, the plants are hardy. Many of the Royal gardens including Buckingham Palace have been supplied with plants from this nursery. The Outdoor Living area stocks a large variety of paving slabs, fencing, decking, summer houses and much, much more.

The staff, all with academic qualifications, are always available to help and assist with any gardening advice. The garden centre shop and gift shop is set within a stone Victorian barn offering a wide array of gardening sundries, unusual elegant gifts, soft furnishings, books, cards and souvenirs to remind you of your visit to Derbyshire and The Peak District. Opening times are 9am to 5.30pm Monday to Saturday and 10am to 4.30pm on Sundays.

The Restaurant and coffee shop offers delicious teas, coffees, snacks, cakes and full lunches. Fruit and cherry almond scones are made in their bakery every morning and most of the produce used is sourced locally. The menu specials are changed daily, Tuesday is Senior Citizens day, special prices apply on a two course lunch, alcoholic beverages can be served to persons having a full meal. The Heathers Restaurant is very popular, should you wish to have lunch booking is advisable.

The Chocolate Shop and Café was introduced four years ago. A chocolate heaven, it offers hot chocolates, Italian coffees, cakes and tea bread and of course a wide selection of exquisite hand made chocolates. Enjoy chocolates with your coffee or have them boxed as an ideal gift. Scotland Nurseries Garden Centre has full disabled and baby changing facilities.

66 THE VAULTS

Coldwell Street, Wirksworth, Nr matlock,
Derbyshire DE4 4FB
☎ 01629 825786

Just a short stroll from the centre of
Wirksworth you'll find **The Vaults**, an early
19th century inn that combines all the
ambience of former times with up to date
amenities, including comfortable
accommodation. It serves a great selection of
drinks
plus
good,
honest
pub fare
that is
hearty
and
filling.
There
are four
fully en

suite guest rooms, and each one is
beautifully furnished and decorated,
ensuring great comfort and convenience for
the discerning guest.

70 WHITE HART HOTEL

10 Church Street, Ashbourne,
Derbyshire DE6 1AE
☎ 01335 344711

Situated right in the heart of Ashbourne, the
picturesque **White Hart Hotel** boasts five
extremely comfortable rooms, four of
which are en suite. In the bar, it has one
regular
real ale
(Marston's
Pedigree)
and
three or
four
guest
ales,
plus, of
course, a
wide
range of

other drinks. Home-cooked food is available
every day (except Monday) at lunchtimes and
in the evenings, using fresh local produce.
This is an establishment that combines
tradition, great service, and value for money.

67 THE NATIONAL STONE CENTRE

Porter Lane, Wirksworth,
Derbyshire DE4 4LS
☎ 01629 824833 or 01629 825403
🌐 www.nationalstonecentre.org.uk

Just think of STONE … Stonehenge, gothic
cathedrals, dry stone walls, precious gems,
sculpture, millstones, perhaps the great debate
about quarrying. But there's so much more – the
sugar and steel we use, our landscapes, technology
from stone axes to computer controls, the rivers, volcanoes, deserts and earth movements which
created stone, even the water we drink depends on stone – we each use 5 tonnes of stone a year.
Our oldest materials shaped by our oldest industry – still providing vital products, with 21st
Century technology.

A dramatic site in the heart of the Derbyshire Dales on the edge of the Peak National Park
and World Heritage Site is a place crammed with ancient tropical reefs, rocks and minerals,
centuries of industrial history and
full of wildlife treasures… a Site of
Special Scientific Interest.

150 Members of the Dry Stone
Walling Association from all over
Britain have built 19 different
sections of dry stone wall in their
own local materials. Wallers and
dykers from as far away as Caithness
and the Cotswolds worked in their
particular styles to make this
wonderful outdoor museum of
traditional walls. The techniques and
geology of the stones are explained.

68 GALLERY CAFÉ

50 St John Street, Ashbourne,
Derbyshire DE6 1GH
☎ 01335 347425
e-mail:info@sjsg.co.uk
🌐 www.sjsg.co.uk

In the heart of historic Ashbourne **The Gallery Café** is situated within a restored 19th century building which was once the towns Magistrates Court. It is undoubtedly one of the finest cafés of its kind in Derbyshire. It sits above the St John Street Gallery,
which showcases contemporary art and crafts in many forms. The Café and Gallery have been owned and run for the last six years by Glen Bentley and Rob Watkin, and has recently been reopened after a complete refurbishment. They want not only to return the café to its former popularity, but surpass it in terms of quality and ambience.

The spacious café seats 40 and is open from Monday to Saturday from 9am to 5.30pm. Glen does all of the cooking, and the majority of the produce is sourced locally, ensuring

freshness and flavour in the range of home-cooked meals and snacks. The Gallery Café is a member of the Peak District Cuisine Group, and in 2006 won three "Great Taste Awards" from the Guild of Fine Food; a gold award for salad dressing and two bronze awards for gluten-free brownies and marmalade.

So if you're in Ashbourne, why not visit the St John Street Gallery and then head upstairs for a snack, a coffee or a meal. Children are more than welcome.

69 THE GREEN MAN ROYAL HOTEL

10 St John Street, Ashbourne,
Derbyshire DE6 1GH
☎ 01335 345783
e-mail: philippagolonko@yahoo.co.uk

The Green Man Royal Hotel is an institution in the lovely old town of Ashbourne. It dates from the 17th century, and its fine, elegant red brick façade has been gracing St John Street for much of that time. It is a firm favourite for good drink, great food and comfortable B&B accommodation, and under Philipa Golonko, its reputation has been enhanced over the last few years.

It has been endorsed by the Campaign for Real Ale for the range of its real ales, which includes Dr Johnson (a local brew), Abbot Ale and a range of rotating ales, which are highlighted on a board. The bar is a great mix of period detail and comfort, just right for a refreshing drink after a hard day exploring the Peak District. It is a meeting place for locals, and you will be made welcome by them.

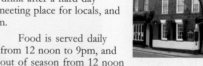

Food is served daily from 12 noon to 9pm, and out of season from 12 noon

to 3pm and 6pm to 9pm. The cuisine is traditional pub food, cooked to perfection and at affordable prices. You can choose from a printed menu or a specials board.

There are 18 fully en suite guest rooms at the Green Man Royal Hotel, and each one is comfortable and cosy, and furnished to an extremely high standard. The bar and dining areas are disabled friendly, but please phone about details of the accommodation.

Osmaston, Ashbourne,
Derbyshire DE6 1LW
☎ 01335 342371
e-mail:
shoulderofmutton.osmaston@barbox.net

Situated in the sleepy, picturesque village of
Osmaston, just off the A52, the **Shoulder of
Mutton** is recognised as one of the best pubs in
Derbyshire. People come from far and near to
sample its great food and its wonderful range of
drinks. Owned and managed by Tina and Paul
since 1993, it goes back centuries, though records were lost in a fire. A date stone of 1803
survives, however.

The exterior is of red brick, which gives it
a charming, warm appearance, and it is an
important feature of a village that boasts the
old Church of St Martin and a village pond.
This is a friendly, welcoming establishment
with plenty of authentic atmosphere and a
great emphasis on high standards of service
and good, old-fashioned value for money. The
customer is king here, and people return again
and again. It is open all day in summer, with
food available from midday until 2pm and
from 7pm to 9pm in the evening,

Only the freshest and finest of local
produce is used in the pub's kitchens, and

guests can choose from a varied menu that
combines the best of English cooking with
influences from abroad. The Sunday roasts are
particularly popular, and the place is always
busy. There is a no booking policy at the
Shoulder of Mutton, so you should turn up
early to ensure a table. So popular is the place
that the owners have recently built an extension
that seats 40 people in absolute comfort. You
can eat here, or in the bar, the lounge, or the
extensive garden in the summer months.

The bar serves a great range of drinks to
suit all tastes. There is a good choice of real
ales - including Bass and Marston's Pedigree -
as well as keg bitters, mild, cider and lager. Plus

there are whiskies, brandies, liqueurs, wines
and a selection of soft drinks should you be
driving. And if you are organising a party or
anniversary, you could do worse than ask Tina
and Paul to supply the outside catering. They
can supply food, outside bar, and all the things
that make an occasion an enjoyable one.

We are on the edge of the Peak District
here, and there is so much to do and see in the
area, from watching motor cycle racing at
Darley Moor to the delights of Alton Towers,
just over the border in Staffordshire. So pay
the Shoulder of Mutton a visit, and sample
good, old fashioned English hospitality in a
friendly, welcoming pub!

Clifton, Nr Ashbourne,
Derbyshire DE6 2GJ
☎ 01335 342654

The **Cock Inn** dates from the 17th century, and is a village local that is not only picturesque and welcoming, but is also full of history. It was originally a coaching inn, and though it has been added to, modernised and altered over the years, it still retains much of the quiet charm of these simpler times. Many of the original features of this whitewashed, stone building have been retained, making it one of the finest pubs in Derbyshire. It is situated in Clifton, which lies two miles south of Ashbourne on the A515.

The interior is equally attractive. It has low beamed ceilings, an open fireplace, old, warm wood and an atmosphere that makes you want to relax, get away from the hustle and bustle of modern life, and enjoy a quiet drink. Mine hosts are the husband and wife team of Andrew and Lorraine Garside, and they have been here for four years, during which time the pub has become very popular with visitors and locals alike. One of the features of the interior is the collection of cockerels on display, many bought for them by the faithful customers.

They keep an immaculate cellar, and were awarded the Cask Marque Beer Award. The preferred pints here are Marstons Pedigree, Bombadier and Timothy Taylors Landlord (all real ales) plus an occasional guest ale in the winter months. And, of course, there is a wide range of beers, wines, spirits, lager and cider. Being a roadside inn, there is also a great selection of soft drinks for people who are driving.

Lorraine is the cook here, producing many fine, traditional dishes that incorporate local produce wherever possible. Everything, as you would imagine, is home cooked to perfection, and the customers' favourites, with good reason, are the home-made steak pies and the roast dinners, which are served every Sunday.

There is seating for up to 60 people in various areas, and the dining room, which seats 16, is no-smoking. When food is being served, the bar areas are also no-smoking. Food times are 12 noon to 2.30pm and 6.30pm to 9pm (8.30pm in the winter months). The pub is closed every Monday at lunchtime, except for bank holidays.

Children are very welcome at the Cock Inn, and all debit and credits cards (with the exception of Diners and American Express) are taken. In the winter months (October to March) there is a quiz on the first Monday of every month from 9pm. The pub is disabled-friendly, and boasts a large beer garden, a great children's play area and plenty of off road parking.

208

73 THE BLACK HORSE INN

Hulland Ward, Derbyshire DE6 3EE
☎ 01335 370206

The Black Horse Inn dates back to the 1690s at least, and is a picturesque building that is full of 'olde worlde' charm, with colourful paintings of horses on the exterior walls, and - surprisingly - a gallows that hangs over the front door! It is on the A517, halfway between Ashbourne and Belper, close to Carsington Water, and makes the perfect base from which to explore the attractions of an area that is rich in heritage and history.

It is a free house, owned and run by Muriel and Michael Edwin for the last eleven years, and they are proud of the reputation the inn has earned, not only among locals, but visitors as well. The interior is equally as picturesque as the outside of the building, with low beams, warm, mellow wood, open fireplaces and featured stone walls.

It has four guest rooms on offer, all en suite and all having a four-poster bed. Such is their comfort and attention to detail that they have been awarded four stars. Each has a colour TV, tea/coffee making facilities, double-glazing and central heating. The bed and breakfast tariff includes a hearty, filling full English breakfast, or something lighter if required.

Food is one of the Black Horse Inn's specialities, with Muriel presiding in the kitchen. The menu features a wide range of delicious dishes (including a wide range of vegetarian options) , and in season game is very popular. Everything is sourced locally wherever possible, except for the venison, which is from Lincolnshire. On Sunday there is a carvery, which is so popular you are advised to book in advance. Food is served from 12 noon to 2pm over seven days, and from Monday to Saturday between 6pm and 9.30pm and on Sunday from 7pm until 9.30pm. Take-away is available on all the dishes, including the carvery.

Good drink is served every session, though there is no all day opening. Four real ales are available which change constantly, and Michael is proud of his ales, which he keeps immaculately. So much so that the inn has featured in the Good Beer Guide for many years, and is about to be featured in the CAMRA beer and bed & breakfast guide. An astonishing fact is that, since Muriel and Michael arrived at the inn, it has featured no less than 693 real ales. Plus, of course, there is a wide selection of beers, wines, spirits, lagers and cider, along with soft drinks if you're driving. There is plenty of off road parking, and a lovely beer garden. All major credit cards are accepted, and the dining and drinking areas will present no problems for the disabled. Please phone about the accommodation, which is upstairs.

This is an inn that you will return to again and again!

74 TIGER INN

232 Ashbourne Road, Turnditch,
Derbyshire DE56 2LH
☎ 01773 550200
e-mail: tigerinn1@btconnect.com

The well-proportioned and whitewashed **Tiger Inn** sits within the picturesque village of Turnditch, on the A517 between Ashbourne and Belper. It is situated within a former coaching inn that dates to the late 18th century, and is filled with history and charm. In fact, the inn places great emphasis on tradition and high standards of service, and has an "olde worlde" interior featuring a collection of distinctive old water jugs. All around is stunning countryside that just cries out to be explored, and to the rear is a veranda where you can sit and admire the view out over the Ecclesbourne Valley.

It is owned and managed by mine hosts Jacquie and Richard. Richard has been here seven years, and in that time has turned it into an inn that is recognised as one of the best in this part of Derbyshire. But that's not all - they want to improve it even further, so that you, the customer, know that you are getting the best of food and drink at the most affordable prices. Already people from all walks of life are singing the praises of its fine food, its drink and the warmth of its welcome!

It is open all day, every day, for fine ales

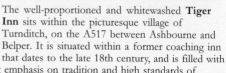

and great food and people come from far and near to sample the great English hospitality on offer here. There are five real ales available, four of them on a rotating basis, with Marston's Pedigree a popular regular.

The spacious dining area seats around 45 people in absolute comfort, and is child-friendly and non-smoking, though a recently constructed outdoor area caters for smokers. The kitchens use only the finest and freshest local produce wherever possible, and the cuisine is an imaginative interpretation of English classics with a hint of other traditions as well. Food is available seven days a week between 12 noon and 9pm. Monday to

Saturday there is a printed menu and a specials board, and on Sunday a traditional Sunday lunch is served. Also popular are the fish dishes served on Fridays and Saturdays. Due to the reputation of the food served in the Tiger Inn, you are advised to book well in advance at all times.

Every Sunday evening at 9pm there is a quiz, and all are welcome. There is plenty of off road parking and a beer garden and children are more than welcome. All major credit cards are accepted.

75 RED LION INN

Main Street, Hognaston, Nr Ashbourne,
Derbyshire DE6 1PR
☎ 01335 370396
e-mail: redlion@w3z.co.uk
🌐 www.redlionhognaston.co.uk

The white-washed **Red Lion Inn** in the picturesque village of Hognaston, near Ashbourne, has a great reputation for its accommodation, its food and its drink. It boasts three en suite rooms, and its food draws customers from near and far. The inn also boasts four real ales, as well as a range of spirits, beers,

wines and soft drinks. This is the place for a dinner on Friday or Saturday evenings, or a Sunday lunch, though you are advised to book.

HIDDEN PLACES GUIDES

Explore Britain and Ireland with *Hidden Places* guides - a fascinating series of national and local travel guides.

Packed with easy to read information on hundreds of places of interest as well as places to stay, eat and drink.

Available from both high street and internet booksellers

For more information on the full range of *Hidden Places* guides and other titles published by Travel Publishing visit our website on

www.travelpublishing.co.uk
or ask for our leaflet by phoning
0118-981-7777 or emailing
info@travelpublishing.co.uk

76 KNOCKERDOWN FARM

Carsington Water, Near Ashbourne,
Derbyshire DE6 1NQ
☎ 01629 540525
e-mail:
info@derbyshireholidaycottages.co.uk
🌐 www.derbyshireholidaycottages.co.uk

Carsington Water is England's ninth largest reservoir, and is now one of Derbyshire's prime leisure facilities. **Knockerdown Farm**, with its self catering holiday cottages, is situated close to the reservoir, and adjacent to the B5035. All of the seventeen cottages are non-smoking, and are housed within

an old farmhouse or in converted outbuildings, offering some of the best self-catering accommodation in the county. The cottages accommodate from two to ten people in absolute comfort, and are tastefully furnished and equipped (including linen). As the cottages are in the countryside, it is regretted that no dogs are allowed.

The on-site facilities are excellent. There is an indoor swimming pool, sauna, treatment room, video library, games area, and children's play area. The restaurant is open from

Wednesday to Sunday each week from 12 noon to 2pm and from 6pm to 9pm. It serves superb food, with the kitchen sourcing its produce locally wherever possible. Non-residents are welcome, though it is advisable to book beforehand.

Holiday cottages are also available at Darwin Lake, at Darley Moor near Matlock. As with Knockerdown Farm, they are furnished and equipped to an exceedingly high standard, and are ideal for people who like to make their own entertainment.

211

Carsington Water Visitors Centre,
Ashbourne, Derbyshire DE6 1ST
☎ 01629 540363
e-mail: enquiries@newleafcatering.co.uk
🌐 www.newleafcatering.co.uk

Carsington Water lies a few miles north east of Ashbourne, off the B5035, and is one of Derbyshire's favourite recreational sites, where you can fish, sail, bird watch or just enjoy the stunning views. At the waterside you will find the Carsington Water Visitors Centre, with its **Main Sail Restaurant**. This is a light, airy, no-smoking place that is both stylish and modern and here you can enjoy the best of food, beautifully cooked and presented, while enjoying wonderful views.

It is owned and run by husband and wife team Janet and Ian Broadbent, who have been here six years. During that time they have created a lively, popular place for people to eat, both summer and winter, and it's superb, contemporary menus have earned it an enviable reputation as one of the best eating places in Derbyshire. It is a member of Peak District Cuisine, which promotes the sourcing of locally grown food products so that diners get dishes that are fresh and flavoursome.

It is open every day of the year with the exception of Christmas Day. From November 1st to December 31st it opens between 10am and 5pm; in January it opens between 10am

and 4pm; in February and March it opens between 10am and 5pm; the rest of the year it opens between 10am and 6pm. The main lunches are always served between 11.30am and 2.30pm. The Main Sail can seat up to 120 people in absolute comfort, and bookings can be taken for parties of over twelve. Coach parties can be accommodated by prior appointment. The daily specials board and the printed menu contain many fine dishes that combine good, fresh produce with flair and imagination, and everything is freshly prepared and cooked on the premises.

Why not have a Christmas lunch or party at the Main Sail? Each year the restaurant prepares a wonderfully evocative menu, ensuring that you enjoy a stress free time while someone else does all the hard work! Carsington Water in winter has a magic all of its own, and enjoying good food and drink while you look out over the reservoir is one of the joys of the winter months.

In addition, the restaurant offers three self-catering cottages to discerning tourists, and they make the ideal base from which to explore the Peak District. Two of the cottages sleep 17, and one sleeps 9, and they represent amazing value for money. There is a minimum stay of three days, and the prices are all-inclusive.

The Main Sail is disabled friendly throughout, with a lift that takes you up to the restaurant. All major credit cards are accepted.

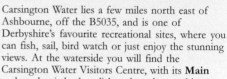

Buxton Road, Tissington, Ashbourne,
Derbyshire DE6 1NH
☎ 01335 350317
e-mail: enquiries@bluebelltissington.co.uk
🌐 www.bluebelltissington.co.uk

Discovering a delightful new pub that offers the very best in English hospitality is always special. And when it's the **Bluebell Inn and Resturant** at Tissington, three miles north of Ashbourne, it is doubly special. This country inn, built of warm stone, has a reputation that goes far beyond its locality for great food and drink.

It consists of a bar, no smoking restaurant and function room, and has bar meals, Sunday lunches, banquets, buffets, conferences, meetings, wedding receptions and so on. The bar seats up to 32 people, and is comfortable, cosy and at the same time spacious. It offers real ales supplied by Greene King brewery, as well as a range of beers, lagers, wines, spirits and soft drinks. It is the ideal place to relax after a hard day exploring the Peak District, or planning your next trip. Hosts Ruth and Phil Sampson have a wealth of experience in the pub trade, and will make you most welcome when you visit.

With its menu containing over 40 main courses, food is important at the Bluebell, and it has achieved a fine reputation for its cuisine.

The no smoking restaurant seats 16 people in absolute comfort, and serves home-made dishes that use only the finest and freshest of local produce wherever possible. In fact, all the meat used in the kitchens is sourced from a local farm, ensuring that you have a meal to remember. In January 2004 the inn was awarded the coveted "Peak District Cuisine" award because of the policy of using local produce, and if you look for the "Peak District Cuisine" logo on the menu you will see which dishes this applies to. Special diets can be catered for, such as gluten-free, dairy-free, wheat-free and vegetarian.

The pub is open from 12 noon until 11pm every day from March to November, with food being served from noon until 9pm (and 8.30pm on Sundays). In November, January and February, Monday to Thursday inclusive, it closes between 3pm and 5.30pm unless booked in advance. There is a large car park that can accommodate approximately 75 cars and a large beer garden with play area.

Tissington is a historic village that continues the Derbyshire tradition of well-dressing, and there are many walks and places to visit in the area. Chatworth House and Alton Towers are close by, as is Haddon Hall.

79 TISSINGTON HALL & GARDENS

The Estate Office, Tissington, Ashbourne,
Derbyshire DE6 IRA
☎ 01335 352200

The Estate came into the hands of the FitzHerbert family as the result of Nicholas FitzHerbert marrying the heiress Cicely Francis in the late 15th century. The family originally came to England with William the Conqueror and settled in Derbyshire when William FitzHerbert was granted the Manor of Norbury in 1125.

The baronetcy was conferred on William FitzHerbert by George III in 1784 for acting as Minister for Woods and Rivers and for his role as a Gentleman Usher to the King. He divided his time between London and Derbyshire and was succeeded by his eldest son, Anthony, in 1791. His brother Henry inherited as a minor in 1798 and built extensively in and around the village during his 60 year tenure. Successive baronets have tended diligently to the estate and village although the total acreage has shrunk from about 4,000 acres at its peak in 1850, to 2,400 acres today. The sales were mainly enforced by twentieth century death duties and the cost of Sir Hugo's divorce in 1922.

Tissington Hall was originally built in the early 17th century, a top floor was added around 1700 and then the well-known Derby architect Joseph Pickford remodelled the west aspect around 1780 by adding a projecting central bay and open arcading on the ground floor.

The Hall and Gardens are open to the public on 28 advertised days per year. Groups, parties and societies are very welcome by arrangement throughout the year.

81 THE SOUTH PEAK ESTATE

The National Trust, South Peak Estate,
Ham Hall, Ilam, Ashbourne,
Derbyshire DE6 2AZ
☎ 01335 350503
e-mail: john.malley@nationaltrust.org.uk
🌐 www.nationaltrust.org.uk

The South Peak Estate, lying within what is called the White Peak area of the Peak District, extends to approximately 4,000 acres. Located to the north of the market town of Ashbourne the main bulk of the estate is located within the two river valleys of the Dove and Manifold. Within the property are popular visitor attractions such as Dovedale and Ham Park. The Estate is centred on Ham Park which contains Ham Hall (now a Youth Hostel), together with the National Trust's visitor facilities. To the north-west lies the Hamps and Manifold Valleys

and to the north-east lies Dovedale stretching seven miles to the north towards Hartington. Some of the finest Peak District limestone grasslands and dales woodland lie within these two valleys under Trust management which are soon to be designated as Special Areas of Conservation under European legislation. Access to the estate is available to the public all year round and visitor numbers are very high with an estimated 2 million visitors a year to Dovedale alone.

Mappleton, Nr Ashbourne,
Derbyshire DE6 2AB
☎ 01335 350305
e-mail: info@okeoverarms.com
🌐 www.okeoverarms.com

Situated in the pretty village of Mappleton, two miles northwest of Ashbourne, the **Okeover Arms** dates from the early 18th century, when it was known as the Griffin Inn. In 1845 it changed its name to the Okeover Arms, after the local estate of the same name, and it has been known by that name ever since, though at one time it was a temperance hotel. Mappleton sits in the Dove Valley, a couple of miles north west of Ashbourne and between the A52 and the A515. It is where the Annual Bridge Jump takes place every New Year's Day, where contestants paddle down the River Dove then throw themselves into the river from a 30-feet high bridge, before heading for the Okeover Arms for something that will warm them up!. Owned and personally run by Selena and Jason Surguy, the pub is open all day and every day between June and September each year, all day at weekends and from 12 noon-3pm and 6pm-11pm weekdays throughout the year.

The inside is cosy and welcoming, as a good English pub should be, and offers six real ales - four hand pulled and two straight from the cask. The real ales are regularly rotated, using micro breweries wherever possible. Plus there is a fine selection of lagers, cider, spirits, wines, liqueurs and soft drinks. This is the place to have a quiet drink and get to know the locals, who will make you more than welcome.

The food here is outstanding. The menu includes such dishes as crab and avocado tian, pan fried scallop and smoked salmon salad with garlic butter and new potatoes, home-made beef Wellington with potatoes and a rich port jus, and rump steak, chips and a black pepper sauce. Only the finest and freshest of local produce is used in the kitchen, ensuring that you have a dining experience you will long remember. Food is served from 12.30 pm and from 6pm until 9pm on weekdays and 12 noon straight through to 9pm at weekends. Varying menus include à la carte, a bar menu and a specials board, so you are sure to find something that will suit your palate. In fact, so good is the food that booking is recommended on Friday, Saturday and Sunday evenings. Jason is a superb chef, and combines flair and imagination when planning his dishes. The restaurant is non-smoking, and seats 38, though you can eat throughout the inn or outside in the summer months. All credit cards except Diners are taken, and there is off-road parking The last Monday of each month is jazz night, and there is a bi-annual jazz festival held in February and August. Every six weeks there is a themed food evening, plus there are occasional wine tastings. Phone for details.

82 LEEHOUSE FARM

Leek Road, Waterhouses,
Staffordshire ST10 3HW
☎ 0538 308439

For first class B&B accommodation, you
can't do better than the no-smoking
Leehouse Farm, in the pleasant village of
Waterhouses, off the A523. It boasts three
fully en suite rooms that have been given a

four
diamond
silver
award by
the Heart
o f
England
Tourist
Board,
that are
comfortable,

spacious and delightfully furnished. It is a
Grade ll listed house dating from 1751, and is
open all year except Xmas. Breakfasts are
hearty and filling, with times being flexible.
No evening meals, but there are many fine
eating houses in the area.

84 PADDOCK HOUSE FARM HOLIDAY COTTAGES

Alstonefield, Ashbourne,
Derbyshire DE6 2FT
☎ 01335 310282
e-mail: info@paddockhousefarm.co.uk
🌐 www.paddockhousefarm.co.uk

A mile and a half out of Alstonefield, on the
Alstonefield to Hulme End Road, are the four-star
Paddock House Farm Holiday Cottages, which
offer outstanding, yet affordable, self-catering
cottages for a holiday that can be as activity-filled
or as relaxed as you like. The five cottages are
within the Peak District National Park, and surround a central
courtyard, amid 35 acres of beautiful countryside. Each one is
furnished and decorated to an exceptional standard.

Ash Cottage, Beech Cottage and Oak Cottage have three
bedrooms, with the first two sleeping 6+2+cot, and the last one
sleeping 5+2+cot. Hazel Cottage has two bedrooms, and sleeps
4+2+cot. Elm Cottage has one bedroom, and sleeps 2+2+cot.
All are double glazed and have central heating. Ash and Beech
cottages also have open fires, and coal is available for purchase.

There is no charge for heating
or electricity, and towels and
crisp cotton linen are supplied. If you book for a week or more,
a complimentary bottle of wine and flowers will await you.

The holiday cottages are open all year, and the arrival day for
a week or more is Saturday. Shorter breaks are also available, and
you should phone for details. These start from Friday or
Monday. Towns such as Buxton or Ashbourne are within easy
reach of the cottages, so buying food and provisions is no
problem.

216

Townend Lane, Waterfall, Waterhouses,
Staffordshire ST10 3HZ
☎ 01538 308279
e-mail: keith@peaklion.co.uk
angela@peaklion.co.uk
🌐 www.peaklion.co.uk

With its prime location on the edge of the Peak District National Park, its picturesque exterior and its high standards of service, it is no wonder that the **Red Lion Inn** is one of the most popular free houses in this area of Staffordshire. Mine hosts are Angela and Keith, who, since they came here in 2005, have built on the establishment's solid reputation as a place for good food and drink. The interior is very attractive and welcoming, with polished wood, an open fire, a well stocked bar, and prints, brass and interesting knick knacks on some of the surfaces.

Situated in the village of Waterhouses, it dates back to the late 19th century, and is built of local stone into a small hill, which has led to the creation of an unusual terraced beer garden. It opens from Tuesday to Friday from 6.30pm onwards, on Saturday from 12 noon to 3pm and from 6.30pm onwards, on Sunday from 12 noon to 3pm and from 7pm onwards, and on Monday from 8pm until closing time. It offers three real ales, Bass regular and two rotating ales, one usually being from the World Top Brewery in North Yorkshire. All are beautifully kept and in addition, of course, there is a good range of beers, wines, spirits

and soft drinks.

Good food is important in the Red Lion, and you can choose from a daily changing blackboard menu so that full advantage is taken of fresh local produce in season. Juicy steaks with all the trimmings are a speciality, and people come from near and far to sample them. Food is served at different times in summer and winter. Summer times for lunches are 12 noon to 2pm from Thursday to Saturday and 12 noon to 2.30pm on Sunday. Summer times for evening meals are 6pm to 9pm Tuesday to Saturday and 7pm to 9pm on Sunday. Winter times for lunches are 12 noon

to 2pm on Saturdays and 12 noon to 3pm on Sunday. No lunches are served on weekdays. Evening meals are served between 6.30pm and 9pm from Tuesday to Saturday and 7pm to 9pm on Sunday. You are well advised to book a table on Saturday and Sunday.

Children are very welcome at the Red Lion Inn, and all major credit cards are taken. There is a quiz night every other Sunday evening from 9pm, and all are welcome. There is plenty of off-road parking at the front. To the rear there is a beer garden, and a terrace at the side of the building.

85 WOLFSCOTE GRANGE COTTAGES

Wolfscote Grange, Hartington,
Nr Buxton, Derbyshire SK17 0AX
☎ 01298 84342
e-mail: wolfscote@btinternet.com
🌐 www.wolfscotegrangecottages.co.uk

Imagine excellent holiday accommodation. Imagine delightful, self-catering cottages that combine history and tradition with all the modern conveniences that holidaymakers expect nowadays. In fact, imagine the **Wolfscote Grange Cottages**, a few miles south of Buxton. Three of them are in a lovely setting overlooking the Dove Valley, while the fourth and fifth are in picturesque Hartington village itself. All are comfortable and full of olde worlde character. There is central heating in each of them, and some have log burning stoves, some with spa/whirlpool bathrooms and dishwashers. All are rated four star by the tourist board. The whole area is ideal for outdoor activities or to just relax amid quiet, rural scenery, while at the same time having access to Ashbourne, Buxton and other towns in the area.

The three cottages named "Swallows Return" (sleeping six), "Wolfscote" (sleeping four) and "Tom Boys Cottage" (sleeping four), are to be found on the edge of the Dove Valley, with breathtaking scenery all round. They have been converted from a 15th century barn and all share a common farmyard which has been landscaped to form a sunny and sheltered patio area. Living quarters are upstairs, with bedrooms on the ground floor. Each cottage has an individual character, and has antique furniture, luxurious bathroom/shower rooms, and comfortable sofas to stretch out on after a hard day exploring in the Peak District! The kitchens are well equipped, with electric cookers and microwaves. Colour TVs, videos and radio and CD player come as standard.

Grace's Cottage and Hillcrest Cottage (both sleeping four) are within the village of Hartington. Grace's Cottage comes complete with many of its original features, such as oak beams, wooden flooring and exposed stonework walls. Living accommodation is upstairs, with the two bedrooms on the ground floor. The living/dining/kitchen area is open plan, and there is a shower room with toilet and basin. There is also a sunny patio with outdoor furniture. Hillcrest Cottage dates from the 18th century, and has recently been restored. It overlooks the old Church of St Giles, and has a ground floor lounge with wood burning stove, separate kitchen/dining area and bathroom with whirlpool bath. The rear garden has outdoor furniture.

Wolfscote Grange farmstead, which was mentioned in the *Domesday Book*, also offers luxurious B&B accommodation.

Biggin-by-Hartington, Nr Buxton,
Derbyshire SK17 0DH
☎ 01298 84451
e-mail: enquiries@bigginhall.co.uk
🌐 www.bigginhall.co.uk

Centrally situated in the beautiful Peak District National Park, historic Biggin Hall dates back to the 17_{th} century. It is now one of the most popular hotels in the area - the **Biggin Hall Country House Hotel**, set in eight acres of glorious countryside. The present owner has completely renovated it in keeping with its original character, retaining many fine period details and marrying them with the modern attributes that make a hotel so friendly and welcoming. Nobody stands on ceremony at the Biggin Hall Country House Hotel - the accent is on informality and good old-fashioned value for money.

Visitors have the choice of two sitting rooms, one with a library, the other with a large, traditional open fireplace, and there is a separate dining room. There are 20 guest rooms, each one individually furnished with antiques and decorated to an exceptional standard. All have a colour TV, tea/coffee making facilities, telephone and silent fridge. As well as the "master suite" in the main house, there are six en suite double/twin

rooms and a suite of two rooms sharing an adjoining bathroom. Within the recently converted 18th century courtyard there are five double/twin rooms and a two-bedroom suite, all fully en suite. The Bothy, which is attached to the main house but accessed from the courtyard, boasts two double/twin rooms, both en suite, and a two-bedroom suite with private bathroom. The Lodge, 70 yards across the lawn from the house, has one single and two double/twin en suite rooms. All guests can avail themselves of the facilities in the main house.

Food is important in this hotel. Dinner is served at 7pm, and is one of the highlights of a stay here. Many guests come back again and again for

the traditional and superb home cooking that forms the mainstay of the menu. Almost all of the produce is sourced locally, so you are assured of a meal that combines great flavour with freshness. Vegetarian options are always available, and special dietary needs can be accommodated by prior arrangement. Continental breakfasts are served between 8am and 9am, and for a modest cost you can have a full English breakfast as an alternative.

The Biggin Hall Country House Hotel combines luxury and informality within stunning surroundings, and affordable prices.

87 FOX AND GOOSE

Foxt, Staffordshire ST10 2HN
☎ 01538 266415

If you want the very best in food and drink in Staffordshire, then it's worth making a diversion off the A52 at Froghall, or the B5053 at Ipstones, to discover the **Fox and Goose**, surely an inn that can be considered one of the gems of Staffordshire. It dates from the 18th century, and its charming exterior blends in perfectly with the surrounding scenery. In fact, the views from the Fox and Goose across open countryside are truly stunning, and worth the visit alone.

It's interior is everything an English inn should be - inviting, warm, friendly and full of olde worlde atmosphere. There is a well stocked bar, plenty of old polished wood, charming prints and knick knacks on walls and shelves, and carpeted floors in many areas. Mine hosts are Louisa and Steven, who have been in charge since March 2006, but who bring a wealth of experience in the licensed trade to the place. They offer great hospitality and good cheer to all who enter the premises, whether local or a visitor.

You can eat in the conservatory-style, no smoking restaurant, which seats 42, and enjoys all the wonderful bucolic views that the place

offers. The food is wonderful, as the Fox and Goose employs a professional chef, who makes sure that only the finest and freshest of local produce in season goes into the dishes. Dishes on the menu include juicy steaks with all the trimmings, Jamaica jerk chicken casserole, salmon steak with prawns and grilled gammon steaks. There is also a 'bangers 'n' mash' menu, featuring such dishes as Cumberland sausage, venison sausage and pork and Bramley apple sausage, with a selection of mashed potatoes and gravy. You can choose from a printed menu or a daily specials board. The bar sells four or five real ales, all immaculately kept by Steven - the regulars being Abbot and Bass, with rotating guest ales.

Plus the selection of beers, lager, cider, wines, spirits and soft drinks is outstanding.

The inn is open every evening through the week, and all day on Saturday, Sunday and bank holidays. Food is served every evening between 6pm and 10pm, and from 12 noon to 10pm on Saturdays and Sundays. Children are most welcome, and all credit cards are accepted. There is an off-road car park, a patio with heating to the rear and seating at the front.

So seek out the Fox and Goose in Foxt for the very best in hospitality, food and drink!

Star Bank, Cotton, Oakamoor,
Staffordshire ST10 3DW
☎ 01538 702489
e-mail: yeoldestarinn@tiscali.co.uk

Ye Olde Star Inn is a rarity nowadays - an old coaching inn that has retained its 'olde worlde' atmosphere while still offering the very modern concepts of value for money, high standards of service and a warm, friendly welcome. It dates from the 18th century, and many of the original features have been retained, such as the low, oak beams, exposed stone and dark, polished wood. Situated on the B5417 a mile of so from the centre of Oakamoor towards the A524, it is a free house owned and run by the Pickles family, who, since they came here in August 2005, have created an establishment that is popular with tourists and locals alike.

It offers three real ales - London pride and two rotating ales - as well as a fine selection of beers, wines, spirits and soft drinks for those who are driving. In addition, it serves great

food, and is the ideal place for a lunch or evening meal. Food is served from Monday to Saturday between 12 noon and 2.30pm and 5pm and 9.30pm, and on Sunday from 12 noon to 8pm. You are best to book at all times in the summer. All the family share the cooking, and there is a menu and a daily specials board which takes advantage of fresh local produce in season. The no-smoking restaurant seats 50, and a family room is available. Children are very welcome, and all credit cards with the exception of American Express and diners are accepted.

Macclesfield Road, Leek,
Staffordshire ST13 8LD

☎ 01538   398823/373867

e-mail: k.barks@btconnect.com
or info@leekwhitelion.co.uk

🌐 www.leekwhitelion.co.uk

The White Lion is a stunning inn on the A52 close to the centre of he historic town of Leek. The building itself is a former farmhouse dating partly from the 18th century, though it has been an inn since the turn of the 19th century at least. Now it is an establishment famed throughout the area for its food. But this is no ordinary pub food - this is restaurant-style food at competitive pub prices, served in a convivial and welcoming atmosphere.

The owner, Kelvin Barks, who has been here five years, has created a family-friendly inn that is relaxed and inviting. The décor places great emphasis on tradition, with old beams, open fires and flagged floors in some areas. And yet the service is efficient and the prices are all highly competitive, attracting people from far and wide to sample the superb eating experience he offers. The decision to change the inn into a non-smoking establishment has made it even more popular.

The inn is open every session for ale and other drinks, and all day on Saturday and Sunday. There are three real ales on offer -

Bombadier, Abbot and a rotating guest ale. There is also a wide selection of beers, lagers, cider, wines, spirits and soft drinks should you be driving.

The menu at the White Lion is exceptional. It is carefully planned by the head chef and Kelvin, whose extensive travels in Europe heavily influence the selection. The produce used in the kitchen is sourced locally and is organic wherever possible, ensuring freshness and flavour. You can choose from a printed menu or from a daily changing specials board. If there is a dish you particularly enjoy, then if the ingredients are

to hand in the kitchen, and you give him advance warning, the chef will endeavour to prepare it for you. Roasts are added to the menu on Sundays, and are very popular

Due to the popularity of the food here, you are well advised to book at all times, and all major credit cards are accepted. Children are more than welcome, and indeed there is a superb children's play area. There is plenty of off-road parking as well as a heated patio area, and the inn is hidden from the main road, ensuring privacy.

12 Sheepmarket, Leek,
Staffordshire ST13 5HW
☎ 01538 385803
e-mail: mickandchez@yahoo.co.uk

The Black Swan is a charming old town pub that dates at least to the 17th century. It was an old coaching inn, and had stables and a smithy to take care of the horses. An outbuilding was also used, at one time, as the town morgue! Today, however, it has a totally charming aspect, being whitewashed, with small-paned windows and hanging baskets to add a touch of colour.

The interior is equally as charming, with old beams, open fireplaces and old, mellow wood. It is cosy and warm in winter, and spacious and cool in summer, but friendly and comfortable all year round. The place is popular with travellers and locals alike, and you'll be made more than welcome by the regulars. Mine hosts Mick and Chez have over 14 years of experience in the licensed trade between them, and first came here two and a half years ago as managers. Now they have taken over the lease, and since they came they have built on the pubs already substantial reputation. Both have open, welcoming personalities, and are full of drive. They will make sure that you enjoy your time here.

The pub is open all day and every day for the sale of a wide range of drinks. There are two real ales on offer, Marston's Bitter and Marston's Pedigree, both beautifully kept so that they are always in tip top condition. There is also the occasional guest ale, plus a wide range of the more usual beers, lager, cider, wines, spirits and soft drinks should you be driving.

The food is great, and home-cooked to perfection on the premises from produce that is sourced locally wherever possible. Mick is a qualified chef, though both Mick and Chez cook. You can choose from a printed menu or, in the near future, a daily specials board. Try the sandwiches, jacket potatoes or their "light and simple" dishes. Or you could choose a juicy steak with all the trimmings, an all-day breakfast or Cajun Chicken etc. Food is served from Monday, Tuesday, Thursday and Friday between 12 noon and 3pm and 5.30pm and 7.30pm, and from 11am to 3pm and 5.30pm to 7.30pm on Wednesday, which is market day. Wednesday night is curry night (with a choice of three or four dishes), and there is no food on Saturday or Sunday evenings.

There are also occasional mid-week quizzes, and you should phone for details. On Saturday evening, before each bank holiday Monday, there is live entertainment. The pub is disabled-friendly, and there is a heated outdoor patio.

Abbey Green Road, Leek,
Staffordshire ST13 8SA
☎ 01538 382865
e-mail: jo@abbeyinn.co.uk
ⓦ www.abbeyinn.co.uk

Jo and Darrel Sargeant offer you a very warm welcome to **The Abbey Inn**, a freehouse that is situated on the outskirts of the historic town of Leek in Staffordshire, and close to the Peak District National Park. It dates from the 17th century, and is a handsome building, a delightful mix of traditional features that you expect from an inn of this age and quality, and modern concepts such as high standards of service and great value for money.

It offers good food, great drink and comfortable and affordable accommodation to the discerning traveller and tourist. Walkers are most welcome, and there are many fine walks within the area. Its food is renowned throughout the area, the cuisine being classic English with a few foreign influences. The kitchen uses only the finest and freshest local produce. You can choose from the printed menu, which features such favourites as warming bowls of soup, mixed grills, a combo for two of chilli and ginger goujons, Brie wedges, onion rings, salad, dips and garlic bread. The specials board also has many favourites, and can include steak and onion pie, liver and onions and chicken breast in a red wine sauce.

It is also famous for the quality of its drinks, and offers two real ales, one of them London Pride and the other a rotating guest ale from a local brewery. It also offers a quality range of beers, lagers, cider, wine, spirits and soft drinks. This is the perfect inn to relax over a glass (or two!) of your favourite tipple as you contemplate a day exploring the Peak District, or planning your next day's foray into an area of England that offers some of the best scenery there is.

Accommodation is superb, as the rooms are comfortable and tastefully decorated. One

room, with its king-sized bed, is suitable for self-catering, though breakfast is available at the inn. The other two rooms are doubles, though one is spacious enough to be considered a suite.

The inn is closed on a Tuesday and serves food the rest of the week at the following times: Monday - Saturday lunchtimes 11am to 2pm; Monday - Thursday evenings 5.30pm to 8pm; Friday - Saturday evenings 5.30pm top 9pm and Sunday 12 noon to 9pm.

92 DEN ENGEL BELGIAN BAR AND RESTAURANT AND EL 4 GATS TAPAS BAR

11-13 Stanley Street, Leek,
Staffordshire ST13 5HG
☎ 01538 373751
e-mail: enquiries@denengel.co.uk
🌐 www.denengel.co.uk

The Belgians love their beer, and now you can share this enthusiasm by visiting the stylish **Den Engel Belgian Bar and Restaurant**, and, from Spring 2007, the **El 4 Gats Tapas Bar**. Opened ten years ago, and having moved to the present premises three years ago, the Belgian Bar is a popular place to sample some of the best beer and food in the Peak District and Staffordshire.

It is one of a dozen or so such bars in Britain, and has been judged as one of the best. It has

certainly been voted by Tim Webb, who writes books about Belgian beer and is a noted authority, as the best he has been to outside Belgium! It is owned by Geoffrey and Hilary Turner, and Geoff, a great Belgian beer enthusiast, makes regular trips to Belgium to keep up to date with the latest brews. This ensures that you, the customer, get to drink some fine beers at really down to earth prices!

On offer are over eleven brews, including the latest, Sparta Pils, a genuine Belgian pils lager. But you can also drink Blanche de Bruxelles, De Koninck, Westmalle Trappist, Chimay Tripel and Liefman's Kriek. No fewer that 110 bottles line the shelves of this popular establishment, together with export Guinness, Kwak, Orval and so much more. Opening times are Monday - Thursday open 4pm, Friday, Saturday, Sunday open 12 noon, Sunday, Monday, Tuesday close 11pm and Wednesday - Saturday close 11.30pm.

The no smoking restaurant features many beer-based dishes. It seats 30 in absolute comfort, and is open from Wednesday to Sunday from 7pm - 10pm. You can choose from a printed menu or a specials board. Menus change monthly with minor changes each week, and you are advised to book for Saturday evenings.

Opening in the Spring of 2007 will be EL 4 GATS, a licensed tapas bar serving traditional;, authentic tapas to discerning customers. It will be open seven days a week from 10am until midnight, and will welcome children. All credit cards, with the exceptrion of American Express and Diners, are welcome.

16-18 Getliffe's Yard, off Derby Street,
Leek ST13 6HU
☎ 01583 373132
🌐 www.thecoffeeclique.co.uk

For a stylish and impressive coffee bar in the centre of Leek, head for **The Coffee Clique** in Getliffe's Yard, off Derby street, the town's main thoroughfare. It is stylish and impressive, with a clean, contemporary ambience about it while at the same time retaining a feeling for the past. Getliffe's Yard was once a uninspired area of the town, but is now trendy and smart - just right for a place as sophisticated as The Coffee Clique.

But for all its modern feel, it is still a friendly establishment that places great emphasis on high quality and value for money. Julie and Kirsty, who own and run The Coffee Clique, have created the coffee house from what was an empty shell (the whole area was once workmen's cottages), designing and decorating it to make it appealing to both young and old alike.

It is open from Monday to Saturday from 8.30 am to 5 pm for breakfasts, light lunches, coffees and snacks. You can choose from a printed menu or a specials board which changes daily. Paninis are very popular, and are served with a salad, coleslaw and potato crisps. Fillings include tuna with mixed pepper salsa, bacon with brie and red onion, feta, Italian herbs and Mediterranean vegetables, and so on. There are also vegan and vegetarian alternatives available. Or how about the The Coffee Clique's

fine range of toasties, which are always tasty? They come with various fillings such as tomato, onion, ham, tuna, etc, and are accompanied by a side salad, coleslaw and potato crisps.

Or you can choose from an extensive range of sandwiches - chicken and bacon with mayonnaise, tuna with sweetcorn or red onion, salsa salad, cheese and onion and so on. Baked potatoes have such fillings as cheese and beans, chilli and cheese, humus and carrot and just plain or buttered. The specials board sometimes carries such favourites as apple and almond slice, Danish pastries or minestrone soup.

The range of coffees and teas is extensive, and all are Fairtrade.

Most of the produce used in the kitchen is sourced locally, and great emphasis is placed on good, organic produce wherever possible. There is seating for 20 upstairs and 20 downstairs. Internet access is provided on both floors as there are three PCs and a laptop available to customers. You'll never be disappointed at The Coffee Clique!

150 Cheadle Road, Cheddleton, Nr Leek,
Staffordshire ST13 7BD
☎ 01538 361449
e-mail: pearl@garden-house.org
🌐 www.garden-house.org

Adjacent to the A520, in Cheddleton, south of the small town of Leek, you will find superb bed and breakfast accommodation at **The Garden House**, owned and run by Pearl and Peter Dalley since 2005. In that time, they have created one of the best establishments of its kind in the area, one that has a great reputation for high standards of accommodation, a friendly welcome and great value for money. It stands in its own small grounds, and is a substantial modern house offering the very best in modern amenities coupled with superb hospitality from a couple who want to ensure that your stay is as comfortable as possible. There are four double en suite rooms on offer, all beautifully furnished and decorated. You will be assured of a good night's sleep here after a hard day exploring the local area, which includes the Peak District and Alton

Towers. One of the rooms is a family room, with an extra sofa-bed, and one contains a four poster.

Children are more than welcome at this no smoking establishment. Breakfasts are normally served between 7.30am and 9am or by arrangement, and there are different breakfasts available to suit different needs. People who are disabled should phone beforehand for details of the house's layout. The owners regret that credit or debit cards are not accepted, and that payment is by cash or cheque only.

11 Cheadle Road, Cheddleton, Nr Leek,
Staffordshire ST13 7HN
☎ 01538 361500
e-mail: james@castros-restaurant.co.uk
⊕ www.castros-restaurant.co.uk

For a taste of authentic Latin American cuisine, head for **Castro's Restaurant and Lounge** in Cheadle Road in the pleasant village of Cheddleton, south of Leek. This modern establishment sits by the A520 right on the Cauldon Canal, and is one of the most popular eating places in the area. It is very much the creation of Jamie, Nikki and Thom, and because of their attention to detail, commitment to fine food and high standards of service, it has become *the* place to eat and be seen in the area.

The exterior is in stylish red brick, with large windows and outdoor eating areas for those warm summer months. The interior is spacious and light, with a contemporary feel to it. Comfortable sofas, tiled floors, tables and chairs in warm pine and exposed brick make for a place that is at once fashionable yet welcoming and warm.

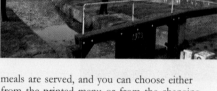

Jamie and Thom are the chefs here, and they create their Latin American dishes with imagination and flair, using locally sourced, fresh produce wherever possible, combined with genuine ingredients that give it that authentic flavour. Both lunches and evening meals are served, and you can choose either from the printed menu or from the changing daily specials board, which is slanted towards produce that is in season.

Why not try their superb nachos, tortilla wraps, fajitas, chimichangas, or tiger prawns wrapped in bacon? They all have a real Latin kick about them, and you certainly won't be disappointed. The evening menu (with fish being a speciality) is strictly Latin American, though traditional English dishes are available at lunchtimes, such as steak and ale pie, scampi and chips, filled baguettes, home-made lasagne or oven baked potatoes with a variety of fillings.

Lunches are served from Tuesday to Friday between 12 noon and 3pm, and evening meals are available from Tuesday to Saturday from 6pm. So popular is the place, and so good is the food, that it is essential to book a table at weekends, and advisable to book at all other times.

The restaurant seats up to 44 people in absolute comfort, but, as the place is licensed, why not drop in just to enjoy a beer, a glass of wine or even just a cup of coffee? The service is fast and efficient, the atmosphere is friendly and informal, and the prices represent amazing value for money!

Denford Road, Denford, Leek,
Staffordshire ST13 7JT
☎ 01538 371819

Think of typical English inn, set beside a slow-paced canal. It has stone-built, whitewashed walls outside, and low beamed ceilings, comfortable seating, dark wood, tiled floors, old copper and brass ornaments and a warm welcoming atmosphere inside. Such an inn really exists - the **Hollybush Inn** at Denford in Staffordshire! The canal in question is the Caldon Canal, while to the rear of the inn is the Leek branch. The inn is a favourite, not only with people who cruise the canal's waters and explore the towpaths, but with locals as well, who have made it their favourite watering hole.

Dating back to the 17th century, the inn was formerly a corn mill before it became a pub, and today's visitors will find a picturesque building with small paned windows and an inn sign incorporating a clock. The bar area is relaxing and cosy - just right for a quiet drink (or two!) as you contemplate a day spent exploring an area that is so rich in history and heritage. It has a roomy no-smoking restaurant area with seating for up to 50 people in absolute comfort, though you can also eat in the conservatory, or in fact, elsewhere in the inn if you want to.

The inn is open all day, every day, for the sale of good drink and excellent, home-cooked food. There are at least six rotating real ales for you to enjoy, as well as a marvellous selection of beers, wines, lagers, cider, spirits and soft drinks if you're driving. Good food is served daily between 12 noon and 9pm, and most of the produce, meat, vegetables, eggs, etc, used in the kitchen is sourced locally for maximum flavour and freshness. You can choose from a printed menu or from the daily changing specials board. There are, in fact, two menus - one for the bar area and one for the restaurant, and you are advised to book a table well in advance of you wish to eat in the restaurant, so good is the food.

All credit cards are accepted with the exception of American Express, and there is plenty of parking available. Every Thursday evening between 9pm and 11pm the live entertainment consists of a live band. The inn presents no problems for the disabled, as everything is on the one level.

The Hollybush is a special inn. It's ambience and general friendly atmosphere harks back to earlier times, when life moved at a slower pace. And yet it has embraced the modern concepts of efficient service, attention to detail and great value for money.

Froghall, Staffordshire ST10 2HAQ
☎ 01538 754782
🌐 www.contrirobe@aol.com

The **Railway Inn** is a handsome, whitewashed building standing on the A52 opposite the Kingsley and Froghall Railway Station, which is on the privately run Churnet Valley Preserved Railway. It sits close to Alton towers, and is also handy for the Peak District National Park, so makes the perfect base from which to explore an area that is rich in tourist attractions and history.

Built as an inn in the late 19th century, it offers five fully en suite bedrooms, each one beautifully furnished and decorated, and two having four poster beds. The place is disabled friendly, as one of the rooms, a family room sleeping up to six, is on the ground floor. The rooms are all clean, spacious and welcoming, and the tariff includes a hearty and filling full English berakfast - just right to set you up for a day exploring the area. Lighter options are also available if required.

The whole place has recently been extensively refurbished, and has the feel and ambience of an "olde worlde" inn, with open fires in the winter months, panelled walls, exposed brickwork and carpeted floors. And being called the Railway Inn, there is some interesting old railway memorabilia for you to examine! It is very popular with locals, which is always a good sign, and you will be made more than welcome by your hosts, brother and sister team Christine and Bob, who have been here since July 2006. It is open all day, every day for the sale of a wide range of beers, lagers, cider, wines, spirits, liqueurs and soft drinks if you're driving. It also serves three to four real ales, with Bombadier and Jennings Cumberland being the regulars and

one to two rotating guest ales.

Superbly cooked food is served every say from Monday to Saturday from 12 noon to 3pm and from 6pm until 9pm. Christine and Bob employ professional chefs, and all the produce used in the kitchen is sourced locally wherever possible, ensuring freshness and great flavour. On Sunday there is a very popular carvery between 12 noon and 4pm. and so good is the food that you are well advised to book on Sundays.

Children are very welcome at this family-friendly establishment, and there is ample off-road car parking space.

Station Lane, Rushton Spencer,
Macclesfield, Cheshire SK11 0QU
☎ 01260 226238
🔳 www.theknotinn@hotmail.co.uk

The **Knot Inn** is a superb hostelry in old, red brick that stands just off the A52 in the village of Rushton Spenser, between Macclesfield and Leek. It stands close to what was a disused branch railway line, and was previously called the Station Inn. It is a handsome building that dates to the 19th century, and has a well-proportioned front with fine, small paned windows and a stately entrance. The whole picture is enhanced by outdoor tables and

seating for those fine, summer months. The interior is a mixture of stylish, modern furniture and fittings and old, polished wood and bare stone pillars. The dining area is especially attractive, with its comfortable seating, its carpets, the sparkling cutlery on every table and the red table cloths.

The inn is managed by Vin Hughes, Gina and their two children Alice and Harriet. who have been mine hosts here since December 2005. They have created a warm, friendly place that is popular with both locals and visitors alike. Here, you feel, you can relax over a refreshing drink after a hard day exploring the Peak District and all it has to offer.

It is open every day and all day Saturday,

Sunday and Bank Holiday Mondays, with the occasional Friday. At other times it is open during the usual sessions for the sale of some of the finest food and drink in the area. Four real ales are on offer. Black Sheep and Charles Wells Bombadier are the regulars. Plus there is the usual range of beers, wines and spirits. Each spring a beer festival is held where you can try up to 30 real ales.

Food is served daily between 12 noon and 2.30 pm and 5.30 pm and 9 pm or thereabouts, while on Saturday and Sunday the times are 12 noon to 9 pm. This is a popular place to eat at weekends, so you are well advised to book in advance. The food is very local, as Vin rears his own Highland cattle,

and Gina's dad rears sheep and lambs. The homemade pies here, as you can imagine, are very popular. Other popular dishes are home-made steak and kidney pie, poached chicken fillet with white wine and mushroom sauce, three lamb cutlets with minted gravy and a selection of juicy steaks. You can choose off the menu or the daily specials board.

All credit cards, with the exception of American Express and Diners Club, are accepted, and children are welcome at this family-friendly inn. There is also occasional entertainment, and you should ring for details. There is a large car park, a play area, a beer garden and a patio to the side and to the rear.

99 THE SILK MILL

Derby's Museum of Industry and History
Silk Mill Lane, off Full Street,
Derby DE1 3AF
☎ 01332 255308
e-mail: museums@derby.gov.uk

The Silk Mill, Derby's Museum of Industry and History, is on the site of the world's oldest factories, the Silk Mills, built by George Sorocold in 1702 and 1717. The foundations and parts of the tower from the 1717 mill are still visible. The displays in the Mill tell the story of Derby's industrial heritage and achievements, and of its people. There is a special emphasis on the development of Rolls- Royce aero engines and the railway industry.

100 DERBY MUSEUMS AND ART GALLERY

The Strand, Derby DE1 1BS
☎ 01332 716659   Fax 01332 716670

Derby Museums and Art Gallery, on The Strand, in the heart of the city, houses collections covering porcelain, paintings, archaeology, geology and wildlife. Paintings by the celebrated 18th Century Derby artist Joseph Wright include portraits, landscapes, subjects from literature and scenes of industry and scientific equipment that represent this exciting period of pioneering discovery. This is the largest collection of the artist's work in any public gallery in the world. The Museum's collection of fine Derby porcelain, produced in the city since c. 1750, is of international importance.

101 THE MARYLAND BED AND BREAKFAST

1083 London Road, Alvaston,
Derby DE24 8PZ
☎ 01332 754892
(mobile 079700 12714)

Situated in Alvaston, on the outskirts of Derby, not far from the A50 and the A5111, the Maryland Bed and Breakfast is one of the finest bed and breakfasts in the whole area. It boasts fifteen rooms, the majority of which are fully en suite. All of them are decorated and furnished to an extremely high standard, and all are comfortable and cosy while still being spacious. Three of the rooms are on the ground floor, and family rooms are also available. It was once two houses, and the present owners, Sharon and Kujeet Sandhu, have converted them into one superb B&B. They have been here for over ten years, and have created an establishment that is a home-from-home.

The Maryland is the perfect base from which to explore the surrounding area. Derby's city centre, with its many shops, restaurants and tourist facilities, is a short distance away, and Castle Donnington Race Track, Nottingham East Midlands Airport, Calke Abbey and Staunton Harold are also close by.

When people discover the Maryland, they seem to return again and again, whether they are business people or tourists. Sharon cooks what must be one of the heartiest breakfasts in Derbyshire - just right to set you up for a day's exploring or shopping! Breakfast times are flexible, though there are no evening meals. However, there are many fine eating places close by.

Children are more than welcome, and there are off-road parking facilities.

102 BLUEBELL INN

Moor Lane, Kirk Langley, Ashbourne, Derbyshire DE6 4LQ
☎ 01332 824423

The **Bluebell Inn** is one of the finest pubs in Derbyshire. It sits in Kirk Langley, just off the A52 west of Derby, and is an attractive, white-washed building that combines modern standards of service with real olde worlde charm. The pub has three real ales, as well as lager, cider, spirits, wines and soft drinks should you be driving. The food is outstanding and reasonably priced, with much of the produce being sourced locally. So popular is the place that you are advised to book at weekends.

104 CULLAND MOUNT FARM

Culland Lane, Brailsford, Ashbourne, Derbyshire DE6 3BW
☎ 01335 360313
e-mail: cullandmount@tiscali.co.uk
🌐 www.cullandmount.co.uk

For superb self-catering accommodation in Derbyshire, there is no better place than **Culland Mount Farm**, a few miles southeast of Ashbourne. The substantial Victorian farmhouse has been divided to offer comfortable, spacious 4-star self catering accommodation among some of the loveliest scenery in the county. It is centrally heated and double glazed, and is well appointed throughout. Sleeping

four, it has two beautifully decorated and furnished bedrooms. Children are very welcome, and short breaks are available.

103 BLACK COW

The Village Green, Dalbury Lees, Derbyshire DE6 5BE
☎ 01332 824297

Looking for a typically English inn? One that served great food, great beer and is situated right on the village green of a picturesque village? Then look no further - the 200-year-old **Black Cow** at Dalbury Lees is for you! You find it by turning off the A52 and Kirk Langley and following the signs to the village, and once you find it you'll be entranced.

This delightful freehouse, with its log fires, friendly atmosphere and warm, old wood, is the hub of the village, and offers three real ales - Banks Bitter, Marston Pedigree and two rotating ales that change mid-week. Plus, of course, there is a fine range of beers, wines and spirits.

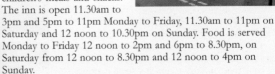

The food is wholesome and filling, and is all homemade on the premises from local produce wherever possible. The menu includes vegetarian, gluten free, "lite bite" meals,

children's meals and snacks. The inn is open 11.30am to 3pm and 5pm to 11pm Monday to Friday, 11.30am to 11pm on Saturday and 12 noon to 10.30pm on Sunday. Food is served Monday to Friday 12 noon to 2pm and 6pm to 8.30pm, on Saturday from 12 noon to 8.30pm and 12 noon to 4pm on Sunday.

Children are welcome and all credits cards, with the exception of American Express and Diners are accepted. There is plenty of parking space, plus a patio and garden.

Derby Road, Doveridge, Ashbourne,
Derbyshire DE6 5JR
☎ 01889 563820

Doveridge is a peaceful, tranquil village near Uttoxeter reached via the A50 dual carriageway, which it stands close to. Legend tells us that it was here that Robin Hood married Maid Marion, under the old yew tree in the churchyard. In the village you will find the **Cavendish Arms**, housed in a substantial, well-proportioned building that has been standing for over 450 years. Whitewashed and picturesque, it was formerly two inns, the Anchor and the Cavendish, and at one time was an old coaching inn with its own stables and smithy.

Times may have changed, but the Cavendish Arms still offers superb hospitality. It is run by Jackie and Dave Jones, who took over here two years ago after having successfully run a pub in nearby Tutbury for over six years. The interior is just as picturesque as the outside, with open fires, old knick knacks and ornaments dotting the walls, plush seating and low, thick beams. It opens every session from Tuesday to Thursday, and from 5.30pm on Monday. On Friday, Saturday and Sunday it opens all day. There are three real ales on offer at the bar - Marston's Pedigree, Bass and a rotating guest ale. They are all beautifully kept by mine host Dave, and are

very popular with both locals and visitors alike. Plus, if you prefer, there is a great range of beers, wines, spirits, lagers, cider and soft drinks on offer. Why not relax here over a welcoming drink after having explored an area that is just so rich in history and heritage?

And, indeed, why not eat here as well? Jackie is in charge of the kitchen, and a superb cook. Food is served from 12 noon to 2pm and from 6pm until 8pm on Tuesday, Wednesday and Thursday, and in the evening from 6pm to 9pm on Friday and Saturday. There is no food on Monday (apart from bank holidays), and on Sunday food is served between 12 noon and 2pm only. On Sunday a traditional Sunday lunch is served, and you are well advised to book, as it is a very popular eating place. Steaks, gammons and steak pie dishes are the favourites here. You can eat in the no-smoking dining area, which seats 18, or in other areas of the inn.

And that's not all – well-appointed accommodation is planned for the near future, and people should phone for details. The inn presents no problems for the disabled, though you should phone regarding the accommodation when it comes on-line. Regrettably, payment is by cash or cheque only.

Children are very welcome, there is occasional entertainment, plenty of off-road parking, and at the back there is extra room in a small marquee. This is also a pub where darts is important, and many famous darts players visit to give exhibition matches.

106 BOARS HEAD HOTEL

Sudbury, Derbyshire DE6 5GX
☎ 01283 820344
⊕ www.boards-head-hotel.co.uk

The AA three-star **Boars Head Hotel** in Sudbury is one of the finest country hotels in Derbyshire. Sitting in its own grounds, it is adjacent to the A515 and close to the A50, and offers 22 luxurious, en suite rooms that have a trouser press, ironing board and iron, hair drier, TV with Teletext and Sky channels, and a direct-dial telephone.

Whether it's a bar snack or a dinner you are after, you are sure of great food at the Boars Head. You can eat in the cosy yet spacious bar or in the elegant "Royal Boar" restaurant. The food is prepared from only the finest and freshest of local produce wherever possible, and the dishes are created with imagination and flair. The restaurant makes an ideal venue for a family celebration such as a party or a wedding reception.

The hotel has an informal atmosphere, and offers weekend breaks which includes two night's bed and breakfast, evening meals on Friday and Saturday, and a Sunday lunch. The price is remarkably reasonable, and you are sure to have a very enjoyable and relaxing time!

All major credit cards are taken, and children are more than welcome. A children's menu is available. There is plenty of off-road parking, and there is so much to see and do in the surrounding area.

HIDDEN PLACES GUIDES

Explore Britain and Ireland with *Hidden Places* guides - a fascinating series of national and local travel guides.

Packed with easy to read information on hundreds of places of interest as well as places to stay, eat and drink.

Available from both high street and internet booksellers

For more information on the full range of *Hidden Places* guides and other titles published by Travel Publishing visit our website on

www.travelpublishing.co.uk
or ask for our leaflet by phoning **0118-981-7777** or emailing **info@travelpublishing.co.uk**

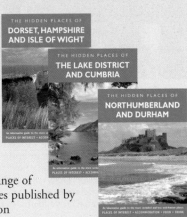

107 THE YARD CAFÉ BAR & RESTAURANT

Belmont street, Swadlincote,
Derbyshire DE11 8JU
☎ 01283 522811
e-mail: info@theyardbar.com

The Yard Café Bar & Restaurant is situated in the centre of Swadlincote, within a listed Edwardian red brick building where once a wood yard flourished. The stunning exterior and interior have a contemporary feel, though traditional features also play a part in making this one of the best establishments of its kind in the area.

It was opened in November 2003 to great acclaim, and since that time has established a reputation which goes far beyond Swadlincote. Food is paramount here, and all the produce is sourced locally to make it as fresh and as full of flavour as possible. Stefan, the chef, combines flair with imagination to prepare dishes that not only please the palate, they please the eyes and the pocket as well! The bar menu, for instance, has such dishes as delicious soups, filled Staffordshire oatcakes, salads, jacket potatoes, lime marinated chicken goujons, burgers and pastas. The Sunday menu features such favourites as honeydew melon with strawberries, pan fried chicken with a chasseur sauce, roast leg of lamb and pan fried loin of pork with pink peppercorns, mushroom and white wine cream.

There is seating indoors for 30, and there is an outdoor area that seats a further 30. The non-smoking air conditioned restaurant seats 56 in absolute comfort. The

décor and furnishings are smart and modern, yet are comfortable and inviting. The bar & restaurant is open seven days a week. From Monday to Thursday the opening times are 11am to 12 midnight, on Friday and Saturday it is open from 11am to 1am, and on Sunday it is open between 12 noon and 12 midnight. Food is served from the bar menu Monday to Saturday between 11am and 6pm. There is no bar menu on Sundays. A traditional Sunday lunch is served from 12 noon until 4pm. The upstairs restaurant is open from Tuesday to Saturday between 7pm and last orders at 9.30pm.

Children are welcome (if eating) up to 5pm, and all credit cards (with the exception of American Express and Diners) are accepted. There is occasional entertainment in the form of live music, and you should ring for details, There are also themed food evenings in the restaurant, and again you should ring for details. Booking for these evenings and at the weekends is advisable. There is plenty of parking close to the bar and restaurant.

Whether it's a cup of coffee you want after a hard day's shopping, a refreshing beer or an intimate dinner in the evening, you need look no further than the Yard Café Bar and Restaurant!

2 High Street, Woodville, Swadlincote,
Derbyshire DE11 7EH
☎ 01283 21753

The **New Inn** at Woodville is owned and run by mine hosts Michelle and Glen Rogers, who have been in charge since 2000, though the pub has been in their family for over 30 ywears. It sits on Woodville's main street, and is found by turning off at junction 22 of the M1 and taking the A511 to Ashby-de-la-Zouch, then continuing on towards Burton on Trent, past Swadlincote, until after about two miles, you reach the village.

The inn, which is housed in an impressive and well-proportioned brick building, dates from the late 18th century, and was the very first pub ever bought by Bass Brewers way back in 1843.

Inside is just as well-proportioned as the exterior, and has a spacious bar that stocks a wide range of beers, lagers, ciders, wines, spirits and soft drinks. There are also two real ales - Marston's Pedigree and a rotating guest ale. They are kept in perfect condition, assuring real ale fans of a treat! It is popular with both locals and visitors alike. The warmth and friendliness of the place marks this pub out as something special, and you are sure to enjoy the convivial atmosphere.

The New Inn is renowned for its food, and serves traditional "pub grub" that is beautifully cooked and served in its 56 seat no-smoking restaurant. The produce is sourced locally wherever possible, and is always fresh and flavoursome. During lunchtimes from Monday to Saturday it offers a delicious range of filling snacks, and on Sunday there is a traditional carvery. In the evenings on Wednesday to Saturday from 6pm until 9pm there is a full menu plus carvery, and, of course, you can order wine from an extensive list. So good is the food that you are well advised to book for the carvery sittings.

Children are most welcome, and most credit cards - with the exception of American Express and Diners Club - are accepted. The pub has an unusual feature - one that makes it even more popular. It has its own bowling green, and there is nothing nicer that sitting out of doors in the summer months, glass in hand, relaxing as you watch a friendly game of bowls - or even a needle match! If you like, you could even be invited to play yourself.

The New Inn offers English hospitality at its finest. You'll get a warm welcome here, and be "welcomed aboard" by the locals. It's one of those places that, if you pay it a visit, you're sure to come back again and again!

237

**Breedon-on-the-Hill,
Derbyshire DE73 8AN
☎ 01332 695129
e-mail: ian@thehorseshoes.com
⊕ www.thehorseshoes.com**

With a history stretching back over 230 years, it's no wonder that **The Three Horseshoes** is one of the best pubs in Derbyshire. But it's not just the age of the place that makes it special - it's the whole ambience. Since arriving here three years ago, owners Jennie and Ian have completely

refurbished the interior, creating a spacious inn that is warm and welcoming, while still retaining many of the original features that make the place so special. Layers have been stripped back to reveal imposing fireplaces, tiled floors and brick walls, while sea grass matting, antique furniture and a mix of collectibles add a dash of warmth.

This is the village pub at its very best - friendly, welcoming and comfortable, and is popular with both locals and visitors alike. The bar serves two real ales, Marston's Pedigree and a guest beer. Plus it has a great selection of beers, lagers, wine, cider, spirits (including some superb malt whiskies) and soft drinks.

But it is the food that marks out the Three Horseshoes Inn. So much so that it has been awarded the "Les Routiers Regional Dining Pub of the Year 2006" award - something that is greatly coveted. Whether it be light snacks, lunches or dinner, all the dishes are carefully prepared from fresh local produce, combined with imagination and flair. Game from local shoots, free-range farm eggs and traditional English cheeses - these are the kind of ingredients used in the kitchen. So whether it's scallops with balsamic, or pasta with salmon and dill cream, or main courses like lamb shank with mustard mash, you know you are in for a gastronomic treat.

The menu is prepared daily, and you can dine either in the non-smoking dining rooms or the bar area. So good is the food, however, that you are well advised to

book in advance.

The building was formerly a farriers, and is found in the centre of Breedon-on-the-Hill. Opposite is the village's old "lock up", where village wrongdoers were once incarcerated until they had seen the error of their ways.

238

109 COFFEE CONCEPT INTERNET CAFÉ

65 High Street, Woodville, Swadlincote,
Derbyshire DE11 7EA
☎ 01283 200646
e-mail: coffeeconcept@btconnect.com
⊕ www.coffeeconcept.co.uk

Woodville High Street is where you will find
Café Concept, an internet café that sells great
coffee and food, and allows you to access
the internet for pleasure, business or
education.

Even if
you don't
want to
surf the
web, it is
the place
to chill
out and
enjoy
great food.
Soup -
cakes - scones - they're all here, as well as
beautifully cooked breakfasts that are served
up until 3.30pm. Children are more than
welcome in this no-smoking establishment.

112 IVY HOUSE FARM GUESTHOUSE AND HOLIDAY COTTAGES

Stanton-by-Bridge, Derby,
Derbyshire DE73 7HT
☎ 01332 863152
e-mail: mary@guesthouse.fsbusiness.co.uk
⊕ www.ivy-house-farm.com

Set in delightful countryside a few miles south of
Derby off the A514, **Ivy House Farm Guest
House and Holiday Cottages** offer the very best
in guest house and self-catering accommodation to
discerning holidaymakers. The no-smoking
guesthouse, which has the coveted four diamonds
and silver award from the English Tourism Council, has six fully en suite rooms (doubles and
twins), four of which are on the ground floor, with one being adapted for the disabled. Two of
the twins and a double are classed as chalets with their own front doors. Each room has a colour
TV, central heating and tea/coffee making facilities. A hearty breakfast is included in the tariff, and
children are most welcome.

Within the adjacent courtyard are five ground floor, self-catering cottages, one of which is
suitable for the disabled. They have been furnished, decorated and fitted out to an exceptional
standard, and sleep three to four. They come fully
equipped, and the price is all-inclusive with the
exception of electricity. People should phone first for
details of availability.

There is so much to do and see in the area around
Ivy House Farm. Stanton-by-Bridge is a sleepy, typically
English village famous for its Swarkeston Bridge and
Stanton Causeway. It was here, in 1745, that Bonnie
Prince Charlie abandoned his march south to take
London for the Jacobites. Derby is only a few miles
away, as is east Midlands Airport and Castle Donnington
Race Track.

111 BAY TREE RESTAURANT

4 Potter Street, Melbourne,
Derbyshire DE73 8HW
☎ 01332 863358
e-mail: enquiries@baytreerestaurant.co.uk
🌐 www.baytreerestaurant.co.uk

Eight miles south of Derby is the small town of Melbourne, home of the **Bay Tree Restaurant**, one of the best known and best-loved restaurants in Derbyshire. It sits in the heart of this small Georgian town, which has so much to offer the tourist and visitor. It has been in the same hands for over 18 years, and during that time its reputation has been made on good, honest cooking, fresh local ingredients and a combination of imagination and flair.

The co-owners are Vicki Talbot and chef Rex Howell, who are determined not only to maintain the high standards they have set, but improve even further on them as well. The restaurant is housed in a warm, old building of red brick that dates back to 1790, and which still retains many of its original features. It features in al the best food guides, and has recently expanded into adjacent premises, creating a restaurant which now seats up to 65 in absolute comfort. However, you are still advised to book, as the place is as popular as ever, if not more so!

The menu changes regularly in this award winning establishment, but always boasts the best of New World cuisine. There is always a great range of nibbles on offer, and, of course, the famous "Bay Tree Champagne Breakfasts". These are served from Tuesday to Saturday each week from 10.30am to 11.45pm. Lunches are served from 11.45am until 3pm, with dinners being from 6.30pm onwards. The Sunday hours are from 12.30pm until 4.30pm, and the restaurant is closed on Mondays.

The wine list has been carefully chosen to reflect the cooking in the Bay Tree, so there is sure to be something that will suit your dinner perfectly. And someone is always on hand to help you choose just the right wine!

There are various menus, including set price dinner menus, set-price lunch menus and à la carte menus. Children are most welcome, and all major credit cards are taken.

Melbourne itself is well worth exploring, with its fine old church (often described as a "miniature cathedral"), the fine old Melbourne Hall (privately owned but open to the public during August, with its gardens open from April to September), and the many places worth visiting within an hour's drive, such as the city of Derby itself, Donnington Park, Calke Abbey and Staunton Harold. So why not visit the restaurant when you're in the area, and enjoy the Bay Tree experience. You'll get a meal which you are going to remember for all the right reasons!

240

113 RISING SUN

**1 The Green, Willington,
Derbyshire DE65 6BP
☎ 01283 702116**

At the crossroads where the A5132 intersects with the B5008, south of the A50, is the small village of Willington. It is here you will find the **Rising Sun**, a picturesque old inn that is popular with visitors and locals alike. This is a typical village "local", full of charm and character, which acts as a focal point for the village and which always offers a warm welcome.

It is family run, ensuring that you always get good service, value for money and friendliness. The spacious and comfortable bar is open all day and every day, and offers two real ales - Marston's pedigree and a rotating guest ale, which are always kept in tip-top condition. Plus there is the usual range of beers, lagers, cider, spirits, wine and soft drinks.

The food served here is delicious, and the finest and freshest of local produce is used wherever possible. Food is available from Tuesday to Saturday, 12 noon - 3pm and 6pm - 9pm, and Sunday 12 noon -

2pm and you can choose from the menu or a specials board for main dishes and desserts. The Sunday lunch is two course and set price, and you are well advised to book.

Children are more than welcome, there are no smoking areas, and credit cards (with the exception of American Express and Diners Club) are accepted. There is plenty of off-road parking, outside seating, a skittle alley and an upstairs function room with bar for up to 60 guests - just right for weddings, parties, anniversaries and conferences.

114 THE BARLEY MOW

**Park Road, Church Gresley,
Derbyshire DE11 9QE
☎ 01283 214662**

Overlooking the large village green at Church Gresley, The Barley Mow is the perfect place to relax and enjoy good ale, great company and wonderful entertainment. It is open all day, every day for real ales plus a wide range of other drinks. No food is served, but snacks such as crisps and nuts are always available. It is a popular meeting place for the locals, who will make you more than welcome. Why not come along on a Friday evening and enjoy the karaoke?

115 DRUM AND MONKEY

Castle Road, Castle Gresley, Swadlincote,
Derbyshire DE11 9LH
☎ 01283 213009
⊕ www.thedrumandmonkey.co.uk

The **Drum and Monkey** is an impressive pub set in the village of Castle Gresley, which stretches out along the A444, and it combines all the ambience of the traditional English inn with the modern concepts of great service and outstanding value for money. Mine hosts are Rob and Adam, and they have been in charge since 2005, and with their combined experience they have created a pub that is popular with both visitors and locals alike.

The interior is welcoming and cosy and is the ideal place to relax over a drink as you chat to the locals or plan your next trip to one of Derbyshire's historic sites. The bar is open at the usual times during the week, and all day on Saturday and Sunday, serving Marston's Pedigree, one of the

county's most popular real ales. Also on offer is a great range of other drinks including the ever-popular Foster's Super Chilled Lager.

Food is served at lunchtimes and in the evenings. The produce is sourced locally wherever possible, and cooked to perfection. There is a beer garden with an aviary, and off road parking. On Friday evenings from 9pm there is live music, and on Sunday evenings at 8.30pm there is a quiz, to which all are welcome.

116 SHOULDER OF MUTTON

64 Church Street, Coton-in-the-Elms,
Derbyshire DE12 8EZ
☎ 01283 761367

The quaintly named Coton-in-the-Elms sits five miles south of Burton-on-Trent, and was named after the many elm trees that once grew there. Within the village you will find the **Shoulder of Mutton**, a superb village pub that is popular with visitors and locals alike. It has recently been taken over by mine hosts Joanne and John, who are determined, not only to maintain the "village pub" feel, but improve on it.

It is open all day, every day, and serves two real ales - Marston's Pedigree and a rotating guest ale. Plus there is a wide selection of beers, lagers, cider, wines, spirits, liqueurs and soft drinks. The interior is as charming as the exterior, and has a cosy feel to it - just right for a village pub.

Food is available every day from 12 noon until 7pm. A no-smoking restaurant that can accommodate up to 30 people is situated upstairs, and opens between 5pm and 7pm. You can choose from a specials board for eating downstairs in the bar, and there is a menu for diners who wish to eat in the restaurant. Entertainment and food evenings include a curry night every Tuesday from 5pm to 7pm, a quiz night on a Wednesday, a "bacon and cabbage" (a well known Irish dish) night on a Thursday, a singalong on a Friday evening and live entertainment - usually a solo singer - on Saturday evenings. There is a patio to the rear and plenty of off-road parking.

117 ROBIN HOOD INN & GLADES RESTAURANT

1 Burton Road, Overseal, Swadlincote,
Derbyshire DE12 6LQ
☎ 01283 760252
e-mail: info@robinhood-overseal.co.uk
🌐 www.robinhood-overseal.co.uk

A short drive south east of Burton-on-Trent, adjacent to the A444, stands the village of Overseal. It is here you will find the **Robin Hood Inn and Glades Restaurant**, one of the best establishments of its kind in Derbyshire. The exterior is whitewashed, and has a quiet charm which is echoed in the interior. It is cosy, warm and friendly, just like a village pub should be. It is open every day (all day on Saturday), and sells three real ales - Marston's pedigree, Banks original and Banks bitter. There is also a superb range of beers, wines, spirits and soft drinks should you be driving.

Bar snacks are available at all times, and great food is served in the Glades Restaurant from 12 noon - 2pm Monday to Friday and from 6pm - 9pm Monday to Saturday. On Sunday it is from 12 noon onwards. The no-

smoking Glades seats 45 people in absolute comfort, and you can choose from a printed menu or a specials board. All the produce is fresh and local, ensuring a great eating experience. On Sundays there is a Sunday roast plus a few optional dishes. All credit cards except Diners are welcome. Thursday and Saturdays from 9pm are karaoke evenings, and between October and December there are cabaret evenings. There is also courtyard seating and a large off-road car park. There are currently four en-suite letting rooms. Refurbishment will see an additional six from April 2007.

118 SHOULDER OF MUTTON

6 Chapel Street, Oakthorpe,
nr Swadlincote, Derbyshire DE12 7QT
☎ 01530 270436

Within the village of Oakthorpe you will find the **Shoulder of Mutton**, a pub that has been owned and managed for over fifteen years by Julie Mole. During that time she has turned it into a delightful and quaint inn, one that is appreciated by locals and visitors alike. Its attractive black and white exterior, with quaint latticed windows and colourful hanging baskets, gives it a traditional air, which is repeated in its cosy, welcoming interior.

The bar serves two real ales, the ever-popular Marston's Pedigree and a rotating guest ale. Plus there is a wide range of other drinks - beers, lager, cider, wines, spirits and soft drinks. The relaxing atmosphere is just the place to enjoy a drink and a friendly chat with the locals.

The food is good, wholesome, unpretentious pub food,

with a few surprises thrown in for good measure. It is served in the no-smoking restaurant, which seats 42 in comfort. Everything is home-cooked from fresh local ingredients where possible, and all the dishes are beautifully presented. It is advisable to book on Fridays, Saturdays and Sundays, as the place is one of the most popular dining destinations in the area. All credit cards are accepted with the exception of American Express and Diners Club, and children are more than welcome.

120 CRICH TRAMWAY VILLAGE

Crich Tramway Village, Nr Matlock,
Derbyshire DE4 5DP
☎ 0870 75 TRAMS (87267)
e-mail: enquiries@tramway.co.uk
🌐 www.tramway.co.uk

Crich Tramway Village offers a family day out in the relaxing atmosphere of a bygone era. Explore the re-created period street with its genuine buildings and features, fascinating exhibitions and most importantly, its trams. Unlimited tram rides are free with your entry fee, giving you the opportunity to fully appreciate the Village and surrounding countryside. Journey on one of the many beautifully restored vintage trams, as they rumble through the cobbled streets past the exhibition hall, workshops, children's play and picnic areas before going on through the woods, and then on to Glory Mine taking in spectacular views of the Derwent Valley.

121 LATTE LOUNGE

15 Church Street, Ripley,
Derbyshire DE5 3BU
☎ 01773 512000

The stylish **Latte Lounge** is in the centre of Ripley, and is a stylish, modern place to dine and stay. The kitchen uses only the finest local produce in its cuisine, which combines imagination and flair. This is the place for that extra special meal or snack! You can choose from the menu or the daily specials board, with its homemade cakes, scones and soups being especially popular. Above the lounge there are two superior rooms to let - one family-sized. The rooms are let on a bed and breakfast basis, with breakfast taken in the lounge downstairs.

Main Road, Morton, Alfreton,
Derbyshire DE55 6GS
☎ 01773 591767
e-mail: janealden15@aol.com

The small, picturesque village of Morton is supposed to lie at the geographical centre of England. It can be found on the B6014, off the A61 and close to the Nottinghamshire border. It is also a historical place, first mentioned in the will of Wulfric Spott, a Saxon nobleman who lived in the ancient kingdom of Mercia.

It is here, in this delightful place, that you will find an equally delightful inn - the **Sitwell Arms**. It too is brim full of

history, and dates back many hundreds of years, having at one time been a farmhouse and later a thatched inn called the Royal Oak, which was opened by the local landowner, Francis Sitwell of Renshawe. It sells a wide range of drinks, including real ales, beers, lager, cider, wine, spirits and soft drinks, and its interior is equally as picturesque as its outside. Old dark wood, low beams and prints on the walls give it that warm, traditional feel that a good pub should have.

You can choose food from either a daily specials board or a printed menu and no matter what you choose, you will find that the dishes are all beautifully cooked and presented, using local sourced produce wherever possible. On Friday, Saturday and Sunday you are well advised to book, so good is the cooking. The no-smoking restaurant can seat up to 32 in absolute comfort. There are themed food evenings once a month which are bookable, and you should phone for details. Children are most welcome, and all credit cards with the exception of American Express and Diners are accepted. On Tuesday evenings there is a quiz, and a music quiz on the last Sunday of the month.

The inn has plenty of off-road parking, and to the rear is a beer garden leading to the village's cricket pitch. The inn soon hopes to have facilities for camping, and you should ring for details.

245

122 EAGLE TAVERN

**94 Ripley Road, Heage,
Derbyshire DE56 2HU
☎ 01773 857235**

The **Eagle Tavern** is very much a family run establishment, and this is reflected in the high standards of service and the warm welcome you get as soon as you step over the threshold! You can choose from three real ales plus a wide range of other drinks, and the food is exceptional. Choose from the menu or the specials board - you won't be disappointed. Everything is freshly cooked from local produce wherever possible. If you pay a visit, you're sure to come back!

123 SPANKER INN

**Nether Heage, Belper,
Derbyshire DE56 2AT
☎ 01773 853222**

Situated in Nether Heage, off the A6 in the Amber Valley, the **Spanker Inn** is a real find - a traditional English pub that puts good ale, great food and a warm friendly welcome at the top of its priorities. Under the new management of mine hosts Laura and Paul Isom, it has earned itself the reputation of being one of the best pubs in the Amber Valley - which is no idle boast!

The interior is cosy and traditional, and here you can enjoy a quiet drink among the friendly regulars. It offers three real ales, the regulars being Marston's Pedigree and Black Sheep, and good, old-fashioned ale from the jug, with two brews a week. Food is served in the no-smoking dining area from 11.30am until 2pm and 6pm until 8.45pm Monday to Saturday. You can choose from the printed menu or a specials board. On Sundays there is a carvery only, with food being served between 11.30am and 3pm in three sittings. The produce used in the kitchen - meat, ham sausages etc - is all sourced from within the county, ensuring freshness and flavour. The traditional dishes are especially popular, and Paul, the chef, is well known in the area for the quality of his cooking. People have come to enjoy it so much that you are well advised to book on Friday or Saturday evenings.

There is ample off-road parking, and children are very welcome. There is also a beer garden and a skittle alley, plus a quiz night every Wednesday from 9.30pm. This is a pub which has everything - a cosy, welcoming atmosphere, good food, great drink and good old-fashioned value for money!

The Denby Pottery Company Ltd, Denby,
Derbyshire DE5 8NX
☎ 01773 740799
🌐 www.denby.co.uk

The Visitor Centre is next to the Pottery in a cobbled courtyard with shops, restaurant and outdoor play area. It is open daily with activities from plate painting to cookery demonstrations.

In the museum you can see examples of pieces from Denby's rich heritage on display. A selection of Heritage Ware in the form of limited editions of Denby animal novelties, created from original moulds, are made by hand in the Craftroom and are on sale in reception.

Discover a selection of prints and original paintings by local artists in the Artists Gallery, and a tempting choice of gifts, jewellery, cards and home accessories are also available in the gift shop.

See hand blown glass being created as your guide explains the processes in the Glass Studio. Tours are available most weekdays for a small charge and a selection of designs from The Glass Studio are on sale in reception.

Cookery demonstrations and an award winning cookware shop are among the other attractions, as well as a garden centre selling seasonal plants and gifts, a Dartington Crystal factory shop and a restaurant and coffee shop..

Ormonde Fields Golf Course,
Nottingham Road, Codnor, Ripley,
Derbyshire DE5 9RG
☎ 01773 744233
🌐 www.pantheon-1.co.uk

Within the well known Ormonde Fields Golf Club, just off the A610, you will find the **Pantheon Restaurant and Bar** - a great place for a meal or just a relaxing drink. It boasts two dining areas (with printed menu and specials board) and two bars - the golfer's bar and the diner's bar. In addition, it has three en suite doubles rooms to let on a B&B or dinner, B&B basis. The Pantheon Restaurant and Bar is different - a place that offers great food, great drink and great accommodation, all at affordable prices.

HIDDEN PLACES GUIDES

Explore Britain and Ireland with *Hidden Places* guides - a fascinating series of national and local travel guides.

Packed with easy to read information on hundreds of places of interest as well as places to stay, eat and drink.

Available from both high street and internet booksellers

For more information on the full range of *Hidden Places* guides and other titles published by Travel Publishing visit our website on

www.travelpublishing.co.uk
or ask for our leaflet by phoning
0118-981-7777 or emailing
info@travelpublishing.co.uk

44 Market Place, Belper,
Derbyshire DE56 1FZ
☎ 01773 823000

Situated right in the market place of the ancient town of Belper, the **Black Swan** is one of the most outstanding pubs in Derbyshire. It is owned and run by Noreen and Neil McCready, who

became owners of the property in April 2004 and completely refurbished the place without stinting on cost or commitment. They opened for business in December 2004, and since then it has become a firm favourite with locals and tourists alike, who appreciate the blending of the English tradition of cosiness and a warm, friendly atmosphere with modern stylish good looks.

It is open all day every day with the exception of Monday, when it opens at 4pm, and sells a full range of drinks, including two real ales - Spitfire and a rotating ale. In addition there is a great range of beers, lager, cider, spirits, wine, liqueurs and soft drinks. This is the place for tourists to enjoy, in comfort, a quiet drink after exploring all that

Derbyshire has to offer.

Plus the Black Swan allows you to dine upstairs (which seats 40 in absolute comfort) or downstairs, in its newly opened Vanilla restaurant, which seats 35. Only the finest and freshest of local produce is used in the kitchens wherever possibly, with the cuisine being traditional English with overseas influences, and all cooked on the premises with imagination and flair. The upstairs dining area serves "posh pub grub", and on Sunday does one of the best Sunday lunches in the area. Downstairs there is an à la carte menu, and you are well advised to book on Friday and Saturday evenings. So there is sure to be something that appeals to your palate. Plus, of course, there is sure to be a wine on

the wine list that accompanies your meal perfectly.

The Vanilla Restaurant is open on Tuesday to Saturday evenings from 6pm until 10pm, and all major credit cards are accepted. Children, unfortunately, can only visit the downstairs restaurant.

The pub is housed in a 17th century building within a conservation area that contains many fine buildings, and Noreen and Neil are committed to improving the pub even further by enhancing its reputation for great food and good drink. Pay it a visit - you won't be disappointed!

127 THE RAILWAY

25 King Street, Belper,
Derbyshire DE56 1PW
☎ 01773 599556

One look at **The Railway** tells you that you have found a pub that is really special. Its white-washed exterior has hanging baskets that are a riot of colour in summer, and its well-proportioned frontage seems to offer a warm and friendly welcome to visitors and locals alike. The beer garden at the back continues the theme, with its pink walls, its shady trees and its relaxed atmosphere.

The interior is equally as impressive. Warm colours, honey coloured wood and print covered walls speak of that fine old English custom of hospitality, great drink and great food. It is, as you would expect with such an inviting hostelry, family run, with all that that implies. The leaseholder is Angela McAuley, and she brings a wealth of experience to managing the pub. She is determined to build on the fine reputation it has in the area, making it *the* pub in Belper for friendly service and outstanding value for money. She also wants to introduce comfortable and affordable accommodation, and you should ring for details.

There are two real ales on offer.

Directors is the regular, plus there is a guest ale that changes every week. In addition, of course, the pub also sells a wide range of beers, lagers, cider, spirits, wines and soft drinks should you be driving.

Angela places great emphasis on her food. It is served on Monday, Tuesday and Wednesday from 10.30am to 3pm, Thursday from 10.30am to 4pm, Friday and Saturday from 10.30am to 6pm and on Sunday 12 noon to 2.30pm. The chef, James, is an excellent cook, and prepares appetising and tasty dishes from fresh local produce wherever possible. He combines flair and imagination to ensure that you have a meal that you will long remember for all the right reasons! His home-made steak and ale pie is very popular. The Railway also offers entertainment, and visitors are welcome to take part. On Tuesday, for instance, there is ladies' darts and dominoes. Wednesday night at 9pm is quiz night, and Thursday is pool night.

The pub also has a no-smoking function room that patrons can hire which seats up to 45 people in absolute comfort. There is plenty of off road-parking and children are most welcome. There is also a beer garden, and the pub is disabled-friendly.

128 TRAVELLER'S REST

**114 Chapel Street, Kilburn, Belper,
Derbyshire DE56 0NT
☎ 01332 880108**

One of the joys of life is discovering a really good pub that serves great drink. Look no further, then, than the **Traveller's Rest** at Kilburn, southwest of Belper off the A608. It dates to the late 18th century, and is a pub for lovers of real ale. It has six regular real ales on offer, plus a rotating guest ale, all kept in perfect condition by mine hosts, Wendy and Terry

Cockroft. On Saturday evening free snacks are available, and a quiz night is held on Thursday evenings from 10.30pm and every other Friday from 9pm. People who enjoy good, traditional ales should certainly make their way to the Traveller's Rest!

131 KING WILLIAM IV

**The Bridge, Milford,
Derbyshire DE56 0RR
☎ 01332 840842
e-mail: kingwilliam.mf@btinternet.com**

Milford lies on the A6 between Derby and Belper, and it is here that you will find the **King William IV**, a pub full of olde worlde charm and character. Famed for its friendly atmosphere and service, it boasts four real ales - three regulars and a rotating ale. Light snacks

and sandwiches are always available. Also on offer are three comfortable, en suite rooms that have been furnished and decorated to an extremely high standard. There is live entertainment every Monday evening.

129 HUNTER ARMS

**23 Church Street, Kilburn,
Derbyshire DE56 0LU
☎ 01332 882907**

Two miles from Belper you will find the village of Kilburn. At its heart is the **Hunter Arms**, a superb pub that has recently been refurbished to an exceedingly high standard. Since September 2005 it has been in the hands of Katrina and Brian Eccleshare, and just one look at it now shows what a great job they are making of it. This is the English pub at its very best - warm, cosy yet spacious, welcoming and offering tremendous value for money.

There are three real ales to enjoy - Deuchars, IPA Regular and a rotating guest ale, plus there is the usual range of beers, wines, spirits and soft drinks. One innovation introduced by the Eccleshares is food - cooked on the premises by Katrina herself. It is served 12 noon - 2pm and 6pm - 9pm, and you can choose from the menu or the specials board, though there are

filled rolls only on a Sunday evening. On Sunday there is a carvery plus specials, Thursday evening is curry night and Saturday evening is steak night. It is advisable to book for these. The pub can seat up to 80 people in absolute comfort both upstairs and downstairs.

Children are very welcome, and the pub is disabled friendly. Payment is by cash or cheque only, and the dining areas are no smoking. There is a rear patio area and beer garden, and on either Friday or Saturday evenings there is live music. Please ring for details. Closed Monday lunchtimes.

120 Ashbourne Lane, Cowers Lane,
Shottle, Derbyshire DE56 2LF
☎ 01773 550271
e-mail: railwayshottle@aol.com
🌐 www.railwayshottle@aol.com

Situated at the junction of the A512 and the B5123, **The Railway** is undoubtedly one of the best pubs in Derbyshire. The tenant, Phil Clarke, has been in the licensing trade for over 25 years, and has brought this wealth of experience to bear on the running of the pub.

The exterior is extremely picturesque, with its whitewashed walls and hanging baskets and, with its warm wood and traditional appearance, the interior is equally as inviting. Open all day, every day, the bar serves Marston's Pedigree and a selection of guest ales, as well as a range of beers, cider, spirits, wines and soft drinks.

However, it is the food that draws people to The Railway. The restaurant is on a raised area, and serves some of the best food in the county weekdays between 12-2.30pm and 5.30pm-9pm, and all day until 9pm Saturday and Sunday. You can

choose from the set menu or from the à la carte menu boards which change regularly to include dishes that take advantage of local seasonal produce wherever possible. Gourmet nights are very popular and booking is advisable on a Sunday.

Children are more than welcome at The Railway, and there is a separate children's menu and a play area outside, close to a decked seating area with heaters for those who wish to dine al fresco.

12 Town Street, Holbrook,
Derbyshire DE56 0TA
☎ 01332 881200
e-mail: info@thespottedcow.co.uk
🌐 www.thespottedcow.co.uk

The picturesque and white-washed **Spotted Cow** sits in the village of Holbrook, a few miles north of Derby between the A38 and the A6. It is packed with history, and dates from at least 1622, when life was lived at a different pace. The inn has managed to preserve this leisurely ambience, and is a relaxed, friendly place that combines all that is best in English hospitality with up-to-date standards of service and good, old-fashioned value for money. The interior especially has that "olde worlde" look that makes an English pub so welcoming and warm.

The customer is king at the Spotted Cow. It is owned and personally managed by Fiona and Andrew West-Hunt, who bought it three years ago, determined not only to maintain the inn's fine reputation, but to build on it. It was their first venture, and so successful have they been that the Spotted Cow is now one of the best pubs in the whole of Derbyshire, popular with both locals and visitors alike.

It is open at regular pub hours from

Monday to Saturday, and all day Sunday, selling four real ales - Marston's Pedigree, Speckled Hen, Jennings Cumberland Ale and a rotating guest ale. In addition, there is a good range of beers, lagers, ciders, spirits, wines and soft drinks.

The Spotted Cow places great emphasis on its food, and it sources most of its produce locally wherever possible, ensuring that the customer has a great eating experience. The menus are inspired both by English cuisine and foreign cuisines, with the chef, Tony, melding imagination and flair. Try the creamy garlic mushrooms, for instance, or home-made spicy salmon fish cakes for starters, or the mixed grill, medallions of fillet or grilled tuna steak for lunch. And the evening menu contains such dishes as frogs' legs, roast silverside of beef, roast breast of duck and chicken and pasta carbonara. There is also a popular Sunday carvery, though a carvery is, in fact, available every day! Food is served between 12 noon and 2pm and 6.30pm and 9pm from Monday to Saturday, and from 12 noon to 8pm on Sunday.

The Spotted Cow also offers superb B&B accommodation in en suite rooms, all situated upstairs.

So come along to the Spotted Cow and enjoy the best in English hospitality!

133 HORSLEY LODGE

Smalley Mill Road, Horsley,
Derbyshire DE21 5BL
☎ 01332 780838
e-mail: enquiries@horsleylodge.co.uk
🌐 www.horsleylodge.co.uk

Horsley Lodge is a golf club, a hotel and a restaurant all rolled into one. It is set in the midst of 175 acres of gently rolling hills in a quiet corner of Derbyshire and offers luxurious surroundings for those people looking for something that little bit extra when it comes to golf, accommodation, food and drink. Owned and run by Richard and Malcolm Salt, it is an independent family business that has been pleasing people since 1990.

The facilities are superb, and great attention has been given to detail. The course is 6400 yards long, par and S.S.S-71. It was originally built in1990, and remodelled by Peter McEvoy OBE, the former Walker Cup captain. Improved and matured over the years, and now a challenge for any golfer who appreciates and enjoys his golf. The greens are said to be the finest in the area, having subtle undulations and, to quote a national golfing magazine, 'the last three holes create a finish that would not be out of place at a major.'

Golf days and exclusive golf breaks are Horsley Lodge's strong points, with the centrepiece of the development being a converted stone country house that has bars, restaurants and banqueting and conference facilities. The Highlander Restaurant offers the best in British cuisine, with food being available all day, every day. It prides itself in sourcing all of the produce used in the kitchen locally, ensuring that it is fresh and full of flavour. Typical dishes are rich beef steak pie, tower of pork medallions, breaded chicken breast with asparagus and chicken or fish risotto. Puddings are made on the premises and the whole menu offers exceptional value.

The Golf Bar beckons when you have finished a (hopefully) satisfactory round of golf, and here you can relax in absolute comfort while contemplating a wide choice of drinks, including real ales and wines to stretch your taste buds.

There are ten superb bedroom suites on offer, each one luxuriously furnished and decorated. Recently upgraded with plasma TV's and free internet, they have been awarded the Tourist Board 4 Star Silver Award.

Conference facilities include all the latest technology, including big screen Powerpoint presentations. If it's friendly staff, luxurious surroundings and an informal atmosphere, then the Horsley Lodge is for you!

134 THREE HORSESHOES

Main Road, Morley, Derbyshire DE7 6DF
☎ 01332 834395

This charming, whitewashed inn epitomises all that is good about England's village pubs. The 19th century **Three Horseshoes**, formerly a coaching inn, sits within Morley, to the north of Derby, and is famous locally for its great drink, its good food and its warmth and character. It serves three real ales and its food is renowned throughout the area. There is plenty of off-road parking, and children are very welcome.

137 MALT SHOVEL INN

14 The Green, Aston-on-Trent,
Derbyshire DE72 2AA
☎ 01332 792256
🌐 www.themaltshovelaston.co.uk

The **Malt Shovel** is an olde worlde inn found in the picturesque village of Aston-on-Trent, two miles from the well-known Swarkestone Bridge. It is open all day, every day, and boasts three to four real ales plus a wide range of beers, lagers, cider, spirits, wines and soft drinks. Freshly cooked food is served, with the produce being sourced

locally where possible. Good, old fashioned English hospitality are the watchwords here, and you'll be assured of a warm welcome if you visit!

135 ALL SAINTS CHURCH

Dale Abbey, Stanton by Dale,
Derbyshire DE7 4PN
☎ 0115 932 4584

All Saints Church, Dale Abbey is the only church in England which shares its roof with a farm. Apart from electrics and some old radiators the interior has not been altered since around 1650 and retains its box pews. There is a medieval wall painting and a leaning pulpit dated 1634. The communion table, actually a Jacobean cupboard, is in front of the reading desk, whereas normally it should be behind and there is in effect a three-decker pulpit arrangement.

In about 1485 the building next door to the church became the infirmary for the nearby abbey and the church became the infirmary chapel, the sick being brought through doors both downstairs and on the gallery where they could see the service from the low balcony.

More recently the adjoining building became the Blue Ball Inn. Clergy would robe in the inn and enter the church through the downstairs door, blocked up in the 1820's but still clearly visible.

Dale Abbey used to be a 'peculiar' and did not come under the authority of the Diocesan Bishop. It had its own lay bishop, Lord Stanhope, whose Episcopal throne is in the church. It was thus Derbyshire's first cathedral.. There was a court at Dale with the authority to issue licences for weddings, which meant that banns did not have to read and so Dale became the Gretna Green of the Midlands in the 17th and 18th centuries, with many weddings being performed. There is a plaque in the church describing one of the lay bishops. It is said to be the smallest Anglican church in England still in regular use.

143 London Road, Shardlow,
Derbyshire DE72 2HA
☎ 01332 792918

The village of Shardlow stands a few miles south east of Derby just off the A50. It is here that you will find a delightful pub - **The Navigation Inn**. It is close to the famous Shardlow Marina on the River Trent, and is a well-run pub - one that makes you want to come back to it again and again. You are always assured of a warm welcome from Kim and Ian Pascoe, which makes it very popular with locals and visitors alike.

The well-proportioned building is over 300 years old, and the interior reflects its "olde worlde" charm. It is cosy yet spacious and full of character, and here you can enjoy the very best of English hospitality. Why not try one of its real ales - you can choose from Marston's Pedigree, Adnams, Greene King Abbot or a rotating guest ale, and all are kept in immaculate condition.

The bar and restaurant menu here has something for

everyone, and food is served 12 noon - 3pm and 6pm - 9pm. Booking is essential for Friday and Saturday evenings and Sunday lunch, when roast dinners are on offer. The produce is sourced locally wherever possible, ensuring freshness and flavour.

On Friday evenings from 9.30pm there is live music. There is also a rear patio and large beer garden. Children are more than welcome, and credit cards are accpeted with the exception of American Express and Diners.

90 Bondgate, Castle Donington,
Derbyshire DE74 2NR
☎ 01332 812214
e-mail: thecrosskeys@ntlworld.com

The **Cross Keys** is a welcoming, friendly pub in the heart of Castle Donington. It is popular with locals and visitors alike, and has a sporty feel to it, as it has three teams attached to it - a rugby team, a cricket team and a football team.

Mine hosts, Donna and Andy Moon, have been in charge for over a year and a half, and have built on the solid reputation the pub had for its great atmosphere, its great drink and its filling snacks. The exterior is very attractive, and well-proportioned, and has colourful hanging baskets that add to its overall attractiveness. The interior is equally as attractive, and is everything a good English pub should be. It is open every session from Monday to Thursday (though it is closed at Monday lunchtime except on bank holidays), and all day on Fridays, Saturdays, Sundays and bank

holidays. It serves four real ales - Deuchars IPA, Black Sheep, Marston's Pedigree and a rotating guest ale, plus a good range of beers, lagers, cider, spirits, wines and soft drinks should you be driving. Snack food is available throughout the opening hours, and include filled cobs, chips and so on.

In the winter months there is a quiz every Tuesday night, and everyone is welcome (ring for details). There is plenty of outdoor seating in the courtyard, and ample parking spaces. Close by is the Castle Donington Race Circuit and East Midlands Airport.

Main Street, Hemington,
Derbyshire DE74 2RB
☎ 01332 810448

Close to the Nottinghamshire border is the village of Hemington. It is well worth seeking out because of the delightful **Jolly Sailor**, a pub that combines charm and friendliness with great food and drink. The building dates back to the 17th century, and the interior reflects its age. There are old beams hung with pint pots and an open fire in the comfortable lounge, and this, combined with its fresh décor, gives it an ambience that visitors and locals appreciate. A recently added extension incorporates modern toilet facilities - including disabled facilities.

The pub has regular opening hours through the week, and is open all day at weekends. There is always a minimum of seven real ales on offer, plus a good range of other drinks, including

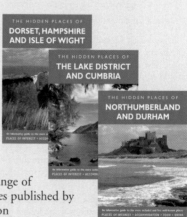

Rosie's Cider on draught. The separate non-smoking restaurant is light and spacious, and here you can enjoy food - cooked mostly from local, fresh produce - in

convivial surroundings, as well as in the bar and outside. Food is served Monday to Saturday lunchtimes from 12 noon - 2pm, and on Thursday, Friday and Saturday evenings from 6.30pm - 8.45pm, when it is best to book. There is no food on Sundays.

Children are most welcome, and all credit cards with the exception of Diners and American Express are accepted. During the first or second week in September an annual mini cider festival is held.

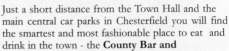

83 Saltergate, Chesterfield,
Derbyshire S40 1JS
☎ 01246 201640

Just a short distance from the Town Hall and the main central car parks in Chesterfield you will find the smartest and most fashionable place to eat and drink in the town - the **County Bar and Restaurant**. Housed in a lovely old building of red brick and half-timbering, it is smart and attractive, and has a faithful clientele - including local businessmen who lunch here - who come back again and again.

If you're visiting the old, historic town of Chesterfield, with its famous crooked spire, then this is the place for you yourself to have lunch, a snack or a dinner. The inside is as attractive as the exterior, and features warm, old wood, wall hangings and smart carpeting to add a touch of warmth.

Mine hosts Claire and Damien have worked hard to create a place where friendly service and value for money are to the fore. And professionally trained chef Martyn Haines brings all his culinary skills to the food, the reputation of which is known far beyond the town itself. He prides himself in using only the

finest and freshest of local produce wherever possible, and his dishes reflect his dedication to really good food. Dishes on the menu range from starters and lite bites, salads, open sandwiches, paninis and pasta, to juicy peppered steaks, burgers, chicken and amazing duck breast and herbs. And the prices are very reasonable! Once a month - usually midweek - there is a speciality food night (ring for details)

It opens during regular pub hours from Monday to Thursday, and all day on Friday and Saturday. On Sunday it remains closed. The bar offers a great range of drinks, from draught keg bitters, lagers and cider to stout, wine, spirits, liqueurs and soft drinks for those who are driving.

Food is served between 12 noon and 3 pm and 5 pm to 9 pm from Monday to Thursday, and from 12 noon to 9pm on Friday and Saturday. The restaurant (where there is table service) seats up to 50 in absolute comfort, and so popular is it that you are well advised to book a table at lunchtime.

Children are very welcome, there is a no smoking area, a rear beer garden, and all major credit cards are taken. Friday evening from 9pm is live music night, and every second Tuesday of the month there is traditional Irish music from 9pm onwards.

Hardwick Park, Chesterfield,
Derbyshire S44 5QJ
☎ 01246 850245
e-mail: batty@hardwickinn.co.uk
🌐 www.hardwickinn.co.uk

Dating from the late 16th century, the **Hardwick Inn** is one of the best known and best loved inns in Britain. It was originally built as a coaching inn for Hardwick Hall which is situated in Hardwick Park adjacent to the inn. It has been run by the Batty family since 1928, with Pauline and Peter Batty as the hosts now in the third generation of the family.

The building itself is of old, mellow stone, with lattice windows, gables and a large beer garden at the front and back of the building. The interior is olde-worldy, warm, friendly and welcoming with an open coal fire in the main bar during the winter months. Traditional English hospitality is important here, coupled with efficient standards of service and value for money, this is undoubtedly one of the finest inns in Derbyshire.

The inn is totally non-smoking, selling real ales including Olde Peculier, Theakstons XB, Old Speckled Hen, Ruddles County and Marstons Pedigree as well as a great range of lagers, ciders, spirits and soft drinks. It also boasted an extensive wine list and over 220 varieties of malt whisky.

People travel from all over to sample the food. It is good, home-made British cuisine, made from the finest and freshest produce. Local produce is used whenever possible, including local meats reared on Hardwick Park Farm adjacent to the inn.

Appetising bar meals, including daily specials, are served all day from 11.30am onwards in the bars and family rooms, where children are most welcome. Alternatively you could sample the Carvery Restaurant where you can have roast meats and fresh vegetables, grills, daily specials and salad bar. Its open Lunch time 12-1.45pm and evenings 7pm-8.30pm, Tuesday - Saturday and Sunday lunch time 12-1.45pm.

142 HUNLOKE ARMS

Derby Road, Wingerworth,
Derbyshire S42 6NB
☎ 01246 232458

The **Hunloke Arms** in Wingerworth is a substantial, well-proportioned inn situated just off the A61 south of Chesterfield. It dates back to the 18th century at least, and was once a well-known coaching inn, named after the surname of the then lord of the manor. With its fine Georgian lines and porticoed front, it looks every inch the welcoming inn.

And welcoming it is. The interior is just as impressive as the exterior. Mellow, old wood and comfortable furnishings combine to give it that 'olde worlde' atmosphere that a real English pub should have. And yet it adheres to the modern concepts of outstanding service and great value for money. It has been run since October 2006 by Gavin Hibbard, who is a vastly experienced chef with over 16 years in the catering trade. He is determined to build on the already enviable reputation the establishment had, and so far has succeeded admirably.

It is open all day and every day for the sale of up to four real ales and a fine selection of beers, lagers, cider, wines, spirits and soft drinks. The regular real ale is one of the most popular in the area - Black sheep, and the others are chosen from a rotating list.

If it is food you are after, you need look no further than the Hunloke Arms! Indeed, due to the outstanding cuisine, it is advisable to book at all times. Food is served on Monday, Tuesday and Wednesday between 12 noon and 2.30pm and 5pm to 8.30pm, Thursday from 12 noon to 2.30pm and 5pm to 9pm, Friday and Saturday from 12 noon to 9 pm and on Sunday from 12 noon to 5pm, when there is a carvery plus vegetarian options. No food is served on Sunday evening.

Dishes are listed on a blackboard, and cooked freshly to order. There is also a sandwich and 'quick bites' menu, and all produce is sourced locally so that it is always fresh.

Children are more than welcome at the Hunloke Arms, and all major credit cards are taken. Tuesday evening is quiz night, which starts at 9pm, and everyone is more than welcome to attend. There is also occasional live entertainment, and you should ring for details. The inn is disabled-friendly, there is a patio area and plenty of off-road parking.

143 BATEMAN'S MILL COUNTRY HOTEL & RESTAURANT

Mill Lane, Old Tupton, Chesterfield,
Derbyshire S42 6AE
☎ 01246 862296   Fax: 01246 865672
e-mail: info@batemansmill.co.uk
🌐 www.batemansmill.co.uk

The award winning **Bateman's Mill Country Hotel and Restaurant** is a conversion of an 18th century mill house, located in a quiet rural area on the edge of the Peak District and in easy travelling distance from many National Park attractions including Chatsworth Estate, Haddon Hall, Hardwick Hall, Bakewell and historic Chesterfield.

Owned and operated by John, Maggie and Steven Roberts since late 2004, the Hotel under their ownership has won a number of awards and accolades, including Winner Outstanding Quality Award 2005/6. With eight lovely en suite bedrooms, all with TV, DVD players WIFI access, tea/coffee making facilities, telephone, iron ironing board and trouser press the hotel offers an ideal base for exploring this part of the Peak District. Ground floor rooms are available along with one larger room for guests with access problems. All bedrooms are non-smoking. Tariffs include full breakfast with choices from a very comprehensive menu.

Families, cyclists and walkers are welcomed at the Mill, and John and Maggie provide a host of local information to assist you in visiting the area. Dogs are also welcome by prior arrangement and the owners can offer a variety of packages including discounted ticket entry to Chatsworth House (subject to availability).

John, a Member of the Master Chefs of Great Britian, produces wonderful dishes, with a policy of purchasing food from local sources wherever possible. Dining at the Mill offers a range of options. Lunches are available in the ground floor bar/restaurant Monday-Sunday from 12 noon -2pm and in the Millers Restaurant on Thursday, Friday and Saturday evenings from 7pm until 9pm. Sunday lunch is available in Millers Restaurant and the ground floor bar/restaurant between 12 noon-2.30pm.

Menus are changed on a regular basis, with dinner menu dishes including locally smoked salmon, pan-fried scallops, with panchetta and minted pea puree, fillet of sea bass with buttered leeks and saffron cream sauce, Chargrilled fillet steak, rosti potato and wild mushroom sauce, roast rump of local lamb, delmonico potatoes, red wine and thyme jus, rich Italian chocolate cake, strawberry creme brulee and sticky toffee pudding. Lighter dishes, steaks and salads are available in the ground floor bar, which with its feature well race, open fire and exposed beams offers a comfortable setting for guests wishing to dine more informally or enjoy a drink from an extensive wine and beverage list, which includes real ales.

A private dining suite is available for parties up to 22 in number with a range of exclusive menus incorporating carefully selected wines.

You are ensured a very warm welcome at this lovely hotel, which prides itself on the quality of food and service, recognised by a number of awards.

144 THREE MERRY LADS

Main Road, Cutthorpe, nr Chesterfield,
Derbyshire S42 7AJ
☎ 01246 277593
e-mail: threemerrylads@btconnect.com

A short drive west of Chesterfield is the pleasant village of Cutthorpe, famous for its well-dressing. It is home to one of the best pubs in the area, the **Three Merry Lads**. This establishment is all that a village local should be, and is extremely popular with both tourists and locals alike. The establishment is open all day and every day for the sale of fine drink and great food. Mine hosts are Caroline and Adrian Close, who have many years experience in the licensed trade.

You can enjoy up to six real ales, with the regular being Jennings Bitter, as well as a great range of other drinks. Food is served from Monday to Saturday between 12 noon and 9.30pm and on Sunday between 12 noon and 8.30pm. So popular is the food here that you are well advised to book for Thursday, Friday, Saturday and Sunday. The produce used in the kitchen is sourced locally wherever possible, and you can choose from a printed menu or a specials

board that changes daily. Dishes containing Derbyshire reared lamb are particularly popular. Caroline is a superb classically trained French chef, so everything is cooked to perfection using imagination and flair. The no-smoking restaurant seats up to 45, and is spacious and elegant.

On the third Friday of the month a folk club meets in the function room, and on the last Friday at 8pm there is an "open mic" night. Children are most welcome and there is also a large decked area, a beer garden and off-road parking.

145 THE ANGEL INN

Main Road, Holmesfield, Dronfield,
Derbyshire S18 7WT
☎ 01142 890336
🌐 www.the-angel-inn.co.uk

Situated three miles northwest of Chesterfield off the B6054, **The Angel Inn** is an inn that is popular with both visitors and tourists alike. It is a modern, brick-built building with hanging baskets that are a riot of colour in the summer months. The interior is cosy, warm and welcoming - just like a good pub should be. It serves great food, and you can choose from an extensive menu or a daily changing specials board. Only the finest and freshest of local produce is used in the kitchen wherever possible, and the dishes are prepared with imagination and flair. Dishes could include grilled haddock topped with garlic and cheddar cheese, sausage and mash in an onion gravy, salmon fillet and chicken breast wrapped in Parma ham with red wine sauce, and so on. Every Tuesday evening all the dishes are gluten

free.

Mine hosts Ruth and James took over here in December 2003, and since then they have been working hard to create an inn that marries tradition with high standards of service and outstanding value for money. They have certainly succeeded.

The inn sells three real ales, all kept in tip-top condition. It also sells a great range of beers, lagers, cider, spirits, wines and soft drinks should you be driving.

261

Tourist Information Centres

ASHBOURNE
13 Market Place, Ashbourne, Derbyshire DE6 1EU
Tel: 01335 343666
Fax: 01335 300638
e-mail: ashbourneinfo@derbyshiredales.gov.uk

BAKEWELL
Old Market Hall, Bridge Street, Bakewell,
Derbyshire DE45 1DS
Tel: 01629 816558
Fax: 01629 814782
e-mail: bakewell@peakdistrict.gov.uk

BURTON UPON TRENT
Coors Visitor Centre, Horninglow Street,
Burton upon Trent, Staffordshire DE14 1NG
Tel: 01283 508111 or 01283 508112
Fax: 01283 517268
e-mail: tic@eaststaffsbc.gov.uk

BUXTON
The Crescent, Buxton, Derbyshire SK17 6BQ
Tel: 01298 25106
Fax: 01298 73153
e-mail: tourism@highpeak.gov.uk

CASTLETON
Buxton Road, Castleton, Hope Valley,
Derbyshire S33 8WP
Tel: 01629816558
Fax: 01433 623726
e-mail: castleton@peakdistrict.gov.uk

CHESTERFIELD
Rykneld Square, Chesterfield, Derbyshire S40 1SB
Tel: 01246 345777 or 01246 345778
Fax: 01246 345770
e-mail: tourism@chesterfield.gov.uk

DERBY
Assembly Rooms, Market Place, Derby,
Derbyshire DE1 3AH
Tel: 01332 255802
Fax: 01332 256137
e-mail: tourism@derby.gov.uk

GLOSSOP
The Heritage Centre, Bank House, Henry Street,
Glossop, Derbyshire SK13 8BW
Tel: 01457 855920
Fax: 01427 855920
e-mail: info@glossoptouristcentre.co.uk

HOLMFIRTH
49-51 Huddersfield Road, Holmfirth,
West Yorkshire HD9 3JP
Tel: 01484 222444 or 01484 223200
Fax: 01484 222445
e-mail: holmfirth.tic@kirklees.gov.uk

LEEK
Leek Tourist Information Centre, 1 Market Place,
Leek, Staffordshire ST13 5HH
Tel: 01538 483741
Fax: 01538 483743
e-mail: tourism.services@staffsmoorlands.gov.uk

MACCLESFIELD
Macclesfield, Town Hall, Macclesfield,
Cheshire SK10 1DX
Tel: 01625 504114 or 01625 504115
Fax: 01625 504116
e-mail: informationcentre@macclesfield.gov.uk

MATLOCK
Crown Square, Matlock, Derbyshire DE4 3AT
Tel: 01629 583388
Fax: 01629 584131
e-mail: matlockinfo@derbyshiredales.gov.uk

MATLOCK BATH
The Pavillion, Matlock, Derbyshire DE4 3NR
Tel 01629 55082
Fax: 01629 56304
e-mail: matlockbathinfo@derbyshiredales.gov.uk

RIPLEY
Town Hall, Market Place, Ripley,
Derbyshire DE5 3BT
Tel: 01773 841488 or 01773 841486
Fax: 01773 841487
e-mail: touristinformation@ambervalley.gov.uk

SHEFFIELD
Tourist Information Centre, 12 Norfolk Row,
Sheffield
Tel: 0114 2211900
Fax: 0114 281 4042
e-mail: visitor@sheffield.gov.uk

SWADLINCOTE
Sharpe's Pottery Museum, West Street, Swadlincote,
Derbyshire DE11 9DG
Tel: 01283 222848
e-mail: tic@sharpespotterymuseum.org.uk

Towns, Villages and Places of Interest

263

TRAVEL PUBLISHING ORDER FORM

To order any of our publications just fill in the payment details below and complete the order form. For orders of less than 4 copies please add £1.00 per book for postage and packing. Orders over 4 copies are P & P free.

Name:

Address:

Tel no:

Please Complete Either:

I enclose a cheque for £ _____ made payable to Travel Publishing Ltd

Or:

Card No: Expiry Date:

Signature:

Please either send, telephone, fax or e-mail your order to:

Travel Publishing Ltd, 7a Apollo House, Calleva Park, Aldermaston, Berkshire RG7 8TN

Tel: 0118 981 7777   Fax: 0118 940 8428   e-mail: info@travelpublishing.co.uk

	Price	Quantity		Price	Quantity
HIDDEN PLACES REGIONAL TITLES			**COUNTRY PUBS AND INNS**		
Cornwall	£8.99	....	Cornwall	£5.99	....
Devon	£8.99	....	Devon	£7.99	....
Dorset, Hants & Isle of Wight	£8.99	....	Sussex	£5.99	....
East Anglia	£8.99	....	Wales	£8.99	....
Lake District & Cumbria	£8.99	....	Yorkshire	£7.99	....
Northumberland & Durham	£8.99	....			
Peak District and Derbyshire	£8.99	....	**COUNTRY LIVING RURAL GUIDES**		
Yorkshire	£8.99	....	East Anglia	£10.99	....
			Heart of England	£10.99	....
HIDDEN PLACES NATIONAL TITLES			Ireland	£11.99	....
England	£11.99	....	North East	£10.99	....
Ireland	£11.99	....	North West	£10.99	....
Scotland	£11.99	....	Scotland	£11.99	....
Wales	£11.99	....	South of England	£10.99	....
			South East of England	£10.99	....
HIDDEN INNS TITLES			Wales	£11.99	....
East Anglia	£7.99	....	West Country	£10.99	....
Heart of England	£7.99	....			
South	£7.99	....			
South East	£7.99	....	**TOTAL QUANTITY:**		
West Country	£7.99	....	**POST & PACKING:**		
OTHER TITLES			**TOTAL VALUE:**		
Off the Motorway	£11.99	....			

VISIT THE TRAVEL PUBLISHING WEBSITE

Looking for:

- *Places to Visit?*
- *Places to Stay?*
- *Places to Eat & Drink?*
- *Places to Shop?*

Then why not visit the Travel Publishing website...

- Informative pages on places to visit, stay, eat, drink and shop throughout the British Isles.

- Detailed information on Travel Publishing's wide range of national and regional travel guides.

www.travelpublishing.co.uk

HIDDEN PLACES GUIDES

Explore Britain and Ireland with *Hidden Places* guides - a fascinating series of national and local travel guides.

Packed with easy to read information on hundreds of places of interest as well as places to stay, eat and drink.

Available from both high street and internet booksellers

For more information on the full range of *Hidden Places* guides and other titles published by Travel Publishing visit our website on

www.travelpublishing.co.uk
or ask for our leaflet by phoning **0118-981-7777** or
emailing **info@travelpublishing.co.uk**

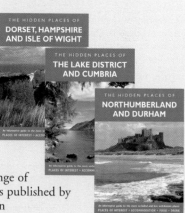

READER REACTION FORM

The *Travel Publishing* research team would like to receive reader's comments on any visitor attractions or places reviewed in the book and also recommendations for suitable entries to be included in the next edition. This will help ensure that the *Country Living series of Guides* continues to provide its readers with useful information on the more interesting, unusual or unique features of each attraction or place ensuring that their visit to the local area is an enjoyable and stimulating experience. To provide your comments or recommendations would you please complete the forms below and overleaf as indicated and send to:

**The Research Department, Travel Publishing Ltd,
7a Apollo House, Calleva Park, Aldermaston, Reading, RG7 8TN.**

Your Name:

Your Address:

Your Telephone Number:

Please tick as appropriate:

Comments ☐   Recommendation ☐

Name of Establishment:

Address:

Telephone Number:

Name of Contact:

READER REACTION FORM

COMMENT OR REASON FOR RECOMMENDATION:

....
....
....
....
....
....
....
....
....
....
....
....
....
....
....
....
....
....
....

READER REACTION FORM

The *Travel Publishing* research team would like to receive reader's comments on any visitor attractions or places reviewed in the book and also recommendations for suitable entries to be included in the next edition. This will help ensure that the *Country Living series of Guides* continues to provide its readers with useful information on the more interesting, unusual or unique features of each attraction or place ensuring that their visit to the local area is an enjoyable and stimulating experience. To provide your comments or recommendations would you please complete the forms below and overleaf as indicated and send to:

**The Research Department, Travel Publishing Ltd,
7a Apollo House, Calleva Park, Aldermaston, Reading, RG7 8TN.**

Your Name:

Your Address:

Your Telephone Number:

Please tick as appropriate:

Comments ☐   Recommendation ☐

Name of Establishment:

Address:

Telephone Number:

Name of Contact:

READER REACTION FORM

COMMENT OR REASON FOR RECOMMENDATION:

....

....

....

....

....

....

....

....

....

....

....

....

....

....

....

....

....

....

Index of Advertisers

PLACES OF INTEREST